Collaborative Problem Solving

Drawing on knowledge from process improvement, organisation theory, human resource management, change management, occupational health and safety, and other fields, the book is a practical, easy-to-read guide to problem solving.

Illustrated with a series of short case studies, this book provides an integrated approach to problem solving in the workplace. *Collaborative Problem Solving* walks through the steps in the problem solving process, introducing dozens of tools, techniques, and concepts to use throughout. Chris J. Shannon describes the behaviours to practice which are most conducive to creating a positive problem solving culture based on curiosity, collaboration, and evidence-based thinking. This book explains why successful problem solving is a collaborative process and provides tools and techniques for responding to other people's behaviour when designing and implementing solutions.

Offering practical advice on problem solving in an easy-to-understand way, this book is aimed at people working in office environments, service industries, and knowledge organisations, enabling them to feel confident in applying the knowledge from the book in their own workplace.

Chris J. Shannon has worked in a variety of financial management and general management roles for the past 25 years, and is currently a manager at The University of Queensland. He has a Bachelor of Business in human resource management, and a Master of Business in leadership. Shannon believes the role of a leader is to create the conditions in which people can thrive, and that organisational success is achieved through developing people. He has previously published a chapter in *Global Lean for Higher Education: A Themed Anthology of Case Studies, Approaches and Tools* (ed. Stephen Yorkstone). This is his first book.

Collaborative Problem Solving

A Guide to Improving your Workplace

Chris J. Shannon

Routledge
Taylor & Francis Group

NEW YORK AND LONDON

First published 2021
by Routledge
605 Third Avenue, New York, NY 10158

and by Routledge
2 Park Square, Milton Park, Abingdon, Oxon, OX14 4RN

Routledge is an imprint of the Taylor & Francis Group, an informa business

Library of Congress Cataloging-in-Publication Data
Names: Shannon, Chris J., author.
Title: Collaborative problem solving : a guide to improving
your workplace / Chris J. Shannon.
Description: New York, NY : Routledge, 2021. | Includes
bibliographical references and index.
Identifiers: LCCN 2020054465 (print) | LCCN 2020054466
(ebook)
Subjects: LCSH: Decision making. | Problem solving. |
Management. | Creative ability in business.
Classification: LCC HD30.23 .S493 2021 (print) |
LCC HD30.23 (ebook) | DDC 658.4/03—dc23
LC record available at https://lccn.loc.gov/2020054465
LC ebook record available at https://lccn.loc.
gov/2020054466

ISBN: 978-0-367-55763-8 (hbk)
ISBN: 978-0-367-55758-4 (pbk)
ISBN: 978-1-003-09505-7 (ebk)

Typeset in Sabon
by codeMantra

To Eloise, for all the love, support and inspiration. Thank you for believing in me.

Contents

Acknowledgements

It turns out that writing a book about problem solving has something in common with problem solving; you cannot do it on your own. Over the course of writing this book, I have drawn on the advice and support of many friends and colleagues.

There are a number of people to thank from The University of Queensland, where I have been a staff member for the past 15 years. I am particularly grateful to Bernard McKenna from the Business School for his support and encouragement during my Master's study and beyond. The research interests I developed in Bernard's courses inform parts of this book. I thank my supervisors for supporting my professional development over the years – Joseph Grotowski and Patrick Testa from the Faculty of Science, and more recently Charles Gilks and Marni Jacoby from the Faculty of Medicine.

I am very grateful to the lean higher education community and the many people I have gotten to know and learn from over the past six years. I had the pleasure of co-facilitating two rapid improvement events with Mark Robinson in 2015–2016 and we have been good friends since. Mark is always willing to share his knowledge with others and provided valuable advice in writing this book. Stephen Yorkstone, editor of *Global Lean for Higher Education: A Themed Anthology of Case Studies, Approaches, and Tools*, has been a great supporter. Having a chapter in Steve's book sparked my desire to keep writing and set me on the path to this book. Bill Balzer has given very valuable advice on the process of putting a book together. I also want to thank Karen Kusler and acknowledge her contributions to the book, most notably the section on automation making problems visible, which we have co-authored.

I must give a special thank you to my friend Julia Faulkner-Figueiredo for reading and giving feedback on sections of the book. Julia's enthusiasm for this project from its early days has been greatly appreciated.

I am very fortunate to have worked with Meredith Norwich as my Senior Editor at Taylor and Francis. Meredith has been an enthusiastic supporter of this book since our first discussion about it in early

2020. She has proven to be an excellent guide through the mysteries and challenges of publishing, and a great source of advice on the structure and flow of the book. That I made it through with the book in hand, unscathed and considering doing it again, is a tribute to her skills. Julia Pollacco joined the Taylor and Francis team on this book later in the process and has also been very helpful.

I had planned to spend part of 2020 living near friends in the north of Italy while writing this book. Then COVID-19 happened. My friends lived in lockdown for months in the epicentre of the pandemic in Italy. Cristina is from Brescia and Davide from Bergamo. They have deep and enduring connections to their region. It was a very troubling time and they were in my thoughts a lot. I thank them for their enduring friendship and promise to visit again as the world reopens post COVID-19. *Prossima volta*!

Thank you to my sons, Dylan and Finley, for their ongoing support. Dylan prepared many of the diagrams in the book and provided feedback on early drafts. It was a great pleasure to have him involved in this project.

Finally, thank you to Eloise O'Toole. This book was conceived in a hotel room in Dublin, Ireland, while Eloise recovered from surgery on a broken ankle. It was written in my office in Brisbane, Australia, in the months that followed, growing in fits and starts from an idea to a proposal and finally a completed manuscript. Eloise was there for all of it, encouraging me, believing in me, asking insightful questions, and making valuable suggestions.

Introduction

People encounter problems in the workplace every day. Some problems are small and relatively straightforward while others are big and complex. What looks like a big, ugly problem might actually be several different problems tangled together. It might be a single, not so complicated problem wrapped up in workplace behaviour which makes the problem harder to solve. Sometimes, people catastrophise the problem they see, making it appear unsolvable. Other times, people understate the problem, glossing over it and subsequently being caught by surprise. Sometimes, people appear to flatly deny the existence of a problem at all, even when other people can see it clearly. Using the payroll function of a business as an example, the incorrect use of a pay code is a simple problem to fix, while a data integration issue between the HR and the finance systems can be a very complex problem. Add in a turf war between HR and IT over who 'owns' the system and you have some workplace behaviour making the problem harder to solve than it would otherwise be. Because the problem relates to people's pay, it is likely to cause distress to the people being paid incorrectly, and therefore, it is critical to fix it quickly. Over the course of a career, you will encounter lots of problems in lots of situations with lots of different personalities at play.

Problems and Opportunities

The language around problems is, well, problematic. Seeing problems is a good thing. Finding ways to bring problems to the surface is important. Solving problems is essential to success. But the word 'problem' is understood to mean something bad. We are accustomed to thinking that problems bring trouble, not only to those who cause them but also to those who find them. We need to change our reaction to problems. Doing this requires behaving in a way which supports honesty and openness in discussing how things really are. It requires willingness to respond to a seemingly bad situation with curiosity and a desire to work with other people to solve the problems. Decisions about how to respond need to be objective and based on evidence. It requires understanding how to go about the business of solving problems and being willing to share that knowledge with other people.

The relationship between problem solving and continuous improvement needs exploring. I refer to problem solving throughout this book because that is what most people understand this work to be. The problem solving model used in this book starts with someone perceiving a 'problem'. But what is a problem as opposed to an opportunity? Is it a matter of whether there is some felt anxiety – a problem causes a shiver up the spine while an opportunity causes a tingle of excitement? Does this reaction to it stem from your level of understanding? Is it a problem when you do not know why something is happening and an opportunity when you do? Is it a matter of scale? Something small which you might work on by yourself or with one or two other people is an opportunity, while something big which runs across multiple business units is a problem. Does it depend on who sees it first? A colleague seeing something is an opportunity, but a customer or a boss seeing something is a problem. Finally, does it relate to its potential impact – what happens if you choose to do nothing? An unfixed problem can put you out of business while an opportunity can sit idle if it has to. It gets even more complex when you consider the relationships between these things. For instance the impact could well be greater if the problem is first spotted by a customer rather than a staff member. The risk has been realised.

In *Four Types of Problems*,[1] Art Smalley describes:

1 'Troubleshooting' problems – a quick response to immediate symptoms
2 'Gap from standard' problems – something causing you to not meet your expected standard of work
3 'Target Condition' problems – raising the standard to a higher level (the new condition you are setting as your target)
4 'Open-ended' problems – innovation and creative processes

In Smalley's model, the first two are about fixing things that go wrong, and the other two are about taking opportunities to improve. Problems and opportunities are part of the same continuum. Similarly, in *The Toyota Way Fieldbook*, Liker and Meier refer to "issues" which can be problems or opportunities.[2]

Personally, I think impact is a relevant factor in calling something a problem or not. What is the impact of what you see? What is the cost of doing nothing about it? Impact creates a sense of urgency and purpose. If the cost of doing nothing is high, let's call it a problem. But let's also remember that the way you approach a problem and an opportunity is the same. Let's also remember that a big opportunity should be prioritised over a small problem. The tools and techniques described in this book work well for both. While the book refers to problems and problem solving, you are encouraged to use this approach to work on improving things before they become problems and to make good business practices into better ones.

The size and complexity of the problem matter as well. The way you approach a big problem is different to how you approach a small one, or a simple one. The bigger and more complex the problem, the more organised and methodical you should be in solving it, and the more people you will likely need to collaborate with to assist in defining and investigating it (Figure I.1).

While the book focuses on collaboration, there are some things you can do on your own. Some of the small problems that you see will be internal to you. That is, they will be about your behaviour, not about processes, policies, systems, or pieces of equipment. That is wonderful; you can start to work on them immediately and it will cost you nothing to do it. A simple example might be that you notice you are often late to meetings, creating waste and ill will because you keep other people waiting. So, resolve to be on time. When you are late, reflect on why and think about how to prevent it in future. Try little strategies to get you there on time. See if they make a difference. I work in universities and it often strikes me that many people arrive late for meetings. It seems to be part of the culture to treat meetings like parties; people are told the start time but invariably arrive fashionably late. If I were to ask questions about why they are late, the reasons would come out – my last meeting ran overtime, it was a ten-minute walk across campus to this one, my boss wanted to

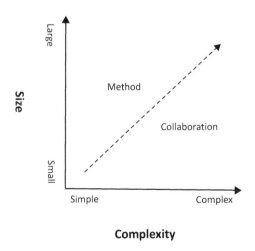

FIGURE I.1 Problem size and complexity.

see me urgently just as I was about to leave for this meeting, or (worst of all) I knew other people would arrive late so figured I would, too.

A more substantial behaviour change to make is to read Chapter 2 and start to practice the three behaviours described in it – curiosity, collaboration, and evidence-based thinking. That will take more time and practice but is certainly achievable and is entirely within your control to do it. It will cost you nothing to reconsider the way you interact with other people, and to start to model the behaviours that will help create a problem solving culture.

Problems that involve other people will require their input to help solve them. This is one of the most important things to remember about this book: the tools, techniques, and behaviours described in this book are all intended to be used with other people. They are all about creating a shared understanding of what is going on, and getting to the root causes of problems in order to solve them. That is the heart of problem solving, and also of improvement opportunities. This is not a solo adventure. It is a team sport. Collaboration is vital to success. How you behave in the problem solving process matters enormously.

The smaller number of big, complex problems you see may well require more resources than you can muster from your place in the organisation. But you can still help to define the problem and feed clear and direct information about the problem to the relevant people. It is my experience that when people are presented with an objective and well considered analysis of a problem, they are more inclined to solve it than if they are presented with a vague or emotional complaint.

It is essential to understand that a problem is not a bad thing. A problem is a learning opportunity. It is a chance to improve the way you and your team work. However, we are accustomed to thinking of problems as bad. The word 'problem' conjures a sense of unease or fear of a bad outcome. Imagine two scenarios in which a problem is identified. In the first scenario, management believes problems are bad news and does not like to hear about them. Management sees problems as evidence of employee failure. Why didn't they get it right first time? Who is to blame? It is not hard to guess what an employee would do if they found a problem in this organisation. There is a high probability the staff member would choose to conceal it rather than raise it. They would be worried they might get in trouble or even lose their job. Where there is a culture of fear and blame, there will likely be very little improvement. In the second scenario, management trusts that staff do their best at work each day. Problems are evidence of a process or a system going wrong and are viewed as learning opportunities. Staff are encouraged to bring the problem to other people's attention so it can be studied and solved. They are thanked for their attentiveness and honesty. Which place would you rather work for?

Do What You Can from Where You Are

There is plenty of research available that shows that business improvement programmes fail anywhere between 50% and 95% of the time.[3,4] Even if every organisation attempted an enterprise-wide improvement programme, 50–95% of people working in organisations do not get the benefit of a successful one. This is a very high failure rate, and means there are a lot of people who would like to do better but do not have the organisational systems and support in place to help them. This book is written for those people. It is very much about what you can do on a daily basis regardless of where you sit in the organisation. You do not have to be an executive, or a manager, or a team leader to use this approach.

This book describes a collaborative approach to problem solving in the workplace. It starts by outlining the steps in the problem solving process; it then introduces tools to use at each step. The book describes useful behaviours for you to practice. Lastly, the book also considers how to respond to other people's behaviour as you set out to solve problems. The book draws on many different fields including process improvement, human resource management, occupational health and safety, psychology, and business management to inform an integrated approach. Practicing this approach not only helps to solve problems but also equips you to share knowledge with other people and contribute to a positive workplace culture. This approach can lead to much greater and longer-lasting benefits than solving the problem at hand.

This book is written for people who want to improve their skills in collaborative problem solving. It is a practical guide for daily use by people in the workplace, regardless of their job title or level of seniority. As with other areas of life, we learn from experience and build skills and knowledge from doing. Given the pervasiveness of problems in everyday life, one would expect that everyone has developed at least some skills in problem solving. If you are reading this book, it is a safe guess to say that you recognise the value of problem solving even if you are not sure of your own ability. As you read through the book, I hope you will see the similarity between problem solving and other things you have probably already done, and you come to realise that you have many transferrable skills to bring into problem solving. You are unlikely to be starting from a blank slate. You will also see that the behaviours and practices described in this book align with other important workplace activities. Practicing this approach to problem solving will develop more skills to take into future endeavours as well. So this book is not just about helping other people and helping your business; it is also about helping yourself.

Even if your company does not adopt this thinking on an enterprise-wide basis, you can apply it. The reality of large organisations is that they have many subcultures within them at business unit or team level.

You can make your unit a better place to work. If you are a manager or leader, you can provide a better and more desirable work environment for your team. They will appreciate it. It is not rocket science to realise that being a good colleague or boss starts with thinking about how you would like to be treated and what sort of workplace you would like to work in. Why not do your best to create that workplace around you? Behaving differently costs you nothing. Create the conditions in which people can thrive. People will see your effort and appreciate it. It is more satisfying than waiting in frustration for your organisation to somehow get into the small percentage with business improvement programmes that work. It is my view that these sorts of change programmes are more likely to be successful if the organisations do some preparatory work on problem solving behaviours before launching anything.

Of course, people do not only encounter problems at work. They occur in our personal lives as well. If you wish, you can also apply this book to problems outside of work. After all, our personal lives are usually much more important than our working lives. I have found that practicing the collaborative approach described in this book is useful in all aspects of life. As John Shook wrote in a Lean Enterprise Institute email in late 2018, "There may be nothing more fundamental to being human than problem solving. We breathe, we eat, we create civilizations – we deal with (solve, tackle) problems every step of the way". However, I have written the book based on office environments.

Solving and Sharing

There is a saying that 'knowledge is power', meaning that knowing some-thing other people do not know gives one an advantage. By extension, hoarding knowledge increases that advantage. This is called informa-tional or expert power.[5] Some people do this to try and increase their personal power and influence. Doing this is inconsistent with the be-haviours needed to solve problems. An alternate approach is to share knowledge and build capacity. Karl-Erik Sveiby observed that unlike conventional assets, knowledge grows when it is shared.[6] This is worth exploring. If I use a machine to make gadgets, and it has an expected use-ful life of 100,000 gadgets before it is likely to need replacing, I consume a portion of the economic life of that machine every time I make a gadget. In so doing, I reduce the residual value of the machine. At least, this is what happens in an accounting sense. However, if I use knowledge to solve a problem, my store of knowledge remains undiminished. It proba-bly grows as I learn something from the situation which I will remember for the future. If I show another person how I am solving the problem, their store of knowledge grows, again with no reduction of mine. The more I use my knowledge with other people, the more both our stores of knowledge grow. A test of whether you truly know something is whether you can teach it to someone else. The more I share my knowledge with other people, the better I become at teaching and the more the total pool of knowledge grows. If they reciprocate and show me something I did not know, my knowledge grows in new areas. The more you use and share knowledge, the greater the value of it, individually and collectively. Knowledge is an asset which grows in value through use.

Hoarding knowledge to build expert power might make an individual more powerful for a while, at least until someone more knowledgeable comes along and displaces them. Sharing knowledge changes the game, making a team or an organisation stronger. Besides, who would want to work with someone who won't share what they know? How would team members learn and improve their work? Showing people how to solve problems together is the real end goal. It is also my experience that this is the most rewarding work. It is personally satisfying and it will help you to build a network of allies and contacts as you become known as someone who develops other people. If you are in a management or leadership role, the success of your team is also your success, so there is immediate benefit to you as well. Good teams reflect well on the team members and on their leaders.

How to Use This Book

You can read this book from cover to cover if you like, and I hope you enjoy doing so. However, it is not necessary to read it that way. It has been written as a guide which you can draw on as required for useful information on each step of the problem solving process and the many tools included. I suggest reading Chapter 1 first, as this is where the problem solving model is set out. Chapter 2 discusses the three key behaviours in more detail. In Chapters 3–8, I elaborate on each step of the problem solving process and describe the use of the tools relevant to that step. There are several case studies and examples with additional information included in the chapters as well. Chapter 9 discusses ways to consider and respond to other people's behaviour. At the conclusion of the book, I give some final thoughts and acknowledge the limitations of this book. It was a deliberate choice to keep this book relatively short in order to make it more accessible to a wide audience. That comes at the cost of going into more detail for some tools.

You will see that there is overlap in use of tools and concepts in problem definition, investigation, and selection. I have tried to explain the problem solving process in a linear way with minimal overlap. However, it is often the case that problem definition is revisited during problem investigation as new information comes to light. Similarly, the choice of measures of success for choosing, implementing, and reviewing the solution really starts with problem definition. As you understand what the problem is, you begin to see what the attributes of a solution will be, even if you don't know what that solution is. As you investigate the problem, you will confirm or adjust your thinking about the relevant measures of success. You will use those measures to assist in selecting the best solution, and then will assess the implemented solution against them when reviewing it.

It is not necessary to apply every tool to every step of the process every time. Consider this book to be a guide to tools and concepts. Use the one(s) you think will best suit the situation. If your first choice does not work as well as you thought, try another. Like all things, you get better with practice. Do try to practice the behaviours in Chapter 2 consistently though. They really are the key.

As stated earlier, this book draws on many different sources. Where I have made an original contribution to a tool, I say so. Where relevant, I have provided references and links to further information. I have not attempted to find the inventor of every single tool in the book. Some are so well known or so widely used that this did not seem necessary. I have given the purpose for each tool and encourage you to adapt them over time as you learn to use them and find what works best for you and your workplace. The habit of borrowing from anywhere and everywhere in an evolving toolkit is a good one to develop. The tools and techniques will change over time, but the behaviours that encourage a collaborative problem solving culture endure.

Notes

1 Smalley, A., 2018, *Four Types of Problems: From Reactive Troubleshooting to Creative Innovation*, Cambridge, MA, Lean Enterprise Institute.
2 Liker J., Meier, D., 2006, *The Toyota Way Fieldbook: A Practical Guide for Implementing Toyota's 4Ps*, New York, McGraw-Hill Companies, p309.
3 Roser, C., 2017, Where Lean Went Wrong – A Historical Perspective (online), Available: https://www.allaboutlean.com/whereleanwentwrong/ (Accessed 18 May 2020).
4 Byrne, A. & Markovitz, D., 2017, Lean Transformation: "Shock and Awe" vs "Slow and Grow" (online), Available: https://www.lean.org/leanpost/Posting.cfm?LeanPostid=767 (Accessed 6 September 2020).
5 Bailey, J. Schermerhorn, J., Hunt, J. & Osborn. R., 1991, *Managing Organisaitonal Behaviour*, Singapore, John Wiley and Sons, p428.
6 Sveiby, K.E., 1997, *The New Organizational Wealth*, San Francisco, CA, Berrett-Koehler Publishers Inc.

Chapter 1

The Problem Solving Model

There are many variations on problem solving models. At the time of writing this book, a Google search on the phrase 'problem solving model' returned 292 million hits. The search brought up links to personal and professional blogs, consulting companies, not-for-profits, small businesses through to multinationals, training providers, and private and public education institutions from all over the world. There were many links to journals, books, and videos. Viewing the Google Images results revealed a startling display of straight lines, circles, squares, ovals, diamonds, funnels, stage gates, ladders, zigzags, animal and tree shapes, and complicated multi-directional charts. The models varied in size from four steps to ten. They came in black and white or a rainbow of colour options. It is easy to be overwhelmed by the many options available.

The model presented in this book has been developed through many years of experience participating in and leading teams in knowledge organisations, along with years of research and study. It is set out in simple language and a logical sequence. The intention is that the readers will quickly make sense of it and use the book to start their own problem solving efforts at a local level. Given the failure rate of organisational process improvement programmes have been estimated at anywhere between 50% and 95%[1] and change management failure has been estimated at up to 75%,[2] it is not feasible for people to sit back and wait for their organisation to change for them. The model borrows from many different sources and assembles them in an easily accessible way. Hopefully, by the end of the book, you will feel empowered to start using this approach.

Problem Solving Overview

The problem solving model in this book can be thought of as three concentric rings (Figure 1.1). The inner ring contains the problem solving process. The middle ring contains the tools that can be used at each step of the process. The outer ring contains the beheviours to practice when solving problems. Each ring is described in this chapter, leading to a more detailed view of the model on page 4.

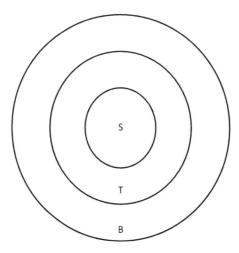

Figure 1.1 Problem solving overview.

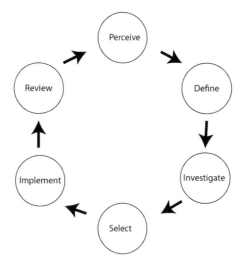

Figure 1.2 Problem solving steps.

Within the inner circle, there is a problem solving process consisting of six steps arranged in a circle (Figure 1.2). The steps are:

1   Perceive the problem
2   Define the problem

3   Investigate the problem
4   Select a solution
5   Implement the solution
6   Review the results (and adjust as necessary)

This model, or something similar to it, will probably look familiar. There are many variations on it, not only in problem solving but in other fields as well (see *Similar Features*). Many problem solving models stop at this point. They describe the steps and you are expected to simply go and do it. That does not seem particularly helpful. You can think of the problem solving process as the frame on which many problem solving tools are hung. However, using the tools in the steps is still not enough. You will achieve better outcomes if you also practice behaviours conducive to successful problem solving. It is the combination of all three which produces a powerful problem solving model that you can work with.

Each of the steps in the problem solving process is described in more detail below. Before getting into the detail, it is worth looking at the process diagram as a whole (Figure 1.2). The choice of a circle is deliberate, as is the use of arrows between each step. Circles signify a holistic approach and interconnectedness. They represent cyclic behaviour rather than specific events that have a beginning and an end. It is not about one-off events or dedicated change projects, but about developing skills to define and fix problems that you can use whenever you need to. The arrows between each step reflect the cyclic nature of problem solving. The arrow between Review and Perceive shows that problem solving is ongoing. There is always more improvement that can be made. It acknowledges that despite everyone's best efforts, attempts to solve problems do not always go to plan. They can sometimes reveal other problems which were not apparent earlier. There might be unintended consequences of the solution which are first noticed as new problems, triggering the cycle to run again. It might seem obvious to start with a circle, but as described above, problem solving models come in many different shapes.

The middle ring of the model represents the tools that support the different steps of the model. The tools are listed near the end of this chapter and described in detail in the following chapters. Due to the number of tools described in the book, they are represented by a single ring around the problem solving process. You will see later in this chapter that they are set out in a table which sits under the circle. As you progress through the book, you will see that the tools presented can take several different forms. Some are document templates (such as a scoping document) or

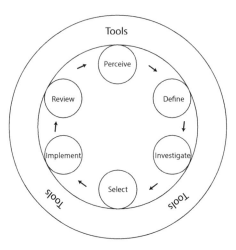

Figure 1.3 Problem solving steps and tools.

diagram templates (such as a fishbone diagram). Other tools are actually concepts (such as the eight wastes) and theories drawn from other disciplines. It is simpler and easier to use the word 'tools' to describe them all rather than using different terms like templates, or models, or concepts throughout the book.

Many of the tools described in the book are applicable to more than one step. For instance, five whys is a classic open-ended questioning approach which can be used at any step of the problem solving process. Similarly, customer journey maps can be used to investigate a problem as well as to review the results of a changed process. In writing the book, it has been assumed this is your first time through the problem solving process and so each tool has been introduced at the point where it is likely to be most useful on first use. However, the reader should not assume the book describes the one best way of doing things. There is no 'one best way' that will work equally well in every organisation. You are encouraged to try the tools at different steps in the model and see what works best for you. This is why all the tools mentioned in this chapter are listed in two different tables – one based on the sequence in which they are linked to the model in this book, and one alphabetical so that you can quickly find the tool you need at the time. You are encouraged to keep looking for other tools which might work for you as well, and to develop your own. Several of the tools in this book are my creations. You will learn over time which ones are best suited to particular situations and which you feel most comfortable using.

Similar Features

If the steps in the problem solving process look familiar to you, it is because they appear everywhere, recurring in many different business and home activities. A few of the more frequently encountered models are set out below.

Hiring New Staff

Most people in the workforce have experienced the hiring process as a job applicant, and many would have participated in selection panels. The steps to hiring someone are very similar to the steps in the problem solving process, as shown in Table 1.1.

Table 1.1 Recruitment and selection = problem solving

Recruitment and selection	Problem solving
• Decide to fill a new or existing position	• Perceive
• Confirm position description, salary, and conditions	• Define
• Seek applicants	• Investigate
• Shortlist applications	• Investigate
• Interview applicants	• Investigate
• Reference checks	• Investigate
• Selection panel decision	• Select
• Hire new staff member	• Implement
• Onboard new staff member	• Implement
• Probation period	• Review

The process starts with seeing the need to hire someone. Then the role is described and the pay and conditions are confirmed. The position is advertised. Possibly a recruitment agency is used and personal networks are activated to attract good applicants. Assessing applicants against the role description, interviews, and referee checks follows. A hiring decision is made, and there may be some negotiation with the person before they commence work. There may be a period of probation to ensure they are a good hire before being confirmed as an employee.

Policy Development

If you have participated in policy development, you may have noticed that the problem solving process looks very similar to steps typically followed when reviewing or developing policy. The typical steps are shown in Table 1.2.

Table 1.2 Policy development = problem solving

Policy Development	Problem solving
• Issue identification	• Perceive and define
• Stakeholder consultation	• Investigate
• Policy formulation	• Investigate
• Decision making	• Select
• Implementation	• Implement
• Evaluation	• Review

Safety Issues

If you have ever been involved in accident investigation, you will see that the models are very similar to problem solving (Table 1.3).

Table 1.3 Safety = problem solving

Accident investigation	Problem solving
• Respond to the accident	• Perceive and/or define
• Plan investigation	• Investigate
• Data collection	• Investigate
• Data analysis	• Investigate
• Corrective actions	• Select and implement
• Reporting	• Review

Procurement Decisions

If you have ever been involved in a procurement process at work or made a major purchase like a car, it probably looked similar to problem solving (Table 1.4).

Table 1.4 Procurement = problem solving

Workplace procurement	Buying a car	Problem solving
• Client identifies need for equipment	• Identify need for a new car	• Perceive
• Prepare procurement brief	• Confirm funding (sale or trade in value of old car, bank loan, other funds) and requirements	• Define
• Go to market with tender	• Search car yards and car sales websites	• Investigate

• Receive tender responses	• Test drive vehicles	• Investigate
• Evaluate responses	• Arrange mechanical and safety inspection	• Investigate/ Select
• Select provider	• Select car	• Select
• Issue purchase order	• Purchase car	• Implement
• Receive and pay for goods	• Receive car	• Implement
• Warranty period	• Warranty period	• Review

When you think of all the different things that you have done, either at work or at home, which follow a similar pattern to solving a workplace problem, you should see that you have a lot of transferrable skills and experience to draw on. It is highly likely that you are starting from a stronger position than you might have thought. You may not have used the problem solving tools described in this book but you have experience in successfully doing similar things.

Steps in the Problem Solving Process

The steps of the problem solving process and the tools introduced in each step are described in more detail below.

The first step in the process is **Perceiving the problem** (Chapter 3). This step is placed at the 12 O'clock position. The key question at this step is "Is there actually a problem to solve?"

When talking about perceived problems, there are often three likely scenarios. The first is a feeling that something is wrong but it is not clear what that is, or why it is not working. The second scenario is people not wanting to believe they need to change and so telling themselves the problem lies elsewhere. The third scenario is that they believe they know exactly what (or sometimes who) the problem is, and have a solution they want you to implement. However, they have no objective evidence to support the claim. They simply insist that it is so. The tools introduced in this chapter will assist in confirming whether there is a problem to solve, and also whether people properly understand the need for an objective and evidence-based approach. The importance of having purposeful conversations throughout the entire problem solving process is discussed as well.

The second step in the process is **Defining the problem** (Chapter 4). The key question at this step is "What is the problem we are trying to solve?"

At this step, you have agreed there is a problem to solve and you are working on a clear definition of it. This is a critical step in problem solving and it warrants the time and attention required to get it right. If you get the problem definition wrong, you will not successfully solve the problem. Skip this step in the rush to a solution and you run the risk of wasting time and money, making things worse rather than better. Properly defining the problem is a highly valuable work. There are a lot of tools introduced in this chapter to help define the problem and scope the work to be done in solving it. You will start to learn about process mapping and be introduced to two widely used problem solving tools: fishbone diagrams and A3 problem statements. The composition of problem solving teams and the importance of choosing the right measures of success are also discussed.

Although defining the problem is a distinct step in the process, you may need to revisit your problem definition as your investigation brings new information to light and gives further insight into the root cause(s) of the problem. The A3 problem statement that you will start at this step is a living document which can be updated through the entire problem solving process.

The third step is **Investigating the problem** (Chapter 5). The key question at this step is "Do we fully understand the problem?"

By this step, you have agreed there is a problem and put effort into defining it. Now you are busy investigating the problem, gathering data and information to ensure there is a clear and shared understanding of the problem. Doing this will generate improvement ideas which should be captured and worked on as potential solutions. Chapter 5 introduces a lot of tools. You should not expect to use all of them on every problem. Two different scenarios are described, with the relevant tools used in each one. The first scenario describes being asked to work with a team from a different unit to help them improve a process. This is done by facilitating a structured process mapping and review activity called a rapid improvement event. This is a very popular structured process improvement activity. The second scenario describes working in a unit responding to unexpected problems arising from a new company-wide payroll system implementation. This scenario uses a fishbone diagram and A3 problem statement, classic tools for finding the root cause of a problem and methodically working through solutions to it.

The fourth step is **Selecting the solution** (Chapter 6). The key question at this step is "Are we confident we have picked the best solution?"

In this step you choose the solution which you believe will best solve the problem. This seems a very simple step and is often glossed over in models. However, it is of great importance as making the wrong decision will cost time, money, and credibility. The tools described in this chapter will help to select the solution. This chapter also explains the difference between reducing cost and creating new capacity. It is critical that you understand this difference when working in an office environment, where you are likely to generate a lot of time savings through problem solving, but not always a lot of cash savings. The payoff to the business will often be in using the saved time to add new value.

The fifth step is **Implementing the solution** (Chapter 7). The key question at this step is "Are we ready to solve the problem?"

At this step, you implement the selected solution. Action plans and RACI charts are discussed. This chapter refers back to the payroll system implementation in Chapter 5 to explore how automation helps to make problems visible to the business, although sometimes at the expense of the internal client.

It is deliberate that implementation is the second last step in the problem solving process. Jumping to the solution without spending the time to properly define and investigate the problem reduces the likelihood of solving it.

The sixth step is **Reviewing the results** (Chapter 8). The key question at this step is "Have we solved the problem?"

Tools introduced at this step help to tell the story of the changes and include customer journey maps and visual displays. The importance of reviewing performance and of reflection on the problem solving process itself is discussed.

Problem Solving Behaviours

The outer ring of the problem solving model shown in Figure 1.1 represents the behaviour needed to successfully solve problems. Three behaviours are discussed in this book: curiosity, collaboration, and use of evidence-based thinking (Figure 1.4). The placement of behaviours at particular points in the model does not mean that the behaviours are only relevant to that part of the process. The use of overlapping arrows circling the model indicates that the behaviours should be used throughout the process where appropriate. However, experience shows that each behaviour is most useful to focus on where they are shown in the diagram. That is, when discussing someone's perception of a problem, using an open and curious approach is more effective than not using one. When investigating the problem and developing potential solutions, curiosity and collaboration are likely to be most useful. It is in this stage of the process that most new tools are introduced, providing a great learning opportunity. When selecting, implementing, and reviewing the solution, the predominant behaviour is likely to be evidence-based thinking. The model builds in complexity as the middle and outer rings are added to it, and the behaviours build in complexity as you progress through the process. You might start with curiosity, asking open-ended questions and trying to draw out information to determine if there is a problem. Then as you define and investigate the problem you will use different tools which require working with other people. This increased focus on collaboration will still require curiosity. When it comes to selecting and implementing a solution, there will be an increased need for evidence-based decisions and objective criteria for measuring improvement. So the

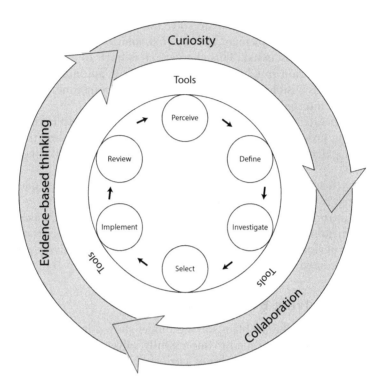

Figure 1.4 The complete problem solving model.

behaviours also layer on top of each other. The behaviours are described in Chapter 2, along with a discussion of how they align with contemporary leadership models.

The final chapter of the book (Chapter 9) contains advice and tools for responding to other people's behaviour. Very few problem solving books consider this. They show you a model, or some tools, and tell you to go for it. However, unless you work in manufacturing or a highly automated transactional job, the way people behave will have an enormous influence over how things get done, and whether improvements will stick. So, it is essential to understand and be able to anticipate how people might act when you are implementing solutions.

Problem Solving Tools

The complete set of tools described in this book is shown in Figure 1.5. This is a view of the tools listed against the step where they are introduced. Table 1.5 is a complete list of the tools in alphabetical order including page numbers so you can easily locate the one you want.

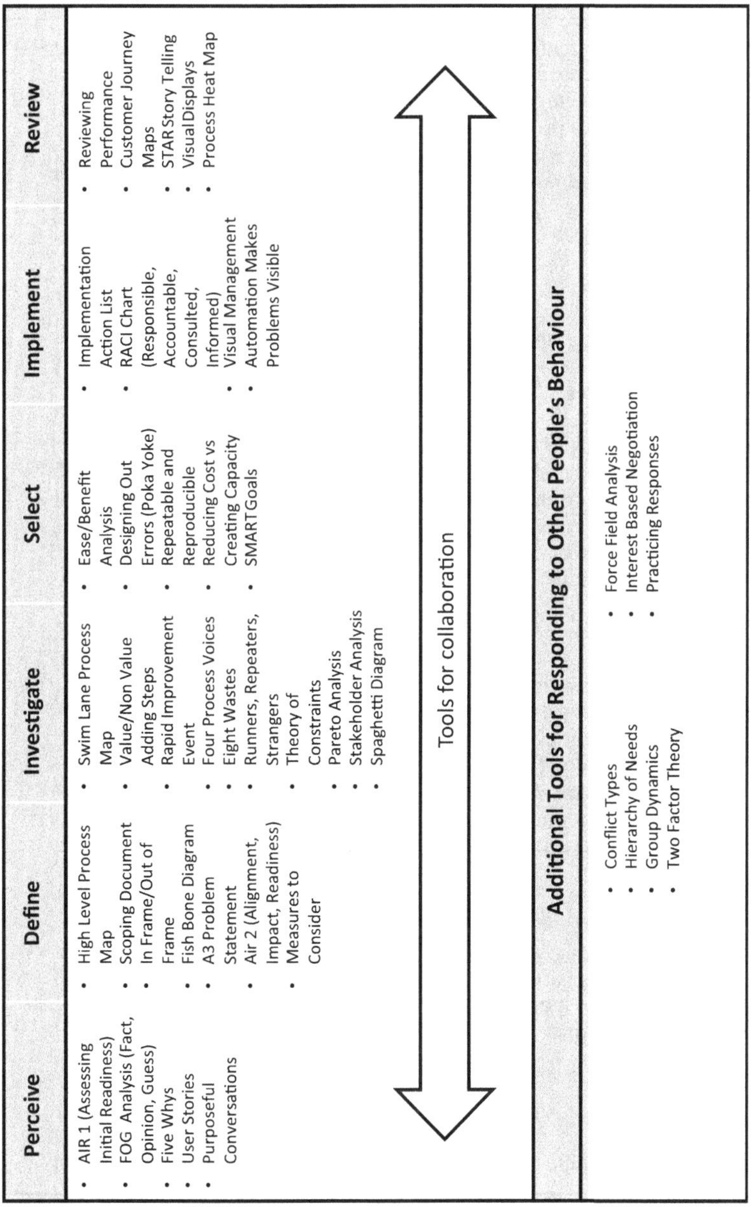
Perceive
AIR 1 (Assessing Initial Readiness)
FOG Analysis (Fact, Opinion, Guess)
Five Whys
User Stories
Purposeful Conversations
Define
High Level Process Map
Scoping Document
In Frame/Out of Frame
Fish Bone Diagram
A3 Problem Statement
Air 2 (Alignment, Impact, Readiness)
Measures to Consider
Investigate
Swim Lane Process Map
Value/Non Value Adding Steps
Rapid Improvement Event
Four Process Voices
Eight Wastes
Runners, Repeaters, Strangers
Theory of Constraints
Pareto Analysis
Stakeholder Analysis
Spaghetti Diagram
Select
Ease/Benefit Analysis
Designing Out Errors (Poka Yoke)
Repeatable and Reproducible
Reducing Cost vs Creating Capacity
SMART Goals
Implement
Implementation Action List
RACI Chart (Responsible, Accountable, Consulted, Informed)
Visual Management
Automation Makes Problems Visible
Review
Reviewing Performance
Customer Journey Maps
STAR Story Telling
Visual Displays
Process Heat Map
Tools for collaboration
Additional Tools for Responding to Other People's Behaviour
Conflict Types
Hierarchy of Needs
Group Dynamics
Two Factor Theory
Force Field Analysis
Interest Based Negotiation
Practicing Responses

Figure 1.5 Tools used in problem solving model.

Table 1.5 Alphabetical list of tools

Tool	Page No.
• A3 problem statement	57, 95
• AIR 1 (assessing initial readiness)	33
• AIR 2 (alignment, impact, readiness)	58
• Automation makes problems visible	116
• Conflict types	132
• Customer journey maps	125
• Designing out errors (Poka Yoke)	103
• Ease/benefit analysis	101
• Eight wastes	82
• Fishbone diagram	54, 91
• Five whys	36
• FOG analysis (fact, opinion, guess)	35
• Force field analysis	138
• Four process voices	81
• Group dynamics	135
• Hierarchy of needs	134
• High-level process map	43, 78
• Implementation action list	111
• In frame/out of frame	48
• Interest-based negotiation	140
• Measures to consider	60
• Pareto analysis	93
• Practicing responses	142
• Process heat map	129
• Purposeful conversations	38, 139
• RACI chart (responsible, accountable, consulted, informed)	112
• Rapid improvement event	74
• Reducing cost vs creating capacity	106
• Repeatable and reproducible	106
• Reviewing performance	124
• Runners, repeaters, strangers	84
• Scoping document	47
• SMART goals	109
• Spaghetti diagram	98
• Stakeholder analysis	95
• STAR storytelling (situation, task/action, result)	127
• Swim lane process map	69, 89
• Theory of constraints	85
• Two-factor theory	137
• User stories	38
• Value/non-value adding steps	72
• Visual display	128
• Visual management	114

Creating Shared Understanding

As you work through this model with a real problem in your workplace, it will very quickly become evident that this is a collaborative problem solving model. All of the tools in this book are intended to be used with other people. Doing so creates a shared understanding of what is happening and strengthens workplace relationships. Many workplaces have siloed units or teams who only work on their part of a process, and who do not have a clear idea of what happens in the process before or after their work takes place. This is especially true of large organisations.

Collaboration is important in all work but perhaps even more so in office work where the 'product' is invisible. One of the challenges in successfully translating process improvement methodologies from manufacturing to offices is the lack of a visible product. If you think of a car progressing along an assembly line, you can see very clearly the parts and materials going into the car, you can see the waste of spare material and the defects of parts that do not fit or do not work as they should. Everything is tangible. The famous Toyota 'andon cord', with which any worker can stop the assembly line when they see a defect, is effective in a setting where the work is visible. However, when the work is electronic and is information based (for instance writing a report), things are harder to see. The person sitting at their desk busily typing away may well be working on an important report for the business. Or they could be preparing their weekly shopping list. Assuming they are doing important work, how they do it could be invisible to you. How would you know if they are doing it the same way as their colleague at the next desk? Or which of the two have the better way of doing it? If they are using a corporate system with an inbuilt workflow which date stamps each person's interaction with an instance of the process, you can collect some information on their work. However, there will still be work they do outside of such systems and your knowledge of how they work will be incomplete. Collaboration and creating a shared understanding of what is actually happening become even more important in such settings. It is worth remembering that what the andon cord actually represents for Toyota is the obligation of every employee to notify colleagues when they see a problem.[3] Building a similar culture in an office environment is a challenge.

As discussed in the introduction to this book, problems are opportunities to improve and to learn. This cannot happen in isolation. It is necessary to use the problem solving model collaboratively in order to take advantage of the learning opportunity. Problems become vehicles to drive learning and knowledge sharing. Doing this inevitably creates a cultural change opportunity too. The culture is not the mission statement in glossy paper on the wall, or the values listed on the website. It is the way people behave on a daily basis. When people start to practice positive behaviours, and other people respond favourably, they begin to change the culture of their team. Practicing the behaviours of curiosity, collaboration, and evidence-based thinking while working with other people to solve problems and improve the workplace can have a positive effect on culture. Individuals and teams become empowered to find and fix problems, and to suggest improvements without waiting for complaints or defects to emerge. Even if your organisation does not attempt to implement this across the board, you can improve the culture locally, making your working life, and the working lives of those around you, more fulfilling.

Notes

1 Roser, C., 2017, Where Lean Went Wrong – A Historical Perspective (online). Available: https://allaboutlean.com/where-lean-went-wrong/ (Accessed 18 May 2020).
2 Raelin, J.D. & Cataldo, C.G., 2011, Wither Middle Management? Empowering Interface and the Failure of Organizational Change, *Journal of Change Management*, 11, p505.
3 Shook, J., 2010, How to Change a Culture: Lessons from NUMMI, *Sloan Management Review*, p66.

Chapter 2

Problem Solving Behaviour

The problem solving behaviours described in this book are curiosity, collaboration, and evidence-based thinking. This is shown in the problem solving model in Figure 2.1. As described in Chapter 1, the placement of the three behaviours at particular points in the model does not mean that they are only relevant to that step. The use of overlapping arrows circling the model indicates that all the behaviours should be used throughout the process, drawing on each whenever appropriate. However, each particular behaviour is shown in the model where they are likely to be most useful. When discussing someone's perception of a problem and subsequently defining the problem, using an open and curious approach is effective. When investigating the problem and developing potential solutions, curiosity and collaboration are likely to be most useful. When selecting, implementing, and reviewing the solution, evidence-based thinking will be very important. It is the integrated use of the problem solving process, the tools, and the behaviours that can lead to great results.

This chapter describes each of the behaviours in more detail, and also explains how they link to leadership. As you become proficient at problem solving and incorporate curiosity, collaboration, and evidence-based thinking in your daily work life, you will be displaying characteristics which align with several contemporary leadership models. This can benefit you in your career. Understanding how these behaviours align with desirable leadership behaviours can help in your interaction with people already in leadership positions. You will be better placed to describe how adopting a collaborative problem solving approach can benefit the business, and also benefit its leaders. Anything you can do to incrementally shift thinking in this way is going to help your future problem solving efforts, and might even assist in changing the alarming situation of 50–90% of business improvement efforts failing.

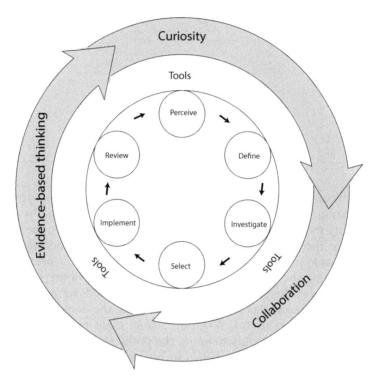

Figure 2.1 The complete problem solving model.

Curiosity

In the busyness of work, and under pressure to complete tasks in short time frames, it is easy to forget to be curious. Hasn't everyone had days when they march into the office with a list of things to accomplish, shut their office door (or put on headphones if they work in an open-plan environment), and then smash out task after task with a growing feeling of satisfaction and accomplishment? Ignore the phone, don't check emails, scowl at anyone who approaches you; do what you have to do in order to get that list checked off. You are in the zone and are a productivity machine! It is sometimes necessary to retreat from distractions and focus on task completion. However, this approach is not likely to be successful if repeated too often. And it is definitely not the best way to go about solving problems.

Curiosity is simply a desire to know. Definitions include "the joy of discovery" and "motivation to seek answers to what is unknown".[1] You have to understand a problem in order to solve it. This means gathering information about the problem, and that information will largely come from other people. Therefore, problem solving requires the ability to make other people feel willing to tell you about things going wrong at work. Depending on their role in the organisation, or the current culture in their workplace, this can be an uncomfortable thing to do. For some people it might feel quite scary. However, in order to improve, it is essential to acknowledge that problems exist and that the solutions are not yet known.[2] This is the challenge of displaying curiosity.

Recent research has shown that asking questions in conversations increases likeability, as you are perceived to be more responsive and attentive.[3] If you think about conversations you have had when getting to know someone new, you probably took turns at sharing information about yourselves. Choosing to disclose something about yourself was seen as a sign of trust in the other person. Asking questions about them demonstrated your interest in them. Each allowing opportunity for the other person to speak helped the conversation to flow. Asking questions with genuine interest and curiosity can also help to establish good working relationships. Curiosity in problem solving is best expressed by displaying genuine interest in understanding what is happening and asking open-ended questions to understand why it is happening. This form of questioning demonstrates a desire to help the other person. Edgar Schein's work on humble inquiry is a great resource for understanding curiosity and helping. Schein defines humble inquiry as "the fine art of drawing someone out, of asking questions to which you do not already know the answer, of building a relationship based on curiosity and interest in the other person".[4]

How you ask the question will make a difference as well. The choice of verbal and non-verbal cues matters. A question as simple as "Why is this happening?" can be received as threatening if delivered in an angry tone, vulnerable if delivered with an anguished cry, or helpful if delivered in a quiet, friendly, and inquisitive tone. The wording of the question matters as well. Questions which only require a yes or no answer are not going to give you much information (for example, "Did you try rebooting the computer?"). An open question to ask instead would be "Can you talk me through the things you did in trying to make the software work?" Using the five whys (explained in Chapter 3) can help to go deeper into why something is happening in order to identify the root cause of a problem. Asking open-ended questions such as "Why do you think this might be happening?" will encourage people to give their ideas and could prompt some new information as well. However, as will be discussed under evidence-based thinking, you do not just want to accept someone's opinion. You also need to understand what information they have to support their view.

Curiosity requires you to be observant. You will need to invest time in understanding what is happening, ask questions about it, and seek information to confirm your understanding. Observation has been defined as "seeing with a purpose" when used to investigate a workplace problem.[5] An early form of observation in an industrial setting is the introduction of time studies by Frederick Taylor in the 1880s, and later time and motion studies by the Gilbreths. The requirement to 'go and see' work where it is occurring in order to grasp the situation[6] is one of the fundamental practices in lean today. There are many other uses of observation such as coaching athletes and dancers in technique, concert performance rehearsals, and so on. Observation is not as straight forward in an office environment as it might be in manufacturing, manual labour or sport. Observing someone working at their desk might not give you much information about a problem or about whether they are following an agreed process. You will need to look for data about process performance, ask questions about how they are doing the work, and seek to observe behaviours and interaction between team members. It is beneficial to already have some understanding of the work or process you will be observing and of the relevant data to look for. You should also be aware that what you observe is what is happening at that moment, and might not be representative of what happens at other times. Seeing something one time only is not enough.

Practicing curiosity is not just about drawing information out of other people by asking questions. It can also be displayed through sharing information (see *Curiosity through sharing*). Curiosity helps to build relationships, and is well suited to problem solving when you will remain part of the team or the organisation into the future. It fosters deeper relationships in order to provide real help. This will strengthen the connection between team members. When you consider that a problem solving team could be an informal group of stakeholders from across an organisation, displaying behaviours conducive to stronger working relationships can have significant long-term benefits. However, this slower build-up of relationships over time is often incompatible with the way consultants and facilitators are engaged. Charging an expensive daily rate tends to concentrate consultancies into short time frames. Seeking to impress the client, the consultant often provides the suggested solution or 'guides' the team to a solution quickly. Consultants, and sometimes internal facilitators or change agents, are given limited opportunity to work with the teams during implementation and review. Learning opportunities are lost as a result. Displaying curiosity from a 'business-as-usual' role in an organisation presents opportunities that other roles might not have.

Curiosity through Sharing

Michael was very busy in last few hours of work before starting a two-week trip to England. He noted in his emails that he
was going to be away from the office for two weeks, but did
not give any details. Michael sent a draft report to a colleague,
asking them to provide feedback. He received a reply from his
colleague, promising to read the report while flying to London
that evening. Realising that they were both about to fly to London, Michael asked about his colleague's travel plans. In a few
short emails they confirmed they were on the same flight and
had some free time on the same day later that week, so arranged
to meet in London. Over lunch, Michael observed that it was
fortunate they had shared their itineraries in time. They might
have seen each other at the airport anyway but it was good to
arrange it in advance, especially as they had wanted to catch
up for several months and had not managed to fix a time. His
colleague replied, "Yes, I always do that. You never know what
might come of it".

"Do what?" Michael asked.

"Give more information than you might think necessary. I chose
to tell you that I was travelling to London that evening. I do that
because I am interested in seeing where it might lead."

"Really? I had not thought of that".

"Some of the best collaborations I have started with giving more
information at the time and seeing where it led. Some people ignore it and some don't. It costs me nothing to share information
and can lead to great things".

As you use the tools described in this book, be prepared to share
your work with people. Put them up on the wall, or online where people can see them. This inevitably draws the curious towards you and
can start interesting and valuable conversations about the problem
you are currently working on, and the problem solving process. Displaying your work becomes an act of change in itself. Problems genuinely become opportunities to learn and to improve things together.
Chapter 8 includes discussion of visual displays, which are simply the
provision of key information in a visual format to encourage discussion and further shared understanding of what is happening in the
workplace.

Collaboration

People who support problem solving efforts perform several different roles during the course of this work. They learn to adjust their approach to the situation and to the level of experience of the people they are working with. This can involve helping people to understand and define problems, teaching people how to use tools they may not have used before, providing directive coaching in the use of those tools, perhaps providing reflective coaching on the success or otherwise of the problem solving effort, and engaging directly in problem solving. This book uses the word collaboration to describe the behaviour conducive to all these things: helping, teaching, coaching, and doing.

Helping is intrinsic to organisations. An organisation is literally an entity which organises people into roles and team structures in order to accomplish more than one person could accomplish on their own.[7] Viewed that way, everyone in the organisation is there to help achieve the organisation's mission. Teamwork, which you can define as people working together to achieve the organisation's goals, is ongoing reciprocal helping. If you think of an organisation in this way, problem solving is an important form of helping as well. It contributes to the organisation achieving its mission more efficiently and effectively. Becoming proficient at problem solving is therefore a way to become better at helping your organisation. As you develop your problem solving skills over time, you can move beyond providing help to providing what is known as 'deep help'.[8] This type of help takes place over a longer time frame in a series of interactions with another person or a team. This form of help is best provided by people in the organisation rather than consultants or contractors. For instance, performing an internal consultant role which assists teams in other parts of the organisation is a form of deep help which can strengthen relationships and contribute to improved performance and team effectiveness.

Teaching is showing someone how to do something that they do not know how to do. For example, when you show someone a fishbone diagram for the first time, you will need to tell them what it is used for, how it is set out, and how it relates to other tools like A3 problem statements. Coaching is more complex than teaching. There are two different types of coaching. One is self-reflective and involves the coach asking questions to draw out personal insights, and guide the other person in a voyage of self-discovery. The other type is directive coaching which can involve providing advice on options, but again without actually providing the answer to a question. Displaying coaching behaviours is not the same thing as claiming to be a coach, but can help to develop and motivate other people.[9] Whether you call it teaching or coaching, it is an essential skill in problem solving. As discussed in the introduction, this is how knowledge is shared and grown.

Actually engaging in problem solving is fun and can be quite addictive. The challenge with participating in the problem solving itself is to make sure you also do the teaching and coaching so there is shared ownership of the solution. You have to think of yourself as being at least part consultant in this activity. Otherwise, the learning opportunity could be lost. Just as importantly, if you try to solve the problem yourself, you are likely to get a less successful outcome. The people closest to the problem are best placed to find the solution. It may be that your role is to guide them to that solution by leading them through the problem solving process.

Problem solving begins with an acknowledgement that we do not know what the solution is, and indeed might still need to properly define the problem. This may sound scary to admit, but is actually liberating. Acknowledging this requires a response. That response is to use a problem solving approach to work through the problem. As someone involved in, or even leading, the problem solving effort, you are not claiming expert knowledge of the problem, or that you personally will find the solution. You are offering to share a structured approach to the problem with other people to help find a solution. Doing this will also increase your own knowledge and skills.[10] Even veteran facilitators or problem solvers will acknowledge that they learn something new in most situations. That is one of the exciting things about working on problems. There is always opportunity to learn something new.

While this book is aimed at individuals and small teams, the potential impact of displaying these behaviours should not be discounted. Rother describes how the actions of one person can make a difference to others: when one person chooses to practice new behaviours every day, this influences other people's thinking and actions, ultimately leading to cultural change.[11] It is important to be realistic about the extent to which one person, or one team, can change an entire organisation via a grassroots revolution. However, there are many different subcultures within organisations and it is possible to positively influence the culture around you. You might have wider impact over time, but even if your influence is local rather than global, you will still improve your own working life and the working lives of your colleagues.

Useful coaching competencies fit very well with the behaviours of curiosity and evidence-based decision making. They include[12,13]:

- Interpersonal skills, including the considered use of body language and other non-verbal cues
- Ability to establish a rapport and communicate openly
- Listening skills and use of observation
- Ability to ask insightful questions
- Responding openly and honestly
- Organisational and time-management skills
- Objectivity

While coaching during the problem solving process is more likely to be directive than reflective, the review step of the process (Chapter 8) is an excellent opportunity to reflect as a team on problem solving process and discuss learnings which each person can take with them in future problem solving endeavours.

Evidence-based Thinking

Evidence-based thinking reinforces the problem solving process. Although it is not typically mentioned in leadership models, it is an important element of process improvement methodology such as Six Sigma. The Six Sigma approach is to understand business performance (or individual process performance) by determining the most appropriate performance measures, then analysing relevant data to identify variations from expected results.[14] Depending on the problem, Six Sigma can sometimes use heavy statistical analysis which is well beyond the scope of this book. However, many problems can be solved using less complicated tools such as Pareto analysis and rolled throughput yield. The case study on problems arising from a new payroll system in Chapter 5 includes the use of Pareto analysis to prioritise the problem solving effort.

A challenge for many knowledge-based organisations is that the quality of available process performance data can be highly variable. For instance, universities generally have a very good understanding of how they compare to other universities, but often do not have robust data on their internal processes. As you start to solve problems in your workplace, be prepared to find that people's understanding of the current state of the work will be incomplete, and often anecdotal. Being evidence-based does not mean insisting on detailed data for everything. It means making decisions objectively, based on the best, verifiable information available at the time. It is quite common in office environments to find there is a lack of robust data to inform problem analyses or assess process performance. While not ideal, you will have to work with it. At the very least, your problem solving effort should clearly identify the information gaps and include ways to improve data quality in the future. In this way, you will be able to establish a more reliable baseline to measure future performance and seek further improvements. Having a baseline also means you can compare your performance to other units or organisations. It is only through looking objectively at performance, and tracking it with evidence, that you can make clear comparisons and assess the gap between current performance and your desired performance.

Here are two examples of the importance of being led by evidence: one in assessing the current state of a process and one in predicting the future state.

Current State Data

People often remember the most extreme example of something happening, even if the extreme example is rare. For instance, when someone is asked how long it takes to complete a task, they might say it can vary from ten minutes to two hours. When asked for details about the variation in time, they tell you in great detail about the incident from hell in which everything went wrong and it took two hours to complete a seemingly simple task. This incident will be burnt into their memory. When asked how often it goes that badly, they look surprised and concede it only happened like that once. On reflection, they tell you that most times it takes 10–20 minutes to complete the task in question. The concept of RRS (runners, repeaters, and strangers), which is explained in Chapter 5, helps with managing this.

Something else to consider is the difference between clock time and perceptual time.[15] Clock time is the actual time it takes to do something. Perceptual time is how quickly or slowly it seems that the time passes. For instance, waiting on hold for someone in a call centre to answer the phone might feel like it takes much longer than it really does (and no, filling the waiting time with recorded messages about how much you value your customer does not make the time go faster). A personal example of this is how my children often commented that the drive back from the beach always seemed faster than the drive to the beach. I suspect it is because time seems to go more slowly when you are excited about spending the day at the beach and want to get there, while it seems to pass more quickly when you are half asleep in the car on the way home after a day out.

Future State Data

In planning the future process, people often get excited and imagine the process running perfectly every time. Even though the discussion of current state performance might highlight many different things happening and many potential points of failure, the future state is imagined as faultless. This can result in an overestimate of benefits from the change, and subsequent disappointment if those benefits are not realised. It is fine to aspire for perfection in the process, but important to be realistic about achieving it quickly. Rolled throughput yield (explained in Chapter 4) is a useful tool to consider when this happens.

It is useful to remember that today's solution may not be the solution in a year. As circumstances change, you may need to revisit your solution. Being evidence-based in your thinking will be very helpful in this situation. The natural tendency will be to defend the changes that were made previously. They represent time and effort, and most likely were delivered with a sense of pride and accomplishment. Objectivity and an evidence-based approach will help to explain the reason for further change.

The behaviours of curiosity, collaboration, and evidence-based thinking are all intended to support problem solving. All of the tools and techniques introduced in this book are collaborative in nature. They are designed to be used while working with other people. It is important to remember that you do not need to wait for a problem to emerge before doing this. Although the book is structured around the steps of the problem solving process, the behaviours and the tools can be used at any time, whenever you think you can improve on some aspect of your work or when you see an opportunity.

Leadership and Problem Solving

Lack of leadership support is one of the most frequently cited reasons for business improvement failure, along with staff resistance to change.[16] This seems intractable – leaders do not support the improvement effort, and even if they did, staff resist the changes! Yet, logically, no one would choose to oppose improvements at work. Why would they? The people doing the work would not choose to continue doing it in a frustrating and mistake laden way. The company leadership would not choose to let the business run in a sub-optimal and wasteful way. There must be a disconnect happening somewhere. Would staff be more open to change programmes if they could see clear leadership support and alignment with shared values and beliefs?

What can you do about this from where you are in the organisation today? As you practice the behaviours of curiosity, collaboration, and evidence-based thinking, you can observe the effect it has on the people around you. You can assess its effectiveness for yourself, and be willing to share this with people when the opportunity arises. You can also understand how these behaviours align with contemporary leadership theories like transformational leadership, exemplary leadership, authentic leadership, and lean leadership. The alignment of each of these theories with the three behaviours in this book is described, both to reassure you of the value of these behaviours and to inform you of their relevance to people already in leadership roles. You do not have to be in a senior role to display leadership behaviours and be a positive influence. People lead in different ways from all levels of an organisation. However, if you do aspire to leadership roles in the future, the problem solving behaviours of curiosity, collaboration, and evidence-based thinking will serve you well.

Contemporary Leadership Theories

Workplace behaviour and motivation theories have evolved over the past century from a basic understanding of the wage-effort exchange and the psychological contract as transactional arrangements, through increasingly sophisticated understanding of extrinsic and intrinsic motivation. The thinking has extended from individuals to teams to entire organisations. Leadership theories have also evolved over the past century. Early leadership theories were 'great trait' theories which tried to identify the unique characteristics successful leaders were believed to have been born with. These traits even included physical characteristics such as height, physique, and appearance, as well as knowledge and intelligence.[17] Subsequent leadership theories focused on leader behaviours and leadership styles, and began to consider the deliberate use of different styles in different situations. Examples of this include the Managerial Grid by Blake and Mouton, and the Situational Leadership model by Hershey and Blanchard. Some theories focused on leader use of punishment or reward to exert control, while others such as Robert House focused on leader charisma, marking a return to traits but linked much more clearly to the ability to inspire others. Recent leadership theories have extended the theme of inspiring others through leader behaviours and characteristics, with consistent themes of forming genuine connections with people, acting with integrity, and inspiring others through actions. As the link between leadership and workplace motivation has become more evident, the models have become more sophisticated and more closely entwined.

This book integrates behaviour and a problem solving framework in order to achieve better results. The behaviours of curiosity, collaboration, and evidence-based thinking were chosen for their effectiveness in contributing to problem solving. They were also chosen for their alignment with leadership behaviours. It is not surprising to consider that the behaviours most conducive to leading problem solving efforts in the modern office environment are also behaviours common to contemporary leadership thinking. Explicitly linking behaviour to problem solving is supported by research into creativity in the workplace, which states that the necessary conditions for creativity (generating ideas) and innovation (putting them into practice) include support at the supervisor, workgroup, and organisational levels.[18] That is, people are more creative at work when they feel supported in doing so.

Table 2.1 maps the three leadership behaviours against the dominant characteristics of the leadership theories. This mapping is done for each of the three behaviours, for the behaviours collectively, and also notes those leadership characteristics which do not align so neatly. You will see there is very good alignment across almost all the characteristics of the models.

Table 2.1 Problem solving behaviours and leadership theories

Problem solving behaviours	Transformational leadership (Bass)	Exemplary leadership (Kouzes and Posner)	Servant leadership (Greenleaf)	Lean leadership
Curiosity	Intellectual Stimulation – encourage innovative solutions	Challenge the Process – work with others to make things better	Listening – be receptive to what others have to say Empathy – see the world from their perspective to understand them	Continuous Improvement
Collaboration	Individual Consideration – listen carefully to the individual needs of followers	Enable Others to Act – build trust and collaboration Encourage the Heart – give praise, show appreciation and encouragement	Awareness – be aware of the impact you have on others Commitment to the growth of people – help people to grow professionally and personally	Respect for People
Evidence-Based Thinking	Inspirational Motivation – communicate high expectations to others		Persuasion – create change through non-judgemental decisions Conceptualisation – provide a clear sense of goals and direction	Continuous Improvement
All Behaviours	Idealised Influence – be a strong role model	Model the Way – find your voice and set an example for others Inspire a Shared Vision – visualise and communicate positive outcomes	Healing – care about the personal well-being of others Stewardship – accept responsibility for leading people and the organisation	Respect for People
Not Fully Aligned	Inspirational Motivation – including emotional appeals to gain buy in		Foresight – act on your understanding of the future	

Transformational Leadership

Transformational leadership involves engaging with people to "create connections which raises the level of motivation and morality in both the leader and the follower".[19] This is distinct from transactional forms of leadership which are based on exchanges or trade-offs between leaders and followers (do this for me and I will do something for you). A transformational leader seeks to infuse the organisation with a different way of doing things. The behaviours in transformational leadership can be used one-on-one, in groups, or in broad organisational culture change. Intellectual stimulation encourages new approaches and careful problem solving. Individualised consideration requires leaders to listen carefully to the needs of followers and for leaders to act as coaches. Both of these behaviours clearly align with the approach described in this book. Inspirational motivation is the communication of high expectations to followers, which aligns with evidence-based thinking. Idealised influence includes being a role model and displaying behaviours that other people seek to emulate. There is a similar characteristic to this in all the leadership models, and it can be considered to relate to all the problem solving behaviours.

Many of these attributes are similar to the problem solving behaviours. Where transformational leadership differs from the problem solving approach in this book is that transformational leaders are typically expected to create a vision for the organisation, and this can include using emotional appeals to promote the vision and gain buy-in to it. These are actions related to senior leadership roles, while this book is for people in any role. Also, given this book is about problem solving, objectivity and evidence-based thinking are more effective than emotional appeals.

Exemplary Leadership

Exemplary leadership describes the "five practices most common to extraordinary leadership achievement".[20] Modelling the way demonstrates personal credibility, standing up for beliefs and demonstrating guiding principles through actions. Inspiring a shared vision requires presenting a clear view of what the organisation can become, and enlisting others in achieving it. It also requires understanding other people's needs and interests and demonstrating how their needs will be met. Challenging the process requires seeking opportunities to improve and accepting ideas from anyone in the organisation. The leader's role is to recognise and support good ideas. Enabling others to act requires leaders to collaborate, to strengthen others, and to build trust. This involves engaging people in making the change and also in living with the results. Finally, encouraging the heart requires recognising the contributions of others and celebrating values and victories. These need not be elaborate celebrations, but must be authentic. Small, genuine acts mean more to people than big, empty gestures.

There is close alignment between the problem solving behaviours and the five practices of exemplary leadership. An important element of exemplary leadership is the belief that leadership skills can be learned, practiced, and developed, as opposed to being something that leaders are born with. Leadership is "an observable, learnable set of practices".[21] The least amount of clear alignment between the problem solving model and exemplary leadership is in evidence-based thinking, although being seen to make decisions based on objective assessment of available information will build trust, which is part of enabling others to act.

Servant Leadership

Servant leadership is based on a belief that leadership is a service to other people. The servant leader starts with a desire to serve others, and ultimately aspires to leadership roles in order to better serve others. Rather than seeing a leadership role as a position of power, the servant leader sees it as a position of influence and opportunity to help others. Robert Greenleaf set out ten characteristics of servant leaders, including listening and empathy, persuasion, stewardship, and commitment to the growth of people.[22] Greenleaf's model of servant leadership was grounded in spirituality, asking questions like "Do the people being served grow through the experience?" More recently, Northouse provided a model of servant leadership which placed the leadership behaviours more in the context of the organisation, including context and culture, leader attributes, and follower receptivity. The leaders' behaviour within that context could influence individual, organisational, and even societal outcomes.[23]

Servant leadership is a model grounded in developing and growing other people. As seen in Table 2.1, the characteristics of servant leadership map evenly on to the problem solving behaviours of curiosity, collaboration, and evidence-based thinking, as well as aligning with the other leadership models in taking responsibility for leading and being a role model. It aligns with curiosity in terms of listening and understanding other people's positions. Awareness and commitment to the growth of other people align with collaboration. Although servant leadership is spiritual in nature, it has a strong alignment with evidence-based thinking through persuasion and conceptualisation. It is only foresight (knowing the future) which does not clearly align. Of particular value to people who are not currently in leadership positions, the focus on influence rather than power makes servant leadership a model that can be applied by anyone.

Lean Leadership

While not widely known as a leadership theory in its own right, lean leadership has steadily gained prominence in business improvement literature in recent years. Lean is a process improvement methodology based on the Toyota Production System. It has become increasingly popular over the past 30 years, since the publication of *The Machine That Changed the World*.[24] Initial attempts to replicate the practices observed at Toyota and described in the book met with limited success. This prompted further study of Toyota, leading to the realisation that it was not the use of particular production methods or improvement tools which sustained their success; it was the integration of continuous improvement practices into jobs across the entire company that gave Toyota its competitive advantage. This has been described in books like *The Toyota Way*[25] and *Toyota Kata*.[26] As interest in Toyota's culture has increased, researchers have written about lean thinking, lean management systems, and lean leadership.

Even within the relatively narrow field of lean leadership, there are multiple definitions. Indeed, a significant difference between lean leadership as a theory and other leadership theories is that there is no single author who developed it. There are many different authors attempting to describe what they see in lean organisations, and particularly in Toyota. Rother describes the role of lean leaders as "increasing the improvement capability of people".[27] Balle offers a similar definition, "Lean leadership is the skill of achieving goals by developing people".[28] Emiliani stresses the need for lean leaders to work on continuous improvement of their own leadership practices and behaviours as well as of the business,[29] explicitly adding a self-reflective element not always evident in other definitions.[30] There are several well-known statements from within Toyota such as "Before we built cars, we built people"[31] and "Go see, ask why, show respect".[32] What these definitions and statements all share is a focus on developing skills and characteristics of people in order to achieve long-term business success.

Lean leadership is one aspect of Toyota's unique business system, and is both complementary to, and supported by, the other elements of that system. It can therefore be thought of as leadership practice rooted in a particular type of organisation. This is very different to other leadership models which describe individual behaviours and characteristics to lead and inspire people, presumably in any organisational setting. This may be a clue to why mature organisations continue to struggle to implement lean. It appears to require a cultural as well as operational rebuild from the top down. While lean leadership behaviours can have a positive impact in any organisation, lean implementation will only succeed when there is commitment to lean leadership. Nonetheless, for people looking to do what they can from where they are in their daily work, the linking of leadership behaviours to continuous improvement and the focus on developing people to achieve long-term business goals is extremely valuable.

Notes

1   Shah, P.E., Weeks, H.M., Richards, B. & Kaciroti, N., 2018, Early Childhood Curiosity and Kindergarten Reading and Math Academic Achievement, *Pediatric Research*, 84, p385.
2   Kofman, F. & Senge, P.M., 1993, Communities of Commitment: The Heart of Learning Organizations, *Organizational Dynamics*, 22, p9.
3   Huang, K., Yeomans, M., Wood Brooks, A., Minson, J. & Gino, F., 2017, It Doesn't Hurt to Ask: Question-asking Increases Liking, *Journal of Personality and Social Psychology*, 113, p436.
4   Schein, E.H., 2013, *Humble Inquiry*, Oakland, CA, Berrett-Koehler Publications Inc., p2.
5   Arumugam, V., Antony, J. & Douglas, A., 2012, Observation: A Lean Tool, *The TQM Journal*, 24, p276.
6   Rother, M., 2010, *Toyota Kata: Managing People for Improvement, Adaptiveness and Superior Results*, New York, McGraw-Hill Education, p135.
7   Schein, E.H., 2009, *Helping: How to Offer, Give and Receive Help*, San Francisco, CA, Berrett-Koehler Publishers Inc., p106.
8   Fisher, C.M., Pillemer, J. & Amabile, T., 2018, Deep Help in Complex Project Work: Guiding and Path-clearing across Difficult Terrain, *Academy of Management Journal*, 61, 1524–1553.
9   Vickers, A., 2009, Can managers be coaches? *Training Journal*, February 2009, p64.
10 Kouzes, J.M., Posner, B.Z. & Birch, E., 2010, *A Coaches Guide to Developing Exemplary Leaders: Making the Most of the Leadership Challenge and the Leadership Practices Inventory (LPI)*, San Francisco, CA, John Wiley and Sons Inc., p214.
11 Rother, M., 2010, p237.
12 Kouzes, J.M. & Posner, B.Z., 2003, *The Five Practices of Exemplary Leadership*, San Francisco, CA, John Wiley and Sons Inc.
13 Thorpe, S. & Clifford, J., 2003, *The Coaching Handbook: An Action Kit for Trainers and Managers*, London, Kogan-Page Limited.
14 Pande, P.S., Neuman, R.P. & Cavanagh, R.R., 2000, *The Six Sigma Way: How GE, Motorola and Other Top Companies are Honing Their Performance*, New York, McGraw-Hill, p16.
15 Womack, J.P. & Jones, D.T., 2015, *Lean Solutions: How Companies and Customers Can Create Value and Wealth Together*, New York, Free Press, p29.
16 Antony, J. & Gupta, S., 2019, Top Ten Reasons for Process Improvement Project Failures, *International Journal of Lean Six Sigma*, 10, pp368, 372.
17 Bailey, J., Schermerhorn, J., Hunt, J. & Osborn, R., 1991, *Managing Organizational Behaviour*, Singapore, John Wiley and Sons, p459.

18 Amabile, T.M., Conti, R., Coon, H., Lazenby, J. & Herron, M., 1996, Assessing the Work Environment for Creativity, *The Academy of Management Journal*, 39, p1178.
19 Northouse, P.G., 2016, *Leadership Theory and Practice*, 7th edition, Thousand Oaks, CA, Sage Publications, p162.
20 Kouzes, J.M. & Posner, B.Z., 2003.
21 Kouzes, J.M. & Posner, B.Z., 2003, p8.
22 Greenleaf, R.K., 1977, *Servant-Leadership: A Journey into the Nature of Legitimate Power and Greatness*, New York, Paulist Press.
23 Northouse, P.G., 2016, p 232.
24 Womack, J.P., Jones, D.T. & Roos, D., 2007, *The Machine That Changed The World*, New York, Free Press.
25 Liker, J., 2004, *The Toyota Way: 14 Management Principles from the World's Greatest Manufacturer*, New York, McGraw-Hill Publishing Company.
26 Rother, M., 2010.
27 Rother, M., 2010, p186.
28 Balle, M., 2017, Lean Leadership, in Netland, T.H. & Powell, D.J. (eds.) *The Routledge Companion to Lean Management*, New York, Routledge, p34.
29 Emiliani, M.L., 1998, Continuous Personal Improvement, *Journal of Workplace Learning*, 10, p31.
30 Emiliani, B., 2008, *Practical Lean Leadership: A Strategic Leadership Guide for Executives*, Wethersfield, CT, The Centre for Lean Business Management, LLC, pp43–44.
31 Dombrovski, U. & Mielke, T., 2014, Lean Leadership – 15 Rules for a Sustainable Lean Implementation, Procedia CIRP 17 (2014) 565–570.
32 Hamalian, J.S., 2015, 6 Key Traits of a Lean Leader (online). Available: https://processexcellencenetwork.com/lean-six-sigma-business-transformation/articles/6-key-traits-of-a-lean-leader

Chapter 3

Perceiving the Problem

Is There Actually a Problem to Solve?

The purpose of this step is to determine if there really is a problem to solve and start to understand what the nature of that problem might be. There will be some overlap with the next step – defining the problem – but each step has a different purpose. At this step, someone perceives there is a problem but may not have clarity as to what the problem is. You are seeking to understand what the other person is experiencing and also testing their willingness to engage in an objective problem solving process. As mentioned in Chapter 1, people who perceive a problem will often be in one of three groups:

1   They feel that something is wrong but do not understand what it is or why;
2   They know something is wrong but are reluctant to change what they are doing, so tell themselves the solution lies in changing something else; or
3   They believe they know exactly what (or who) the problem is, and they want you to do something about it. Sometimes they even know what it is they want you to do.

The first group is one where you can help to clarify their understanding and initiate a problem solving effort. The second group is potentially more challenging as you will need to understand what will be required to get them to agree to change their own behaviour if needed. The third group is the most challenging. You will need to understand why they are convinced something (or someone) is the problem, and why they want you to be the one to intervene. You might ultimately decide not to work on the problem presented by someone in the third group if you do not trust their motives.

The tools introduced in this chapter help to explore these questions. AIR 1 (assessing initial readiness) explores their willingness to engage in objective problem solving and helps you to prioritise this problem against other work you may have. It will help you to draw out any misconceptions they might have. Crucially, it makes clear that problem solving includes looking at what they do and how they do it. There is no assumption of perfection on their part, much as they might like there to be one. FOG (fact, opinion, guess) analysis helps to set the expectation of evidence-based thinking throughout the process. The five whys will be used throughout the entire problem solving process. Introducing them at the start also reinforces objectivity and determination to get to the root cause.

At this stage you should lead with curiosity. Collaboration and a determination to make evidence-based decisions are important as well. However, for establishing the relationship and drawing information out, curiosity is crucial. You should also explain the problem solving process so that people understand what will happen as you work through the problem with them.

AIR I (Assessing Initial Readiness)

AIR is a tool which I developed to assist with the initial conversations about whether there is a problem, and if so, what the impact of the problem is. AIR 1 (assessing initial readiness) is used in the Perceive step of the process. AIR 2 (alignment, impact, readiness) is used in the Define step. The main thing to assess during the Perceive step is the other person's readiness to engage in an objective problem solving process. This is necessary in organisations which do not have enterprise-wide continuous improvement cultures. As already mentioned, this is somewhere between 50% and 95% of organisations! In an ideal world, you would not have to test people's readiness. However, it may well be the case that your organisation does not have a shared understanding of what problem solving entails. It is in your interest to 'test the AIR' before you start.

I use AIR very early in the process as I want to understand where the person raising the problem is coming from. Speaking frankly, you should be wary of anyone who tries to present a 'problem' for you to fix, and it becomes evident that they believe they know what the problem is, who the person responsible is, and what the solution is. You need to be clear that if you are to engage with the problem, you will use an objective, evidence-based approach. You might even ask them, "Why do you need me? If you are so certain of things, why not just fix it yourself?" Fortunately, most people will genuinely want help solving problems and will respond positively to the approach used in this book. It is very unfortunate that some organisations allow internal politics and game playing, but they do so please be aware of the possibility. With practice, you will become very good at spotting it early.

Table 3.1 provides examples of the sort of questions that are useful in starting this discussion.

Table 3.1 AIR 1 – Assessing initial readiness

Question or statement	Likely response	Comments
Tell me what is happening. Why do you feel there is a problem?	Some information is provided, and yes they do feel there is a problem	You are leading with curiosity and being collaborative.
Can you describe the problem?	More detail re the problem	You are not asking them to diagnose it, just to describe the symptoms. Steer them away from diagnosis at this point.
Can you tell me what the impact of the problem is? How does it affect the business?	They may not have thought about this in advance but should be able to tell you why the problem matters	This is useful for AIR 2 in prioritising the problem against other work you may have.
Who needs this work to happen and what are the dependencies in getting it done?		This is a good follow up question re impact and also starts to inform your stakeholder list and high-level process map in the Define step.
Do you have evidence to support your assessment of what the problem is?	This can vary from quite specific evidence to generalisations or 'gut feel'	At this stage, remain curious and draw more information out. You are introducing evidence-based thinking early.
Let's discuss the evidence. I would appreciate you explaining it to me.		Use of words like 'let's' and 'we' reinforces the collaborative nature of problem solving. You might choose to introduce FOG at this point or to keep it for later in the conversation. From here, you could ask several different questions.
I see you have attempted to solve it already by doing X. Let's try and understand why this solution did not work. Have you considered using any other approaches to solving it? Are you willing to explore other ways of solving the problem? In solving this problem, are you ok with an outcome in which you might need to do things differently in the future?		These questions are to test their own readiness for change as part of the solution while reinforcing the three behaviours of curiosity, collaboration, and evidence-based thinking.

The purpose of this line of inquiry is to explore their understanding of what is happening, and also assess their personal readiness for change in this situation. This is particularly important if their perception of the problem is that they are doing good work and the cause lies elsewhere. It is not necessary to gather all the information for AIR 2 at this step in the process. However, the information you have gathered in your initial discussion will inform AIR 2 in the problem definition step.

Using this tool gives you the opportunity to display all three behaviours in your initial discussion about the potential problem. You are displaying curiosity by asking open-ended questions and being genuinely curious about what is happening, what they have already tried, and what they are open to considering. You are being collaborative in your approach, and are already beginning to coach them in your approach to solving the problem, and you have introduced the need for objective evidence up front.

FOG (Fact, Opinion, Guess)

A critical first step in determining if there is a problem is to separate facts from opinions or guesses. Separating facts from opinions *and* guesses certainly makes sense. Establishing the facts is very important. Separating opinions from guesses is somewhat more abstract. The purpose of using FOG is to introduce evidence-based thinking from the start of the problem solving process. FOG is useful in removing subjectivity and emotion from considering whether a problem exists. It will help to think of FOG as a hierarchy of evidence:

1   A fact is verifiable and has evidence to support it. Something not being completed by an agreed due date is a fact.
2   An opinion is an interpretation of current events based on some evidence.
3   A guess is not informed by evidence in the current situation, although it may be based on past experience.

For example, imagine there is a spreadsheet which is updated monthly and saved under a different file name each month. In the month after the end of financial year, there is an incorrect formula which causes the spreadsheet to give an incorrect calculation. You could categorise the information you gather as shown in Table 3.2.

Describing FOG as a hierarchy of evidence enables you to relate its use directly to the behaviour of evidence-based decision making. Not only are you starting to get clarity around the problem by differentiating facts from opinions and guesses, you are also beginning to coach people in the importance of evidence. It is also useful in removing

Table 3.2 FOG analysis

Statement	FOG
There is a team of three people who can all access the spreadsheet on a shared drive	Fact – verifiable by checking share drive permissions
The current version of the spreadsheet has the incorrect formula	Fact – verifiable by viewing the current version of the spreadsheet
The previous version of the spreadsheet does not contain the incorrect formula	Fact – verifiable by viewing the previous version which was saved under a different file name
The current version of the spreadsheet was last updated after the end of financial year	Fact – verifiable in file properties
The error occurred due to workload pressure at a busy time of the year	Opinion – based on consideration of the time of year and changing the workload of the team. This is an interpretation based on current events
James made the mistake	Guess – based on James being responsible for a similar mistake a few months ago. This is not based on any evidence from the current situation

subjectivity from the process. Focusing on facts reinforces objectivity and will assist with getting to the root causes of problems. In the same way as you need to 'test the AIR' with the earlier tool, you also need to 'clear the FOG'.

Five Whys

The five whys are synonymous with conducting root cause analysis and can be used at every step of the problem solving process to reinforce the behaviours of curiosity and evidence-based thinking. It is literally a matter of continuing to ask why in order to go deeper into the problem and understand what the underlying causes are. It is not necessary to have only five whys; you can have as many as you need to get to the root cause. An example of five whys is shown in Table 3.3.

What started as a complaint that people were making too many mistakes was eventually revealed to be the organic growth of work in a system that people liked using, until the demand outgrew its functionality. Bear in mind that sometimes you will open multiple paths for more Why questions. For instance, if we were to continue the questions in Table 3.3, we could ask 'why wasn't system A fixed?', then 'Why wasn't system B fixed?', and so on. There would most likely be different reasons

Table 3.3 Five whys

Problem statement	Why
People are making too many mistakes completing forms in the system.	Why are people making so many mistakes?
One reason is they have to re-enter the same information whenever they raise a new form in the system. It is repetitive and annoying and leads to mistakes.	Why do people have to enter the same information every time?
Forms do not pre-populate with information already held in the system. Doing so would reduce the amount of data entry.	Why doesn't the system pre-populate?
There are no user IDs stored in the system. It treats every person as a first time interaction	Why doesn't the system have user IDs stored?
User IDs were never linked to the system. The use of the system has grown much more than was expected.	Why has the use of the system grown so much?
It is a good system and we have added forms to it that were previously handled by other systems we do not like.	

for each system. Conceivably, you could do a fishbone diagram on the root cause of problems in each of the different systems and describe lots of long-standing problems to be solved. Using five whys is not always a neat linear process. You will need to focus on getting to the root cause of the problem you are currently looking at, and have a way of parking the other ones for a future time.

A variation that has been suggested is 'five whats' rather than 'five whys'. The rationale is that 'what' questions are more likely to be open-ended and sound less accusatory than 'why' questions (e.g. 'What has been happening?' rather than 'Why is this happening?'). One could simply soften the language of the whys ('why do you think this might be happening?' or even 'what are your thoughts on why this is happening?') while still using 'why' questions. This might sound pedantic but the wording of questions is important, particularly if you have not already established a working relationship with the person. More information on this is provided in Chapter 2. The way people answer questions is informative as well. For instance, distancing language can be very important in assessing people's willingness to take responsibility. Consider the difference in meaning in the responses "The job did not get done on time" and "I did not do the job on time".

The five whys are useful for introducing the three behaviours you need to display – curiosity, collaboration, and evidence-based thinking. In asking why something is happening, you can start to also ask questions like

'What data is there to support your view of why that is happening?' or 'What evidence would we need to consider to confirm your understanding of why this is happening?' In this way, from the very beginning, while displaying curiosity you are also reinforcing the need for evidence-based thinking. It is not necessary in five whys to ensure that every single question is a why question. The purpose of five ways is to structure your approach to drill deeper and find the root cause of the problem.

User Stories

User stories are used in Agile software development to describe how a user interacts with a system. They can also be helpful in clarifying why something is considered a problem. The standard format for a user story is:

"As a [role], I can [activity] so that [business value]".[1]

An example of this is "As a manager, I can view new applications for leave as well as leave that has already been approved so that I can ensure we are not understaffed at any time".

Although primarily used for software development, user stories are a very good technique for understanding how people perceive problems. They are constructed in a de-personalised way (the story is about the role, not the individual) so that they reinforce objectivity. They are similar to the 'who does what' format used in process mapping (explained in Chapter 5) which ensures consistency of approach in different stages of problem solving. They assist in determining whether the perceived problem is a 'gap from standard' problem (an established standard of work that is not being met)[2] or is a new and previously undescribed expectation being felt as a problem. An example of this is "As a manager, I need to be able to track all of my team member's work at all times to ensure they are all working hard. The system does not do this". You can then point out that the system was never designed to do that, and managers are expected to engage with staff on their work, rather than watch it all remotely. This is not a 'problem' with the existing system; it is a request for new functionality based on a more distanced approach to managing staff. It may be a desirable change, or may not.

In an office environment where a lot of work is done electronically, learning to construct user stories is a valuable skill. It will assist you in discussing problems and potential fixes with IT staff in a format that they are accustomed to.

Purposeful Conversations

A purposeful conversation is a planned and deliberate interaction with another person to progress the problem solving effort. The importance of having purposeful conversations will become clear as you work through the problem solving model and see how much of what happens in an office environment is influenced by the actions and behaviours of other people. Purposeful conversations can take place at any step in the process. You could use a purposeful conversation to build consensus, influence a decision, challenge a misconception, provide coaching to a team member, or to discuss sustaining the solution over time. This section provides advice on preparing for purposeful conversations. More information is provided in Chapter 9 on strategies to support purposeful conversations.

While problem solving is presented as a circular model which is iterative in nature, you could also think of a specific problem solving activity as being a shorter, linear process. That is, when you identify a problem, you could form a small team to investigate and solve it. Once a solution has been implemented, sustaining the change over time becomes the responsibility of the teams who work in the process. Should further problems (or improvement opportunities) arise in the future, a new problem solving team can be formed and the process repeated. So, responsibility for solving the problem could sit with one group formed for a short period of time, while responsibility for sustaining the solution in the future could sit with a different group which remains in place. This is why it is vital to form the problem solving team from people who work closely with the problem in their daily work. They will have the best knowledge of the problem, and will live with the change afterwards. The work done by the problem solving team is a form of intervention to help the organisation. This is shown in Figure 3.1. The careful use of purposeful conversations can help make this intervention more successful.

When preparing for a purposeful conversation with someone, you should think about:

1   Why you are having the conversation (the purpose)
2   What you want to achieve from it (your objectives)

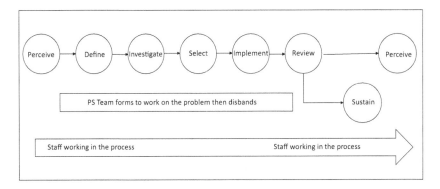

Figure 3.1 A linear view of problem solving.

3   What information or evidence you need to have with you at the time (your supporting material)
4   What the likely reactions might be (their reaction). It is good to consider several different possible reactions
5   How you can respond to each of those reactions (your response)
6   What anecdotes you might use in the discussion (illustrate your points with stories)
7   What the next steps after the conversation might be (the future actions)

Anecdotes can be very effective in purposeful conversations when they clearly relate to the topic and are thought provoking. They are used to make new concepts relatable and to link ideas together in ways that people might not otherwise see. They can be very persuasive, especially when you are able to find alignment between the practical and the symbolic. See *Standing up for Desks* for an example of this. Alignment between the practical and the symbolic can also occur in the problem solving process itself. While the purpose of a specific problem solving effort is literally to solve a workplace problem, it is also an opportunity to transfer knowledge and to build a positive workplace culture. The process you go through to improve the workplace matters as well. Supporting improvement efforts can become powerful symbolic as well as practical acts for people in leadership positions.

Standing Up for Desks

A hospital administration office wanted to purchase adjustable height desks for their staff. An adjustable height desk is an office desk with a small electric motor or a spring loaded lever, which allows the user to raise or lower it throughout the day. They can work sitting down or standing up, and easily alternate between them. Some organisations consider these desks to be an unnecessary expense, and will only purchase them when an employee produces medical evidence of an injury. The hospital initially resisted buying the desks for budget reasons. The administration office argued that it is the wrong message for a hospital to send. If you work in a hospital or any allied health industry, promoting actions that maintain wellness and prevent injury or disease should be a priority. The hospital executive agreed that promoting wellness for staff was consistent with hospital values and the desks were purchased.

Another view of purposeful conversations is provided by the lean concept of *nemawashi* or consensus building.

Consensus Building

Nemawashi is a Japanese gardening term which is used in lean process improvement. *Nemawashi* refers to the preparation for transplanting a tree, both in the careful removal of the tree from its existing location and preparation of the location it will be moved to. In process improvement, *nemawashi* refers to the informal discussions and quiet consensus building which occurs in the background to ensure a change is successful. It is the "informal feedback gathering process by which we establish the causes and conditions necessary to arrive at a successful decision".[3] This is similar to the change management concept of socialising ideas prior to implementation, and can be effective in overcoming the silo effect of large, functionally structured organisations.[4]

Nemawashi is an elegant concept to keep in mind when problem solving, and also in other aspects of your working life. It makes sense that the more care you take in relocating a tree, including preparing the soil it will be planted in, the more likely the tree is to thrive after being moved. It is a useful reminder that successful changes do not happen quickly, require the people who will work with the change to be engaged in the change process, and that the result of the change will not be known until after the change takes place. Does the tree live or die in its new location? What care will it need after being moved? The more care you take in defining and investigating the problem and the more care you take in preparing to implement the solution, the greater the likelihood of success. However, like the tree, knowing whether the solution ultimately lives or dies will take time, and will require some ongoing maintenance.

Notes

1 Leffingwell, D., 2011, *Agile Software Requirements: Lean Requirements Practices for Teams, Programs, and the Enterprise*, Boston, MA, Addison-Wesley, p109.
2 Smalley, A., 2018, *Four Types of Problems: From Reactive Troubleshooting to Creative Innovation*, Cambridge, MA, Lean Enterprise Institute, p47.
3 Jackson, S., 2019, Standard Work for Decision Makers: Avoiding the Waste of Rework, in *Lean Higher Education Conference 2019*, Ann Arbor, MI.
4 Liker, J., 2004, *The Toyota Way: 14 Management Principles from the World's Greatest Manufacturer*, New York, McGraw-Hill Publishing Company, p242.

Chapter 4

Defining the Problem

What Is the Problem We Are Trying to Solve?

Properly defining the problem is the most important step in the problem solving process. Get the definition wrong, and you will not successfully solve the problem. Skip this step in the rush to a solution, and you risk wasting time and money in trying to solve the wrong problem. You will frustrate your clients and your colleagues, and risk derailing your attempt to adopt a problem solving approach at work. Whether it is a localised activity in a business unit or an enterprise-wide business improvement program, poor problem definition is frequently cited as a cause of failure.[1]

In the problem definition step, issues of scope, ownership, and identification of key stakeholders will need to be resolved. You can start to define the objectives of the problem solving process and review what data is available to you. As you work through problem definition, you will start to understand the relevant measures of success for the problem. If performance measures already exist, you will have a baseline against which you can compare any changes you make. At this step, you can start to manage expectations regarding the timeline for solving the problem and also what the benefits of solving it might be. Careful problem definition has been called "The single most underrated skill in all of management practice".[2]

All three behaviours are valuable at this step. You will need curiosity to draw out the information needed to define the problem. Collaboration is important because no one solves a problem on their own, and the problem solving process is also an opportunity to share knowledge and skills. You will need to use evidence-based thinking in problem definition. Problem solving is an iterative process. Do your best to properly define the problem at this step. However, bear in mind that the next step, investigating the problem, will bring new information to light. This may cause you to revisit your problem definition. Some of the tools introduced in this chapter are living documents which will develop as you work through the steps. This is especially true of the A3 problem statement, which is the storyboard of your problem solving adventure.

High-Level Process Map

Creating a high-level process map is very useful for defining a problem relating to a process, particularly when the process runs across multiple units in an organisation. A high-level process map is typically no more than seven to ten steps long and is used to answer several early questions:

1   What is the scope of the process? It is important to understand where the process starts and ends.
2   What is the purpose of the process? It is important to understand why the process is done and who it serves.
3   Who are the key players in the process? This will help to inform the composition of the team needed to improve it.
4   Who is the process owner? It will be necessary to ensure they are aware of the problem and are willing to support your effort to solve it.

An example of a high-level process map for reconciling a credit card is shown in Figure 4.1.

This tool, like several others used in this book, contains a section for relevant information, including:

• Process name
• Process purpose
• Names of people who have worked on the map
• Date updated
• Version

The first draft of the high-level process map can be created with the person who raised the problem. It should then be checked with the process owner and with the key stakeholders in the process. Checking the process map accuracy is a good opportunity to progress the discussion about solving the problem and socialising the work to be done. Confirming the scope of a process can be more difficult than it sounds, particularly if you are in an organisation which is not used to clearly defining and documenting processes. Don't be surprised if confirming the scope of a process takes several goes. This is also true of the process purpose. It is common to find that people have different understandings of the purpose of a process and who the customer really is. You might find that no one person in the process properly understands it from end-to-end, including the process owner. Organisations are typically structured vertically by function, while processes run horizontally across organisations.

Process Name: Credit card reconciliation – High level process map
Process Purpose: To ensure that credit card transactions are appropriate to the business and comply with policy

Prepared By:
Date Updated:
Version:

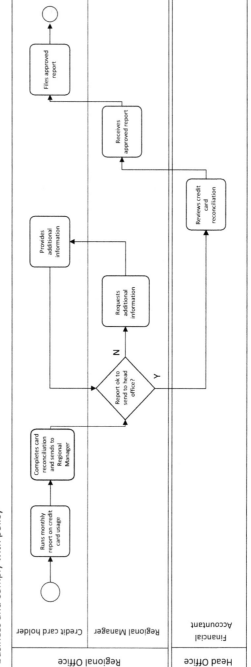

Figure 4.1 High-level process map.

Also, many processes are dependent on stakeholders from outside your own organisation (see *Networked Business*), making it more challenging to understand and solve problems in them.[3]

Identifying the process owner can be surprisingly difficult. It is a feature of large organisations that formal process ownership sometimes sits a long way from where the process is enacted. For instance, in the credit card reconciliation process shown in Figure 4.1, the Chief Financial Officer (CFO) might be the processes owner. Since card reconciliations will be happening across the organisation, the CFO may have very little knowledge of what is really happening in the process. This is not negligence on the part of the CFO. They are in a busy role and they have lots of other things to focus on. Presumably they rely on the Financial Accountant and controls (for example, spot checks of reconciliations and periodic audits) to alert them of problems. When it comes to improving the process, the CFO might have very little appetite for changing the process unless they are personally aware of problems with it. Ensuring they will be supportive of a change will require being able to describe the current situation and the benefits of the proposed change.

Networked Business

Every business, regardless of size or complexity, relies on a network of suppliers, stakeholders, and employees to keep it running. This network extends well beyond the boundary of the business, and in a larger organisation will run horizontally through the business. Consider the following examples of a micro business, a small- to medium-sized enterprise, and a large institution.

The Market Stall

Greg sells gourmet goods at farmers markets on weekends. He specialises in Mediterranean flavours and has established a strong client base for his infused olive oils, green and black olives, *dukkah* and dry rubs for slow cooked meat. He sources olives and oil from a farm in another state via a supplier in his city, and makes his own infusions for the oil from fresh herbs and spices he sources from several local farms in his region. He makes his own *dukkah* and dry rubs from ingredients he sources from several different suppliers around town. He insists on using high-quality products, and takes pride in the goods he sells and in supporting local farmers. Although not a farmer himself, his stall is very popular and he enjoys chatting with the regular customers. Sometimes when he sells out the goods at the market, he accepts additional orders and delivers them during the week. He is given a good location for his stall within the markets due to his relationship with the market managers and the popularity of his stall. Greg believes his supply chain relationships and customer relationships are essential to his business.

The Online Ticket Seller

Travelling circuses work in many countries, providing traditional or contemporary circus entertainment for families. When they arrive in town, they set up their 'big top' tent and put up signage in nearby streets so people know they are there. People can buy tickets at the circus at the time of the show or, increasingly, can purchase tickets online before the show. Joanne runs an online ticketing business which sells tickets for several travelling circuses. She has helped them to set up websites and operates her business as 'middleware'. People visit the circus websites, click on 'pay here', and are taken to specially skinned pages on Joanne's site. She processes the orders and generates electronic tickets which are emailed to customers. They can print them or display them on a mobile device at the big top. Joanne has several staff who provide online support to ticket buying customers and also to the circus operators. Her business takes a small amount for each ticket sold and does a weekly dispersal of all other funds to the circuses. In order to generate more business for the circuses, Joanne visits them in person, taking videos and doing short interviews with performers, which she edits into online content. Joanne believes her relationship with the circuses and her work in building up their online profiles are essential to her business.

The Medical School

The medical school is a part of the university but is collocated with a major hospital. It also has connections with several other hospitals in the city. Students spend most of their time in the early part of their degree in the classroom. As they progress through their study, they spend increasing amounts of time in the hospital as they complete a series of placements. After graduating, they will be required to do an internship at a hospital to consolidate their learning and demonstrate that they can work effectively as doctors. The school is highly networked with hospitals, private practices, government agencies, doctors, alumni, philanthropists, medical equipment suppliers, secondary schools, and other universities and research institutes.

Scoping Document

Depending on the size and complexity of the problem you are working on, you may wish to prepare a scoping document. They can be very valuable documents when working with problem solving teams drawn from across the organisation. If you run a rapid improvement event with a team of people (described in chapter 5), it is definitely worth using a scoping document to ensure everyone has the same understanding of the work. They are also good for structuring your thoughts and prompting questions. There are many different scoping templates available. BOS-CARD is a comprehensive document used as "a consultative approach to securing group agreement on the problem definition"[4] and the scope of problem solving work. Although it may not be necessary to use a BOSCARD or similar document for every problem, it is described in this book for use with more complex problems. It is also useful for responding rapidly to situations. The University of Texas Arlington used BOSCARD as a condensed project planning tool to manage their rapid transition to online teaching and remote work during the COVID-19 pandemic in 2020, with support staff working directly with senior executives to quickly define and scope the work to be done.[5]

The elements of a BOSCARD are shown in Table 4.1.

It is helpful to schedule a meeting specifically for scoping rather than trying to catch individual people in between other tasks. Given the importance of scoping to problem solving, this work warrants ensuring

Table 4.1 BOSCARD

Category	Information sought
Background	Relevant information on the current state of the problem, any previous decisions or actions in relation to it.
Objective	Aspirational statement regarding solving the problem.
Scope	If the problem relates to a process, the scope includes a statement describing where the process starts and ends. It is important to consider both what is in scope and what is out of scope.
Constraints	Known factors that could impede or prevent the problem solving effort. This is important information for the team to have. This can help to inform the resources required to successfully solve the problem.
Assumptions	Factors considered to be true and which will contribute to the problem being solved. This can be useful in identifying assumptions to test (e.g. is the policy really as prohibitive as people say?).
Risks	Known risks of doing nothing, and of selecting the wrong solution.
Deliverables	Key outcomes to achieve the objective. Be realistic about time frames and measures of success.

Source: Adapted from Robinson, 2020.[6]

Table 4.2 BOSCARD with SPLITBAR

Background	*Objective*	*Scope*	*Constraints*	*Assumptions*	*Risks*	*Deliverables*
Stakeholders		Process				Benefits
Later (parking lot)		Team				
Information/Data						
Actions						
Reporting						

Source: Provided by Mark Robinson in private correspondence.

people focus on it together. The BOSCARD does not have to be completed in sequential order. You can complete sections as you go, depending on the flow of the discussion, ensuring it has all been addressed during the meeting.

There is a variation on this called BOSCARD+, which includes additional sections using the acronym SPLITBAR (stakeholders, process, later, information including data and documents, team, benefits, actions, reporting). The SPLITBAR was created by the process improvement team at the University of St Andrews. They found they were putting so much information into the Background in their BOSCARDs that it was becoming unmanageable. The BOSCARD+ format provides a place to record additional information during the problem solving process. This makes it more than a scoping document (Table 4.2).

One of the biggest risks in problem solving or process improvement is scope creep. Documenting the objective, scope, and deliverables is essential to preventing this. If it becomes apparent during the problem solving effort that the scope needs to change, you will need to revisit your scoping document and use it to inform a discussion on what a change of scope means, particularly with regard to time frames and measures of success.

In Frame/Out of Frame

This is a diagram to show visually what is in scope (in frame) and what is not. You can simply draw a large picture frame on a sheet of paper (see Figure 4.2). As issues are raised, write each one on a post-it note and place the note on the page. If it is agreed that issue is in scope, it goes inside the frame. If it is agreed it is out of scope, it goes outside the frame. If you are not able to decide whether it is in or out of scope, you can place the post-it note on the frame for a decision to be made at a later time. However, the work should not proceed until all issues are either in the frame or not.

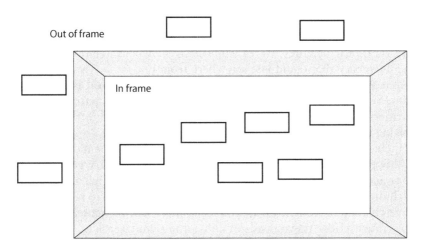

Figure 4.2 In frame / out of frame.

While this seems very basic, it can assist in clarifying the scope of a problem to be solved. It is a mistake to underestimate the importance of confirming the scope, and also the complexity of doing so. Using the 'in frame' diagram can help to clarify what is recording in the 'scope' section of the BOSCARD. If there is disagreement about whether something is in scope or not, the question then becomes 'Why is there disagreement'?, prompting discussion about the underlying reasons for different people thinking something should be in scope or not.

Problem Solving Teams

Deciding who will be involved in the problem solving effort is vital to success. It must be the people closest to the problem (or process) and who know it best. It might seem politically astute to select their manager, or their manager's manager, but this is not going to help solve the problem (see *Iceberg of Ignorance*). Ensuring decision makers are on board as stakeholders is important. They do not need to be included in a problem solving team to achieve that. Proximity to the problem matters more than job title, status, or personal ambition.

When reviewing a process, it is valuable to include a customer of the process in your team whenever possible. This can be a confronting thought for people, especially if the process is considered to be in poor shape. Why reveal your inadequacies to your customers? In a large organisation, the 'customer' of a process is often another part of the organisation. They are colleagues as well as customers and should be included with the expectation they will contribute to benefit the entire organisation. In an institution like a university, where a student is defined as a customer, they should be included. The student as customer is a high-value, long-term customer. They are not buying something once and disappearing; they are in a mutually beneficial relationship with the university that could last anywhere from one to six years or more. As an alumnus of the university, their relationship could last for decades. Similarly, in many organisations, customers are actually critical partners in long-term success. They should be included in the problem solving effort.

Including carefully selected customers in improvement activities is highly beneficial. First, the customer usually has a pretty good idea of your actual performance and so you are not really hiding anything by excluding them. Second, the customer is the best person to tell you what your customers want. Third, your customers will be acutely aware of how much effort they spend on consuming your service,[7] something you may not have considered before. Customers can give you insight to the whole process, whereas people working in the process often only know their part of it (see *Ordering new bins*). Understanding this can inspire improvements you would not have considered otherwise. Finally, involving someone in an improvement or problem solving effort tells them that you value them and that you are seeking to improve. These are positive messages that can help strengthen your relationship with them.

Iceberg of Ignorance

The iceberg of ignorance is widely attributed to Sydney Yoshida. The iceberg model states that senior management only know 4% of the problems in the organisation, middle managers know 9%, supervisors know 74%, and frontline workers know 100% of the problems in the organisation. Referring to the iceberg, 96% of problems in the business are invisible to senior management as they are below the waterline (see Figure 4.3). Some people have disputed the model, arguing that nobody actually knows 100% of the problems in the organisation. How could the frontline employees know all the problems that senior management are facing? The message to take from this model is the closer you are to the work being done, the better you know the problems in it. The frontline workers know 100% of the problems they face, and know those problems better than anyone else does. Therefore, the frontline

Figure 4.3 Iceberg of ignorance.

workers have to be involved in solving those problems. One example of this being done at organisational level is described in the book, *Moments of Truth*.[8] The title refers to Carlzon's belief that every interaction that a customer has with anyone in the business is a moment of truth for the business. With this mindset, you cannot afford to restrict decision making capacity to senior people. It is the workers on the frontline who the customers interact with most.

As with so many popular models, there is an alternate version of the iceberg which says that 100% of problems in the organisation are visible to 'employees' rather than to 'front line staff' specifically. There is still a valuable message from this version as well. No one person will know every problem in the organisation because the problems exist at different levels and are not all visible to one person. But the employees collectively know the problems. Therefore, the way to solve the problems is to collaborate.

Ordering New Bins

James called the city council to request a replacement garbage bin. His bin was old and had split on one side. It was also missing one of the pins holding the lid in place, so the lid did not open and close properly. He had been meaning to replace it for months but only thought about it when putting the bin out for collection. Because he always did this on a Friday morning, he was usually running late for work and had no time to spare. He would make a mental note to call the council, then forget it during the day. However, due to COVID-19 he was working from home and so on this Friday morning, he decided to make the call.

James patiently listened to the recorded message asking him to press 1 to pay a council bill or fine, press 2 to report a sidewalk or storm water issue, and various other options before being asked to press 9 to speak to an operator. He pressed 9. James waited on hold for three minutes (although it felt like ten), during which time he listened to recorded messages about council's pride in their service and commitment to the community. Eventually he was answered by one of their call centre staff. She identified herself as Fiona, enquired as to how he was that morning, and then asked how she could assist him. Upon hearing he wanted a replacement bin, she asked him to verify his identity by giving his council rates account number or, if he did not know his council rates account number, his full name, address, date of birth, and mobile telephone number. Once Fiona was satisfied that he was indeed James, he was asked to describe the faults with the bin, placed on hold for several minutes (again listening to pre-recorded messages about how valued he was), and then told he was approved to receive a replacement bin.

Fiona told him,

> I have placed a request for a replacement bin for you. Under our service agreement, the bin will be delivered sometime before next Wednesday evening. Please place your current bin on the sidewalk. Replacing the bin is a manual process so please refrain from placing any rubbish in the bin until the new one arrives. We will not be able to take the old bin away if there is rubbish in it.

"OK", replied James, "I guess I can find somewhere else to put my rubbish for a few days".

"That would be grand", Fiona said. "Is there anything else I can assist you with this morning?"

"Actually", James said, "I've been meaning to get a green waste bin as well. Can we do that now?"

"Certainly, sir, please hold the line". James was placed on hold for several more minutes, and then Fiona told him that she had also raised a request for him to receive a green waste bin. This was for grass clippings, leaves, and branches which the council would use to make compost for use in public parks. It too would be delivered sometime before Wednesday evening the following week. His council rates notices would be adjusted in the future to include the additional cost of the green waste service.

"Is there anything else I can assist you with this morning?" asked Fiona.

James was tempted to ask Fiona why it was necessary to provide so much information about his identity in order to replace a bin. Bins were provided to every dwelling in the city, and replacing it was at no additional cost to him as it was funded from his quarterly rates payments. He was also tempted to ask who had agreed the terms of the service agreement with the council. He did not think three working days to deliver a bin was particularly fast, especially when he was not allowed to use his existing one in the meantime. The council was telling him their promised delivery time without asking what the customer's required time was. He could also have asked why the council's record message while he was on hold waiting to be answered did not request he have his rates account number ready. However, it was Friday morning, the weekend was fast approaching, and the bin was not that big a deal to him. After all, he had put up with a broken one for months. Why take on the bureaucracy? Besides, he had remembered to get the green bin as well so felt it was a worthwhile phone call.

On Monday, a council truck pulled up outside James' house.

"That was quick", James thought to himself, as the driver unloaded a new general waste bin from a large cage full of them on the back of the truck and placed it on the sidewalk. James saw the driver lock the cage and climb into the truck cabin. He opened his window and called out "Do you have a green bin for me as well?"

The driver grabbed a clipboard from the cabin and checked his delivery list for the day. "Must be due for delivery on another day", the driver called out, then drove away.

On Tuesday, the same driver pulled up outside James' house and unloaded a green waste bin. James opened his window again and called out, "Thanks. Shame you had to come here twice, though".

The driver laughed and replied, "That's council for you. They send the jobs and I deliver them".

"Aren't you council?", thought James?

A short time later, James received a text inviting him to click on a link to rate council's service. "Hmmm", he thought,

What do I think of their service? They delivered both bins ahead of their promised time, but wasteful to come here twice. Why didn't Fiona put both bins on the one job? Why didn't the driver check with the office yesterday and if there was an order for a green bin, give me one yesterday instead of coming here twice?. Why does he have a printed job list anyway instead of using an iPad?

Fishbone Diagram

The fishbone diagram, also known as a *cause and effect diagram* or an *Ishikawa*, is one of the most widely used root cause analysis tools available. It is called a fishbone because the template resembles the bone structure of a fish. The head of the fish contains the problem statement, the backbone runs through the middle of the template, and there are usually six large bones attached to the backbone. The template (Figure 4.4) includes a section in the top right corner for the version, date updated, and names of people who worked on it. This is an important reminder that the fishbone diagram is a collaborative tool. It is also one of a number of tools which contribute to an excellent visual display of your problem solving work (refer Chapter 8).

The purpose of the fishbone diagram is to prompt discussion about the potential root causes of problems to guide your problem solving efforts. The category headings provided are commonly used ones, but if you find it necessary to change some or remove them due to some unique circumstance of your workplace, then go for it. The tool is a prompt, not a sacred relic.

Depending on the number of people in the discussion, you can work on an A3 size diagram or could draw it on a large sheet of paper on the wall and put post-it notes on it as people raise potential causes. If working remotely, you can display the fishbone diagram using a shared screen function when video-conferencing, and type or write on the screen as you go. When working on the fishbone diagram with people, don't dismiss ideas straight away. Discuss them and record them, even if you discount them later as you investigate the problem.

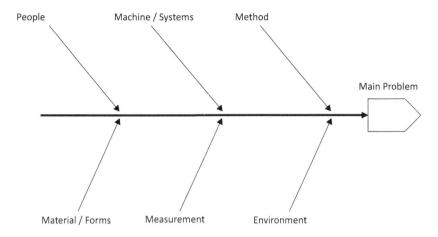

Figure 4.4 Fishbone diagram.

Examples of causes that could be listed under each category in the office variation are shown in Table 4.3.

Table 4.3 Sample causes

Category	Examples
Method	The process is not clearly documented.
	Roles and responsibilities are not clear to the people doing the work.
Systems	The system is not intuitive to use.
	There are data migration issues between systems.
People	Training was not provided to people on the changed process.
	People are doing the same work in different ways.
Materials / Forms	The forms are confusing to complete.
	Training material that was provided is incorrect.
Measurement	There is inadequate measurement information currently available to establish a baseline.
	Reporting is ad hoc and inconsistent across business units.
Environment	The organisation has a blame culture and people are afraid to raise problems.
	There is a lack of privacy due to open plan office space.

It can be helpful to develop greater understanding of the tool by discussing which bone a potential cause fits on, but do not let the discussion of causes be derailed by prolonged debate about one bone over another. The purpose of the tool is to encourage discussion about potential causes and capture them somewhere on the diagram so they can be considered further. As you progress through the discussion of the potential causes, you can incorporate five whys to get to the underlying causes. Table 4.4 is the five whys table from Chapter 2, with a column added to show which fishbone you might put causes on as you work through them.

Table 4.4 Using the fishbone diagram

Problem statement	Why	Fishbone(s)
People are making too many mistakes completing forms in the system.	Why are people making so many mistakes?	People – people are making mistakes Forms – forms are confusing or difficult to use
One reason is they have to re-enter the same information whenever they raise a new form in the system. It is repetitive and annoying and leads to mistakes.	Why do people have to enter the same information every time?	Forms – forms are not user-friendly
Forms do not pre-populate with information already held in the system. Doing so would reduce the amount of data entry.	Why doesn't the system pre-populate?	System – system does not pre-populate forms
There are no user IDs stored in the system. It treats every person as a first time interaction.	Why doesn't the system have user IDs stored?	System – no user IDs stored
User IDs were never created for the system. The use of it has grown much more than was expected.	Why has the use of the system grown so much?	System – no user IDs exist System – limited functionality
It is a good system and we have added forms that were previously handled by other systems we did not like.	Why weren't the other systems fixed instead of working around them?	System – problems in other systems not fixed, work diverted to this one Forms – paper-based forms replaced by using this system

Fishbone diagrams are living documents which you can revisit, showing different people over time or with the same people as you keep working on the problem. As you investigate the potential causes, you could use colour coding to show the ones you have ruled out while not actually removing them from the diagram. You can also use a code to show which unit each cause is assigned to for resolving (the case study in Chapter 5 includes this). The diagram shows the story of your progress through the root cause analysis over time.

A3 Problem Statement

The A3 problem statement is another widely used problem solving tool. It was developed by Toyota as a means of sharing information in a concise and consistent format.[9] It is called an A3 problem statement because it is prepared on a single sheet of A3 paper. Telling the problem solving story within that limited space requires you to distil the problem and solutions down to their most important elements. When using an A3 problem statement, I sometimes think of the quote attributed to Mark Twain, "I did not have time to write a short letter, so I wrote a long one instead". Take the time to understand the problem and be able to describe it in a short letter.

The A3 problem statement has been adjusted and changed by different organisations as required. There are many versions available as templates. The template provided in Figure 4.5 follows a basic plan-do-check-act format. Think of the A3 problem statement as a storyboard. Its purpose is to explain to other people what is happening in the problem solving (or improvement) effort. It is not feasible to capture all the detailed information relevant to a problem on a single sheet of paper, so you will have other material you are working with; but the A3 problem statement is a critical part of your visual display of the problem (refer Chapter 8).

As with the fishbone diagram, the A3 problem statement includes a section for recording the date, version, and who has contributed to it. This is useful to share and primarily a reminder that this is a collaborative tool. It cannot be successfully completed alone.

A3 problem statements have been widely used in manufacturing, and there are some excellent books available that describe using them in great detail. However, the books tend to use manufacturing examples and so may not be as accessible to people in knowledge organisations. For office-based problems, it is an excellent collaborative and storytelling tool which is likely to invite comment when displayed. You don't have to be experienced in using it to understand the story it tells. They are useful in communicating across functions and facilitating teamwork.[10]

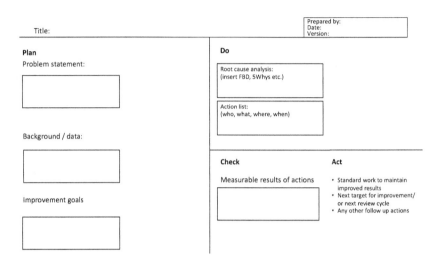

Figure 4.5 A3 problem statement template.

You will continue to refer back to and update the A3 problem statement throughout the problem solving process, culminating in it being part of your visual display when reviewing the solution. Worked examples of both the fishbone diagram and A3 problem statement are provided in Chapter 5.

AIR 2 (Alignment, Impact, Readiness)

AIR 1 was introduced in Chapter 3 to assist in testing readiness to engage in objective problem solving, including people's willingness to consider their own behaviour and actions. Readiness is one of three criteria to consider in AIR 2, along with alignment and impact.

Alignment refers to the extent to which the problem aligns with the core business of the organisation or of its current priorities. This alignment should be evidenced by an agreed plan (for instance, a strategic plan or operational plan) rather than just stated verbally by a stakeholder.

Impact refers to the difference that solving the problem will make to the organisation. It may be an issue that is important to a small number of people, and solving it will not have much impact on the business or its customers. Examples of impact could be the number of people who benefit from the solution, how much time (or money) will be saved by the change, and whether the solution will have a wider community benefit.

Readiness refers to stakeholder willingness to engage in objective problem solving and to change their own actions and behaviours in solving the problem. Readiness is necessary for implementation and sustaining the result. You will already have a good sense of that from having 'tested the air' when they first raised the perceived problem with you.

Alignment and impact are about the importance of solving the problem to the business. Readiness is about the likelihood of a solution being successfully implemented and sustained. It may be that you have identified a problem which will have significant impact for the business but you assess the readiness to engage as being very low. This puts the problem solving effort at risk. You could refer to the tools described in Chapter 9 at this point (for instance force field analysis) to understand why readiness is low and what would be required to change it. Doing this can inform a plan to improve readiness prior to taking on the problem. The plan may well include having a purposeful discussion with key stakeholders.

In assessing AIR, you can use a Likert scale (rating of 1–5 from not important through to very important) for each criterion. You can weight the criteria for their relative importance. For instance, if alignment with core business is considered most important, you can weight alignment so its score is worth more. If you have several different problems to work on and need to prioritise them, AIR 2 provides a means of comparison. In a situation where you only have one problem to assess, you will need to determine what a 'pass' mark would be, or whether one of the criteria is essential. That is, you could decide you will not work on problems with less than four out of five on readiness. Alternatively, there may be times when you take on a problem which does not score that highly but which has other appealing features (it could serve as a good proof-of-concept case leading to more problem solving in the future or it is an opportunity to work with a particular team and share knowledge). A sample AIR test is provided in Table 4.5.

In Table 4.5, although problem 2 has greater alignment and the same impact as problem 1, you have assessed readiness as being low compared to problem 1 which has very high stakeholder readiness. On the basis of this assessment, you would prioritise problem 1. An option at this point is to go back to the stakeholders for problem 2 and have a further conversation with them to confirm your view of their readiness. This could also assist you in developing a plan to improve readiness for this

Table 4.5 Sample AIR test

Problem	Alignment (w2)	Impact (w1)	Readiness (w1.5)	Total
Problem 1	4 (score of 8)	3	5 (score of 7.5)	18.5
Problem 2	5 (score of 10)	3	2 (score of 3)	16
Problem 3	3 (score of 6)	2	3 (score of 4.5)	12.5

problem. You might end up deciding to work on problem 1 and see if a successful outcome from that problem increases stakeholder readiness for tackling problem 2.

AIR is one set of criteria which you can use, and is based on experience working in organisations without an enterprise-wide improvement culture. If these criteria ultimately do not suit your organisation, you can always develop your own. Toyota has used importance, urgency, and tendency.[11] Importance and urgency are similar to alignment and impact. Tendency refers to trends in performance – if a problem is showing a tendency to get worse, it is a higher priority. The purpose of having the criteria is to help prioritise problems when you have to decide between them, and to give you a basis for making a decision about whether to take on solving a particular problem or not.

Measures to Consider

It is important to start considering measures of performance and of success early in the problem solving process. Understanding what the expected performance should be will assist in defining the problem (for instance, is it a gap against expected standard or an opportunity to improve beyond the current standard). Knowing what the actual performance currently is will help to establish a baseline to measure improvements against. Knowing what matters most to your customers will help to determine the critical-to-quality measures, which will assist in selecting the preferred solution to implement. Once you implement the solution, you will need to ensure that someone is measuring performance over time to see if anticipated benefits are being realised. All of this requires you to use evidence-based thinking as well as curiosity and collaboration.

Some of the more common types of performance measures are described in Table 4.6.

Error Reduction Measures

This is probably the most 'technical' section of the book, so please take your time working through the examples and revisit them as needed. The error reduction measures are drawn from Six Sigma and are very useful for providing greater insight to how a process is performing and where to focus improvement efforts.

Defects per unit (DPU): This is the number of defects (or errors) made per completed piece of work. It is simply a count of identified errors per day or week, divided by the number of completed pieces of work, with no closer analysis of what the errors are or why they are occurring.

Table 4.6 Measures to consider

Metric type	Examples or description
Critical-to-Quality (CTQ)	These are the things the customer says they value most. For example, if the customer says that a rapid response is the most important thing, a CTQ measure could be "number of minutes to respond to customer query"
Cost measures:	
Cost reduction (discussed further in Chapter 6)	Specific and identifiable costs which can be saved in the process (e.g. printing of brochures, unique software license costs, offsite storage costs)
Cost of poor quality (COPQ)	This is the cost associated with things not being as good as they can be. These costs can include the cost of maintaining a checking system (e.g. periodic reviews, audits), internal failure costs (often based on time spent to correct errors and to investigate accidents), and external failure costs (customer complaints, warranty or insurance claims, lost business)
Error reduction measures (explained in detail below)	Defects per unit, defects per million opportunities, rolled throughput yield, cycle time
Use of new capacity (discussed further in Chapter 6)	What you do with the time saved in a process (for instance, increased workload absorbed without increased cost, new revenue-generating ideas, or activities)
Behaviour or cultural change (explained below)	Examples include a number of improvement ideas suggested, increase in the number of respectful interactions, decrease in complaints about behaviour/attitude, increase in positive feedback on service

Is Checking Necessary?

Part of the cost of poor quality is maintaining a checking system. Is checking really necessary, or should you keep working to build quality into your processes to the point where you do not need additional steps to check the quality at all? This is the view of lean advocates: build quality into your process and you don't need to allocate specific resources to check if the work is right. There is an alternate model used in occupational health and safety called the Swiss cheese model. This model is based on the view that all controls put in place will have some risk of failure (visually a piece of Swiss cheese). Accepting this, you mitigate risk by putting in extra layers of protection, that is, several slices of Swiss cheese. An accident can only occur if something passes through all the layers, which can only happen if the holes in the Swiss cheese overlap each other (Figure 4.6).

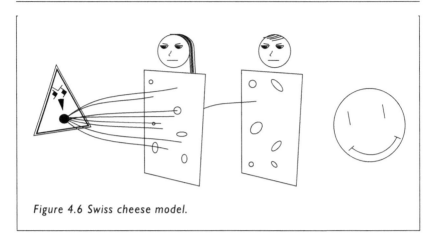

Figure 4.6 Swiss cheese model.

However, if you think of the extra checking steps in a process as slices of Swiss cheese, with the goal of limiting the ability of anything to pass through the holes, you can see that the effectiveness of checking as a protection depends on the quality of the checking being done. How often is the job of checking allocated to a team leader or manager on top of their other work? How much time to do they have to dedicate to that checking work? If they are rushed and do a cursory check (perhaps telling themselves it is ok because they have good staff who they trust), are they really adding to the quality? You could say the holes in their slice of Swiss cheese are made much bigger by their workload and consequent inability to check things carefully. Using the Swiss cheese model, the effectiveness of adding layers of checking into a process is compromised if you ask busy people to do more (Figure 4.7). The same applies to requiring team leaders to approve things (checking is implicit in approving). Stories of people approving without checking or even of senior people giving their assistants their login details to approve on their behalf are common.

Figure 4.7 Compromised Swiss cheese model.

Defects per million opportunities (DPMO): This is a count of the number of errors, divided by the number of error opportunities (i.e. how many things could go wrong when doing the work), then expressed as the likely number of errors per million opportunities. This is more complex than DPU as it introduces error opportunities. Thinking about DPMO helps to pursue simplicity in work design. The more opportunities for things to go wrong, the more likely that something will go wrong.

An example of this is running an end of month report. Imagine if your process at the end of each month was to run a report from the finance system, and then export the report into a spreadsheet, create a pivot table in the spreadsheet, and select half a dozen different objects in the pivot table to display the specific information your manager needs to see. You have to do this because no one has built the report in the finance system that you really need. If that report existed, your action each month would be to press a button to generate the report with none of the extra work. With DPMO you can map the process and highlight all the error opportunities created through this manual process. It will show that the likelihood of making a mistake is much higher when you have to download and manipulate data to produce the information.

Rolled Throughput Yield: This is another valuable way of looking at errors. In Figure 4.8, you can see two different situations in which four staff are working, with each staff member achieving 90% accuracy in their own work. When all four people are doing the same work (for example, four call centre staff answering customer questions), the overall accuracy rate is 90%. This seems obvious – four people working at 90% accuracy gives an overall accuracy rate of 90%. However, look at what happens to the overall accuracy when the four staff work on different steps in a single process (for example, delivering a council bin); one person (Fiona in the case study provided) receives the order over the telephone, a second person sets the delivery schedule for the warehouse, a third person loads the truck for delivery, and a fourth person (the driver James spoke to) delivers the bins. The overall accuracy rate is just 65%. This is because the work is handed from person A to B to C to D in a four-step process. Each person has a 10% error rate. The chance of the first step in the four-step process being done correctly is 90%. The chance of the second step of the process being done correctly is also 90%. This means the chance of a piece of work passing correctly through both Step 1 and Step 2 is 81% (90% × 90%). This is set out in Table 4.7. The more steps in the process, the less chance the work has of passing through the entire process error-free.

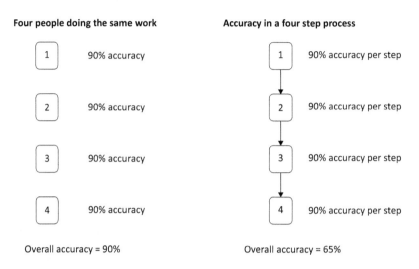

Four people doing the same work

1	90% accuracy
2	90% accuracy
3	90% accuracy
4	90% accuracy

Overall accuracy = 90%

Accuracy in a four step process

1	90% accuracy per step
2	90% accuracy per step
3	90% accuracy per step
4	90% accuracy per step

Overall accuracy = 65%

Figure 4.8 The cumulative effect of errors in a process.

Table 4.7 Calculating rolled throughput yield

Process step	Accuracy	Rolled throughput yield
Step 1	90%	90%
Step 2	90%	81% (0.9 × 0.9)
Step 3	90%	73% (0.9 × 0.9 × 0.9)
Step 4	90%	65% (0.9 × 0.9 × 0.9 × 0.9)

Table 4.8 An example of rolled throughput yield

Process	Error-free work per step	Error-free work for the process (rolled throughput yield)
Step 1	100%	100%
Step 2	90%	90% (1.0 × 0.9)
Step 3	80%	72% (1.0 × 0.9 × 0.8)
Step 4	90%	65% (1.0 × 0.9 × 0.8 × 0.9)
Step 5	90%	59% (1.0 × 0.9 × 0.8 × 0.9 × 0.9)

It is the cumulative effect of errors at each step of the process that reduces the yield. A more complex example is set out in Table 4.8.

Even though each step in the process is being done to a seemingly high standard, the cumulative effect is that less than 60% of all work being done is error-free. That is, because almost every step of the process has a possibility of error, the likelihood of a piece of work passing through all the steps with no error is much lower. Rolled throughput yield, like DPMO, gives you a different perspective on how to improve a process. If you could eliminate a step from the process, even without improving the error rates in the other steps, your RTY would immediately go up. For example, if you can change your process to eliminate Step 4, the RTY for the process increases to 65% because you have fewer opportunities for errors to occur. The RTY would be:

$$1.0 \times 0.9 \times 0.8 \times 0.9 = 0.65.$$

Having this level of detail about accuracy in each process step also helps to prioritise what to improve in the process. For instance, improving Step 3 from 80% to 100% would increase your RTY from 59% to 73%

$$1.0 \times 0.9 \times \mathbf{1.0} \times 0.9 \times 0.9 = 0.7$$

Targeting the step with the highest error rate gives the biggest improvement in overall accuracy.

As you can see from these measures, you can start with a simple count of errors and that will tell you something. You can look at the number of error opportunities to see the risk inherent in overly complex processes. You can look at the cumulative effect of errors at each step of the process to understand what the customer is likely to be experiencing. You can use your understanding of errors at each step of the process to help prioritise your solutions. It all reminds us that simplicity is elegant.

Cycle time: This is the length of time to complete an instance of the process. There are two parts to cycle time. They are 'hands on time' (the time taken to actually perform a step in the process) and 'lag time' (the time in between actually performing the steps in the process). As you get into mapping processes and looking at the cycle time, you will find almost all of the time it takes to complete a process is lag time. Do not be surprised to find that 90–95% of cycle time is lag time. It is shocking at first, and also exciting. Think of all the time you can take out of the cycle time as you eliminate the causes of lag time! Examples of this can include something waiting in a manager's inbox to be approved, something waiting for missing information to be provided, or something waiting because the person who does that step is unexpectedly away.

The requirement to have managers and executives approve work is the natural enemy of cycle time. The further up the organisational hierarchy the approval sits, the worse it will be. Some executives even have 'signing meetings' scheduled once or twice a week, where they allocate an hour for their staff to bring them all the requests they need to approve and try to work through them in a sitting. This batching of work is convenient for them, but not for anyone else. It means that a routine decision could take up to a week to be taken. If the executive has a question that cannot be answered at the time, the decision might be deferred to the next signing meeting for more information to be gathered or it has to be handled out of session. This has the effect of causing everyone to prepare briefing papers to accompany the decision. Consider the psychology of this. When you get one chance a week to get a decision, you will likely decide it is better to provide more information than less. This leads to a waste of effort in preparing the briefing paper, and creates more work in the signing meeting trying to get through a lot of additional (and unnecessary) accompanying material. Also, how much attention can the executive be paying to each decision if they are batched and presented in one sitting?

Behavioural or Cultural Change

When thinking about measures of success in a process or in solving a problem, you may need to think beyond measures of the process itself. You can also include measures which observe changes in behaviour. For example, a veterinary teaching hospital which wanted to streamline its procedure for scheduling animal surgery recognised that staff behaviour was contributing to the problems they faced.[12] In changing their process, they specifically considered measures of success relating to process performance and hospital culture. This is shown in Table 4.9. Including these behavioural measures sent a clear message to staff that the hospital was implementing change for their benefit as well as for the benefit of their clients.

Table 4.9 Outcomes and measures of success

Outcomes	Measures of success
The hospital will know the process is improving through:	Increase in the number of days when staff finish work at scheduled time
	Decrease in the number of procedures rescheduled because of delays in completing procedure inputs (request form, bloodwork, Vetpay consent, clinical discussion)
	Reduction in patient waiting time in shared services (Anaesthesia and Diagnostic Imaging)
	Reduction in downtime in shared services
The hospital will know the culture is improving through:	Observable increase in respectful interactions between staff and reduction in complaints about disrespectful behaviour
	Observable increase in staff using data to inform problem solving and decision making
	Increase in the number of ideas coming from staff and percentage of those ideas which are implemented

Source: Shannon, 2020.[13]

Notes

1 Corrigan, S., 2010, 10 Reasons Why Change Management Programs Fail, Loanhead, Vanguard Scotland Ltd, pp9–10.
2 Repenning, N.P., Kieffer, D. & Astor, T., 2017, The Most Underrated Skill in Management, MIT Sloan Management Review, 58, p40.
3 Womack, J.P. & Jones, D.T., 2015, Lean Solutions: How Companies and Customers Can Create Value and Wealth Together, New York, Free Press, p178.
4 Robinson, M., 2020, BOSCARD: A Scoping Tool for Lean Continuous Improvement Projects, in Yorkstone, S. (ed.) Global Lean for Higher Education: A Themed Anthology of Case Studies, Approaches, and Tools, Boca Raton, FL, Taylor and Francis Group, LLC, p187.
5 Berkman, C. & Kusler, K., 2020, Acceleration of Process Improvement Culture because of COVID-19, Lean HE Global Festival (online).
6 Robinson, M., 2020 pp187–188.
7 Womack, J.P. & Jones, D.T., 2015, p68.
8 Carlzon, J., 1987, Moments of Truth, New York, Bellinger Publishing Company.
9 Liker, J., 2004, The Toyota Way: 14 Management Principles from the World's Greatest Manufacturer, New York, McGraw-Hill Publishing Company, p244.
10 Balle, M., 2017, When Should We Do An A3 Or Use a Different Problem Solving Tool? (online). Available: https://www.lean.org/balle/DisplayObject.cfm?o=3573
11 Liker, J. & Meier, D., 2006, The Toyota Way Fieldbook: A Practical Guide for Implementing Toyota's 4Ps, New York, McGraw-Hill Companies, p338.
12 Shannon, C., 2020, Lessons from Implementing Lean at the Veterinary Teaching Hospital, in Global Lean for Higher Education: A Themed Anthology of Case Studies, Approaches, and Tools (S. Yorkstone, ed.), Boca Raton, FL, Taylor and Francis Group, LLC, pp311–328.
13 Shannon, C., 2020, p319.

Chapter 5

Investigating the Problem

Do We Fully Understand the Problem?

How you go about investigating a problem will depend on what the situation is. This chapter describes processes and process maps, and gives two different problem solving scenarios. In the first scenario, you are working with a regional manager to improve onboarding of new staff, using a swim lane process map in a rapid improvement event (RIE). This is the kind of planned and structured process improvement activity you will see in organisations around the world. In the second scenario, you work in a hospital responding to unforeseen problems arising from the implementation of a new corporate payroll system. The team formed within the hospital use a fishbone diagram to conduct root cause analysis and an A3 problem statement to track their progress in solving the problems they encounter. This is an approach to defining and responding to problems that is used in many workplaces.

As you investigate the problem, you will need to draw on all three behaviours at different times. Curiosity is at the heart of investigation, as you seek to find all the relevant information which will confirm the problem definition and enable solutions to be identified. Collaboration is essential as a complicated problem involving multiple teams or stakeholders cannot be solved on your own. Evidence-based thinking is also essential to ensure that the proposed solutions will actually solve the problem. Being swayed by opinion or guesses at this point could lead to a proposed solution that won't succeed.

Understanding a Process

A process is a sequence of actions that are performed in order to accomplish something. Just as an organisation is an arrangement of people into roles and teams to accomplish more than a single person can, processes are the arrangements of the work those people do. Viewed that way, every process should have a purpose that contributes to the organisation's mission, and every process should be arranged to achieve its purpose as efficiently as possible.

A process consists of three elements: roles, tasks (or actions), and tools. Roles are positions in the organisation which people occupy. For instance, Finance Officer is a role which can perform tasks in many different finance processes. Tasks are particular actions taken in the process. Checking for unusual transactions is an example of a task a Finance Officer might perform in the credit card reconciliation process. Tools are the things the people in roles use to perform the tasks. The Finance Officer might use a transaction report generated from the finance system to perform the checking task. When you map a process using a swim lane map, the interaction between these three elements becomes obvious.

There are two levels of process decision making: decisions taken in the process and decisions taken about the process. Decisions taken in the process (e.g. to approve a purchase or not) are shown as tasks in the process map. Decisions taken about the process are not shown in the map as they are not a step in the process. However, they can have a significant impact on how the process works even though they may not be documented anywhere. Ideally, every process has a nominated process owner who makes decisions about the process. The role of the process owner is to maintain order in the process, acting as the escalation point for instances when people seek to change the current process. This is an important role because without order, the process will not run effectively. In practice, there is not always a process owner. If you work in a decentralised organisation, there is a good chance that you will see the same process being done differently across the organisation. Each unit will have their reasons why they do it a particular way. This can make improving a process more challenging as each unit will probably think theirs is the best way of running the process.

Swim Lane Process Map

A swim lane process map (also known as a cross-functional process map) is a diagram of a process showing all the steps taken in the process and who they are taken by. Like the high-level process map in Chapter 4, and the fishbone diagram and A3 problem statement, this map contains information, including:

- The name of the process
- The process owner
- The details of who prepared the process map and when
- The version number

The process map reads from left to right across the page, and the process starts in the top left corner. The map consists of a series of parallel lanes running left to right. Each of these is called a swim lane.

Visually, the outline of the process map looks like a swimming pool divided into multiple lanes. Each role in the process occupies a single lane. A role does not leave its lane. The swim lanes show you how many different roles are in the process and from how many different units. It is a common approach to have lanes and pools. Each lane is occupied by a single role, and each pool is a set of all the roles in the process from a particular business unit. A hand-off of work in the process is shown by the line moving from one lane or one pool to another.

Figure 5.1 is a more detailed look at part of the credit card reconciliation process which was shown as the high-level process map in Figure 4.1. The steps are described in greater detail and the map includes documents used at different steps of the process, and also indicates where email is used to route documents. The symbols used in the process map are important. They are drawn from a standard notation system known as BPMN (Business Process Model and Notation). Using BPMN will mean that your process map is drawn in a consistent way with maps from all over world, making them easy to share and read. However, you do not need to worry about using BPMN when you first start to draw the map, particularly if working with a team of people in a group discussion. A long sheet of paper and a set of sticky notes will get you started.

Each step in the process should be described in a 'who does what' format. Be informative in your description of each step, particularly if working with a group drafting the process on paper, with someone intending to draw the map in a software program later. It is surprising how much knowledge is assumed when a team is working together, and how uninformative a map can be later on when someone is reviewing it. For example, write the step as "Credit card holder runs monthly report on credit card usage", with a note as to which report it is and where they run it from rather than "Report is downloaded".

In process improvement language, there are three process states:

- Current state – the way it is right now
- Interim future state – an improved state that you can move to quickly and easily
- Ideal future state – how you want the process to be in the future

It is important to create a shared understanding of the current state of a process. Without a shared understanding of the process, there is unlikely to be agreement on the root causes of problems and what the best solutions are. This is why working with other people in problem solving is essential. Understanding the current state means ensuring that you understand what really happens in the process, not what people think should happen, or what happens once in a while when everything goes right. You need to know the way it is right now, warts and all, in order

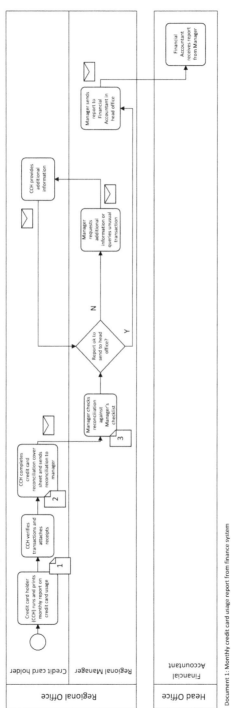

Process Name: Credit card reconciliation

Process Purpose: To ensure that credit card transactions are appropriate to the business and comply with policy

Prepared By:
Date Updated:
Version:

Document 1: Monthly credit card usage report from finance system
Document 2: Credit card reconciliation cover sheet from sales team share folder
Document 3: Manager's checklist of elements to check in credit card reconciliation from Manager's resource kit

Figure 5.1 Swim lane process map – credit card reconciliation.

to find solutions. This is where the three behaviours are vital. Be curious about understanding what is really happening. Be collaborative so people will trust you with the truth. Be evidence-based and test opinions or guesses about what is happening. Look for evidence to support the claims.

When you look at improving a process, start with behaviours and practices (the way people perform tasks in roles), then look at the tools used to complete the tasks. After doing that, look at the larger systems which support the process (e.g. the corporate finance system). Consider the improvements in that order. It is remarkable how often people will tell you that a new system is the required solution when there may be many improvements that can be made by changing behaviours and practices, or by using tools differently. The saying "spend ideas, not money" is useful to remember.

Value vs Non-value-Adding Steps

The steps of a process can be grouped into three categories:

1   Value-adding
2   Non-Value-adding but necessary
3   Non-Value-adding

A process step is considered to be value-adding if the customer of the process sees value in that step being done. This is an important concept, and can be a difficult one for people to accept. Remember that a process exists in order to do something that the business needs done. Somebody must be the customer of that process. The only value-adding steps in a process are the steps which the customer values and is willing to pay to have done.

A non-value-adding but necessary step is one which the customer does not see value in, but which must be done. This usually involves some form of compliance with legislation or unavoidable policy. It is arguable that a customer should care about steps required for compliance with legislation as the legislation might exist in order to protect their safety in using the end product. But if your customers tell you they do not care about these steps, they are non-value-adding, although necessary.

A non-value-adding step is one which does not fit into either of the other two categories. You should remove these steps from your process since they do not serve the customer or the organisation. The concept of a non-value-adding step can be difficult to accept. People take pride in their work and labelling some of the tasks they do as non-value-adding can be hurtful. See *The Welcome Back Event* for an example of this.

The Welcome Back Event

Most universities offer a study abroad experience, in which students can spend a semester studying at an overseas university during the course of their degree. While these opportunities have not been available during the COVID-19 pandemic in 2020, they have been in the past and one can expect will again in the future. In one university, a small team oversaw the process. Each semester, several hundred students would travel to different universities all around the world. It was a wonderful experience for the students, and the team who arranged this took great pride in helping them. At the end of each semester, the staff would hold a welcome back event for the students to share their experiences with each other and with the staff. These events were never particularly well attended. The team attributed this to the timing of the events, potential conflicts with exams, or some other reason.

The team decided to review the study abroad process and held an RIE. They invited several students to participate in the event to provide the voice of the customer. The team spent time mapping the current state of the process from end to end in order to create a shared understanding of the process. When they got to the steps for arranging the welcome back event, the staff were quite surprised, and somewhat disappointed, to be told that the students did not see value in the event. For the students, the excitement was in the trip itself. The steps that added value for them were those directly related to arranging the overseas experience. When they came back, they were keen to share their experiences with their family and friends, not with other students they had not met. The students appreciated the work the staff had done, but actually were not interested in a social event with them afterwards. The staff who worked in the process really enjoyed and valued the welcome back events because it was their chance to hear the stories of the students they had helped. So the voice of the employee said the welcome back event mattered. However, the voice of the customer said it did not.

From a process efficiency point of view, the answer to this is clear. Remove the welcome back event from the process because the customer sees no value in it, and it is not a necessary step in the study abroad process. However, the voice of the employee says the event matters. Using the five whys to explore this (i.e. seeking to understand 'why does the event matter to the staff?'), it became evident that the welcome back event was viewed by staff as recognition of their effort. They ended up agreeing that the event was not really for the students, it was for the staff, and could understand why the students did not value it. In a situation like this, it is important to balance the needs of the employee with those of the customer. Before removing the event from the process, the team discussed other simpler ways to acknowledge their effort so they did not feel undervalued as a result of the change.

Rapid Improvement Event

An RIE is a structured workshop in which a team work on improving a preselected process. They are also known as *kaizen* events or *kaizen* blitzes. *Kaizen* is a Japanese word used in lean process improvement, which is generally translated as improvement or change for the better. An alternate name is process improvement events (PIE). Calling these events 'rapid' can cause confusion for people if they are scheduled for several days. The rapidity refers to the desired speed of implementing changes during or after the event rather than the lead time to prepare for them or the duration of the event itself. RIE can be immersive (a team commits up to five consecutive days) or intermittent (shorter blocks of time scheduled over several weeks).[1] An intermittent approach can be easier to get agreement to, as it does not involve taking people offline for several days straight. However, there is considerable merit in giving a team sufficient time to thoroughly work through a process without interruption or distraction. There are many different variations on running RIE. In general, they will involve:

1 Preparatory work prior to the actual event to confirm process scope and team membership, gather relevant data, and have purposeful conversations about the process
2 In the RIE, prepare a swim lane process map of the process as it currently is
3 While doing this, identify and record all ideas for improving the process
4 Discuss the improvement ideas generated by the team
5 Prepare a swim lane process map of the agreed future state process (and an interim future state map if required)
6 Prepare an action plan to implement changes to move from current state to future state

There is a wealth of material available on RIE, including very detailed walkthroughs of the full five-day immersive event.[2] For this reason, this book does not go into great detail about running an event. Table 5.1 provides a summary of the steps in running an RIE, showing which of the tools described in this book can be introduced at each step.

Assuming that you are able to work together in the same room, it is good to give each person a notepad or a post-it note set at the start of the RIE, so they can write down ideas about the future as they map the current state process. Those ideas can then be discussed to inform what the future state process should be. Moving from the current state to future state of the process will require an action plan. RIEs are action oriented; set out to implement as many of the agreed changes as possible during or immediately after the event. This will be possible if you consider behaviours and actions, tools, and systems, in that order.

Table 5.1 RIE and relevant tools

RIE Step	Tools
Request	AIR 1 and 2, FOG, high-level process map
Scoping	Scoping document, in frame/out of frame
Training the RIE team	Introduce tools as required
Planning	Confirm the scoping document with the RIE team
Event	Swim lane process map, eight wastes, four voices, RRS, theory of constraints, ease/benefit analysis, SMART goals
Implementation	Implementation plan, RACI, Visual management
Review	Customer journey map, Visual display, STAR

Source: RIE steps based on Robinson and Yorkstone, 2014.[3]

Virtual RIE in Tasmania

The COVID-19 pandemic in 2020 has forced a global rethink of how people work. In many countries, the default changed from attending a workplace to working remotely from home, unless in a job which could not be done remotely. At the time of writing this book, vaccines were still in development and it was not known when (or if) people would return to their pre-COVID ways of working. During this time, work went on, including the work of running RIEs at the University of Tasmania.[4] They have been running RIEs since 2018 and had already shifted from the four consecutive days of immersive event to a 'two plus two' model with days 1 and 2 run consecutively, then a seven-day break before days 3 and 4 being run consecutively (Figure 5.2). The sudden need to work remotely forced a rapid rethink of their approach. Within months, they had re-imagined their RIE as much more modular, with increased pre-training and pre-work, then the RIE itself delivered virtually in shorter blocks of time. This compensated for the difficulty in sustaining momentum and interest over video conferencing software. The virtual format also increased the opportunity to include people from other locations, something they were not easily able to do when the RIE was always delivered face-to-face in a single room.

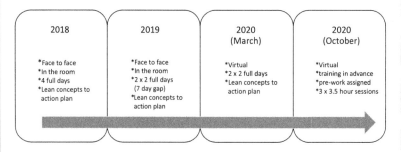

Figure 5.2 Adjusting the RIE for COVID-19.

While these sorts of events are popular as a means of introducing process improvement to an organisation, and can be a very powerful cultural change activity, they are actually one of the most expensive forms of process intervention due to the time commitment of everyone involved. They also tend to attract a lot of attention, especially if run as an immersive multi-day event, and so can become high profile within the organisation. For this reason, RIE should only be undertaken when there is clear leadership support for implementation of change. To launch into an RIE without explicit support for implementing the changes the team agrees on risks creating false expectations, leading to disenchantment and increased dissatisfaction. Implicit in leadership support is ensuring that leadership knows what it is in for with RIE. These events require an understanding that the organisation trusts the team members to solve a problem on the organisation's behalf. The RIE team might spend days working on the problem. They have the right to expect their solution will be tried. Equally, you cannot expect leaders to give a blank cheque to an RIE team. You will need to have some principles and parameters agreed in advance so your leadership is not caught off guard by a funding/solution implementation request they did not anticipate.

Some things to consider in running a RIE[5] are:

- Be clear on why you are running the improvement events. Are they for cultural change and training and development of participants or purely for process improvement with an expected return on investment?
- Use your understanding of why you are running the RIE to inform the measures of success you set for them. For instance, it is ok to include cultural change measures of success as well as process efficiency measures of success.
- Depending on the complexity of the process and the amount of process improvement experience in your organisation, the lead time to properly prepare for an RIE can be several months. Don't skip over this; it is as bad as jumping to the solution in problem solving.
- Review the end-to-end process during the RIE but if necessary, prioritise your top few changes and make sure they happen. It is dispiriting to be part of an RIE and then not see the changes actually made afterwards.
- Monitor and celebrate improvements as part of the cultural change required.

Case Study: Improving the Onboarding Process (Part 1)

You have been asked to assist the regional manager of a government agency with improving their staff onboarding process. The region has a small number of administrative staff in the office and also rely on several head office teams for support, including human resources (HR), information technology (IT), and occupational health and safety (OHS). The HR team process the appointments, IT set up user accounts, and OHS oversee safety inductions and monitor completion of mandatory online training. The local administrative staff arrange building and room access, computer equipment and office supplies, and do the local area induction. The local IT staff set up computers and provide on-site support. The new staff member's supervisor then takes over to discuss the work they will be doing and introduce them to their colleagues. Each of the teams involved in onboarding reports to a different manager, either in the regional office or in head office. The managers talk regularly about common issues, but have not previously attempted to improve processes together. Onboarding is considered to be an important organisational activity as it is the first significant interaction a new staff member has with the department, but is currently being done poorly.

After an initial discussion with the manager, you work together to draft a high-level process map, and agree the process purpose is "to successfully introduce new staff to the office" (Figure 5.3). The purpose will be checked with stakeholders, along with other elements of the map.

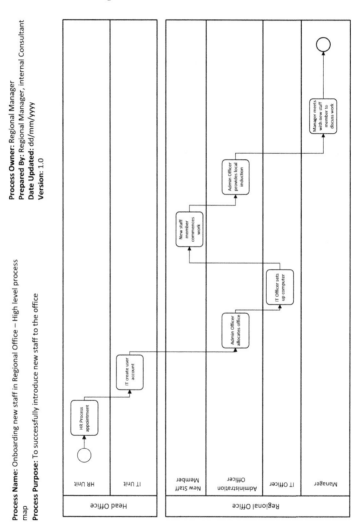

Figure 5.3 High-level process map – onboarding.

It is quickly evident that there is no process owner for onboarding. In fact, onboarding does not look like a single process at all. Further discussion leads to the suggestion that the work involved in onboarding a new staff member is a series of processes which contribute to the employee's onboarding experience. The manager concludes that they are the process owner for the activities that occur in the regional office, while managers of the different head office units would be process owners for the work which each of their teams do. The other significant learning for the manager from this initial discussion is the amount of work that occurs prior to the new staff member starting. In the seven-step high-level map shown in Figure 5.3, the new person starting work is step five.

The manager arranges a meeting of the key stakeholders identified to discuss the current state of onboarding. In preparation for the meeting, you agree to a small number of messages to convey. They are:

- We know everyone is doing the best they can with our current way of doing things. This is about improving the process, not blaming or questioning the commitment of our staff.
- However, we also know our new staff are not having a great onboarding experience, and this is a risk for the department, not just for the region.
- We know the staff from all of the teams doing the onboarding are frustrated as well. They would like to provide a better experience.
- The measures of success for this improvement will be based on an improved experience for new staff being onboarded, and also an improved experience for the staff working in the onboarding processes.

Framing the problem this way acknowledges the effort from all of the teams and the frustrations of everyone involved in. It commits you to improving the process in a no-blame way.

In the meeting, it becomes evident that each manager has a different view of why onboarding matters. The HR representative talks about the importance of onboarding in shaping a new employee's impression of the department. The IT representative talks about needing to maintain the integrity of their systems when setting up user accounts. The OHS representative talks about the need to ensure that the new employee completes mandatory online training so that the department is seen to be compliant with policy. The regional manager talks about a positive introduction to the workplace and getting the new staff member set up to work quickly and smoothly. There is agreement among everyone that it is an important process to get right.

The decision to start the onboarding process with "HR processes appointment" (refer Figure 5.3) is questioned. Is that really when onboarding starts? One person suggests that onboarding starts when new staff member arrives at work. However, it is evident from the high-level map that a lot happens prior to their first day at work. Eventually, the decision is upheld on the basis that new staff need to have an IT account in order to log into their computer on their first day, and IT cannot create the account until HR has processed the appointment. They are both agreed to be necessary precursors to a successful first day of work. It is also agreed that starting onboarding with "HR process appointment" also means that 'onboarding' could follow 'recruitment and selection' as a high-level process in an employee life cycle, if they decide to pursue wider improvements in the future. The managers actually share a moment of optimism about further possible improvements in the future.

The meeting is a success and you secure an agreement from the stakeholders to support their staff in participating in the improvement exercise. You have also agreed to amend the measures of success to include the phrase "while ensuring we meet our employer obligations" at the request of both the HR and OHS managers. The measures of success are now agreed to be "based on an improved experience for new staff, and also for the staff working in the process, while ensuring we meet our employer obligations". It is agreed that you will review onboarding as scoped in the high-level process map, but will start with improvements you can make within the regional office before seeking to implement changes that will need to be led from the head office. In return, the other managers commit to leading those improvement activities as the scope of that future work becomes clear.

In preparation for the RIE, you work with stakeholders to identify the team members. As discussed in chapter 4, the problem solving team should consist of the people who work in the process and who know the problems first hand. While the initial improvements will be based in the region, the head office teams provide staff for the RIE team as well in order to understand the end-to-end onboarding experience, and to see how an RIE works. The team also includes two relatively recent hires as customers of the process. They can tell you first hand what it is like to experience the process. You gather whatever data is available on the process.

Examples include IT helpdesk statistics and an estimate of the number of follow ups with support staff based on a review of email inboxes. Based on email dates, you can work out roughly how long it took from date of commencement to all onboarding tasks being completed. It is not great data but is the best you can do with the current information and gives you something to start with as a baseline. As you gather this information, you can prepare a draft scoping document such as a BOSCARD.

Looking at the department's strategic plan and other material, you see statements about the importance of staff and the department's ambition to make staff feel valued. While these statements are sometimes considered to be 'corporate wallpaper', displayed in posters and vision statements and then ignored, you include reference to them in the scoping document. If the region can demonstrate an improved onboarding experience, aligning this with the department's strategic plan could help to influence more senior decision makers in the future.

You organise a scoping and training session with the team to discuss what will happen during the RIE and some of the concepts and tools they need to be aware of. The discussion about scoping is important, given the decision to treat onboarding as an experience consisting of a series of processes, with the RIE focusing on what can be improved in the regional office. Issues relating to head office activities will be captured, but the action plan from this first event will be focused on what the regional office has the ability to improve. After working through the scoping document, you provide training in process mapping and improvement. Additional training material to include in this session is set out below, followed by the rest of the onboarding case study.

Four Voices

The four voices is a very powerful concept to understand in assessing a process. The four voices are voice of the customer, voice of the business, voice of the employee, and voice of the process.

The **voice of the customer** is the information you get from the customer of a process about its performance and the quality of its output. This can be formal or informal feedback. It could be in writing, via a survey, or could be verbal. Depending on the process, the customer could be external to the organisation or internal. Since the onboarding process exists for new staff, it is an internal process. You are already aware the new employees are unhappy with the induction process, but do not yet know what the new staff consider most important in the process.

The **voice of the business** will tell you the needs and expectations of the organisation. You have already heard that HR, IT, and OHS have different expectations from onboarding. This reinforces that onboarding is not a single process but a set of different process, each delivering something different for the business.

The **voice of the employee** is the voice of employees working in the process. It is not the voice of employees from other units who are actually internal customers of the process. Their voices are expressed through the impact (positive or negative) that the process has on their work.

The **voice of the process** is the information you can gather on the performance of the process. Examples of the voice of the process include:

- Cycle time – average length of time it takes to run the process
- Work-in-process – the number of jobs in the process at any one time
- Hands on time – the time taken to actually perform each step of the process
- Lag time – the time spent waiting in between steps for something to happen
- Error rate – how many mistakes are detected during the process
- Defects/rework – specific examples of things going wrong in the process

Eight Wastes

The eight wastes is a concept from lean which relates to the different types of waste which typically occur in processes. There are several acronyms used to remember the wastes. This book uses 'WISDOM TO change' (provided by Karen Kusler). Two other common ones are DOWNTIME and TIM WOODS. They are very similar as shown in Table 5.2.

Table 5.2 The eight wastes

WISDOM TO change	DOWNTIME	TIM WOODS
Waiting	Defects	Transportation
Inventory	Over-production	Inventory
Skills	Waiting	Motion
Defects	Non-utilised talent	Waiting
Over-production	Transportation	Over-production
Motion	Inventory	Over-Processing
Transportation	Motion	Defects
Over-processing	Extra Processing	Skills

Following the WISDOM TO change sequence:

Waiting is the time spent in between doing the steps of a process. Processes consist of 'hands on time' (the time taken to actually do the work in that step) and 'lag time' or waiting. It is usually the case that most of the time it takes to run a process is actually waiting in between steps. This could be due to handoffs from one person to another in a process, something waiting for approval before it can progress, or the unscheduled absence of the only person who can do a particular step (single point of failure).

Inventory is a stockpile of parts or materials used in the process. This is a waste more easily understood in a manufacturing setting. An office example of this could be a large collection of forms used in processes. As the forms become outdated and are discarded, the waste is evident. Another view of inventory is the large amount of information held in duplicate on different share folders, intranets, hard drives, and so on. When an electronic form is stored in many different places, there is a greater chance of the old version remaining in the system after it is officially replaced.

Skills (or non-utilised talents) refer to the waste of not using people to their full potential and letting some skills go unused, or the waste created from not training people to do their jobs properly and expecting them to find their own way through the work.

Defects are mistakes which occur in the process. In manufacturing this can result in wasted materials or the need to fix the product before it is ready to ship to customers. In an office environment, it could be an error in preparing a budget or a report which results in rework.

Overproduction is making too much of something, resulting in inventory. This could be multiple copies of a report or a brochure which sit in boxes in the cupboard, quietly going out of date.

Motion is the unnecessary movement of people during a process. An example could be hand delivering a form instead of sending an electronic copy.

Transportation is the unnecessary movement of materials during the process.

Over-processing (or extra processing) is making something more complicated than it needs to be. This could be a briefing paper or a quarterly or annual report. The temptation to add more information is always there, but does the information add value rather than volume?

The eight wastes are a useful concept for getting people to critically review the way they work. Once people start to understand the different types of waste, they will begin to see this waste in their workplace. It is useful to give people a common language to talk about processes and about improvement. However, do not fixate on whether a particular activity is one type of waste or another. It does not matter which category it fits into; the main thing is learning to see waste.

RRS (Runners, Repeaters, Strangers)

A process map is an illustration of all the steps in a process from start to finish. Every time the activity described in the process is undertaken, it is an instance of the process being run. Each instance will tell you something about whether the process is working as it should or not. However, not every instance of something going wrong will require a change. RRS is a categorisation of instances into three categories:

1   Runners are instances of the process running as it runs most of the time. It is the normal result (good or bad) from the process. Runners are the default expected result of the process.
2   Repeaters are instances of the process running with an identifiable variation which recurs (repeats) on a regular or semi-regular basis. You will see a trend of repeaters occurring.
3   Strangers are instances of the process running with a rare variation or sequence of variations occurring. However, it is a rare instance of the process and not likely to occur again.

The best way to know for sure if a particular outcome of a process is a runner, repeater, or stranger is to keep records so you have evidence to rely on in decision making. In general, in an office environment you do not change your process for a stranger. As you will see with the Pareto analysis, addressing the errors that occur most frequently will give you the best return. An exception to this is if the stranger yields a process outcome which is considered too high a risk to allow it to happen again. An example of this is the space shuttle Challenger exploding after take-off, killing all the astronauts on board.

RRS is a useful concept when investigating a problem or mapping a process and working with people who do not have good baseline data to work from. As discussed in Chapter 2, people sometimes vividly remember the worst instance of a process being run and describe it as though it were the norm. Something that has only happened once in hundreds of incidents is not an indication of the current state of the process. This often comes up when attempting to determine how long a process takes. When most people say it takes 15 minutes and one person says it can take up to three hours, it is worth asking what happened in the three-hour instance. Why did it take so long? What other factors might have been at play? Were all the problems they encountered actually related to that process? How many times has it taken three hours instead of 15 minutes?

You also need to be aware of the tendency for people to tell you what they think the process should be. You may give a description of the 'happy path' – what it would look like if everything went right. This can be as far removed from reality as the instance from hell. What you need to know is what actually happens most of the time. Unless you can get a shared understanding of what is actually happening, you will be unlikely to solve the problem. This is a situation in which displaying curiosity and discussing the need for objective evidence is important.

Theory of Constraints

The theory of constraints relates to processes and states that the entire process can only move at the speed of its slowest step. There may be several constraints in a process. The worst of these (i.e. the slowest step) is the bottleneck. According to this theory, the way to improve process performance is to first focus on alleviating the bottleneck. Once that is improved, the second worst constraint becomes the new bottleneck, so you shift your focus to improving that one. Over time, you improve all the steps, improving the flow and speed of the overall process. The five steps in approaching this are:[6]

1   Identify the constraint
2   Exploit the constraint (do what you can to improve it without major expenditure)
3   Subordinate other processes to the constraint (e.g. provide additional assistance from other people)
4   Elevate the constraint (invest in further improvements, if required)
5   Repeat the cycle

While the theory of constraints comes from manufacturing, it is applicable to office work as well. Rather than simply blaming the person who is slowing the process down, this theory requires you to do what you can to assist them, including getting other people to help, before looking at a larger solution. In a scenario where there is a multistep process involving several handovers of work and one step (or one person) is identified as the bottleneck, it is necessary to ask why (use the five whys) to understand what is happening. Possible reasons include:

•   The person is an approver for multiple processes and so work of different kinds all queue up, waiting to be actioned

- The person takes the more complex work which requires more time per transaction to be completed
- Some of the work being sent to the person contains errors which the person fixes rather than sending back to be fixed

Being identified as 'the bottleneck' is not pleasant, and can be received as suggesting poor performance. Asking why a particular step is the bottleneck is essential to understanding what is really happening and determining what to do. For instance, a veterinary hospital was seeking to streamline its process for scheduling small animal surgery. Anecdotally, they had identified diagnostic imaging (taxing X-rays before and after surgery on broken limbs) as a bottleneck. When they mapped the process in detail, they realised that the problems that were evident in diagnostic imaging were caused earlier in the process, resulting in periods of time with no patients followed by several animals arriving at once. This meant the process bottleneck had periods of downtime and periods of being overloaded. Ensuring a smooth flow of patients through diagnostic imaging required making the earlier steps of the process flow first.

Case Study: Improving the Onboarding Process (Part 2)

Once the training is completed and the RIE is scheduled, the team gathers any additional data they think will be useful. At the start of the RIE, it is good to revisit the scope and purpose of the process, and the goals to be achieved in the RIE itself.

During the RIE, the team agrees that 'onboarding' is not a single process; it is a set of processes with dependencies and which contribute to the new staff members starting experience. The team prepares a detailed map of the current process and discuss many ideas to improve things. Each team member has been given a set of large post-it notes or something similar, and told to write down ideas as they go, with one idea per sheet of paper. If several people have the same idea or agree with someone else's idea, they should each write it down. It is quite common for a team of six to eight people to write down hundreds of ideas during an RIE, and literally cover a wall with them once they are all put up for discussion. You confirm during the RIE that the new staff (customers of the process) are unhappy with the process. They find it difficult to identify the right person to talk to about different things they need. Also, the compliance elements are not of value to them, although everyone concedes they are necessary.

As a result of mapping the process, you are able to describe the extent to which the different voices are currently being heard:

- Voice of the customer – dissatisfaction being heard via follow up emails and calls. These are initiated by the customer, not the department. The department does not solicit feedback from its new employees.
- Voice of the business – compliance elements being heard through mandatory requirements, 'positive onboarding experience' not being heard.
- Voice of the employee – not being heard, although they do talk to each other about how bad the process is.
- Voice of the process(es) – not being heard in a systematic way.

Finding alignment between the voice of the customer and the voice of the employee is important. Both are frustrated by the process, although possibly for different reasons. However, when the customer and the service provider are both frustrated by the current state of the process, getting agreement to change it will be easier. Looking to the future, you agree on the following statements for three of the voices, written in a user story format:

- Voice of the customer: As a customer, I want to be enabled to work effectively as quickly as possible, and to be assisted in understanding how to interact with the department when I need something.
- Voice of the business: As an employer, we want our new staff to have a positive onboarding experience, and we need to ensure compliance with departmental policy.
- Voice of the employee: As employees, we want to perform the onboarding tasks quickly and efficiently and provide a positive experience to our new colleagues.
- You also discuss the indicators to measure in the future as the voice of the process.

These statements help you to distinguish between the value-adding processes (those which contribute to the voice of the customer statement) and non-value-adding but necessary processes. This improved understanding of onboarding as an experience rather than a single process can lead to different measures for each process within it, which become the voice of the processes.

Using the eight wastes, you go through the current state map and discuss waste at each step. You find a lot of waste, mostly waiting. This is typically in the form of work waiting in a queue to be actioned, and then being delayed when it is actioned because information is missing or incorrect. As the team explores the waste in the current process, they are amazed at the amount of it, and also excited about the opportunities to improve. A valuable observation from the customers in the team is that no one is considering their overall experience. While each unit treats a call as a new task which has its own time frame for responding, no one has previously considered the cumulative effect of this for the customer. This is not surprising given there are different units involved and each unit has their own call logging and queuing system. However, it is the cumulative effect of all these discrete processes with their own waste which is so off-putting to new staff. This provides an idea for improving the process within the regional office, which quite a few people in the team write down on their notepads. The regional office would benefit from having one person assigned with coordinating the different tasks to be completed in the onboarding experience, monitoring progress for the new employee, and ensuring that processes happen concurrently rather than being done one at a time. This is a change from the current situation in which the employee engages with each unit separately in a fragmented and at times confusing experience. This coordinator could also gather the information needed to discuss specific future improvements to other processes within the head office.

Having completed the current state map, the team goes through all the ideas they generated, discussing them and deciding whether to include them in the future state process. They then produce a future state process map, and an action plan which lists all the things that need to happen to move from the current state to the future state. Ideally, the team will start to implement these changes immediately (Figure 5.4).

The team comes up with recommendations about reducing waiting time in the different units. Many of these can be actioned quickly and at low (or no) cost, using the lean principle of "spend ideas, not dollars" and are recorded in an action plan which states each action, who is responsible for it, and when it will be completed. The most substantial change in the regional office is the decision to assign responsibility for overseeing onboarding to one of the existing administrative staff. This person will act as a guide to the regional office, explaining what is required and assisting new

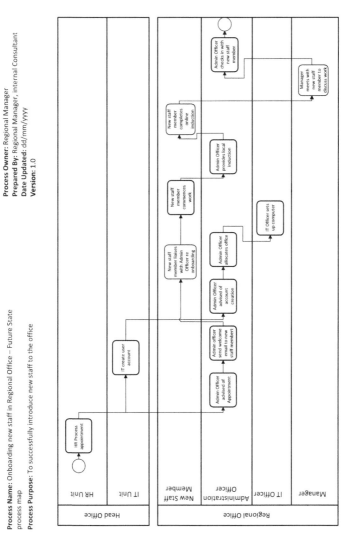

Process Name: Onboarding new staff in Regional Office – Future State process map

Process Purpose: To successfully introduce new staff to the office

Process Owner: Regional Manager
Prepared By: Regional Manager, internal Consultant
Date Updated: dd/mm/yyyy
Version: 1.0

Figure 5.4 Future state map – onboarding.

employees with completing forms, providing information, and getting established more quickly. It is anticipated this will contribute directly to the department's goal of "making staff feel valued and supporting them in successful work". Doing this will require some reallocation of work between the other staff. However, the team feels it will not be a significant addition of work overall when they factor in the time currently being spent by different team members in following up on things for new employees already. This new role will be encouraged to identify further opportunities to streamline processes and improve the user-friendliness of forms. The head office representatives agree to work closely with this role to understand how their work impacts on the onboarding experience.

Case Study: The New Payroll System

This section uses the example of a payroll system implementation to describe using root cause analysis to identify and solve problems. This case study is also referred to in Chapter 7, in the section on automation making problems visible.

You are a member of the administration team in a hospital which is part of a network of hospitals in your region. The hospital network has implemented a new payroll system and the first pay run from the new system has taken place. You come into the office to find your phone is running hot and email inbox is full of messages from people saying they have been paid the wrong amount, and in some cases, have not been paid at all. The payroll project was managed by head office with some user consultation. While you have received some training on using the system in a test environment and been provided access to online training material, you have had limited opportunity to interact with the new system or engage with the project team. You know that the pay run took place two nights ago and that people have been sent electronic timesheets to show the details of the pay deposited into their bank accounts.

As you read through the emails and listen to the phone messages, you take notes and start to see some early patterns forming in the complaints you are receiving:

- Most people were not paid for all of the hours they worked
- Some of the hours worked were paid at the wrong pay rate
- A small number of people were not paid at all

Seeking more information about what has happened, you run a payroll report and start to look more closely at transaction details. The HR officer and finance officer in the hospital have also received many calls and messages about the pay issues as well. The three of you meet with a laptop and the payroll report to discuss the situation.

Fishbone Diagram

The team might start the discussion with the three broad categories identified from the messages and draw a table on the whiteboard similar to Table 5.3.

Table 5.3 Error categories

Not paid for all hours	Wrong pay rate used	Not paid at all

As you start to put notes into each category, you realise this is not going to be the most useful way forward. Each of the three categories is a type of error, but what do they all have in common? Deciding to use a fishbone diagram instead, you draw the fishbone template and ask what is the question or statement to go in the fish's head? Thinking about the payroll errors from the customer point of view (i.e. the staff being paid), you agree to try the statement "My pay is incorrect". Having described the problem from the customer point of view (based on the emails and messages from customers of the process even if they are not in the room with you), you can now start to list potential root causes on the bones of the fish.

Over the course of several days of investigation with the staff who were not paid correctly and with the payroll project team, you populate the fishbone diagram as per Figure 5.5 with likely causes of the pay problems and which unit you think is best placed to address the cause. Keeping track of the changes in the fishbone diagram as you proceed through the investigation step is very important. As you investigate further, you could grey out the font of causes which you reject, but keeping them on the diagram as a record. You could use a code for different teams or units who are best placed to solve each root cause. This keeps all the relevant information about the problem solving story on the diagram as part of a concise but informative visual display.

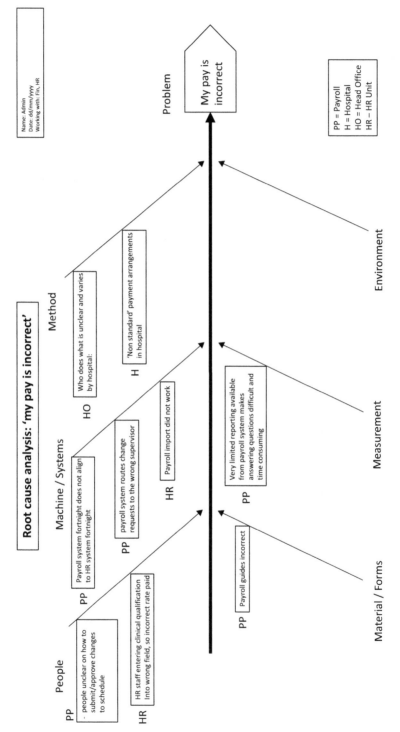

Figure 5.5 Fishbone diagram – my pay is incorrect.

Pareto Analysis

Pareto was an economist in the early 20th century who is best known for devising the '80/20' rule. Based on his analysis of wealth distribution in Italy at the time, he said that 80% of the wealth was owned by 20% of the population. The 80/20 rule has been broadened to many other fields, including problem solving. In this context, it is believed that 80% of the observed problems are attributable to 20% of the causes. Conducting a Pareto analysis is quite simple. As you gather evidence about what is actually happening and determine the root causes, you can compile a bar chart as a visual representation of this. In a Pareto chart, the number of events is shown on the Y axis and the cause of events is on the X axis. The saying "Y to the sky" is an easy way to remember which is Y. The results are shown in a bar chart which any standard spreadsheet package such as Excel can generate using the chart wizard.

The team prepared a spreadsheet listing all the impacted staff and the type of errors affecting each. Then they performed a Pareto analysis on it to show which problems are occurring most often (Figure 5.6). You can quickly see that most of the payroll errors are attributable to a couple of root causes. Solve them and you can take a lot of heat out of the situation by fixing the errors for most people. The Pareto analysis also shows how

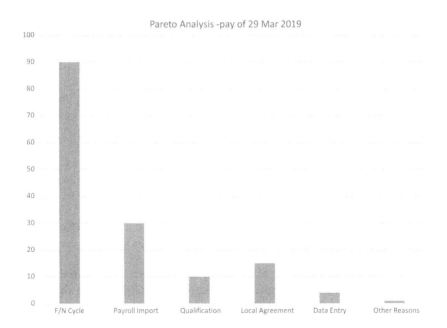

Figure 5.6 Pareto analysis – my pay is incorrect.

many of the errors originate in the new payroll system and how many were actually caused by other systems or by local practices. This information will be very useful for the payroll project team.

What the unit's analysis led to discovering about the casual pay system included:

- The casual pay system had a different pay fortnight (Monday week 1 to Sunday week 2) than the HR system (Sunday week 1 to Saturday week 2). Any work not scheduled for a specific time in the casual pay system (e.g. an allocation of time for completing reports) was automatically scheduled in the new system to day 14, which was actually day 1 of the following pay fortnight in the HR system. So the staff did eventually get paid the correct amount, but a fortnight later than they expected.
- The casual pay system did not recognise that a casual staff member could work for more than one hospital at a time. It routed all time sheet approvals to the first recorded supervisor. This meant hospitals were getting approval requests for work being done in other hospitals in the region. This caused confusion and stress for supervisors.

What the unit's analysis led to discovering about other systems contributing to incorrect payments included:

- The HR system which had been in use for over a decade had two different fields in which clinical qualifications could be recorded. Only one of those fields was linked to the pay rates table to ensure that people were paid at the higher rate if they had the clinical qualification. However, HR staff across the network had been updating qualifications using either of the two fields, since both resulted in the qualifications appearing in the staff members personnel record. The choice of field had never mattered before.
- The payroll import function did not work properly in the HR system, but had not been used before; so the problem had remained undetected.

What the unit's analysis led to discovering about local practices and behaviours included:

- Hospitals, and in some cases wards within hospitals, entered into a variety of 'local agreements' with casual staff resulting in different payments to staff for the same type or work depending on where they worked. This had not been observable in the paper-based system due to a large volume of timesheets being processed.

These variations had developed over time and were well intentioned, often based on someone's subjective assessment of what work descriptor best suited the work that was being done. While staff across the network were quick to blame the new system for all the incorrect payments, this was not true. In many cases, the incorrect payments were not caused by the new system at all. It had simply brought other problems to the surface.

A3 Problem Statement

Having developed a clear understanding of all the root causes, the team produced an A3 problem statement to describe and monitor progress in fixing the problems (Figure 5.7).

As you can see from the completed A3 problem statement, it provides key information on the problem, the data used to confirm the causes, the actions planned to solve the problem, and progress against the action plan. This shows how the A3 problem statement follows the "plan, do, check, act" format. As the team moved into implementing solutions, they updated the A3 problem statement every fortnight as they assessed the improvements in payment accuracy and were able to confirm that problems were solved. For instance, they could see from the payroll information that the correct pay rates were being used for clinical qualifications and that the fortnight cycle issue had been resolved. The A3 problem statement is an excellent storyboard to show the improvements over successful pay cycles.

As discussed in Chapter 4, fishbone diagrams and also A3 problem statements are collaborative tools which can also form part of your visual display of the problem you are working on. Both are documents you will return to during the investigation step. Using the fishbone diagram when defining the problem is important as it can assist in identifying the root cause(s) of the problem. As you investigate the problem, you will be able to confirm or reject the potential root causes. You may also find new information which leads to a different root cause being uncovered.

Two other tools to be aware of during the investigation stage of problem solving are stakeholder analysis and spaghetti maps.

Stakeholder Analysis

Conducting a stakeholder analysis consists of listing all the stakeholders in a problem solving process and considering:

1   The extent to which they currently support potential changes or not, and
2   The level of support you think you need from them to successfully make a change.

Title: Incorrect payments to staff

Name:
Date: 30 March 2019
Working with:

Plan

Problem statement:

A new casual payroll system was introduced in 2019. It has created problems with paying staff through system bugs and errors, and made visible other errors in previously unconnected systems. It has also made visible process problems within the hospital.

Ensuring casual staff are paid correctly (or that pay errors are corrected as quickly as possible) is proving to be very time consuming and frustrating for staff in the process, and for casual staff.

Background / data:

Allocating staff to activities in the system:

Admin staff were unsure how to use the system correctly, and had to rely on online training material. Casual staff received very little training in how to use the new system.

250 staff paid 29 March 2019 – 90 F/N cycle issue, 30 payroll import errors, 10 qualification not recorded (wrong pay rate), 15 local agreements don't align with pay rates, 4 data entry, 1 other. 150/250 = 60% impacted staff

Improvement goals:

2nd pay fortnight: (in bank 12 Apr 2019)
250 staff to be paid – 0 F/N pay cycle issue,
0 qualification error, 0 data entry

4th pay fortnight: (in bank 10 May 2019)
0 local agreement discrepancies

6th pay fortnight (in bank 7 June 2019)
No preventable errors

Issues - pay F/N 1

(chart)
100
50
0
F/N Cycle | No import | Part, PhD Flag | Tutor TTE, Course

Do

Refer to attached fishbone diagram

Action list:

What	Who	When
Provide clearly described problems to Payroll team for resolving as appropriate		5/04/19
Provide information to staff and supervisors on how to 'read' pay information in Payroll		10/04/19
Provide clearly described problems to Head Office team for resolving as appropriate		10/04/19
Resolve local agreement discrepancies with supervisors and staff		24/04/19

Check

4th pay fortnight – 5 casual staff identified problems (as at 28/4)

5th pay fortnight – track errors and Resolve with casual staff

6th pay fortnight – track errors and Resolve with casual staff

Act

- *Monitor errors per fortnight, correct them for staff and identify root causes of errors*
- *Monitor who is doing what in system via audit trails*
- *Reconcile payments in finance system each month*

Figure 5.7 A3 statement – my pay is incorrect.

Sometimes the relative importance of stakeholders to an issue will be obvious. For instance, the process owner is a key stakeholder required to support a change to that process. At other times though, identifying which stakeholders to focus on winning the support of can be more complex. Another way to view your stakeholders is to use a matrix to consider how important they are and how influential they are (Figure 5.8). The high importance/high influence stakeholders are the highest priority to win the support of.

Once you have confirmed which stakeholders are most critical to success, you can assess their current level of support and your desired level of support from them. You can use a simple Likert scale for the ranking (e.g. 1–5 with 1 being the lowest and 5 being the highest level of support). An example of this is provided in Table 5.4. The letter A denotes current level of support and the letter B denotes the required level of support. You can see in Table 5.4 that Susan and Ella have been assessed as being respectively neutral and strongly against the proposed change, but also assessed as being required to be somewhat strongly in favour of the change to make it successful.

Stakeholder Analysis can be a useful exercise as part of understanding the current state of a problem. When you identify that a stakeholder is not at the level of support you require, you can consider what actions will be needed to ensure you gain their support. This could involve a purposeful conversation (refer to Chapter 2) or using interest-based negotiation (discussed in Chapter 9). Stakeholder analysis is conceptually similar to force field analysis (also discussed in Chapter 9). A weakness of stakeholder analysis is that it can be based on the opinions of the people performing the analysis. Using the five whys during this analysis will be useful in helping to understand why people think stakeholders have particular views on the problem. You can also assess the comments about stakeholders via a FOG analysis (Chapter 3).

Figure 5.8 Stakeholder analysis matrix.

Table 5.4 Stakeholder analysis

Name	Strongly against	Somewhat against	Neutral	Somewhat in favour	Strongly in favour
Joe		A	B		
Susan			A		B
Ella	A			B	

Spaghetti Diagram

A spaghetti diagram is a floor plan or map used to observe the movement of people or products through a process or over a period of time. It can be useful in highlighting inefficiencies in processes or in the physical layout of a workspace. For instance, the diagram might reveal that someone working at a service counter has the most popular brochures stored at the far end of the counter and out of their reach rather than right next to them. Another example is two people working on a project together who might not realise how often they are going up and down in the lifts to see one another. The spaghetti diagram becomes a usual source of evidence to inform a discussion with their manager about moving desks to be collocated for the duration of the project.

How useful a spaghetti diagram is will depend on the circumstances in which you use it. For instance, a spaghetti diagram showing lots of people moving back and forth to a single printer throughout the day will give the impression of inefficiency. A solution would be to add more smaller printers throughout the office so people have to walk less distance. This would reduce the waste of *motion*. However, there may be other good reasons for having one large printer rather than lots of smaller printers. These could include lower print rates per copy on a high volume copier, better print quality on a more advanced device, use of a multi-function device rather than a series of printers as well as scanners and faxes, or a desire to make people move away from their desks during the day so they interact with each other and for their physical well-being. The information from the spaghetti diagram would need to be considered in context.

In the example shown in Figure 5.9, two staff work on a front desk in a busy service centre. They have forms and brochures stored in a small storeroom behind their desk. The left-hand diagram shows their current movement through the day, with many visits to the store room to bring forms to a small cabinet behind the desk. The person sitting nearest the cabinet does most of the back and forth to refill it. The right-hand diagram shows their movements after reviewing the diagram and

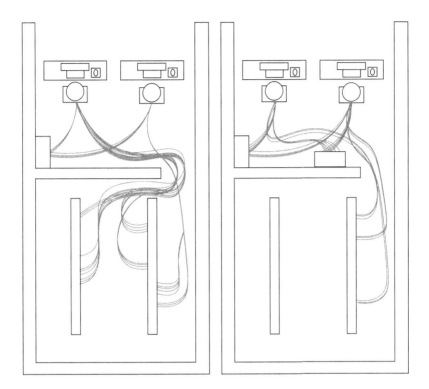

Figure 5.9 Spaghetti diagram.

deciding to install a second cabinet behind the desk. They now have a cabinet each located where they sit, and have rearranged the store room so the forms they use the most are located next to each other. They now have fewer trips to the storeroom through the day to replenish the cabinets, and are sharing the work of refilling cabinets more evenly between them.

Notes

1 Balzer, W.K., 2020, *Lean Higher Education: Increasing the Value and Performance of University Processes*, 2nd edition, New York, Taylor and Francis Group, LLC, pp145–146.
2 Robinson, M. & Yorkstone, S., 2014, Becoming a Lean University: The Case of the University of St Andrews, *Leadership and Governance in Higher Education*, 1, pp41–72.
3 Robinson, M. & Yorkstone, S., 2014.
4 Ghosh, B. & di Palma, L., 2020, Virtual Rapids: Optimising the Rapid Improvement Event Model for the Virtual Environment, Lean HE Global Festival (online).

5 Shannon, C., 2020, Lessons from Implementing Lean at the Veterinary Teaching Hospital, in Yorkstone, S. (ed.) *Global Lean for Higher Education: A Themed Anthology of Case Studies, Approaches, and Tools*, Boca Raton, FL, Taylor and Francis Group, LLC, pp313–319.
6 Nave, D., 2002, How to Compare Six Sigma, Lean and the Theory of Constraints, *Quality Progress*, 35, p73.

Chapter 6

Selecting the Solution

Are We Confident We Have Picked the Best Solution?

As you work through investigating the problem and determining potential solutions, you will most likely be assessing the options as you go. Try to keep an open mind and not jump to a solution. Establishing objective measures of success when defining and investigating the problem will assist with this. This chapter explains the use of ease/benefit analysis for decision making. The concept of *poka yoke* (designed to avoid mistakes) is introduced. The difference between cost reduction and capacity creation is discussed, along with the use of SMART goals. It will not be a surprise to see that evidence-based thinking is the essential behaviour at this point. You will still need to maintain curiosity and collaboration but at the decision making stage of problem solving, being evidence-based is vital to success.

Ease/Benefit Analysis

An ease/benefit analysis can help with solution selection. It is a two × two matrix used as a visual display of possible solutions positioned against two axes – the ease with which the solution can be implemented and the likely benefit to be achieved from the solution. The model presented in Figure 6.1 is typical of many ease/benefit analyses based on a two × two matrix diagram.

Solutions which are easy to implement and have a large benefit (in the top right quadrant of the diagram) are the highest priority to implement. Easy to implement solutions with smaller benefits and hard to implement solutions with large benefits are the second level of priority to consider. Hard to implement solutions with small benefits are unlikely to be useful and can quickly be discarded. As with many of these two × two matrices, the goal is to have as many options in the top right quadrant as possible. With that in mind, you could review options currently seen as being medium priority to see if you can make any changes that would make them easier to implement or to increase their likely benefit.

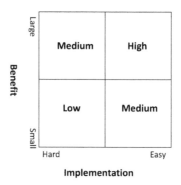

Figure 6.1 Ease/benefit analysis.

Determining Ease

Determining the ease with each a solution can be implemented could consider factors such as:

- How long it would take to implement
- The likely cost of implementation
- Whether the solution would require a change of policy
- Whether other groups need to be consulted prior to making the change
- How many different units need to change behaviour to make this work?

Determining ease requires considering both the actual implementation and the follow up work. For instance, writing a policy and sending an email to announce it is easy. Ensuring that people follow the new policy is much harder, and should be considered in the ease/benefit analysis.

Determining Benefit

A benefit is "a positive impact achieved from implementing or using the deliverables" of a problem solving process.[1] Determining the benefit of implementing a solution requires assessment of each potential solution against the performance criteria already established for the process. You can do this via a discussion of the merits of each solution in order to determine whether they will deliver large or small benefits, or using a points system as shown in Table 6.1.

There may be additional benefits which could be realised but which do not align with the performance criteria. These could be considered 'nice to have' but do not form the basis for the decision (see *Cars and Phones*).

Table 6.1 Benefits scorecard

Solutions	Criterion 1 (w2)	Criterion 2 (w1.5)	Criterion 3 (w1)	Total
Solution 1	3 (score of 6)	4 (score of 6)	5	17
Solution 2	5 (score of 10)	4 (score of 6)	3	19
Solution 3	3 (score of 6)	2 (score of 3)	4	13

It is important to come back to the problem definition question, "what is the problem we are trying to solve?" and assess solutions against the criteria which were agreed to be most important in the process. You will use these criteria to measure performance over time and assess the effectiveness of the solution. Consistency in the use of performance criteria from definition through investigation to selection and review will give you the best chance of ensuring you solve the problem.

Designing Out Errors (*Poka Yoke*)

You will recall from Chapter 5 that a process involves people in roles performing tasks by using tools and systems. In considering how to improve a process, it was suggested to start with actions and behaviours, then look at tools, and look at systems last. This is consistent with the process improvement maxim "spend ideas, not money". There are many small and low cost changes that can immediately improve the way work is being done. You also saw in Chapter 4 that one of the costs of poor quality is the cost of maintaining a checking system. Checking can find errors but not eliminate them, unless you investigate the cause of the error and prevent it from recurring. The use of rolled throughput yield showed that errors have a cumulative effect in a process, and highlighted the value of simplicity in process design. *Poka yoke* is a Japanese term for error prevention by design which has become popular through lean process improvement. However, the concept is universal and not tied to lean.

Physical examples of *poka yoke* are everywhere in our daily lives. The overflow hole in a bathroom sink is a great example of *poka yoke* at home. It is part of the sink design and ensures that you cannot overfill your sink, flooding the bathroom, and causing you to slip on the wet floor tiles.

Here are some examples of *poka yoke* related to putting petrol into your car:

- Your car dashboard has a gauge to show you at a glance how much petrol you have in your tank. Some cars have a detailed display predicting how many kilometres of driving till you run out of gas.

- A warning light appears on your dashboard when you are getting low on petrol.
- The petrol gauge on your dashboard has a little arrow pointing to the left or the right, indicating which side of the car your petrol cap is on.
- You cannot insert a diesel pump nozzle into a car that takes un-leaded petrol (at least not in Australia), physically preventing you from damaging the motor with the wrong type of fuel.
- The petrol cap is attached to the car by a plastic cord so you cannot drive away without it.

These are all designed to make the process of putting petrol into your car that little bit easier and minimise the risk of something going wrong.

Examples of *poka yoke* in an office include:

- Elevator doors fitted with sensors so they do not close on people entering or exiting the lift
- Surge protectors on power boards to prevent damage to computers and other equipment
- Smoke detectors linked to security systems to alert you and the fire brigade if there is a fire
- Mandatory fields in electronic forms so the form cannot be submitted with essential information missing
- Auto-calculation functions in electronic forms that total the amounts entered for you
- The requirement to enter an email address twice when registering with a website to ensure it is entered correctly
- 'field masking' on input fields in electronic forms which defines the input format (for example, a date of birth must be entered dd/mm/yyyy)
- Automatic backups to file servers so important information is not lost
- Pop up boxes that display information when you hold the cursor over them
- Pop up reminders 15 minutes before a meeting is due to start

Cars and Phones

When I decided to buy a new car, it was because my old one was out of warranty and I did not want to incur expensive repair bills as parts inevitably wore out. When I replaced my mobile phone, it was specifically to get a higher resolution camera and also a larger screen for ease of use. Neither purchase had anything to do with an imagined futuristic lifestyle. But it turned out that the combination of my new car and my new mobile phone provided previously unknown benefits through pairing my phone to my car with blue tooth technology. One could argue that this pairing ability is *poka yoke* as it can prevent me from getting lost while driving around. I can simply say "Hey Siri, give me directions to Mockingbird Lane" and a few seconds later Siri will start to provide directions to my destination.

But my car/phone combination can do much more than that. I have lots of songs saved to my phone. I can say "Hey Siri, play Neil Young" and Siri will reply with "Here's some music by Neil Young", or sometimes "Neil Young, coming right up", and the music will play through my car speaker system. It is very cool. The car/phone combination also allows me to make or receive hands-free phone calls. "Hey Siri, call Eloise" quickly connects me to my partner. It has become a running joke with my father that I almost always call him when I am driving somewhere. My old car could pair a phone as well, but the reception in it was so bad that I rarely used it. My new car has very good phone reception, an attribute that never entered my mind when buying it. Making use of this improved technology allows me to use the car as an extension of my office, turning the commute into a productive part of the day. I will often get in the car with a list of calls to make on the way to or from work. It also makes the perceptual time of the trip seem much shorter.

My car/phone combination has some other interesting features as well. When I get in my car on a weekday (Monday to Friday), the phone connects to the car, then displays a message telling me the estimated travel time to my office, and suggests an alternate route if the traffic is very slow on my normal route. But when I get in the car on a Saturday morning, the phone displays a message telling me the estimated travel time to the local farmers market I usually shop at. The phone recognises my travel pattern for a particular day and gives me helpful, if unsolicited, information. This is apparently because I have something called 'location services' activated on my phone. Use of location services was not in my mind when I purchased the phone. These are all cool features, but none were features that formed part of my decision making process when purchasing the car or the phone.

Repeatable and Reproducible

The concept of repeatable and reproducible processes comes from Six Sigma. A repeatable process means the process can be done by the same person multiple times and they will get the same result each time (within an acceptable range of variation). A reproducible process means the process can be done by different people multiple times and they will get the same result as the first person got each time.

In an office environment, these are useful tests to keep in mind. When using a system with a built-in workflow, repeatable and reproducible results are much more easily achieved as the system forces a particular way of doing things. However, when doing other forms of knowledge work (for instance writing a report, or preparing a business case), the likelihood of variation in approach and in outcomes is much higher. In many large organisations, common tasks can be done by people who occupy a variety of different roles and who have different levels of expertise. An example of this is reconciling corporate credit cards. This could be done by a purchasing officer using a credit card issued to them for a high volume of purchases, a personal assistant who reconciles a card issued to an executive for travel, or a junior technician who uses the card for routine orders of consumables for a research laboratory. If you were to change the credit card reconciliation process, you would need to be confident that each different type of card reconciler could understand the new process and complete it successfully. You would need to ensure it is repeatable and reproducible.

Reducing Cost vs Creating Capacity

This is a potentially contentious and confusing issue for problem solving teams in office environments. You might recall from Chapter 4 that cost reduction refers to specific and identifiable costs which can be reduced. Examples of this include printing brochures, software licensing costs, and offsite storage costs. If you can remove the need for these things, you will spend less money as a result.

The concept of cost reduction is straightforward and is easily expressed using the Ohno equation from Toyota. The Ohno equation is:

Price − Cost = Profit

This is similar to the layout of a Statement of Income and Expenditure:

Revenue − Expenditure = Profit / Loss

The important thing to remember about the Ohno equation is that it is driven by cost reduction. If the price is set by an external force (such as a market or a regulator), the way to increase profit is to reduce cost. As Ohno said, "costs exist to be reduced, not to be calculated".[2] In a manufacturing workplace that uses materials to produce goods, the Ohno equation makes sense. If you reduce the inputs to the finished product, you reduce cost. If you reduce the number of defects in the production process, you reduce cost by reducing the waste of materials used to make products. If you reduce the amount of machine time required in making the finished product, you reduce cost. However, in an office environment, where the work is often done by people applying knowledge and skills to electronically held data, reducing cost is not so simple. The primary input is not materials, it is people's time. Time saved in a process does not automatically result in lower cost because you will still be paying the people to work there.

When you improve a process and reduce the time taken to perform a task from 30 minutes to 15 minutes, you do not release 15 minutes worth of salary expense that can be spent on something else. You free up 15 minutes of someone's time which can be used on a different activity. There are two critical things to remember about this:

1   The cost to the business does not go down by 15 minutes worth of salary, so do not claim the value of the time as a 'savings' from the improvement.
2   The way the business benefits from the time savings is by staff doing something else with the 15 minutes of spare time or spare capacity that has been created. The benefit must be measured by the value of the new thing the person does.

It is amazing how often people calculate the value of time saved in a process and present that to management as a 'savings' from the process improvement. Imagine a manager's pleasure at hearing there was $20,000 worth of time savings from the improvement, and then their subsequent frustration when they find out later they don't really have $20,000 to spend on something else. That was a 'notional' saving based on the cost of time previously spent on the process.

The instances in which there might be genuine cash savings from time savings are:

1   A genuine reduction in cost if you were paying overtime to your staff to get everything done by working extra hours, and now you do not need to
2   A genuine reduction in cost if you were paying casual or temporary staff in addition to your normal staffing in order to get everything done, and now you do not need to
3   A genuine reduction in cost if you were outsourcing work to external providers because your staff were overloaded, and your staff can now do that work themselves

All three of these examples are payments to people in addition to your salaried staff because of the way the work was being done. Once you 'right size' your team, you are into the time saved for people who will remain with the business. The way to track the benefit of their time saving is to record what they do with the time you have saved them and put a value on it. It is the *value* of the new activity, rather than the *cost* of the time being saved, that is the *benefit* in an office environment. In considering benefits, you have to look at what is happening in the process and what else can happen as a result of the process being improved. This can be expressed in several different ways, including:

1   Additional work from growth in business which can be completed with the existing staff numbers due to the time savings (absorbing new work)
2   Planned work which had been on hold due to capacity issues (e.g. fixing known problems)
3   New product and service development resulting in new clients and new income (generating new business)

It is true that a business could choose to 'cash in' savings by letting more people go (i.e. not just the ones who were there in addition to your salaried workforce). However, it is easy to see the danger in this. Why would anyone contribute their discretionary effort towards solving problems or improving processes if they think the outcome is that people will lose their jobs? There is no incentive for the employee, and no prospect of doing the planned improvement work that kept being put off, or the new product/service development which could generate new income. Focusing on cost cutting and downsizing is not conducive to a problem solving culture. In a situation such as the COVID-19 pandemic in 2020, where there was clearly an unprecedented external factor threatening the existence of businesses (in the case of COVID-19, entire economies were at risk), you probably would get buy-in to driving down costs at the expense of some jobs in order to preserve the business. However, under normal operating conditions, there is no chance of staff buy-in if the goal is to cut costs and shed staff. A company director might say a legitimate goal is to maximise profit and provide greater returns to shareholders. That is fine, if you maximise profit by increasing revenue rather than just cutting cost. There is no guarantee that pursuing a cost reduction strategy will benefit the business. A particularly startling report produced in 2006 stated that 80% of companies using downsizing strategies experienced significant drops in morale, only 30% experienced reduced costs, and 22% had terminated the wrong people.[3]

When assessing the potential solutions and the different benefits you could realise from successful implementation, please be sure to distinguish between cost reduction and capacity creation when describing the benefits. It might be tempting to assign a high dollar value to 'savings', but when talking about time saved in a process, it is much better to talk about capacity creation.

SMART Goals

SMART goals are widely used in strategic and operational planning, project management, and other business activities. They can also be used for personal goals. SMART is an acronym most commonly known as Specific, Measurable, Attainable, Relevant, Time-bound. However, as with many other tools and concepts, there are multiple variations on them, as set out in Table 6.2.

The purpose of using SMART is to ensure that the goals you set are focused (specific, relevant, and attainable) and objective (measurable and time-bound). This format is very useful for reinforcing evidence-based thinking as a problem solving behaviour. Referring back to the staff onboarding case study in Chapter 5, the aspirational statement for the voice of the customer was:

> As a customer, I want to be enabled to work effectively as quickly as possible, and to be assisted in understanding how to interact with the department when I need something.

Assuming your organisation has a set of induction material prepared in a folder or something similar, a SMART goal to measure performance against achieving this statement for the customer could be:

> To ensure the new staff member is provided with an induction folder, and on-site support so they have agreed system access and onboarding completed within 48 hours of commencing work.

This is very specific in describing what will be done (provide the kit and on-site support), it is measurable (agreed system access and onboarding

Table 6.2 SMART goals

Common	Alternatives
Specific	Simple, Sensible, Significant
Measurable	Meaningful, Motivating
Attainable	Acceptable, Achievable, Assignable
Relevant	Realistic, Reviewable
Time-Bound	Timely, Trackable

Source: Adapted from Rubin, 2002.[4]

completed), and time-bound (within 48 hours). It is directly relevant to the onboarding process, and is attainable.

Interim Solutions vs Future State Solutions

Chapter 5 introduced the three different process states:

- Current state – the way it is right now
- Interim future state – an improved state that you can move to quickly and easily
- Ideal future state – how you want the process to be in the future

As the name suggests, the ideal future state is the one you want to move to, ideally as quickly as possible. Sometimes, this is not possible and you will need to accept improving the process to an interim future state. This is still an improvement, but not all the change you might like to make. Reasons why you might not be able to implement the ideal future state straight away include:

- It is too expensive to implement at the time
- There is too much work already scheduled for the next x months, and the company does not want to lose that business through downtime
- It requires government policy change or some other external agency change, which is not yet done
- The CEO is about to retire and some decisions are being held over till a new one is appointed

These are circumstances you may have to accept, making the improvements you can, and waiting for the time to do more.

Sometimes, you may not find a solution which will fully solve the problem. If you have three critical-to-quality measures, and you can fulfil two of them with a change to the process, you should do that while understanding that the job is not yet complete. It is still an improvement on the current state.

Notes

1 Lawrence, H. & Cairns, N.J., 2017, *A Guide to Evidencing the Benefits of Change in Higher Education*, Business Improvement Team, University of Strathclyde, p18.
2 Miller, J., 2013, *Taiichi Ohno's Workplace Management, Special 100th Birthday Edition*, New York, The McGraw Hill Companies, p22.
3 Bhasin, S., 2012, Prominent Obstacles to Lean, *International Journal of Productivity and Performance Management*, 61, p404.
4 Rubin, S., 2002, Will the Real SMART Goals Please Stand Up? *The Industrial-Organizational Psychologist*, 39, pp26–27.

Chapter 7

Implementing the Solution

Are We Ready to Solve the Problem?

By the time you implement the solution, you will have developed a thorough understanding of the problem and selected a solution based on objective measures of success. Ideally, you will have had purposeful conversations with stakeholders and they are confident the problem solving team has the information and skills necessary to make the best decision. During implementation, you will need to display all the behaviours described in this book. Evidence-based thinking will help to respond to unexpected responses you may encounter. It will help to calm yourself and the team if unexpected issues come up. Coupled with curiosity to understand exactly what is happening and why, and collaboration to assist others in their understanding, using an evidence-based approach can help you be the island of calm in a rough sea.

Implementation itself can be very quick. In *The Toyota Way*, Liker describes making decisions slowly and implementing quickly.[1] As discussed in Chapter 5, when running a rapid improvement event, the team endeavours to implement solutions while the event is still in progress so the benefits are realised as quickly as possible. However, it must be remembered that making the change is one thing, seeing it used consistently and ensuring its effectiveness over time is another. That requires other people to change what they do and not revert back to their earlier actions and behaviours. It is at this stage of the problem solving process that the ideas and tools described in Chapter 9 could prove most useful to you.

Implementation Action List

In order to implement your solution, you need to have a clear understanding of what each person will do in making the changes, and how their work will differ after the changes are made. This must be documented and described to people. In both examples of problem investigation in

Chapter 5, the team developed action plans with tasks assigned to people and agreed due dates for completing them. The rapid improvement event resulted in a future state map of the onboarding experience and an action list. Investigating the payroll problems led to an A3 problem statement which included actions and checks on progress.

There are many different forms of implementation plans and charts you could use, some of which go into great levels of detail. Software packages like Microsoft Project are designed for this purpose and include useful features to show the dependencies between tasks, allocation of people to tasks, and the critical path of a project. In many cases, a spreadsheet, set out like the example shown in Table 7.1, will suffice. However, if you feel you will need something more sophisticated, there are many options available.

Table 7.1 Sample action list

Action	Aligned to goal	Assigned to	Supported by	Due by

The sample action list includes the titles 'Aligned to goal' and 'Supported by'. If you have used SMART goals, you can ensure that every action on your list supports one of your goals. If the action does not align to one of the goals, you should question whether you need the action or whether you are missing something from your goals. The 'Supported by' column is useful for identifying which senior staff member will be available for problems to be escalated to. This provides support to the RIE team in implementing changes. In the onboarding case study from Chapter 5, the managers who supported the RIE would be asked to provide this support.

RACI Chart

RACI is a useful tool for describing agreed changes to roles in the process. RACI is an acronym for Responsible, Accountable, Consulted, Informed, and is typically used in a chart to clearly explain the involvement each role has in each step in a process. Definitions of each are:

- Responsible: the person who must perform the work
- Accountable: the person who must approve the work that is performed

- Consulted: person whose opinion is sought while performing the work
- Informed: person who is kept up to date on the progress of the work

A RACI chart can be prepared to accompany a swim lane process map, as shown in Table 7.2. This is a RACI chart to accompany the future state process map from the onboarding case study. Given the nature of many of the tasks in the process are routine, there is not likely to be a lot of consultation required. The regional manager is consulted on allocation of office space and on the nature of the work the new person will do, but there is no need to consult people on account creation, set up of the computer etc. The significant thing about the changed process is that the regional administration officer is informed of the completion of actions throughout the process so they can coordinate the onboarding experience for the new staff. The regional administration officer can consult

Table 7.2 RACI chart for regional onboarding process

	Responsible	*Accountable*	*Consulted*	*Informed*
HR process appointment	HR Officer	HR Manager		Regional Admin Officer
IT create user account	IT Officer	IT Manager		Regional Admin Officer
Admin Officer sends welcome email to new staff member	Regional Admin Officer	Regional Manager		
Admin Officer allocates office	Regional Admin Officer	Regional Manager	Regional Manager	
Local IT Officer sets up computer	Regional IT Officer	Regional Manager		Regional Admin Officer
New staff member commences work	New Staff Member			Supervisor, Regional Admin Officer, Regional Manager
Admin Officer provides local induction	Regional Admin Officer	Regional Manager		OHS Manager/Unit
Supervisor meets with staff member to discuss work	Supervisor	Regional Manager	Regional Manager	Regional Admin Officer
Admin Officer checks in with new staff member	Regional Admin Officer	Regional Manager	Other staff as required (to resolve any outstanding issues)	Regional Manager

with any of the other people in the process to resolve outstanding issues and assist in completing the onboarding successfully.

RACI charts are particularly useful for new or changed processes, and also are useful in workplaces where role confusion or scope creep has been evident. These charts can be displayed on the wall, or stored in shared electronic folders for ease of access, to minimise confusion over who should be doing what. When implementing a change, having a RACI chart gives people a clear guide to refer to. Aside from using RACI for a particular problem or process, RACI charts are also useful for reviewing workload at a team level. Compiling a RACI chart for all the activities of a team can show if particular team members are being overloaded with responsibilities, and also to perform a check that all the activities that teams perform have responsibilities properly assigned. They are also very useful for inducting new staff to the team as they are good visual guides to the activity of the team.

Visual Management

The terms visual management, visual controls, and visual display are often used interchangeably in process improvement. Visual management is often described as part of a lean daily management system, while visual controls are an important part of implementing approaches such as 5S. A lean daily management system is an integrated management model using key performance indicators, standard work and procedures, visual displays, short interval controls and frequent check ins (e.g. daily stand-up meetings) to embed continuous improvement in the workplace. 5S is an organised approach to the physical workspace which supports a broader lean management system. The 5S's are Sort, Set in Order, Shine, Standardise, and Sustain. Sort, Set in Order and Shine relate to cleaning and organising the physical workspace. Standardise and Sustain relate to work procedures and putting practices in place to maintain the changes you have implemented.

The term 'visual display' is often used to describe the use of posters, signs, floor marking, and display boards in both visual management and visual control. In this book, *visual management* is used in performing the business process (i.e. the visual aids used to help manage the process over time), and *visual displays* are used to describe the problem solving effort and to review the effectiveness of the solution. Visual management is in the business process, while visual displays are about the problem solving process.

Visual management is everywhere. Visual management is often used to provide instructions, and also to alert when something is going wrong. Think back to the examples of *poka yoke* in Chapter 6 – the petrol gauge and warning light are examples of visual management giving you information and warning when something might go wrong. Staying with the motoring analogy, while driving to the petrol station you may well see lane lines painted on the road, speed limit signs, give way or stop signs, traffic lights, pedestrian crossings, and turning arrows. These are all forms of visual management, intended to keep you safe while driving.

Almost every workplace already has visual management in place, whether it is emergency exit signage, 'no smoking', 'staff only', 'hours of business', or other signs. Visit a sick friend in the hospital and you will see visual management everywhere. This can include signs for the different departments, colour coding of departments, including different coloured lines painted on the floor to follow in order to find the department you want, chemical and other warning signs on cupboards and rooms, and many more. Some of the tools you have used in problem solving can be used for visual management. A printout of the future state process map and the RACI chart described above are excellent visual reminders to staff of what is expected in the new process.

Most of the examples given above are static displays to instruct or inform you. The other aspect of visual management is giving information about current performance and to alert when something is going wrong. Of the examples given above, the fuel gauge and fuel warning light are examples of real-time information on performance. A well-known example of this in an office setting is a display board in a call centre or a service desk, giving real-time updates on the number of calls waiting in the queue, how long they have been waiting, and so on. Takeaway food places use similar displays, giving updates on where your order sits in the queue and how long till it is ready. Returning to the hospital, patient monitoring systems installed beside hospital beds give real-time updates on vital statistics, and are connected to hospital systems to store the information, and alert hospital staff if a patient's condition changes.

Seeing New Behaviour Emerge

The implementation phase is when you find out what people really think of your solution and what the culture in your organisation is really like. People who may have been 'diplomatic' during the define and investigate steps will feel compelled to act once the solution becomes real in the workplace. This is why communication is so important in problem definition and investigation. One could argue that organisations should not be like this, and that problem solving efforts should be supported with employees using the changed procedures. After all, they are paid by the organisation and should do what it says. However, people are complex and sometimes act in seemingly irrational and unhelpful ways, at least to those who do not understand the reasons for their behaviour. In knowledge organisations, people truly are the most valuable asset and understanding them is vital to success.

This chapter contains some practical tools and techniques for implementing solutions. Chapter 9 looks at responding to other people's behaviour. There are linkages between the two, just as implementation logically follows from investigating the problem and selecting a solution. During implementation, things might not go as you expect them to. Problems you had not anticipated will be revealed. People will surprise you (for better and for worse) with their behaviour when this happens. It is at this stage of the problem solving process that the people working on the problem can suffer. We plan, we implement, and we expect it to look like the plan. We get stressed when it does not. It is important to embrace the unexpected results as learning opportunities, even if the timing seems terrible.

Automation Makes Problems Visible

Co-authored with Karen Kusler.

Chapter 5 describes the use of a fishbone diagram and A3 problem statement to lead the problem solving effort when a new payroll system is implemented in a network of hospitals. In identifying the root causes of problems, the team categorised them as:

- Issues in the new casual pay system (different fortnightly pay cycle, issues with multiple appointments)
- Issues with other corporate systems (recording of clinical qualifications in the HR system, payroll import function not working in the HR system)
- Issues with variation in local practice (local agreements on different pay rates)

The first category is related to problems or bugs in the new payroll system. The other two categories were problems or behaviours that already existed, but were not known to the project team. Ideally in a new system implementation, every problem would be identified and solved in advance. However, this is often not possible. The problems within the payroll system were preventable through better design. But how many of the other problems were truly the responsibility of the payroll project team? The two problems in the HR system (qualifications field and payroll import) had existed for years. The behaviour in the hospitals had developed over years as well. More testing and greater consultation might have surfaced them before the system went live, but some might have still emerged as problems after the system was implemented.

A common reaction in this situation is to blame the project team for poor implementation, and to declare the new system a failure. If you have seen this happen before, be assured you are not alone in that experience. It would be a better organisational response to anticipate that unforeseen problems will emerge and be ready to respond positively when they do, rather than express frustration and assign blame. A positive reframing of this situation is to say that automation of paper-based processes helps to make hidden problems visible to the business. This is a good thing, even if the problems first surface at a challenging time. They could be problems that were latent for years and making them visible creates the opportunity to solve them.

Understanding this will help to shift from frustration and blaming to understanding and solving. Examples of how previously hidden problems become visible through the use of technology include:

- Electronic workflows enforcing a particular path, with desired variations to the path (previous practice in the paper-based process) manifesting as complaints about the process not suiting people's needs
- New reports and dashboards highlighting bottlenecks in processes and supplying objective evidence of their existence. People may have been aware of them anecdotally, and now the system can provide objective evidence that they exist
- Variations in decision making surfacing as 'errors' (e.g. local payment agreements surfaced as incorrect payments to staff)
- Record keeping errors (e.g. the qualifications field problem surfaced as incorrect payments to some staff)
- System integration issues (e.g. this surfaced as failed payroll imports in the case study)

This is a different way of thinking about system implementation issues. As you saw in the payroll system case study, this approach led to an objective analysis of the root causes of the problems in order to solve them. The project team appreciated the clarity around the issues, and felt supported by a hospital seeking to understand the issues rather than blame the team. This objective and constructive approach can help to build strong working relationships which will pay off in the future.

The Visibility Paradox

While it is true that technology can make problems visible, there is a paradox about automation and process visibility which is important to understand. While automation improves visibility for the business, it often reduces visibility for the internal customer of the process (the end user). This loss of visibility creates new frustration for the internal customer, and increases the likelihood that they will want to declare the new system a failure. Once you understand this paradox, you are in a much better position to anticipate how people will respond to anything going wrong with the system.

There is a tendency to think of new system implementations as solely technology projects. System development progresses through technical staff working with a sample group of operational staff to understand the business needs and the process logic (how things are done). They might negotiate or sometimes mandate new process logic if there are system design constraints, or if the project steering committee insists on a particular way of doing things. They will almost certainly want one version of each process rather than lots of variations on it. Those rules and requirements are coded into the system by the developers, at which point they become invisible to all but a few system administrators. If you were not part of the sample group, you could feel as though you had no input to the new system.

If you think back to earlier points made in this book, you can see that system implementations are much more than technology projects. Remember that:

- An organisation is made up of people organised into roles and teams to accomplish more than one person could on their own
- Processes are sequences of activities performed by people, using tools, to accomplish tasks that contribute to the organisation

A system, such as a payroll system or a finance system, is the technology that supports a set of processes, which are performed by people. Technology is an enabler of people performing tasks. Electronic workflows do enable tasks, but unlike paper-based systems, they enforce a particular way of performing the task. When people find that the technology requires them to perform the task in a different way, it does not feel like they are being enabled. It feels like they are being constrained. To the individual, the new system can be seen as a problem rather than a solution.

Imagine Jeffrey is a long-term employee in a large department who has worked with paper-based systems for years. Jeffrey has a direct working relationship with Catherine, the person administering the process. In fact, Catherine may have been the local administrator for a lot of different paper-based processes; a local 'one stop shop' for administration. They developed a working relationship in which Jeffrey was able to introduce local variations on processes which suited his needs. Catherine supported this because it felt like good customer service to do so. This is not to suggest that they were breaking any rules, simply that they altered the process to suit their circumstances. Their behaviour may have been moderated by local management, but not by an organisational process owner seeking consistency of application across the entire organisation.

The process owner, if there was one, would have had limited visibility of what was happening in paper-based activity across the organisation.

Then the new automated system is implemented and Jeffrey realises:

- He can no longer do the work in the same way he used to
- He is required to interact with the system rather than ask Catherine to complete the paperwork for him (but is told it is a user-friendly system which he can easily learn)
- The training material is available online and describes one way of doing things
- Catherine has no influence over any of this and cannot help Jeffrey adapt the system to his preferred way of working

If you were to capture the four voices of the process at this point, the different perspectives on visibility in the new system would be dramatic (Table 7.3). Jeffrey is unhappy, Catherine feels somewhat powerless, and other people (further removed from the actual task completion) see the benefits of the change.

Table 7.3 Four voices in new system implementation

Voice	User stories
Customer (Jeffrey)	As a customer of this new system, I am outraged! It does not allow me to continue with the practices I have had in place for years and which have served me well. Even worse, I don't know what my options are other than the one way described in the training material. This system is no good.
Employee	Employee 1 (Catherine): As an employee, I am being inundated with complaints about the system. People are very unhappy about being forced to use a process that is different to what they did before. I think the system is good but most people don't like it. Employee 2 (system administrator): As a system administrator, I have learned a lot about problems in other systems which we had not seen before. There were data architecture and system dependency issues which we can fix to make future system implementations easier.
Business	Business 1 (Team Manager): As a manager in the business, I can see what is happening in the process much more clearly. I can get reports on things like cycle time, volume of work, where work is queued, where work has been rejected at a step due to an error. The system really helps to see what is going on. Business 2 (Unit Director): As a director, I am pleased to see that the system enforces a consistent way of doing this process. We finally have confidence in the governance of this important work!
Process	New information available from the system on cycle time, where work is backing up, volume of work.

The automated system suits the business much more than it suits the customer of the processes it enables. Even worse for Jeffrey, he might find that each new conversion of a paper-based process to an automated one is a similar experience for him. He is increasingly expected to interact with systems rather than relying on people like Catherine. Jeffrey might find that several different systems are used to automate processes over time (e.g. all the HR forms are now routed via a web-based HR interface while the finance forms are via a web-based finance interface). His experience of this is a gradual shift away from an established relationship with one very helpful admin person to interacting with multiple systems which force particular behaviours and only offer online help documents or short videos. It is an impersonal experience for the 'customer'.

Helping the Customer Accept and Adopt

Automating paper-based processes usually is better for the business. However, the sense of frustration among staff is real and needs to be addressed as well. The question is how to help staff who feel alienated by the change to accept it and adopt it. Project teams often attempt to do this by including a selection of staff in focus groups to describe the business needs, user acceptance testing to interact with the system during development, piloting the system with selected business units, and preparing a communication strategy for the launch of the system. These are all activities typically related to large-scale system implementations. If you are working on a smaller problem and do not have access to the resources required for this level of activity, you can still borrow from this thinking. A few useful ideas to keep in mind are:

- Training people in any process change should include explaining changes in both the process or technology steps (the 'what' and 'how') of the process, and also the business logic (the 'why'). Remind people of the why at every opportunity.
- Use simple analogies and stories to explain why automation is needed. For example, when people first learn mathematics, they start with memorising and reciting tables: "Two times two is four. Three times two is six". Then they learn to perform more complex calculations using long division on a sheet of paper. Then, as they get into more complex calculations, they learn to use a scientific calculator. Eventually, 'learning' becomes learning how to use the functions of the calculator properly rather than how to do the calculations on paper. They rely on the technology to perform the more advanced work. Businesses increasingly rely on technology to perform business processes quickly, at scale.

- Use visual controls to guide them through the process. Make following the process as intuitive as possible.
- Where possible, be consistent across processes and systems. Having the same 'look and feel' is reassuring as the customer gains proficiency in navigating similar screens. It is similar to developing the skills to work the scientific calculator, which could be the common tool for many different calculations.
- Be open to some change in process over time. Workflow systems run on programmed paths for the work to follow. Some workflow systems allow the user to add additional people to the path (for instance a manager might want someone to give expert advice prior to making a decision so adds that person to the workflow for a particular job). The systems track and report on the amount of variation, providing information which can inform changes to the process. This is a form of desire path.

Desire Paths

Imagine a newly completed public park, with grassed areas, stands of trees, a small lake, a children's playground, and a half-size basketball court. Connecting the different sections of the park are brand new concrete paths. The park opens and families start to use it. It gets very busy on the weekends and is a success. You come back to the park six months later and are surprised to see several dirt paths worn into the grass fields. It is evident that people did not walk along the concrete paths but took different routes, with many thousands of pairs of feet wearing away the grass and defining new paths between attractions. These footworn paths are *desire paths*, created by the actual users of the park as they interact with the space over time and decide their own preferred paths between attractions.

The local council would be wise to install new concrete paths along the desire paths. It is clear that people want paths there. The only way to enforce the use of the existing concrete paths would be to fence off all the grassed areas, possibly ruining the atmosphere of the park as a family friendly space. Automated workflows effectively fence off the grassed areas by only allowing the prebuilt flows to be used. A solution to a genuine need for more flexibility in the workflow paths could be to add more user roles over time, and optional inclusion of them in workflows where there input is needed to make a decision. The risk the organisation runs in not allowing some flexibility in design over time is the addition of 'off process' steps handled via email and the creation of satellite reports in spreadsheets or other packages to manage this. As this happens, the organisation starts to lose visibility of the process, and the emerging problems, again.

Note

1 Liker, J., 2004, *The Toyota Way: 14 Management Principles from the World's Greatest Manufacturer*, New York: McGraw-Hill Publishing Company, p237.

Chapter 8

Reviewing the Results

Have We Solved the Problem?

The review step of the problem solving process is primarily to assess the effectiveness of the solution and decide if any further changes are required. While you might formally review the solution at a set time (e.g. three months after implementation), reviewing results and responding to challenges in implementation can occur frequently. Similarly, the completion of a formal review does not mean measuring performance stops. This should become part of your 'business as usual' activity in the future. You may also wish to have a six- or nine-month review scheduled to ensure that the changes are still delivering the expected benefit. It is sometimes the case that people revert to the old ways of doing things over time, and the benefits of change are lost. It could also be that some other factors change, such that the solution you chose is no longer the best option and you need to change again.

It is easy to imagine a situation in which a changed process was put in place with enthusiasm and a genuine intention of using it. But then everyone got busy with their ongoing volume of work. They were aware of the change and supported it (in principle at least), but it was not second nature to do the work that way. In learning language, they have conscious competence at best (see Table 8.1). Under pressure,

Table 8.1 Stages of learning

Stage of learning	*Description*
• Unconscious incompetence	• Not aware of the need for the skill
• Conscious incompetence	• Aware they lack a needed skill
• Conscious competence	• Able to perform the task when focusing on it
• Unconscious competence	• Able to perform the task without thinking about it

they revert to the way they used to doing things. This is a critical moment for the lasting success of the change. If no one questions why they have reverted back to the old way, there is no reason for them to return to the new. Someone has to keep an eye on the behaviour over time to ensure that the new way of doing things becomes the new normal. It is not feasible for the problem solving team to sustain the change. You will need to create the expectation of team leaders putting effort into sustaining benefit over time. You might recall from the section on purposeful conversations that sustaining goes well beyond the formal end of a change process, so it is essential to engage the relevant stakeholders where the work takes place. Monitoring the success of the change over time could be assigned to someone in the RACI chart.

Not every change or solution is going to be a success. Some will be partial successes and some might not be successful at all. It is very important to review them all and to openly and honestly discuss why changes did not achieve the results you were expecting. If the barrier to success is related to organisational culture or to particular people undermining the change, you will need to be aware of this and devise strategies to prevent this recurring in the future.

All of the behaviours in this book are useful at this time, particularly curiosity and evidence-based decision making. It may be tempting for people to declare something to have been more successful than it really was. After all, their pride could be on the line. This is as risky as overstating the potential benefits when investigating the problem and selecting the solution. Focusing on objective evidence of success or otherwise will be important here. Equally, if there are people opposed to the changes that were made, they may seek to understate the results or to attribute the results to something else. Evidence is your ally in this situation.

Reviewing Performance

An important part of reviewing the solution is to check progress against the measures of success that you identified earlier. As you have worked through the problem solving process, you will have:

- Considered what data is relevant at the time of defining the problem
- Gathered data or identified data gaps during the investigation of the problem
- Chosen some specific measures of success when you selected the solution
- Included establishing tracking performance against these measures in your plan when you implemented the solution

Having done all this, you will be well placed to use the data to inform your assessment of the success or otherwise of the solution. While all this sounds obvious, it may be new work arising from the change of process and is at risk of being overlooked if people are busy.

Remember also to track performance against any cultural or behavioural measures you set. These measures are the most likely to be overlooked when the change is implemented as they are likely to be qualitative and less easily recorded. Measuring cultural changes might require doing short surveys of customers (voice of the customer) and staff working in the process (voice of the employee).

Something not going according to plan is not a failure, so do not be discouraged if you do not achieve the improved performance you were expecting. The important thing is to understand why the result was not achieved and to determine what next to do about it. Initiating a problem solving process can be an event, but it is not the entire journey in itself. Remember that the term 'continuous improvement' implies an ongoing process of improvement – literally, *continuous*. If you expect to see a 10% improvement and you see a 2% improvement, that is still an improvement and means there is still another 8% or more to be gained.

Track Your Capacity Creation

This is a reminder to track the capacity creation from the change. This is often forgotten when assessing the benefits of a change. As discussed in Chapter 6, saving five hours a week of time is great, but it often does not translate to a reduction in cost for the business. Unless you are going to make someone work reduced hours and receive less pay, you cannot cash that saving in. The benefit to the business is realised through the new activities people do with the time freed up by the changes. It is absolutely valid to track and report on that. If you had not solved the problem or improved the process, they would still be spending their time doing the old work. This cost of inefficiency would still be incurred, perhaps without anyone noticing, because it is just the way things have always been done.

Customer Journey Maps

Once you have implemented the new process in your workplace, you can discuss your customer's experience of the process by preparing a customer journey map. It is simply a map of the new process discussed step by step with the customer, with notes or illustrations on the map to reflect their experience. In its simplest form, it could be the map with the customer's name and date of the discussion, with 'smiley' or 'frowny' faces at each step depending on their experience of it (Figure 8.1). You

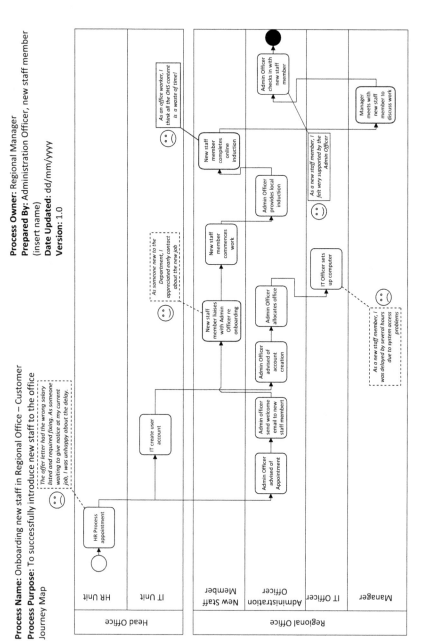

Figure 8.1 Customer journey map.

can use a user story format to record the problems they encountered along the way. The marked up version of the process map is a customer journey map, as it tells the story of that customer's experience of the process. It is a great way to engage with customers as it shows you are serious about improvement, and focuses their feedback on specific steps in the process rather than generalised statements.

You can see from the customer journey map above that the new staff member's experience starts badly with an incorrect offer letter being sent. It improves through early contact from the Admin Officer. They have a problem with user access on their first day, which is eventually resolved by the local IT staff. The new person appreciates the single point of contact provided by the Admin Officer and generally feels supported. The customer journey map highlights two preventable issues (offer letter and system access) and one which you may not be able to do a lot about (relevance of OHS training). The user story format is important for capturing the customer's voice as it includes the impact of the problem. For instance, they were delayed in resigning from their current job because the offer letter was wrong and had to be re-done. In a large organisation where you may need to talk to other units about problems encountered in their steps in the process, the customer journey map is very useful. Because it provides direct feedback from the customer of the process, it cannot be dismissed as 'that person/unit complaining again'. Direct feedback with specific examples in user story format are very powerful statements. Each user story is an opportunity to further improve the process. Over time, as you prepare more customer journey maps, you can use the set of them to identify recurring issues. They become a valuable input to the voice of the customer. Depending on the feedback you receive from the customer, you could use the map to review a particular step in the process, or you could use one of their user stories to start a new fishbone diagram to conduct root cause analysis.

STAR Storytelling

STAR is a simple format for telling the story of how you did something. It is widely used in responding to scenario questions in job interviews. The acronym stands for Situation/Task, Action, Result. An example of this in an interview is:

Q: Can you tell us about a time when you used your initiative to improve something in the workplace?
A: I was asked to assist with improving the onboarding process in the regional office *(situation/task)*. After meeting with the manager to define and scope the process to be reviewed, we met with the key stakeholders and proposed running a rapid improvement event *(actions)*. I facilitated the event, the team proposed some improvements, which we implemented, and over the next six months, received very

positive feedback from new staff about their onboarding experience. We also received great feedback from managers about how much the process had improved (*result*).

In job interviews, it is surprising how often people forget to say what the results of their actions were. The STAR format helps to tell a story with structure, including the results. This suits telling business improvement stories well, and serves to reinforce the importance of identifying the right measures of success, and then following through on measuring them after implementing a solution.

Visual Displays

Visual displays tell the story of your problem solving effort. If you use the problem solving tools described in this book, there should be very little additional work involved in preparing a visual display. The tools are the display. Recording the names of people involved in preparing them is the evidence of collaboration in solving the problems and also a very good way to acknowledge their contribution to the work. Thinking back to the two different examples of problem investigation in Chapter 5, those teams could have visual displays using the items listed in Table 8.2 with no additional work required.

These tools could be put up on the wall or stored on a share drive to access remotely. You can have them up during the problem solving effort and gather around them for team meetings (often called 'huddles' or 'stand ups'), and can leave them up in the workplace afterwards to invite comment and interest from other people as a way of further promoting the problem solving efforts. If you do that, be ready to talk to people about the display when they stop to check it out. It is a great opportunity to talk about the collaborative nature of the problem solving effort and focus on understanding what the customers value from the process.

Table 8.2 Visual displays

Onboarding process	Casual pay system
• Current state process map	• Fishbone diagram
• Future state process map	• Pareto analysis
• RACI chart	• A3 statement (updated with performance results)
• Action plan	• Sample or subset of data used to track improvements
• Performance results against agreed measures	
• Customer journey maps	

Table 8.3 Process heat map

Finance	Human resources	Information technology	Health and safety
• Issue new credit card	• Process new staff appointment	• Establish user account	• Prepare risk assessment
• Purchase of low risk items	• Process leave application	• Reset user password	• Ergonomic assessment of workspace
• Credit card reconciliation	• Process staff termination	• Reimage computer	

Process Heat Maps

The visual displays discussed above relate to specific problem solving activities. However, visual displays need not be limited to that. A process heat map is a longer-term visual display for a team. This is a diagram or a table of the main processes that the team works with and your collective assessment of their current state. A sample start of this is shown in Table 8.3. You can code this in colour, with cool colours for processes which are currently meeting expectations, changing to a hot colour for processes which have the most evident problems. An alternative colour scheme is traffic lights using the acronym RAG (red, amber, green) with red being high priority to work on, amber for lower priority, and green for the process going well.

This sort of display works well if you are a manager or a team leader and want to instil a continuous improvement culture in your team. When updated periodically (perhaps every quarter or every six months), the changes in the heat map over time will show the progress in reviewing and improving processes in the unit. The heat map can be used in team meetings to acknowledge the improvement efforts and prioritise the next process(es) to be reviewed. You will need to be objective in assessing the state of the processes, and of course should use data to measure them.

Reflection on the Problem Solving Process

Reviewing the results of the solution also provides an excellent opportunity to reflect as a team on the problem solving process itself. An easy way into this is to start with reviewing the solution and then move into debriefing the problem solving steps you undertook, and facilitate a discussion of what worked well or not. It will be valuable to consider what each of you can learn from this experience to take forward into the future. Doing this is consistent with the view that knowledge is an asset which increases in value through use. Sharing your knowledge with another person will increase their store of knowledge without diminishing yours and vice versa. Experienced facilitators and consultants will tell you that they learn from every job, refining their approach, learning new techniques and tools, and sometimes challenging long-held beliefs. Helping other people to develop new skills can be very rewarding work, and in the practice of helping other people, you will build your own skills and expertise. Doing this reflection as a group is a reminder that problem solving is a team sport, not a solo adventure. All of the problem solving tools are designed to be used in collaboration with other people.

Reviewing the problem solving process as a group can also help to strengthen working relationships and position you and the other team members to work well in the future. It can assist in moving your own efforts from help to 'deep help' in your organisation.[1] Deep help takes place over a longer time frame in a series of interactions with teams and can contribute to you positively impacting your organisation. You can reinforce the three problem solving behaviours by doing this reflection as well – curiosity about what worked or did not work in order to improve next time, collaboration through doing this as a group exercise, and evidence-based thinking through seeking clear examples and any supporting information about parts of the process working well or not. Reflective exercises are not data driven, but tools like FOG can assist in working through them. This provides opportunity to remind everyone of the importance of creating a shared understanding of things in order to improve on them.

You can do this individually as self-reflection as well. This is part of the practice of continuous improvement of yourself which will build your strengths and skills as a problem solver and as a leader. The lean concept of continuous improvement can be viewed as continuous improvement of self as well as of business processes.[2] Contemporary leadership theories emphasise the ability to encourage others to have ideas and to listen to them, and also to create trusting relationships. Unlike the early 'great trait' theories which suggested people were born leaders, it is understood that leadership skills can be developed through practice. Practicing the three behaviours of curiosity, collaboration, and evidence-based thinking, and keeping them in mind while using the problem solving tools, will improve your problem solving ability and also help to develop leadership skills. Using interest-based negotiation and practicing your responses in order to have purposeful conversations will help as well.

Notes

1 Fisher, C.M., Pillemer, J. & Amabile, T.M., 2018, Deep Help in Complex Project Work: Guiding and Path-Clearing Across Difficult Terrain, *Academy of Management Journal*, 61, pp1524–1553.
2 Emiliani, M.L., 1998, Continuous personal improvement, *Journal of Workplace Learning*, 10, pp29–38.

Chapter 9

Responding to Other People's Behaviour

Learning how to effectively solve problems can be an exciting and liberating experience. Applying the tools and seeing how they can make a positive difference is empowering. Working with other people and sharing the light-bulb moments as you strive to solve workplace problem for everyone's benefit is a lot of fun. It can be hard work, but is also very rewarding. It is understandable to think that other people will appreciate the effort and will want to see the solutions implemented. As you become proficient in problem solving and see the potential benefits, it is possible to imagine a grassroots revolution occurring in your workplace as people see the wisdom of a collaborative problem solving approach. It may come as a surprise to find that not everyone appears to share your enthusiasm. Be curious as to why that is. Use a collaborative approach to better understand why people feel the way they do. Be evidence-based in your thinking, politely asking what data or information they have to support their concerns about the solution.

There is an enormous amount of literature available that says organisational change programs fail far more often than they succeed. Organisation-wide business improvement programs fail a lot too. Estimates vary wildly and can be anywhere from a 50–95% failure rate.[1] The most frequently cited reasons for change program failure are lack of alignment between the program and the strategic goals of the business, lack of senior leadership commitment, lack of resources, employee resistance to change, and lack of understanding of the culture change required for success.[2] These are daunting reasons for failure. People who have experienced failed programs can become wary of change, and appear cynical when they hear about another attempt to improve things. They might think this is just the latest flavour-of-the-month approach.

This book is about what each person can do as an individual. It is about doing what you can from where you are in the organisation. This chapter provides several different frames for considering and responding to behaviour you might encounter. Understand up front that this is not about assigning blame. If you think about the people you work with, it is unlikely that you would say many of them do not want things to improve or that many of them are genuinely resistant to change. They may well be cynical about organisational change programs, but that is not the same thing. It is convenient for the people running unsuccessful change programs to say the program failed because the staff were resistant to change. However, this is rarely true. People adjust to change all the time, and in many cases they embrace change. The internet is a great example of this. Developed countries were able to respond much more effectively to prolonged periods of COVID-19 lockdown in 2020 thanks to the internet supporting hundreds of millions of people working from home, meeting via video conferencing software, ordering groceries online instead of going to supermarkets, and maintaining connections with loved ones via social media platforms. If people in general were resistant to change, we would not even have the internet, or if we did, people would not have embraced alternate ways of working in 2020. In fact, lack of internet as an essential enabler has been identified as one of the great challenges less developed countries face in an increasingly connected world.[3] It is not that people do not like or adjust to change. What is true is that people sometimes do not like the way change is done to them. They need to understand why the change is important and what the benefit of it will be.[4]

All of the tools and models described in this chapter are useful for any workplace situation. They are not specific to problem solving, and are drawn from HR and negotiation theories. They are included to provide insight to what might be driving the behaviour you observe in other people, and advice as to how to respond.

Types of Conflict

When you encounter resistance or observe conflict, it is important to understand where it is coming from. In the workplace, there are several different types of conflict, and understanding which one you are facing can help to resolve it.

Intrapersonal Conflict

Intrapersonal conflict takes place within the individual. The most common example of intrapersonal conflict is difficulty deciding between two alternatives. This could be because both alternatives are appealing (called approach-approach conflict) and the individual does not understand how to choose one, both alternatives are unappealing (avoidance-avoidance conflict), or the alternatives have both appealing and unappealing aspects (a promotion comes with higher pay but a larger workload and longer hours).[5] In a problem solving setting, intrapersonal conflict could manifest as inability to decide on a preferred option. Evaluating options using objective evidence against agreed measures of success will assist in resolving this.

Intrapersonal conflict can also occur when people cannot see themselves in the solution. They might see that it is a good solution, but fear for their own job security. Thus the solution contains both appealing and unappealing elements. For example, you could be running a rapid improvement event in which the team maps the current state of a process, identifies waste, and develops a new, streamlined future state process. People who previously had roles in the process may be worried if they do not have roles in the future state process. This is where measuring capacity creation becomes important. They will feel more secure once they understand that the benefit of the change will include the new, value-adding work they can do, outside of the new process. Counting capacity and value creation rather than cost becomes an important part of the change management involved in implementing and sustaining the changed process.

Interpersonal Conflict

Interpersonal conflict takes place between individuals. It is generally defined as either substantive (relating to tasks, resource allocation, policy content, i.e. to the substance of something) or emotional (relating to beliefs and values). Sometimes interpersonal conflict is based on both substantive and emotional issues. There may be underlying emotional differences between people which a substantive issue brings to the surface. In a problem solving setting, being clear on the purpose and scope of the work being done, the measures of success, and the decision making process, will assist in resolving interpersonal conflict. This will be more effective with substantive conflict than emotional conflict if individuals have very different values or personalities. However, resolving the substantive issue can release some of the emotion as well.

Role Conflict

Role conflict takes place within the individual as they attempt to fulfil the expectation of their role(s). This type of conflict can be 'person-role' (their personal beliefs or values conflict with the expectations of the role) or 'inter-role' (the individual occupies several different roles and feels the expectations of the roles are incompatible).[6] When working with a problem solving team, inter-role conflict can be common. In the example of improving onboarding in Chapter 5, a rapid improvement event team was formed from representatives of the different teams in the regional office and in head office. They were asked to work together to improve the process. But each individual also belonged to a team which they will continue to work with after the changes are implemented. It is understandable that they will look at potential solutions with an eye on their team's reaction to it, and may feel conflict due to that.

Intragroup Conflict

Intragroup conflict takes places between members of a group. It is more complex than interpersonal conflict as it can involve other members of a group becoming engaged in an interpersonal substantive conflict, effectively taking sides over a task or resource issue. Resolving intragroup conflict also requires being clear on the purpose and scope of the work being done, the measures of success, and decision making process. The section of this chapter on group dynamics will assist with intragroup conflict.

Hierarchy of Needs

Maslow's hierarchy of needs is one of the classic models in human resource management and is used to help understand individual motivation and behaviour. It describes the different levels of needs that people feel. As shown in Figure 9.1, Maslow identified five levels of need. The bottom three are lower-order needs and top two are higher-order needs. The theory is that people will increasingly seek to satisfy the higher-order needs once they have satisfied their lower-order needs.

A later modification to this model was developed by Alderfer who proposed three categories of needs rather than five, and added a 'frustration–regression' principle. In both models, people seek to satisfy lower-order needs before higher-order needs (e.g. physiological and safety needs before social needs). Once a need is satisfied, people innately seek to satisfy the next level need. For instance, having secured a job, people naturally seek to become proficient in their work and to be recognised by other people for their proficiency. In Maslow's model, people constantly work to satisfy the next level need. Alderfer's 'frustration-regression' principle states that if someone is blocked from satisfying their next level need, they will become frustrated and revert to reinforcing satisfaction of their currently met needs. In a work environment, this can explain why people stop trying to implement changes or improvements. If they have felt blocked in the past and unable to make progress, they will be less inclined to try in the future. Similarly, if they have had a bad encounter with a former boss or organisation which had a strong blame culture, they will be unwilling to make suggestions or take responsibility for implementing

Figure 9.1 Hierarchy of needs.

change until they can be sure it is safe to do so (meeting their lower-order need for safety before seeking to satisfy the higher-order need for esteem).

Not everyone seeks to self-actualise at work. Some people find self-actualisation in volunteer work or a hobby which they do outside of work, and do not seek to do more in the office. This does not make them bad people or bad employees. It might explain why they have less enthusiasm for problem solving at work than you do. Further, not all self-actualising work is widely known. Some people perform very important acts in the workplace which are largely 'invisible', such as maintaining social networks or providing emotional support to other people.

Group Dynamics

Group dynamics is a very well-known theory on how groups form and interact. It is useful to be aware of group dynamics when working with a problem solving team formed around a specific problem or process.

The team members may not be used to working with one another, and so the group will go through the stages of group development. These stages are shown in Table 9.1.

Additional points to bear in mind about the stages of group development:

- While the stages are sequential, it is possible for groups to move backwards as well as forwards. For instance a group could move from storming to norming and then back to storming again.
- A change of group membership can cause the group to repeat some stages. For example, the addition of a team member or replacement of someone in the team can cause renewed forming and storming.
- What appears to be the rapid formation of a functional group might only be the forming stage of development.

Group dynamics is useful to understand in work and non-work contexts. It is particularly relevant to problem solving when a team-based approach is used to transfer knowledge and diffuse it throughout the workplace. Group dynamics is also increasingly relevant as the nature of work continues to change and evolve. The likelihood of working for one

Table 9.1 Stages of group development

Forming	Group members learn about one another and seek to understand the purpose of the group and how it will interact. This can be complicated by people belonging to multiple groups at the same time. People tend to be polite and deferential.
Storming	Group members can experience conflict with each other as they spend more time together and as work pressure builds. Personalities are revealed and sub-groups or cliques can form. Some individuals try to exert themselves on the group.
Norming	Group members learn to work together and begin to conform to an agreed set of norms. Some members develop a sense of closeness and of commitment to the group's purpose. Consensus might exist, but in a fragile state.
Performing	The group has matured and is functioning well. It has established norms and a stable structure. The group is able to respond successfully to changes.
Mourning	Something has happened to cause the group to disband. This could be the successful completion of a project or could be an organisational change. Group members may feel a sense of accomplishment but will also feel a sense of loss that the group will not continue working together.

Source: Adapted from Bailey et al. (1991).[7]

organisation for your entire career is very low. Modern career theory describes careers as boundaryless, portfolio, free agent, and other similar terms. Careers are said to be a series of experiences in which people gain knowledge and experience, increasing their future employability through the acquisition and development of transferable skills. These experiences can take place in a paid role in the workplace, unpaid roles in social settings like sporting clubs, volunteering for a charity, and at home. Employers increasingly use contract or casual employment in an attempt to manage changing resource needs and revenue constraints. In this career context, understanding group dynamics is very useful. Being able to adapt to working with different groups is an important skill set. Understanding how groups interact and being able to guide them to successful outcomes are important leadership skills to develop.

Two-Factor Theory

Herezberg's two-factor theory is another classic human resource management theory. It was developed by analysing all the factors that can impact on someone's experience at work. Herzberg grouped them into two categories: hygiene factors and satisfiers. Hygiene factors are potential sources of dissatisfaction and are mostly related to the work context (the environment and setting); they are external to the individual. Satisfiers are potential sources of motivation and are linked to the work itself. They are internal to the individual. This is shown in Table 9.2. The premise of the model is that improving a hygiene factor will not motivate staff. The best it will do is decrease the risk of dissatisfaction occurring. Motivating staff requires focusing on satisfiers. This theory challenged the notion that increasing pay and conditions would motivate staff to higher levels of performance. Somewhat ironically, the payroll function is a frequently cited example of a hygiene factor. People are unlikely to call the payroll team to say 'Thank you for paying me correctly again this week'. But if they are paid incorrectly, they will be on the phone very quickly!

Table 9.2 Herzberg's two-factor theory

Factors leading to dissatisfaction	*Factors leading to motivation*
Company policy and administration	Achievement
Relationship with supervisor	Recognition
Work conditions	The work itself
Relationship with peers	Responsibility
Personal life	Advancement
Relationship with subordinates	Growth

Source: Adapted from Bailey et al. (1991).[8]

This model is of interest in problem solving for several reasons:

- Some problems will relate to hygiene factors. Solving them will help to minimise dissatisfaction but will not increase staff motivation. Therefore, people may struggle to be excited about the improvements.
- Involvement in problem solving teams can contribute to staff motivation if the problem solving work provides responsibility, recognition, and achievement. The problem solving process can be a satisfier in itself, and adopting a collaborative approach to problems at work will draw people to you.
- Starting an improvement effort which is subsequently blocked or abandoned by senior management will create dissatisfaction. This is important for people in leadership roles to be made aware of.

Force Field Analysis

Force field analysis is a very useful tool for understanding why an action or decision appears to be blocked and is not progressing. Developed by Kurt Lewin, force field analysis proposes that every situation progresses at a pace dictated by the forces which act for it and those which act against it. A situation is said to be held in equilibrium if the forces for and against it are of equal strength. It makes progress when the forces in favour of it are stronger than those opposing it. Similarly, it regresses when the forces opposing it are stronger.

Performing a force field analysis involves writing the decision or change in the centre box, then listing the forces for or against it on each side of the page. You can show the relative strength of each force by lengthening or shortening the arrows. A longer arrow applies greater force. Once you have agreement on the forces for and against, you can discuss what to do. The outcome of a force field analysis is a plan to strengthen the forces in favour of your desired change and weaken the forces opposing your desired change. In the example provided in Figure 9.2, the decision being sought is shown in the centre box, and forces for and against are shown on each side.

Force field analysis is a good visual representation of the identified forces impacting a decision or action. It is another tool that is designed to be used collaboratively in discussing a situation. You will need to be aware of the sensitivity involved in discussing opposing forces. The intention is not to get furious agreement that "Fred opposes this decision". If it appears that Fred does oppose the decision, apply the five whys to understand why Fred opposes the decision. What is the root cause of his concern? No one knows? Go ask him. Part of your action plan will be to understand why Fred appears to oppose it. He might have a very good reason you might not have considered, or he might be misinformed and

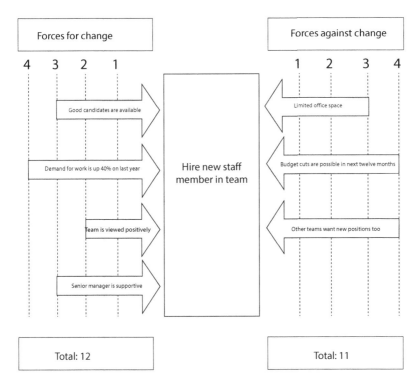

Figure 9.2 Force field analysis.

you can clarify the situation for him. Find a way to have a purposeful conversation about it.

A risk in using force field analysis is that it becomes subjective. It is your (or your team's) view on why something is not happening, and so is limited to the wisdom in the room. It can help to identify and describe opposing forces but cannot always tell you for certain why that is. It is therefore necessary to practice all three behaviours in using it, particularly curiosity and evidence-based decision making.

Supporting Purposeful Conversations

As discussed in Chapter 3, a purposeful conversation is a planned and deliberate interaction with another person to progress the problem solving effort. You can use a purposeful conversation at any stage of the problem solving process. The diagram shown in Figure 9.3 was introduced in Chapter 3 to explain how the problem solving effort can be viewed as

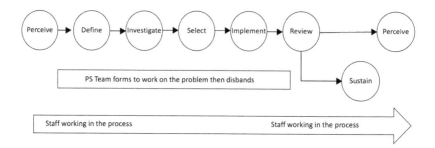

Figure 9.3 A linear view of problem solving.

a specific intervention with responsibility for finding a solution resting with the problem solving team and responsibility for sustaining the solution resting with the business units working on the process.

In Chapter 3, it was suggested that you think about these things in preparing for purposeful conversations:

1   Why you are having the conversation (the purpose)
2   What you want to achieve from it (your objectives)
3   What information or evidence you need to have with you at the time (your supporting material)
4   What the likely reactions might be (their reaction). It is good to consider several different possible reactions
5   How you can respond to each of those reactions (your response)
6   What the next steps after the conversation might be (the future actions)

The information on interest-based negotiation and practicing your responses may be helpful in your preparation.

Interest-Based Negotiation

As you work through the problem solving process, having purposeful conversations and assessing what obstacles there might be to achieving a successful outcome, it might feel like you are negotiating for the solution to be implemented. Interest-based negotiation[9] is an excellent framework to keep in mind during these times, as it aligns very well with the problem solving behaviours described in this book. The behaviours and tools in this book are all designed to bring problems to the surface so they can be carefully investigated and solved. Interest-based negotiation focuses on bringing different people's interests to the surface so they can be met with mutually satisfactory outcomes. The approaches are very similar. Interest-based negotiation has three criteria by which negotiations should be assessed:

1. It should result in a 'wise agreement', if possible
2. It should be efficient
3. It should improve, or at least not harm, the relationship between the parties

A wise agreement is defined as "one which meets the legitimate interests of each side to the extent possible, resolves conflicting interests fairly, is durable, and takes community interests into account".[10] The three criteria would work equally well for considering the solution to a problem. Careful selection of measures to assess options is likely to result in a wise choice. Understanding many of the tools described in this book will assist in ensuring you implement an efficient solution. The behaviours described in the book, particularly collaboration, all contribute to improving workplace relationships.

There are four principles to follow in using interest-based negotiation, and they are all similar to the problem solving approach described in this book:

1. Separate the people from the problem
2. Focus on interests, not positions
3. Invent options for mutual gain
4. Insist on using objective criteria

Separating people from problems is important because negotiations often take place in the context of a broader relationship. Each person will need to be aware of the substantive issue (in this case, the problem being solved) and also the broader relationship. The ideal solution will enhance both. As per the section on group dynamics, members of a problem solving team may belong to several different teams, and have relationships within and possibly between each. It is important to understand their perspective and seek solutions that will satisfy everyone's needs. If this is not possible, you will need to acknowledge that and be ready to explain how the solution is the best available.

Focusing on interests rather than positions is extremely important. People adopt positions for a variety of different reasons. Once someone has taken a position, they may feel compelled to hold it, and that shifting from their stated position will look like weakness. Understanding what interest they are trying to serve by adopting that position is the key. As Fisher and Ury wrote, "Your position is something you have decided upon. Your interests are what caused you to so decide".[11] This relates to force field analysis, where it was identified that Fred opposes the change (his position) but no one understood why (his interest). Achieving this understanding may require displaying curiosity and using the five whys. Focusing on interests can help when assessing potential solutions to a problem. If some of the team or some of the stakeholders adopt positions against a potential solution, you need to look beyond their positions to understand and address their interests.

Once you understand other people's interests, you can consider options for mutual benefit. Fisher and Ury identify four obstacles[12] to developing successful options: premature judgement, searching for the single answer, the assumption of a 'fixed pie', and thinking that "solving their problem is their problem". Not surprisingly, these four blockages are very similar to the difficulties encountered in problem solving. Premature judgement is the same as jumping to a solution. Searching for the single answer is narrowing the options quickly, instead of taking the time to properly define and investigate the problem. The assumption of a fixed pie is that there is only so much to be gained, and therefore any negotiation will have a winner and a loser. The alternative approach is to 'grow the pie' by seeking outcomes which yield greater returns for all. The final obstacle ("solving their problem is their problem") is clearly at odds with a collaborative, problem solving approach. Insisting on using objective criteria is self-explanatory, and is also very effective at removing the emotion from decision making. It can assist decision makers in handling role conflict and the expectations of other teams that their interests will somehow take preference. When a decision is clearly based on objective measures, it is easier to explain and defend. It clearly separates the people from the problem. It supports the longer-term relationship while providing a clear way to resolve the substantive issue. Agreeing on the criteria will require careful problem definition. The measures of success should link directly back to the critical-to-quality measures identified early on. Fisher and Ury use the term "frame each issue as a joint search for objective criteria".[13]

Practicing Responses

You might be in the situation of having investigated a problem and are ready to select the solution and implement it but are being blocked from doing so. You might have completed a force field analysis and identified a concern or misconception that people hold. You feel the potential benefit to your organisation is at risk. You also feel a responsibility to the people who have put effort into solving the problem. You need to speak up, but are not sure how. Your next step is deceptively simple, but is very powerful. You need to prepare to speak up; to practice your response. This includes not only knowing the facts of the situation but practicing how to speak up when the time comes. The *Giving Voice to Values* framework is very useful in this situation.[14] Although it was developed as a framework for assisting people in handling ethical conflicts in the workplace, it works equally well in other settings, including problem solving. Elements of it, which are particularly helpful in problem solving, are:

- taking a rational approach to a stressful or emotional situation;
- thinking through what you will say or do when the time comes; and
- practicing this in advance.

Because the framework is designed for values-based issues, it also includes sections on setting a powerful example, knowing that you are not alone, and affirming that speaking up for your values is important. These sections may be beneficial to you beyond problem solving. Even without the overlay of ethical issues, the idea that responding to a potentially challenging situation by preparing in advance and practicing for it is very useful. It is no different to practicing for a job interview or for a presentation. It is quite similar to critical incident training, in which a stressful or emergency situation is simulated, and your actions in the moment are observed and debriefed. As with other skills and competencies, practice will help to improve your ability over time and will give you some reassurance in the moment. You have prepared and you are ready for this.

Notes

1 Roser, C., 2017, Where Lean Went Wrong – A Historical Perspective (online). Available: https://www.allaboutlean.com/where-lean-went-wrong/ (Accessed 18 May 2020).
2 Sreedharan, R.V., Gopikumar, V., Nair, S., Chakraborty, A., & Antony, J., 2018, Assessment of Critical Failure factoRs (CFFs) of Lean Six Sigma in Real Life Scenario, *Benchmarking: An International Journal*, 25, p3377.
3 Mackintosh, E., 2020, Almost Half the World is Living through this Pandemic without the Internet (online). Available: https://edition.cnn.com/2020/06/07/world/internet-inequality-coronavirus-int/index.html (Accessed 8 June 2020).
4 Fiume, O., 2007, Lean Strategy and Accounting: The Roles of the CEO and CFO, in Stenzel, J. (ed.) *Lean Accounting: Best Practices for Sustainable Integration*, Hoboken, NJ, John Wiley and Sons Inc, p67.
5 Bailey, J., Schermerhorn, J., Hunt, J., Osborn, R., 1991, *Managing Organizational Behaviour*, Singapore, John Wiley and Sons, p 408.
6 Bailey, J., Schermerhorn, J., Hunt, J. & Osborn, R., 1991, p407.
7 Bailey, J., Schermerhorn, J., Hunt, J. & Osborn, R., 1991, pp221–233.
8 Bailey, J., Schermerhorn, J., Hunt, J. & Osborn, R., 1991, p49.
9 Fisher, R. & Uty, W., 1991, *Getting to YES*, London, Random House Business Books.
10 Fisher, R. & Ury, W., 1991, p7.
11 Fisher, R. & Ury, W., 1991, p24.

12 Fisher, R. & Ury, W., 1991, p31.
13 Fisher, R. & Ury, W., 1991, p46.
14 Gentile, M., 2009, *Giving Voice to Values: How to Speak Your Mind When You Know What's Right*, New Haven, CT, Yale University Press.

Conclusion

This book describes a collaborative approach to problem solving, using an integrated model consisting of the steps in the problem solving process, a set of problem solving tools, and the three key behaviours of curiosity, collaboration, and evidence-based thinking. There are many other books or articles which focus on the problem solving steps alone, or the tools, or aspects of behaviour. Other books which discuss some of these together tend to be set in manufacturing industries, focused on a specific methodology, or heavy academic texts that are 350–400 pages long and very expensive to purchase. They are simply not accessible to a wide audience. I set out to make this book simple and accessible, with the goal of encouraging people to start applying this approach in their own workplace today. A theme of this book is to *do what you can from where you are*, regardless of whether your workplace has a formal improvement programme in place. We all start from somewhere. A limitation arising from this approach to the book is that I do not go into detail in describing some complex ideas, and almost certainly have left some good ideas and tools out.

There may be advocates of particular methodologies who say I missed key parts of their approach. For instance, I have chosen not to include any of the more complex statistical work used in Six Sigma. My experience is that most problem solving in an office environment does not need it. I also have not used Plan Do Check Act (PDCA) in an explicit way. The reason for this is that the successful implementation of PDCA links strongly to management behaviour and action. It requires acceptance that changes do not always bring the expected result, and that this is a good thing because it provides additional information to help in solving the problem. PDCA is iterative and experimental in nature. Without a supportive culture in place, attempting PDCA can leave you open to criticisms that 'your solution did not work'. I acknowledge that most organisations do not have this supportive culture in place and therefore have not suggested doing something that could leave the reader exposed. People interested in learning more about different methodologies are encouraged to do so.

At the time of writing this book, the long-term impact of COVID-19 on how people work was not known. In my home country of Australia, working from home started in earnest in April 2020 and restrictions eased in most states through the second half of the year. The manuscript for the book was completed by October 2020. Australia has fared much better through the pandemic than many other countries and as this book has gone into production, Europe is experiencing a second wave of cases, and the United States, India, and countries in South America are still experiencing many cases and, sadly, many deaths. This presented a di-lemma for the book– should I write as though a return to face-to-face office work is a likely future scenario or not? A further complication is that at the time of writing, there was limited published information available on how business was responding. The book is written based on experience, which is largely in face-to-face settings, with some examples of remote work where they were available to include.

In many cases, I provide references and links to further information. These are not exhaustive. Aside from anything else, new material is writ-ten every day. If you read this book two years after publication, there will doubtless be new references and perhaps new tools to apply. The beauty of the approach used in this book is that you can adapt it to your own needs and situations over time. You could recreate the tools table from Chapter 1 in a spreadsheet or some other format and add new tools and ideas as you come across them. In writing this book, I used a spreadsheet with cell comments and cross-referencing to keep the various threads of thought together. You are welcome to do the same and build your own modified toolkit over time. Don't get lost in a never ending search for new tools though. The tools can change over time, but the behaviours will endure.

The model presented in this book has been developed over time and is based on a combination of my own work experience and personal research. Where I have contributed new work in the form of models or flow charts, I have said so. I have also created a website to support the book, www.collaborativeproblem.com, where you will find electronic versions of all the models presented in the book, along with other infor-mation I hope you will find useful.

Index

Note: **Bold** page numbers refer to tables and *italic* page numbers refer to figures.

Discrete Models of Financial Markets

This book explains in simple settings the fundamental ideas of financial market modelling and derivative pricing, using the No Arbitrage Principle. Relatively elementary mathematics leads to powerful notions and techniques – such as viability, completeness, self-financing and replicating strategies, arbitrage and equivalent martingale measures – which are directly applicable in practice. The general methods are applied in detail to pricing and hedging European and American options within the Cox–Ross–Rubinstein (CRR) binomial tree model. A simple approach to discrete interest rate models is included, which, though elementary, has some novel features. All proofs are written in a user-friendly manner, with each step carefully explained, and following a natural flow of thought. In this way the student learns how to tackle new problems.

MAREK CAPIŃSKI has published over 50 research papers and nine books. His diverse interests include mathematical finance, corporate finance and stochastic hydrodynamics. For over 35 years he has been teaching these topics, mainly in Poland and in the UK, where he has held visiting fellowships. He is currently Professor of Applied Mathematics at AGH University of Science and Technology in Kraków, Poland.

EKKEHARD KOPP is Emeritus Professor of Mathematics at the University of Hull, UK, where he taught courses at all levels in analysis, measure and probability, stochastic processes and mathematical finance between 1970 and 2007. His editorial experience includes service as founding member of the Springer Finance series (1998–2008) and the CUP AIMS Library Series. He has authored more than 50 research publications and five books.

Mastering Mathematical Finance

Mastering Mathematical Finance is a series of short books that cover all core topics and the most common electives offered in Master's programmes in mathematical or quantitative finance. The books are closely coordinated and largely self-contained, and can be used efficiently in combination but also individually.

The MMF books start financially from scratch and mathematically assume only undergraduate calculus, linear algebra and elementary probability theory. The necessary mathematics is developed rigorously, with emphasis on a natural development of mathematical ideas and financial intuition, and the readers quickly see real-life financial applications, both for motivation and as the ultimate end for the theory. All books are written for both teaching and self-study, with worked examples, exercises and solutions.

[DMFM]   *Discrete Models of Financial Markets*,
         Marek Capiński, Ekkehard Kopp

[PF]   *Probability for Finance*,
         Ekkehard Kopp, Jan Malczak, Tomasz Zastawniak

[SCF]   *Stochastic Calculus for Finance*,
         Marek Capiński, Ekkehard Kopp, Janusz Traple

[BSM]   *The Black–Scholes Model*,
         Marek Capiński, Ekkehard Kopp

[PTRM]   *Portfolio Theory and Risk Management*,
         Maciej Capiński, Ekkehard Kopp

[NMFC]   *Numerical Methods in Finance with C++*,
         Maciej Capiński, Tomasz Zastawniak

[SIR]   *Stochastic Interest Rates*,
         Daragh McInerney, Tomasz Zastawniak

[CR]   *Credit Risk*,
         Marek Capiński, Tomasz Zastawniak

[FE]   *Financial Econometrics*,
         Marek Capiński, Jian Zhang

[SCAF]   *Stochastic Control in Finance*,
         Szymon Peszat, Tomasz Zastawniak

Series editors Marek Capiński, *AGH University of Science and Technology, Kraków*; Ekkehard Kopp, *University of Hull*; Tomasz Zastawniak, *University of York*

Discrete Models of Financial Markets

MAREK CAPIŃSKI
AGH University of Science and Technology, Kraków, Poland

EKKEHARD KOPP
University of Hull, Hull, UK

CAMBRIDGE
UNIVERSITY PRESS

CAMBRIDGE
UNIVERSITY PRESS

Shaftesbury Road, Cambridge CB2 8EA, United Kingdom

One Liberty Plaza, 20th Floor, New York, NY 10006, USA

477 Williamstown Road, Port Melbourne, VIC 3207, Australia

314–321, 3rd Floor, Plot 3, Splendor Forum, Jasola District Centre, New Delhi – 110025, India

103 Penang Road, #05–06/07, Visioncrest Commercial, Singapore 238467

Cambridge University Press is part of Cambridge University Press & Assessment, a department of the University of Cambridge.

We share the University's mission to contribute to society through the pursuit of education, learning and research at the highest international levels of excellence.

www.cambridge.org
Information on this title: www.cambridge.org/9780521175722

First published 2012

A catalogue record for this publication is available from the British Library

Library of Congress Cataloging-in-Publication data
Capinski, Marek, 1951–
Discrete models of financial markets / Marek Capinski, Ekkehard Kopp.
pages   cm. – (Mastering mathematical finance)
Includes bibliographical references and index.
ISBN 978-1-107-00263-0 – ISBN 978-0-521-17572-2 (pbk.)
1. Finance – Mathematical models.   2. Interest rates – Mathematical models.
I. Kopp, P. E., 1944–   II. Title.
HG106.C357   2012
332.01´5111 – dc23   2011049193

ISBN   978-1-107-00263-0   Hardback
ISBN   978-0-521-17572-2   Paperback

Additional resources for this publication at
www.cambridge.org/9780521175722

To Ewa and Margaret

Contents

Preface

In this first volume of the series 'Mastering Mathematical Finance' we present discrete-time mathematical models for the pricing and hedging of derivative securities, as well as an initial analysis of fixed income securities. Throughout, the sample space of possible scenarios is assumed to be finite, and there are finitely many trading dates. This greatly reduces the need for sophisticated mathematical tools, while providing sufficient complexity to highlight the key aspects of arbitrage pricing techniques.

Keeping the mathematical requirements to a minimum makes the text accessible to students from a wide variety of backgrounds, while the large number of exercises, which should be regarded as integral to the text, include routine numerical examples and test understanding of basic techniques as well as providing more challenging problems. Solutions and additional exercises are available on the linked website www.cambridge.org/9781107002630, where, if necessary, a list of errata will be updated regularly.

While most of the material is well known, we have sought to develop ideas gradually through simple examples, leading to careful proofs of the key results for option pricing in finite discrete models. While the setting of the final chapter is standard, the discussion of binomial term structure models, though close to the Ho–Lee model, contains features we believe to be novel.

1

Introduction

This volume introduces simple mathematical models of financial markets, focussing on the problems of pricing and hedging risky financial instruments whose price evolution depends on the prices of other risky assets, such as stocks or commodities. Over the past four decades trading in these **derivative securities** (so named since their value derives from those of other, **underlying**, assets) has expanded enormously, not least as a result of the availability of mathematical models that provide initial pricing benchmarks. The markets in these financial instruments have provided investors with a much wider choice of investment vehicles, often tailor-made to specific investment objectives, and have led to greatly enhanced liquidity in asset markets. At the same time, the proliferation of ever more complex derivatives has led to increased market volatility resulting from the search for ever-higher short-term returns, while the sheer speed of expansion has made investment banking a highly specialised business, imperfectly understood by many investors, boards of directors and even market specialists. The consequences of 'irrational exuberance' in some markets have been brought home painfully by stock market crashes and banking crises, and have led to increased regulation.

It seems to us a sound principle that market participants should have a clear understanding of the products they trade. Thus a better grasp of the basic modelling tools upon which much of modern derivative pricing is based is essential. These tools are mathematical techniques, informed by some basic economic precepts, which lead to a clearer formulation and quantification of the risk inherent in a given transaction, and its impact on possible returns.

The formulation and use of dynamical models, employing stochastic calculus techniques or partial differential equations to describe and analyse market models and price various instruments, requires substantial mathematical preparation. The same is not true of the simpler discrete-time

models that we discuss in this volume. Only a modicum of probability theory is required for their understanding, and we gradually introduce the main ingredients, trying to make the volume self-contained, although familiarity with basic probability may give the reader some advantage.

Discrete-time models, using finitely many possible trading dates and a finite collection of possible outcomes (scenarios), have intuitive appeal, since the world we inhabit is finite and, as Keynes famously observed: 'in the long run we are all dead'. Moreover, even the simplest models already embody the principal features of the modelling techniques needed in more complex settings, and it may be easier to 'see the wood for the trees' in the friendlier environment of a simple model. At the same time, one must recognise that models are only useful to the extent that they agree with the observed data; hence the need to reflect actual market practice more accurately must inevitably introduce ever greater complexity.

These more realistic models, and the necessary mathematical background to understand them fully, will be introduced and studied in the companion volumes in this series.

2

Single-step asset pricing models

In this chapter we explore the simplest option pricing models. We assume that there is a single trading period, from the present date (time 0) to a fixed future time T. We examine mathematical models for the behaviour of the prices of one or more underlying stocks, beginning with the simplest case of a single stock whose price at time T takes one of just two possible values. This analysis is extended to a model with two stocks, models with three possible prices for each stock, and finally to a general pricing model with $d > 1$ stocks, each with m possible outcomes for its price at T.

The principal economic requirement, arising from the assumption that the financial markets being modelled are efficient is that, provided all market participants share the same information about the random evolution of the stock price, an investor in this market should not be able to make a profit without incurring some level of risk. This assumption is cast in mathematical terms and underlies the methods we develop to establish how to determine the value of financial instruments whose price depends only on the price of the underlying stock at time T: the so-called European derivative securities, whose study is the principal topic of this and the next two chapters.

2.1 Single-step binomial tree

The most important feature of financial markets is uncertainty arising from the fact that the future prices of various financial assets cannot be predicted. We begin by examining the simplest possible setting and construct a 'toy model' whose two dimensions – time and uncertainty – are illustrated by means of the simplest possible tools.

We take time as discrete and reduced to just two time instants: the present 0 and the future T. To simplify the notation and emphasise the fact that we are now dealing with one step we will write 1 instead of T, so we have in mind a single step of length T.

The uncertainty is reflected by the number of possible scenarios, which in this section is minimal, namely two: 'up' or 'down'. This deceptively simple model reflects many of the key features of much more general pricing models, and we examine it in detail.

Assets

At time 0 assume we are given some asset, which is usually thought of as a stock and is customarily referred to, in defiance of proper grammatical usage, as **the underlying** – since its price will determine the prices of the securities we wish to study.

The current price $S(0) > 0$ of the underlying is known, while its future price $S(1)$ is not known, but we consider possible future prices and the probabilities of attaining them. This is performed formally by first choosing a set Ω, called a **sample space**. The elements of this set are related to outcomes of some random experiment (either specific, tossing a coin, or quite vague, the future state of the economy) and we call them **scenarios** or **states**. In this volume Ω will always be a finite set.

Just for the current section we take $\Omega = \{u, d\}$ and we let the future price of our asset be a function

$$S(1)\colon \Omega \to (0, +\infty).$$

In general, a function defined on Ω is called a **random variable**. Since $S(1)$ takes just two values, so does the **return**

$$K_S = \frac{S(1) - S(0)}{S(0)},$$

which determines the price

$$S(1) = S(0)(1 + K_S)$$

and we will define $S(1)$ by first deciding the shape of K_S. Assume that

$$K_S(\mathrm{u}) = U,$$
$$K_S(\mathrm{d}) = D,$$

where

$$-1 < D < U$$

to avoid negative prices. Then

$$S(1,\mathrm{u}) = S(0)(1 + U),$$
$$S(1,\mathrm{d}) = S(0)(1 + D).$$

It is convenient to introduce the following notational convention: $S(1,\mathrm{u}) = S^{\mathrm{u}}$, $S(1,\mathrm{d}) = S^{\mathrm{d}}$, which gives the random variable of stock prices as

$$S(1) = \begin{cases} S^{\mathrm{u}} = S(0)(1 + U), \\ S^{\mathrm{d}} = S(0)(1 + D). \end{cases}$$

The probabilities are given by prescibing one number p from the interval $(0, 1)$ writing

$$P(\{\mathrm{u}\}) = p,$$
$$P(\{\mathrm{d}\}) = 1 - p.$$

Here we are careful with notation since P assigns numbers to subsets of Ω, but the following simplified version is quite useful: $P(\{\omega\}) = P(\omega)$ for $\omega \in \Omega$. Furthermore, the probability P is assumed to be zero for the empty set and 1 for the whole Ω and so it is defined for all subsets of Ω, called **events**, satisfying additionally the so-called **additivity** property: for any $A, B \subset \Omega$, such that $A \cap B = \emptyset$,

$$P(A \cup B) = P(A) + P(B).$$

(The choice of such A, B in our case is rather limited!)

The accompanying non-random asset is the money market account with deterministic prices $A(0)$, $A(1)$, where

$$A(1) = A(0)(1 + R)$$

for some $R > 0$.

Investment

Suppose we have at our disposal a certain sum of money, which we invest by purchasing a portfolio of x units of the above risky asset and y units

of the money market account. We build a portfolio (x, y) with initial value given by

$$V_{(x,y)}(0) = xS(0) + yA(0).$$

The value of this portfolio at time 1 is

$$V_{(x,y)}(1) = xS(1) + yA(1),$$

that is

$$V_{(x,y)}(1) = \begin{cases} xS(0)(1 + U) + yA(0)(1 + R), \\ xS(0)(1 + D) + yA(0)(1 + R). \end{cases}$$

We assume that the market is **frictionless:** we do not impose any restrictions on the numbers x, y, so that unlimited **short-selling** is allowed: at time 0 we can borrow a share, sell it, and purchase some other asset, while at time 1 we buy the share back to return it to the owner. The assets are assumed to be arbitrarily **divisible,** meaning that x, y can take arbitrary real values. We do not impose any bounds on x, y, thus assuming unlimited **liquidity** in the market. Finally, there are no transaction costs involved in trading, i.e. the same stock price applies to **long** (buy: $x > 0$) and **short** (sell: $x < 0$) positions. Moreover, risk-free investment ($y > 0$) and borrowing ($y < 0$) both use the rate of return R.

Our most important modelling assumption is the No Arbitrage Principle (NAP), which asserts that trading cannot yield riskless profits. In general, the form of this assumption depends crucially on the class of trading strategies that we allow in the market. In the present context, with no intervening trading dates, this is trivial, since a 'strategy' consists of a single portfolio chosen at time 0.

Definition 2.1
A portfolio (x, y), chosen at time 0, is an **arbitrage** opportunity if $V_{(x,y)}(0) = 0$, $V_{(x,y)}(1) \geq 0$, and with positive probability $V_{(x,y)}(1) > 0$.

The last statement for our choice of Ω reduces to saying that we have strict inequality for at least one of the two possible scenarios.

Assumption 2.2 No Arbitrage Principle
Arbitrage opportunities do not exist in the market.

This has an immediate consequence for the relationship between the returns on the risky and riskless assets:

Theorem 2.3

The No Arbitrage Principle implies that

$$D < R < U.$$

Proof If $R \le D$, that is

$$S(0)(1 + R) \le S^d < S^u,$$

we put $x = 1$, $y = -S(0)/A(0)$. At time 1

$$V_{(x,y)}(1) = S(1) - S(0)(1 + R) \ge 0,$$

which is strictly positive in the 'up' state, i.e. with probability $p > 0$.
  If $R \ge U$, that is

$$S^d < S^u \le S(0)(1 + R),$$

we take the opposite position: $x = -1$, $y = S(0)/A(0)$ and

$$V_{(x,y)}(1) = -S(1) + S(0)(1 + R) \ge 0$$

and this is strictly positive with probability $1 - p > 0$. In each case we have
constructed a portfolio that leads to arbitrage. Hence neither inequality can
hold and the theorem is proved. □

The converse implication is also true.

Theorem 2.4

The condition $D < R < U$ implies the No Arbitrage Principle.

Proof Suppose (x, y) is a portfolio with zero initial value. By definition
of portfolio value

$$V_{(x,y)} = 0 = xS(0) + yA(0),$$

$$y = -x\frac{S(0)}{A(0)}.$$

We compute the terminal value with y as determined above:

$$\begin{aligned} V_{(x,y)}(1) &= xS(1) + yA(0)(1 + R) \\ &= x(S(1) - S(0)(1 + R)), \end{aligned}$$

thus

$$V_{(x,y)}(1) = \begin{cases} x[S^u - S(0)(1 + R)] = xS(0)(U - R) > 0 \\ x[S^d - S(0)(1 + R)] = xS(0)(D - R) < 0 \end{cases}$$

for any positive x, under the given assumption that $D < R < U$. If $x < 0$ the
above signs are reversed and they remain opposites. So (x, y) cannot be an
arbitrage for any choice of x. □

Definition 2.5

Suppose the asset X has value $X(1)$ at time 1. Its **discounted** value (to time 0) is given by

$$\tilde{X}(1) = X(1)(1 + R)^{-1}.$$

For the stock S we have

$$\tilde{S}(1) = S(1)(1 + R)^{-1},$$

and define the discounted stock price process $\tilde{S} = \{\tilde{S}(0), \tilde{S}(1)\}$ by also setting $\tilde{S}(0) = S(0)$. Clearly $\tilde{A}(1) = A(0)$. Similarly the discounted value process becomes

$$\tilde{V}_{(x,y)}(1) = V_{(x,y)}(1)(1 + R)^{-1} = x\tilde{S}(1) + yA(0),$$
$$\tilde{V}_{(x,y)}(0) = V_{(x,y)}(0) = xS(0) + yA(0),$$

yielding

$$\tilde{V}_{(x,y)}(1) - \tilde{V}_{(x,y)}(0) = x\tilde{S}(1) + yA(0) - (xS(0) + yA(0))$$
$$= x[\tilde{S}(1) - \tilde{S}(0)],$$

so the change of the discounted portfolio value results exclusively from the change of the discounted value of the risky asset.

2.2 Option pricing

A **European call option** provides profit for the holder of a long position if the price of the underlying at time 1 is above a predetermined level K, the **strike** or **exercise** price, but eliminates the possibility of losses. We define the **payoff** of a call as

$$C(1) = \begin{cases} S(1) - K & \text{if } S(1) > K, \\ 0 & \text{otherwise,} \end{cases}$$
$$= (S(1) - K)^+,$$

where we use the notation $f^+(\omega) = \max\{0, f(\omega)\}$ for any function f on Ω and $\omega \in \Omega$. (The reader should take care not to confuse the return K_S on the stock S with the strike price K of the option.) The effect of holding a call option is the right (without the obligation) to buy the underlying at the **expiry** time 1 for a price that cannot exceed K since if the asset is more expensive, the option pays the difference. If the underlying can be bought in the market for less than K at time 1 the option is simply not exercised. The right to sell the asset for at least K is called a (European) **put option** and its

payoff is of the form $P(1) = (K - S(1))^+$. It is clear from the No Arbitrage Principle that options cannot be issued for free at time 0, since the payoffs are always non-negative and can have positive probability of being strictly positive. Finding 'rational' prices $C(0)$ (resp. $P(0)$) for a call (resp. put) option in a given market model is one of the major tasks of mathematical finance. The initial price $C(0)$ (resp. $P(0)$) is called the option **premium**.

To avoid trivial cases, assume that the strike price K satisfies

$$S(0)(1 + D) \le K < S(0)(1 + U).$$

We now look for a portfolio (x, y) (of stocks and bonds) with the same value at time 1 as the option, the so-called **replicating** portfolio

$$V_{(x,y)}(1) = C(1).$$

This gives a pair of simultaneous equations

$$\begin{cases} xS(0)(1 + U) + yA(0)(1 + R) = S(0)(1 + U) - K, \\ xS(0)(1 + D) + yA(0)(1 + R) = 0, \end{cases}$$

which are easily solved

$$\begin{cases} x_C = \dfrac{S(0)(1 + U) - K}{S(0)(U - D)}, \\ \\ y_C = -\dfrac{(1 + D)(S(0)(1 + U) - K)}{A(0)(U - D)(1 + R)}. \end{cases}$$

We claim that the price of the option should be the initial value of the replicating portfolio. This is based on the intuition that two portfolios identical at time 1 should have the same values at time 0. The justification involves the No Arbitrage Principle: in the case of different initial values, at time 1 we buy the cheaper and sell the more expensive asset and at time 1 we keep the profit. To do this requires trading in options, which leads us to extend the notion of the market.

We extend the notion of a portfolio by including the position in options: the extended **portfolio** is now a triple (x, y, z), where x represents the number of units of stock S, y the risk-free position (the money market account A), and z the number of units of the call option C held (z can be negative, which corresponds to taking a short position by writing and selling z options).

The definition of the **portfolio value** is extended in a natural way:

$$V_{(x,y,z)}(0) = xS(0) + yA(0) + zC(0),$$
$$V_{(x,y,z)}(1) = xS(1) + yA(1) + zC(1).$$

Remember that the second equation asserts equality of random variables! This allows us to formulate our key assumption in the same way as before.

Definition 2.6

We say that (x, y, z) is an arbitrage opportunity if $V_{(x,y,z)}(0) = 0$, $V_{(x,y,z)}(1) \geq 0$, and with positive probability $V_{(x,y,z)}(1) > 0$.

Assumption 2.7 No Arbitrage Principle

Arbitrage opportunities do not exist in the extended market.

In future models we shall always assume that the notion of portfolio is adjusted similarly to cover all securities in question.

Theorem 2.8

The No Arbitrage Principle implies that the price of the European call with strike price K is the value at time 0 of the replicating portfolio

$$C(0) = x_C S(0) + y_C A(0)$$

with x_C, y_C as above.

Proof Suppose $C(0) > x_C S(0) + y_C A(0)$. Then if we sell the expensive asset (option), and buy the cheap (portfolio (x_C, y_C)) we obtain the positive balance $C(0) - (x_C S(0) + y_C A(0))$. To construct an arbitrage we invest this amount in the money market account in addition to $y_C A(0)$ already held, so our portfolio is

$$(x, y, z) = \left(x_C, \frac{1}{A(0)}(C(0) - x_C S(0)), -1\right)$$

and its current value is zero. At time 1, in each scenario the value of this portfolio is

$$
\begin{aligned}
V_{(x,y,z)}(1) &= xS(1) + yA(1) + zC(1) \\
&= x_C S(1) + (C(0) - x_C S(0))(1 + R) - C(1) \\
&= (C(0) - (x_C S(0) + y_C A(0)))(1 + R)
\end{aligned}
$$

since by replication $C(1) = x_C S(1) + y_C A(0)(1 + R)$. But $C(0) - (x_C S(0) + y_C A(0)) > 0$ by our assumption, so we have a strictly positive outcome in each scenario at zero initial cost, more than is needed to contradict the No Arbitrage Principle.

If $C(0) < x_C S(0) + y_C$ we take the opposite position with the same result. $\square$

Remark 2.9

The fact that the probabilities of the stock movements do not appear in the pricing formula is a paradox. One might expect that a call option where

the probability of the up movement of the stock is high should cost more as it is more likely to be exercised, but this is not the case. This surprising effect arises from the fact that the No Arbitrage Principle and replication do not directly involve the probabilities of up or down movements of the stock.

An example of placing bets is quite illuminating. To determine the pay-out ratios a bookmaker follows the proportion of bets placed, not 'true' probabilities based on his own perceptions of likelihoods. So if 1000 bets are on team A and 2000 on team B, then the ratios are 3/1 for A and 1.5/1 for B. The bookmaker is safe and cannot lose money. On the other hand, in casinos the pay-outs for roulette depend on the probabilities being 34/1 since there are 34 equally likely fields. The house here can go bankrupt. In reality in both examples the ratios are slightly unfavourable to the players so the bookmaker has a steady guaranteed income and the casino has an income in the long run.

Exercise 2.1 Show that the option price increases if U increases. Show that it also increases if D goes down.

Exercise 2.2 Show that the option price does not necessarily increase if the 'spread' $|U - D|$ increases by analysing the following examples: for $R = 0$, $S(0) = 1$, $K = 1$, $h = 1$ consider two cases: $U = 5\%$, $D = -5\%$ or $U = 1\%$, $D = -19\%$.

2.3 General derivative securities

A **derivative security**, also called a **contingent claim**, is a security whose payoff depends on the prices of some underlying asset (henceforth simply called the **underlying**, S) which can be a stock, an index, an exchange rate, an interest rate or any other quantity that can be traded or otherwise observed in the market. Within this chapter, a derivative security is represented by a random payoff of the form

$$H(1) = h(S(1))$$

for some payoff function $h: (0, \infty) \to \mathbb{R}$. In fact, any random variable $X: \Omega \to \mathbb{R}$ can be written in such a form. We simply write $h(S^u) = X(u)$,

$h(S^{\mathrm{d}}) = X(\mathrm{d})$, and extend h to the whole of $\mathbb{R}$ arbitrarily. This definition makes use of the fact that $S^{\mathrm{u}} \neq S^{\mathrm{d}}$.

For example, the call option has a payoff function of the form

$$h(x) = \max\{x - K, 0\} = (x - K)^+$$

where $a^+ = \max\{a, 0\}$.

Replication of $H(1)$ gives the system of linear equations

$$\begin{cases} xS^{\mathrm{u}} + yA(0)(1 + R) = h(S^{\mathrm{u}}), \\ xS^{\mathrm{d}} + yA(0)(1 + R) = h(S^{\mathrm{d}}). \end{cases}$$

The unique solution is

$$x_H = \frac{h(S^{\mathrm{u}}) - h(S^{\mathrm{d}})}{S^{\mathrm{u}} - S^{\mathrm{d}}}$$

which is known in the markets as the **delta** of the derivative security since it has the form of 'differential ratio' of h. This becomes

$$x_H = \frac{h(S^{\mathrm{u}}) - h(S^{\mathrm{d}})}{S(0)(U - D)}.$$

Moreover,

$$y_H = \frac{(1 + U)h(S^{\mathrm{d}}) - (1 + D)h(S^{\mathrm{u}})}{A(0)(U - D)(1 + R)}.$$

We claim that the derivative price is the present value of this portfolio, namely $H(0) = V_{(x_H, y_H)}(0) = x_H S(0) + y_H A(0)$, which becomes

$$H(0) = \frac{h(S^{\mathrm{u}}) - h(S^{\mathrm{d}})}{U - D} + \frac{(1 + U)h(S^{\mathrm{d}}) - (1 + D)h(S^{\mathrm{u}})}{(U - D)(1 + R)}. \tag{2.1}$$

The proof of the following theorem is exactly the same as in the case of the call options above. We need only replace $C(1)$ by $H(1) = h(S(1))$. The details are left for the reader.

Theorem 2.10

The No Arbitrage Principle implies that the price of the security with payoff $H(1) = h(S(1))$ has the form (2.1).

Write the right-hand side of (2.1) in the form $ah(S^u) + bh(S^d)$:

$$h(S^u)\left(-\frac{1+D}{(U-D)(1+R)} + \frac{1}{U-D}\right)$$

$$+ h(S^d)\left(\frac{1+U}{(U-D)(1+R)} - \frac{1}{U-D}\right)$$

$$= h(S^u)\frac{R-D}{U-D}(1+R)^{-1} + h(S^d)\left(1 - \frac{R-D}{U-D}\right)(1+R)^{-1}$$

since $\frac{U-R}{U-D} = 1 - \frac{R-D}{U-D}$. Denoting $q = \frac{R-D}{U-D}$ we have

$$H(0) = (1+R)^{-1}(qh(S^u) + (1-q)h(S^d)). \tag{2.2}$$

Since $D < R < U$, we have $0 < R - D < U - D$, so that $0 < q < 1$ and we can interpret q as the probability of an 'up' move. Together with $1 - q$ this defines a probability Q on $\Omega = \{u, d\}$ and we call it the **risk-neutral probability**. The expression

$$qh(S^u) + (1-q)h(S^d)$$

is called the mathematical **expectation** (or **expected value**) of the random variable $h(S(1))$ and is denoted by $\mathbb{E}_Q(h(S(1)))$ and so the pricing formula can be written in the form

$$H(0) = \mathbb{E}_Q\left((1+R)^{-1}h(S(1))\right).$$

Such a notion can be defined for any random variables $X, Y: \Omega \to \mathbb{R}$ and for any probability. In the case where the probability used is the original one (called **physical** or **real** probability in contast to the risk-neutral one) the subscript P is often dropped so that

$$\mathbb{E}(X) = pX(u) + (1-p)X(d).$$

For any real numbers a, b we have **linearity** of the expectation

$$\mathbb{E}(aX + bY) = a\mathbb{E}(X) + b\mathbb{E}(Y),$$

the proof boiling down to some elementary algebra. The formula is valid for any probability.

Theorem 2.11
The price of a derivative security is the expected value of the discounted payoff with respect to the risk-neutral probability.

Consider the discounted values of the asset prices and compute the expectation

$$\mathbb{E}_Q(\widetilde{S}(1)) = q\frac{S(0)(1+U)}{1+R} + (1-q)\frac{S(0)(1+D)}{1+R}$$
$$= \left(\frac{R-D}{U-D}\right)\frac{S(0)(1+U)}{1+R} + \left(\frac{U-R}{U-D}\right)\frac{S(0)(1+D)}{1+R}$$
$$= S(0) = \widetilde{S}(0).$$

Saying that the expected value of the discounted prices is the same at both instants means that the sequence $\widetilde{S}(0), \widetilde{S}(1)$ is a (one-step) **martingale** under Q ($\widetilde{S}(0)$ is a constant, so $\mathbb{E}_Q(\widetilde{S}(0)) = \widetilde{S}(0)$). Accordingly, we often call Q a **martingale probability**.

The reason why Q is also called 'risk neutral' becomes clear when we calculate the expected return on the stock under this probability:

Theorem 2.12
The expected return, with respect to Q, on the stock is equal to the risk-free return if and only if Q is a martingale probability.

Proof Recall that the return on the stock is $K_S = \frac{S(1)-S(0)}{S(0)}$, which equals U in the up-state and D in the down state. If $q = \frac{R-D}{U-D}$ then

$$\mathbb{E}_Q(K_S) = qU + (1-q)D = \frac{R-D}{U-D}U + \frac{U-R}{U-D}D = R.$$

On the other hand, if $qU + (1-q)D = R$, then solving this for q gives $q = \frac{R-D}{U-D}$. □

Risk and return

We now compare the return K_S on the stock with the return K_H on a given European derivative security with payoff $H = h(S(1))$. We denote the expectations under P of these random variables by μ_{K_S}, μ_{K_H} respectively, so that

$$\mu_{K_S} = \frac{pS^u + (1-p)S^d}{S(0)} - 1 = D + p(U-D),$$

$$\mu_{K_H} = \frac{pH^u + (1-p)H^d}{H(0)} - 1,$$

(using the notation $H^u = h(S^u)$, $H^d = h(S^d)$).

The variability of the return embodies the risk inherent in the investment, and this can be expressed by its **variance**. In general, this is given by

$$\text{Var}(X) = \mathbb{E}\left[(X - \mathbb{E}(X))^2\right] = \mathbb{E}(X^2) - \mathbb{E}(X)^2.$$

Exercise 2.3   Prove that for $\Omega = \{u, d\}$ we have

$$\text{Var}(X) = p(1 - p)(X(u) - X(d))^2.$$

Exercise 2.4   Show that $\text{Var}(aX) = a^2\text{Var}(X)$.

To obtain linear scaling we use the **standard deviation** as the measure of risk

$$\sigma_X = \sqrt{\text{Var}(X)}$$

and so we write σ_X^2 for the variance of X. Consequently we have

$$\sigma_{K_S}^2 = p(1 - p)(\frac{S^u - S^d}{S(0)})^2 = p(1 - p)(U - D)^2$$

and the standard deviation is $\sigma_{K_S} = \sqrt{p(1 - p)}(U - D)$ so we see that the risk is proportional to the spread of the two possible values of $S(1)$.

The next goal is to compare this with the risk of the derivative security H written on the stock. Exactly as for the stock, the variance of the return on H is given by

$$\sigma_{K_H}^2 = p(1 - p)(\frac{H^u - H^d}{H(0)})^2.$$

The relation between two random variables X, Y is measured by their **covariance**, as defined by

$$\text{cov}(X, Y) = \mathbb{E}[(X - \mathbb{E}(X))(Y - \mathbb{E}(Y))].$$

The covariance of the returns K_S and K_H, normalised by the variance of K_S, is known as the **beta** (sometimes called the elasticity), denoted by

$$\beta_H = \frac{\text{cov}(K_S, K_H)}{\sigma_{K_S}^2}.$$

Again this is easy to compute in our model:

$$\beta_H = \frac{p(1-p)\frac{H^u - H^d}{H(0)}\frac{S^u - S^d}{S(0)}}{p(1-p)(\frac{S^u - S^d}{S(0)})^2} = \frac{\frac{H^u - H^d}{H(0)}}{\frac{S^u - S^d}{S(0)}} = \frac{h(S^u) - h(S^d)}{S^u - S^d}\frac{S(0)}{H(0)}$$

$$= x_H \frac{S(0)}{H(0)}$$

by our earlier computation of the delta x_H in the replicating portfolio. A similar calculation shows that

$$\sigma_{K_H} = \beta_H \sigma_{K_S}.$$

In other words, the standard deviation of the derivative security H is proportional to that of the underlying stock, and the constant of proportionality is β_H.

The **excess mean return** of a risky asset is defined as the difference between the return on that investment and the return on a riskless investment. In our context, with a fixed riskless return $R > 0$, this involves comparing $\mu_{K_H} - R$ with $\mu_{K_S} - R$. The calculation is left to you as the next exercise.

Exercise 2.5   Show that the excess mean returns for a derivative $H = h(S(1))$ and an underlying stock S in the single-step binomial model are related by

$$\mu_{K_H} - R = \beta_H(\mu_{K_S} - R).$$

By considering the risk-neutral probabilities, deduce that for a European call option C we always have $\beta_C \geq 1$.

The exercise shows that the excess mean return for the option is at least that of holding the stock, but equally the risk inherent in the option is also at least as great as that in the stock (and both are usually much greater). Greater returns can only be achieved if we accept greater risks! Note that Theorem 2.12 shows that the excess mean return is always zero under the risk-neutral probability.

Exercise 2.6   Verify that for any given p (with $P(u) = p$)

$$\mathbb{E}_P(K_H) - \mathbb{E}_Q(K_H) = (p - q)\frac{H^u - H^d}{H(0)}.$$

Exercise 2.7 Assuming $\mathbb{E}_P(K_H) \geq R$ show that

$$\mathbb{E}_P(K_H) - R = (p - q)\frac{\sigma K_H}{\sqrt{p(1 - p)}},$$

where q is the risk-neutral probability, implying in particular that $p \geq q$.

This again illustrates the term 'risk neutral': the excess mean return under P is proportional to the standard deviation of the return. But the mean return under Q is just the return on riskless investment, irrespective of the 'riskiness' of the investment as calculated under any other measure. The investor using Q is therefore entirely indifferent to calculations of risk for individual instruments, i.e., is risk neutral. Of course, in real markets investors do not use Q. If Q were the actual probability, no risk-averse investor would choose any risky security, since he can obtain the expected return under Q by investing in the money market account, without any risk! It is important to remember that Q is an abstract object, created to achieve a pricing method for derivatives that is consistent with the No Arbitrage Principle.

Exercise 2.8 Find the relationship between the risk-neutral probability and the **market price of risk**, defined as

$$m_S = \frac{\mu_{K_S} - R}{\sigma_{K_S}}.$$

Exercise 2.9 Show that for any derivative security H on the stock S its market price of risk $m_H = \frac{\mu_{K_H} - R}{\sigma_{K_H}}$ is the same as m_S. Also give a heuristic explanation of this result.

Exercise 2.10 Find a random variable G playing the role of a 'density' of Q with respect to P, considered on $\Omega = \{u, d\}$, i.e., satisfying $q = G(u)p$, $1 - q = G(d)(1 - p)$. Prove that $\mathbb{E}_P(G) = 1$, so that a sequence $G(0) = 1$, $G(1) = G$ is a martingale with respect to P.

2.4 Two underlying securities

We discuss the possibility of modelling the prices of two stocks in a binomial model. This is a very natural step towards reality, where we face a large number of stocks traded on markets. Even when we restrict to a single stock, we may wish to add an international perspective, since if the stock is traded on some foreign market we should include in our model the home currency on this market. Finally, some derivative securities may involve many underlying assets.

The initial prices of our two stocks will be denoted by $S_1(0)$ and $S_2(0)$. Their future prices are determined by random returns, denoted by K_1, K_2 and assumed to be defined on the probability space $\Omega = \{u, d\}$ for simplicity, with obvious modifications if a general space is needed. So we have

$$S_i^u = S_i(0)(1 + K_i(u)),$$
$$S_i^d = S_i(0)(1 + K_i(d)),$$

$i = 1, 2$. In general, we do not expect both returns to agree with the 'up' and 'down' meaning of the elements of $\Omega = \{u, d\}$: for instance we may have $K_1(u) > K_1(d)$ but $K_2(u) < K_2(d)$. However we always assume distinct values with the natural notation $K_i(u) = U_i$, $K_i(d) = D_i$ for $i = 1, 2$, $U_1 \neq D_1$, $U_2 \neq D_2$.

Exercise 2.11 Show that there exist real numbers $a \neq 0$, and b such that $K_1 = aK_2 + b$.

We can interpret this result in terms of the covariance of K_1 and K_2. Given a random variable X we obtain the centred (mean-zero) random variable $X_c = X - \mathbb{E}(X)$ by subtracting its expectation. So the covariance of X and Y can be written as $\mathrm{cov}(X, Y) = \mathbb{E}(X_c Y_c)$; normalising this we obtain the **correlation coefficient**

$$\rho_{X,Y} = \frac{\mathrm{cov}(X, Y)}{\sigma_X \sigma_Y},$$

since $\sigma_X = \sigma_{X_c}$ and similarly for Y. Note that we always have $|\rho_{X,Y}| \leq 1$. The linear relationship between K_1 and K_2 shows that they are perfectly correlated, that is $|\rho_{K_1,K_2}| = 1$.

Exercise 2.12 Show that the correlation coefficient for the returns $K_1 = aK_2 + b$ and K_2 is $\rho_{K_1,K_2} = 1$ if $a > 0$ and $\rho_{K_1,K_2} = -1$ otherwise.

We can regard S_2 as a derivative security with S_1 as the underlying; a function h such that $S_2(1) = h(S_1(1))$ can be easily found.

Exercise 2.13 Find h using the relation between the returns.

Exercise 2.14 Find the replicating portfolio (x, y) such that $S_2(1) = xS_1(1) + yA(1)$.

Denote by Q_1 the risk-neutral probability determined by S_1, that is $Q_1 = (q_1, 1 - q_1)$ with

$$q_1 = \frac{R - D_1}{U_1 - D_1}.$$

We know that the no-arbitrage price of the derivative security S_2 is given by

$$S_2(0) = \mathbb{E}_{Q_1}(\tilde{S}_2(1)). \tag{2.3}$$

Introduce the risk-neutral probability Q_2 given by S_2, that is, with

$$q_2 = \frac{R - D_2}{U_2 - D_2},$$

and by the martingale property for $\tilde{S}_2$ (i.e. the equality of expectations) we have

$$S_2(0) = \mathbb{E}_{Q_2}(\tilde{S}_2(1)). \tag{2.4}$$

From (2.3) and (2.4) we get

$$\mathbb{E}_{Q_1}(K_2) = \mathbb{E}_{Q_2}(K_2) = R.$$

This gives $q_1 U_2 + (1 - q_1)D_2 = R$ which implies $q_1 = q_2$. We have thus proved

Theorem 2.13
No-arbitrage implies $Q_1 = Q_2$.

The converse is also true.

Theorem 2.14
If $Q_1 = Q_2$ then the market composed of a risk-free asset and two stocks does not admit arbitrage.

Proof Seeking a candidate for arbitrage, suppose that for some portfolio we have

$$xS_1(0) + yA(0) + zS_2(0) = 0$$

and

$$V_{(x,y,z)}(1) = xS_1(1) + yA(1) + zS_2(1) \geq 0.$$

Take the expectation with respect to Q_1

$$\begin{aligned}
\mathbb{E}_{Q_1}(V_{(x,y,z)}(1)) &= x\mathbb{E}_{Q_1}(S_1(1)) + yA(1) + z\mathbb{E}_{Q_1}(S_2(1)) \\
&= x\mathbb{E}_{Q_1}(S_1(1)) + yA(1) + z\mathbb{E}_{Q_2}(S_2(1)) \\
&= xS_1(0)(1 + R) + yA(0)(1 + R) + zS_2(0)(1 + R) \\
&= 0.
\end{aligned}$$

In general, a non-negative random variable with zero expectation must be zero almost surely. Here this expectation is a weighted average of non-negative numbers with positive weights, so each of the numbers must be zero, and arbitrage is excluded.   □

Exercise 2.15 Find an arbitrage if $S_1(0) = 50$, $U_1 = 20\%$, $D_1 = -10\%$, $S_2(0) = 80$, $U_2 = 15\%$, $D_2 = -5\%$, $A(0) = 1$, $R = 10\%$.

Exercise 2.16 Find the form of S_2^d as a function of the remaining parameters so that there is no arbitrage.

Remark 2.15
Above we could regard S_1 as a derivative security with S_2 as the underlying with the same arguments and conclusions.

Remark 2.16
What the above results show is that the binomial model does not allow us sufficient freedom to include two arbitrary stocks in the model: under the No Arbitrage Principle, we find that their risk-neutral probabilities are identical and the stocks are perfectly correlated. Thus, in order to construct models which reflect real markets more closely we are forced to increase their complexity; first we shall increase the number of possible random outcomes.

2.5 The trinomial model

An immediate generalisation of the binomial model is the **trinomial** one, where at time 1 the stock price has three possible values. To describe this we introduce an intermediate return M in addition to U, D considered before. So the rate of return for the stock is a random variable of the following form:

$$K = \begin{cases} K^{\mathrm{u}} = U & \text{with probability } p_{\mathrm{u}}, \\ K^{\mathrm{m}} = M & \text{with probability } p_{\mathrm{m}}, \\ K^{\mathrm{d}} = D & \text{with probability } p_{\mathrm{d}}, \end{cases}$$

with $p_{\mathrm{u}}, p_{\mathrm{m}}, p_{\mathrm{d}} \in (0, 1)$ such that $p_{\mathrm{u}} + p_{\mathrm{m}} + p_{\mathrm{d}} = 1$ assuming that $\Omega = \{\mathrm{u, m, d}\}$. The definition of the expectation of a random variable X defined on Ω takes the form

$$\mathbb{E}(X) = p_{\mathrm{u}}X(\mathrm{u}) + p_{\mathrm{m}}X(\mathrm{m}) + p_{\mathrm{d}}X(\mathrm{d}).$$

We assume that the three returns are different and without loss of generality we may further assume $D < M < U$. A derivative security will be a random variable $H(1) = h(S(1))$ as in the binomial model and again we note that any random variable $X: \Omega \rightarrow \mathbb{R}$ is of this form by defining h on the three (different!) values of $S(1)$ to agree with those of $H(1)$ and extending it arbitrarily.

If R is outside the range of stock returns, the model makes no sense since it is always preferable to either invest risk free or in the stock; in other words, the model admits arbitrage, and as in the binomial case the converse is also true.

Theorem 2.17
No-arbitrage is equivalent to $D < R < U$.

Proof   The proof of the implication from the left to right is the same as in the binomial case (Theorem 2.3).

Conversely, a candidate (x, y) for an arbitrage opportunity must satisfy

$$V_{(x,y)}(0) = 0, \quad xS(0) + yA(0) = 0, \quad y = -x\frac{S(0)}{A(0)}.$$

We investigate the terminal value

$$\begin{aligned} V_{(x,y)}(1) &= xS(1) - xS(0)(1 + R) \\ &= xS(0)(K_S - R) \\ &= \begin{cases} xS(0)(U - R) > 0 \\ xS(0)(M - R) \\ xS(0)(D - R) < 0. \end{cases} \end{aligned}$$

Hence (x, y) cannot be an arbitrage: if R lies between U and D then the three above values cannot all have the same sign. Therefore the model is arbitrage-free.   □

In real life stock prices change in a discrete way, quite frequently, but the movements are limited to the so-called **ticks**. So for example, given $S(0) = 30$ the possible values after one time step are 30.50 or 29.50, say. However, the price may not change at all, hence introducing the medium return is quite realistic.

Unfortunately, this leads to mathematical complications since replication (using only risk-free investment and the single stock) of random pay-offs at time 1 is no longer always possible. To see this, we try to replicate a random payoff $H(1)$ with three values H^u, H^m, H^d, which requires finding a portfolio (x, y) with $V_{(x,y)}(1) = H(1)$:

$$\begin{cases} xS^u + yA(0)(1 + R) = H^u, \\ xS^m + yA(0)(1 + R) = H^m, \\ xS^d + yA(0)(1 + R) = H^d, \end{cases}$$

obtaining a system of three equations in two variables which in general has no solution. Thus typically a replicating portfolio for $H(1)$ does not exist.

Exercise 2.17 Given a trinomial single-stock model with $R = 0$, $S(0) = 10$ and $S^u = 20$, $S^m = 15$, $S^d = 7.5$ show that the derivative security H can be replicated if and only if $3H^u - 5H^m + 2H^d = 0$.

Exercise 2.18 Let $S(0) = 100$, $A(0) = 1$, $U = 20\%$, $M = 10\%$, $D = -15\%$, $R = 5\%$, $H^u = 25$, $H^m = 5$. Find H^d such that there is a unique replicating portfolio.

Exercise 2.19 For general H^u, H^m, H^d find a relation between these three numbers so that there is a unique replicating portfolio with arbitrary $S(0), U, M, D, R$.

The no-arbitrage interval

Since the replication $V_{(x,y)}(1) = H(1)$ is impossible in general, we relax the condition somewhat:

Definition 2.18
A portfolio (x, y) **super-replicates** the option with payoff $H(1)$ if

$$V_{(x,y)}(1) \geq H(1).$$

The holder of such a portfolio is protected against the option payoff. Super-replication is satisfactory from the point of view of the trader who sold the option, for whom the option payoff is a liability. This is a source of risk and super-replication **hedges** (i.e. eliminates) this risk completely. Whatever happens, the trader will have sufficient funds to cover the amounts due to the option holder. Therefore, the party selling the option would willingly accept the following price:

Definition 2.19
The **super-replication option price** H^{super} is the minimal initial value of a super-replicating portfolio:

$$H^{\text{super}} = \inf_{(x,y)\in\mathbb{R}^2} \{V_{(x,y)}(0) : V_{(x,y)}(1) \geq H(1)\}.$$

Exercise 2.20   Let $S(0) = 30$, $A(0) = 1$, $U = 20\%$, $M = 10\%$, $D = -10\%$, $R = 5\%$, $H(1) = (S(1) - 32)^+$. Find the super-replication price.

We should analyse the problem from the point of view of the buyer. He wishes to spend no more than he would need for a portfolio that will yield him the same sum as $H(1)$ at time 1. This should therefore be the highest initial price of a **sub-replicating** portfolio (x, y), that is one for which $V_{(x,y)}(1) \leq H(1)$. However, the payoff of the super-replicating portfolio is greater than the option payoff, so from his point of view the option should be cheaper than H^{super}.

So it seems natural to seek a lower bound on the price:

Definition 2.20
The **sub-replication option price** H^{sub} is the maximal initial value of a sub-replicating portfolio:

$$H^{\text{sub}} = \sup_{(x,y)\in\mathbb{R}^2} \{V_{(x,y)}(0) : V_{(x,y)}(1) \leq H(1)\}.$$

Remark 2.21
In fact, H^{sub} is a maximum (and similarly, H^{super} is a minimum) since we are optimising the linear function $V_{(x,y)}(0)$ over a closed subset of the plane, so that the supremum and infimum are attained at elements of the set.

> **Exercise 2.21**　Using the data of Exercise 2.20 find the sub-replicating portfolio price.

If, given two portfolios (x, y) and $(\bar{x}, \bar{y})$, we have

$$V_{(x,y)}(1) \le H(1) \le V_{(\bar{x},\bar{y})}(1)$$

then $V_{(x,y)}(0) \le V_{(\bar{x},\bar{y})}(0)$ since otherwise we can initiate an obvious arbitrage strategy. This implies $H^{\text{sub}} \le H^{\text{super}}$ since the inequality will be preserved after taking the supremum over all (x, y) and then the infimum over all $(\bar{x}, \bar{y})$. Thus an interval of possible prices emerges. We call the open interval with the endpoints at H^{sub} and H^{super} the **no-arbitrage interval**. The next Proposition justifies the terminology.

Proposition 2.22
If $a \in (H^{\text{sub}}, H^{\text{super}})$ then taking $H(0) = a$ does not lead to arbitrage opportunities.

Proof　Let (x, y, z) be such that $V_{(x,y,z)}(0) = xS(0) + yA(0) + zH(0) = 0$ and suppose that $V_{(x,y,z)}(1) \ge 0$. We may assume $z = 1$ or $z = -1$ without loss of generality (divide both sides by $|z|$). Suppose $z = 1$ so $H(0) = -xS(0) - yA(0) = V_{(-x,-y)}(0)$ and $-xS(1) - yA(1) \le H(1)$ so $(-x, -y)$ is sub-replicating. Thus $V_{(-x,-y)}(0) \le H^{\text{sub}} < H(0)$ – contradicting our assumption that $V_{(x,y,z)}(0) = 0$. Similarly, when $z = -1$ we find that (x, y) is super-replicating, yielding the contradiction $V_{(x,y)}(0) \ge H^{\text{super}} > H(0)$. □

Next, consider the possibility of using risk-neutral probabilities, which in the binomial model served as an alternative to replication for pricing. We use Q to denote a probability measure on the three-point sample space $\Omega = \{u, m, d\}$, represented by a triple $q_u, q_m, q_d \in (0, 1)$ with $q_u + q_m + q_d = 1$. The definition of a risk-neutral probability remains the same, namely $\mathbb{E}_Q(S(1)) = S(0)(1 + R)$, with equivalent form $\mathbb{E}_Q(K) = R$, that is, in the trinomial model,

$$q_u U + q_m M + q_d D = R.$$

We have two equations with three variables and such a linear system has many solutions, potentially giving infinitely many risk-neutral probabilities. Of course we still have to identify which of these solutions give genuine probabilities, that is, take all their values in the interval $(0, 1)$. The next proposition will show that in a pricing model consistent with the No Arbitrage Principle there are always some that do.

Exercise 2.22 Given a trinomial single-stock model with $R = 10\%$, $S(0) = 10$ and $S^u = 20, S^m = 15, S^d = 7.5$ find all risk-neutral probabilities.

Proposition 2.23

If the trinomial pricing model is consistent with the No Arbitrage Principle then there is a probability Q such that the underlying stock prices satisfy

$$S(0) = \mathbb{E}_Q[\tilde{S}(1)].$$

Proof To find one such probability, note that the absence of arbitrage (Theorem 2.17) ensures that $S^d < S(0)(1 + R) < S^u$, or, equivalently, $\tilde{S}^d < S(0) < \tilde{S}^u$. Now, either $\tilde{S}^m > S(0)$ or $\tilde{S}^m \leq S(0)$. In the first case let $A = \frac{1}{2}(\tilde{S}^u + \tilde{S}^m)$ and let $B = \tilde{S}^d$; in the second take $A = S^u$ and $B = \frac{1}{2}(\tilde{S}^m + \tilde{S}^d)$. In both cases we obtain $B < S(0) < A$, so there exists $c \in (0, 1)$ such that $S(0) = cA + (1-c)B$. Hence either $S(0) = c\frac{1}{2}(\tilde{S}^u + \tilde{S}^m) + (1-c)\tilde{S}^d$ or $S(0) = c\tilde{S}^u + (1 - c)\frac{1}{2}(\tilde{S}^m + \tilde{S}^d)$. In each case we can find the required probability measure $Q = (q_u, q_m, q_d)$: in the first, we take $q_u = q_m = \frac{c}{2}$, $q_d = 1 - c$; in the second we use $q_u = c, q_m = q_d = \frac{1}{2}(1 - c)$. □

In the binomial model the risk-neutral probability is unique and gives the price of any derivative security as the discounted expectation of the payoff with respect to the risk-neutral probability. Since here we have many such probabilities we cannot expect the same result, but we now show that they determine the range of prices consistent with the No Arbitrage Principle. Let

$$I = \{(1 + R)^{-1}\mathbb{E}_Q(H(1)) : \mathbb{E}_Q(K) = R\},$$

where the expectations are taken over all risk-neutral probabilities Q. Note that the set I is an interval, since the set of martingale probabilities is obviously convex and the map

$$(q_1, q_2, q_3) \rightarrow (1 + R)^{-1}\mathbb{E}_Q(H(1)$$

is linear. This interval can be also called a 'no-arbitrage interval'.

Proposition 2.24

Each number in the interval I is a price of H consistent with the No Arbitrage Principle.

Proof Let $a \in I$, write $H(0) = a$, so that $H(0) = (1 + R)^{-1}\mathbb{E}_Q(H(1))$ for some risk-neutral Q. Consider a portfolio (x, y, z) in the extended market

with $V_{(x,y,z)}(0) = 0$ and $V_{(x,y,z)}(1) \geq 0$. Compute the expectation of discounted $V_{(x,y,z)}(1)$ with respect to Q

$$\begin{aligned}
\mathbb{E}_Q((1+R)^{-1}V_{(x,y,z)}(1)) &= x\mathbb{E}_Q((1+R)^{-1}S(1)) + yA(0) \\
&\quad + z\mathbb{E}_Q((1+R)^{-1}H(1)) \\
&= xS(0) + yA(0) + zH(0) = 0
\end{aligned}$$

hence $V_{(x,y,z)}(1) = 0$. But zero expectation of a non-negative discrete random variable forces this random variable to be zero. $\square$

Finally, we show that the two 'no-arbitrage intervals' coincide.

Theorem 2.25
Let H be a European derivative security in the single-period, single-stock trinomial market model, and assume that $H^{\text{sub}} < H^{\text{super}}$. Then

$$I = (H^{\text{sub}}, H^{\text{super}}).$$

Proof First, we show that I is contained in $[H^{\text{sub}}, H^{\text{super}}]$. We assume $A(0) = 1$ without loss of generality.

Suppose the portfolio (x, y) is sub-replicating

$$xS(1) + y(1+R) \leq H(1).$$

Take any risk-neutral Q and compute the expectation of both sides:

$$\mathbb{E}_Q(xS(1) + y(1+R)) \leq \mathbb{E}_Q(H(1)).$$

By linearity and the martingale property $\mathbb{E}_Q(S(1)) = S(0)(1+R)$ we have

$$\mathbb{E}_Q(xS(1) + y(1+R)) = xS(0)(1+R) + y(1+R)$$

which implies

$$xS(0) + y \leq (1+R)^{-1}\mathbb{E}_Q(H(1)).$$

Take the supremum over all such portfolios

$$\sup(xS(0) + y) \leq (1+R)^{-1}\mathbb{E}_Q(H(1))$$

so that

$$H^{\text{sub}} \leq (1+R)^{-1}\mathbb{E}_Q(H(1)).$$

In the same manner we prove that $H^{\text{super}} \geq (1+R)^{-1}\mathbb{E}_Q(H(1))$ by considering portfolios (x, y) such that

$$xS(1) + y(1+R) \geq H(1).$$

which implies

$$xS(0) + y \geq (1 + R)^{-1}\mathbb{E}_Q(H(1)).$$

Taking the infimum over all super-replicating portfolios we conclude that

$$H^{\text{super}} = \inf_{(x,y)}\{(xS(0) + y) \geq (1 + R)^{-1}\mathbb{E}_Q(H(1))\}.$$

Hence I is a sub-interval of $[H^{\text{sub}}, H^{\text{super}}]$.

Next, for notational convenience assume that $\Omega = \{\omega_1, \omega_2, \omega_3\}$ and let $A = \{(\widetilde{S}(1, \omega_i), \widetilde{H}(1, \omega_i)) : i = 1, 2, 3\} \subset \mathbb{R}^2$. Let C denote the closed convex hull of A, i.e. the set of all, not necessarily strict, convex combinations of these points. The closed set C is either a triangle or a line segment in $\mathbb{R}^2$. Now recall that $H(1) = h(S(1))$ for some function h. To obtain $\widetilde{H}(1, \omega_i)$, set $g(x) = (1 + R)^{-1}h(x(1 + R))$, then $\widetilde{H}(1, \omega_i) = g(\widetilde{S}(1, \omega_i))$. The vertices of C are therefore of the form $(\widetilde{S}(1, \omega_i), g(\widetilde{S}(1, \omega_i)))$, hence (as g is a function) none of the sides of C can be vertical. Similarly, if the three points in A are collinear, this line segment is not vertical.

Assume first that the three points of A are not collinear, so that C is a triangle in $\mathbb{R}^2$. The No Arbitrage Principle ensures that $S(0)$ lies strictly between the smallest and largest value of $\widetilde{S}(1, \omega_i)$ for $i = 1, 2, 3$. This follows since $S(0)(1 + D) < S(0)(1 + R) < S(0)(1 + U)$, so that $S(0)$ lies strictly between the two extreme discounted values. Thus the intersection of the triangle C with the vertical line through $(S(0), 0)$ is a non-empty line segment with endpoints $(S(0), a), (S(0), b)$, say.

Clearly $(a, b) = \{u : (S(0), u) \in \text{int}(C)\}$, where $\text{int}(C)$ denotes the interior of C. Moreover, we can express any $(S(0), u)$ in $\text{int}(C)$ as a strictly convex combination of the points of A, that is,

$$(S(0), u) = \sum_{i=1}^{3} c_i(\widetilde{S}(1, \omega_i), \widetilde{H}(1, \omega_i)), \text{ where } c_i > 0, \sum_{i=1}^{3} c_i = 1.$$

These three positive numbers define a probability measure Q on 2^Ω by putting $q_u = c_1, q_m = c_2, q_d = c_3$. The identity

$$S(0) = \sum_{i=1}^{3} c_i\widetilde{S}(1, \omega_i) = \mathbb{E}_Q[\widetilde{S}(1)] = (1 + R)^{-1}\mathbb{E}_Q[S(1)]$$

shows that Q is a risk-neutral probability, which, together with the identity

$$u = \sum_{i=1}^{3} c_i\widetilde{H}(1, \omega_i) = \mathbb{E}_Q[\widetilde{H}(1)] = (1 + R)^{-1}\mathbb{E}_Q[H(1)],$$

shows that $u \in I$, in other words $(a, b) \subset I$.

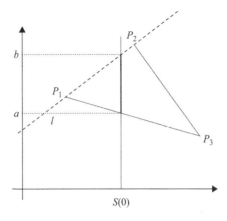

Figure 2.1

We have therefore shown that:

$$(a,b) \subset I \subset [H^{\text{sub}}, H^{\text{super}}].$$

Now observe that, since the above triangle has no vertical edges, there is a straight line l with gradient x and intercept y passing through the point $(S(0), b)$ such that the set A is contained in the half-plane below this line. In fact, this is a line containing one side of the triangle (see Figure 2.1, where $P_i = (\widetilde{S}(1, \omega_i), \widetilde{H}(1, \omega_i)))$.

In other words, $\widetilde{H}(1) \leq x\widetilde{S}(1) + y$ or equivalently

$$H(1) \leq xS(1) + y(1 + R),$$

which means that (x, y) is a super-replicating portfolio. Because the line passes through $(S(0), b)$ we have

$$b = xS(0) + y \geq H^{\text{super}}.$$

Similarly, since $a = \inf I$, there is a straight line, again containing one side of the triangle, with gradient x' and intercept y' passing through $(S(0), a)$ such that A is contained in the half-plane above this line (in Figure 2.1 this would be the line passing through P_1 and P_3), so that $\widetilde{H}(1) \geq x'\widetilde{S}(1) + y'$. It follows that

$$H(1) \geq x'S(1) + y'(1 + R),$$

so that (x', y') is a sub-replicating portfolio. Since the line passes through $(S(0), a)$, we have

$$a = x'S(0) + y' \leq H^{\text{sub}}.$$

Hence we have shown that (a, b) contains $(H^{\text{sub}}, H^{\text{super}})$, so that, finally, $I = (H^{\text{sub}}, H^{\text{super}})$. This completes the proof for the case when C is a triangle. □

Remark 2.26

It is clear from the above proof that this result also holds for any single-step, single-stock model with $n \geq 3$ possible outcomes at time 1: the convex hull is then an n-gon in the plane, otherwise the proof is essentially the same.

Special case: $H^{\text{super}} = H^{\text{sub}}$

Finally, we still should discuss the case where sub- and super-replicating prices meet. In the trinomial model this is unusual but it may take place. The situation then basically reduces to the binomial model and we will demonstrate this by a series of exercises. The ideal solution is to have replication; one may suspect that this is trivial in the case in question, but actually some work is needed to prove it.

Exercise 2.23 Show that if $H^{\text{sub}} = H^{\text{super}}$ then there exists a replicating portfolio.

Such a portfolio gives a no-arbitrage price but it it would be nice to sort out the uniqueness issue. In general, two portfolios might give the same price, but as it turns out, we do not have to worry too much.

Exercise 2.24 Show that the replicating strategy is unique.

Going to the analysis of the set I we are relieved to find that in the current circumstances it is a singleton.

Exercise 2.25 Show that the existence of a replicating strategy implies uniqueness of the risk-neutral probability.

In summary: if $H^{\text{sub}} = H^{\text{super}}$ then this number is the expectation of the discounted payoff of the derivative security with respect to the unique risk-neutral probability and also the time zero value of the replicating portfolio, precisely as in the binomial case.

Going back to our geometric proof of Theorem 2.25 this can be seen very clearly. When C is a line segment (i.e., the three points of A are collinear) the intermediate point $(\widetilde{S}(1, \omega_2), \widetilde{H}(1, \omega_2))$ is a (known) convex combination of the other two, so there are only two sources of uncertainty. Thus we are back in the binomial model, and there is a (unique) replicating portfolio. Geometrically, the intersection of the line segment C and the vertical line through $(S(0), 0)$ is a single point (again, it is non-empty by our no-arbitrage assumption).

We will show in Theorem 2.40 that the existence of replicating portfolios for every derivative security ensures that I is a singleton in a general setting as well.

Replication with two stocks

An alternative way of approaching the replication problem and obtaining a unique price is to 'complete the market' by adding a third variable in our three equations: in other words, in our trinomial model we assume that, in addition to the money market account, we have two stocks S_1, S_2 with returns K_1, K_2

$$
\begin{aligned}
K_1^{\text{u}} &= U_1, & K_2^{\text{u}} &= U_2, \\
K_1^{\text{m}} &= M_1, & K_2^{\text{m}} &= M_2, \\
K_1^{\text{d}} &= D_1, & K_2^{\text{d}} &= D_2,
\end{aligned}
$$

working on $\Omega = \{\text{u}, \text{m}, \text{d}\}$. The role of the index $\text{u}, \text{m}, \text{d}$ is to indicate the branch and is not related to the size of return. The stock prices are then given by

$$
S_1(1) = S_1(0)(1 + K_1),
$$
$$
S_2(1) = S_2(0)(1 + K_2).
$$

For replication of a claim H in this model we need (x_1, x_2, y) so that

$$
\left\{
\begin{aligned}
x_1 S_1^{\text{u}} + x_2 S_2^{\text{u}} + yA(0)(1 + R) &= H^{\text{u}}, \\
x_1 S_1^{\text{m}} + x_2 S_2^{\text{m}} + yA(0)(1 + R) &= H^{\text{m}}, \\
x_1 S_1^{\text{d}} + x_2 S_2^{\text{d}} + yA(0)(1 + R) &= H^{\text{d}}.
\end{aligned}
\right.
$$

In matrix form:

$$
AX = H,
$$

where

$$A = \begin{bmatrix} S_1^u & S_2^u & A(0)(1+R) \\ S_1^m & S_2^m & A(0)(1+R) \\ S_1^d & S_2^d & A(0)(1+R) \end{bmatrix}, \quad X = \begin{bmatrix} x_1 \\ x_2 \\ y \end{bmatrix}, \quad H = \begin{bmatrix} H^u \\ H^m \\ H^d \end{bmatrix}.$$

Depending on the coefficients, this linear system has either no solution or a unique one, or infinitely many. However, provided the determinant of A is non-zero, we can invert A and obtain a unique solution:

$$X = A^{-1}H.$$

The solution gives the option price $H(0) = x_1 S_1(0) + x_2 S_2(0) + yA(0)$. A model which has a unique solution for every choice of random payoff H is called **complete**. We rephrase this as a general definition.

Definition 2.27
A market model is **complete** if every random payoff $H(1)$ can be replicated.

We now seek a risk-neutral probability so that both discounted stock prices satisfy the martingale condition, in other words we solve the system

$$\mathbb{E}_Q(K_1) = R,$$
$$\mathbb{E}_Q(K_2) = R,$$

which reads

$$\begin{cases} q_u U_1 + q_m M_1 + q_d D_1 = R, \\ q_u U_2 + q_m M_2 + q_d D_2 = R. \end{cases} \tag{2.5}$$

A system of three linear equations (the third one is $q_u + q_m + q_d = 1$) with three variables can be solved apart from some singular cases. However, the question for us is whether the solution represents a genuine probability measure, that is, if the three probabilities belong to the interval $(0, 1)$. We illustrate this with examples.

Example 2.28
For an example where Q is not a genuine probability, consider stocks S_1, S_2 with $U_1 = 30\%$, $M_1 = 5\%$, $D_1 = -20\%$, $U_2 = -5\%$, $M_2 = 0\%$, $D_2 = 10\%$, $R = 5\%$. Solving the above equations we find $q_u = 1$, $q_m = -1$, $q_d = 1$. This model allows arbitrage:

If $S_1(0) = 100$, $S_2(0) = 50$, $A(0) = 1$, the portfolio $x_1 = -0.5$, $x_2 = -2$, $y = 150$ is an arbitrage: $V_{(x_1,x_2,y)}(0) = 0$, $V_{(x_1,x_2,y)}(1) \geq 2.5$ in each scenario. Note that here the two stocks do not go 'up' together.

This example illustrates the first fundamental theorem of asset pricing, which will be proved more generally in the next section.

Theorem 2.29
When Ω is finite there is no arbitrage if and only if there exists a risk-neutral probability measure, with positive probabilities for each scenario.

Consider some further examples:

Example 2.30
Let $H(1) = (S_1(1) - X)^+$ which is a call option on stock 1. Let $R = 5\%$, and let $S_1(0) = 30$, $A(0) = 1$, $X = 32$, $U_1 = 20\%$, $M_1 = 10\%$, $D_1 = -10\%$. Suppose now that $S_2(0) = 30$ and the movements of this stock are given by $U_2 = -5\%$, $M_2 = 15\%$, $D_2 = 10\%$. We can find a replicating strategy which provides the option price $H(0) = 1.6402$. To do this we simply solve the matrix equation

$$
\begin{bmatrix} 36 & 28.5 & 1.05 \\ 33 & 25.5 & 1.05 \\ 27 & 33 & 1.05 \end{bmatrix} \begin{bmatrix} x_1 \\ x_2 \\ y \end{bmatrix} = \begin{bmatrix} 4 \\ 1 \\ 0 \end{bmatrix}
$$

and compute $H(0) = x_1 S_1(0) + x_2 S_2(0) + y$.

There is a unique risk-neutral probability Q and

$$H(0) = (1 + R)^{-1} \mathbb{E}_Q(H(1)) = 1.6402,$$

as you may check.

This seemingly positive result requires some critical thinking. We have obtained a unique price of H but this was obtained as a result of completing the market by introducing a second underlying security. The option price therefore depends on this choice, which contradicts common sense – why should some other stock influence the price of a call option written on stock 1? So in fact we still have a range of prices, this time related to the variety of securities which can be chosen to complete the market. To see a possible use of the above ideas suppose that a derivative security H written on S_1 is traded; its market prices available. Now we can choose H as the additional security making the market complete and we may price other derivatives using the unique risk-neutral probability. In this sense a statement often found in the financial literature, that 'the market chooses the risk-neutral probability', gains substance.

Example 2.31

With $U_2 = 10\%$, $M_2 = 5\%$, $D_2 = -20\%$ and the remaining data as before, the replication problem can be solved with $H(0) = -1.2698$ which is nonsense (a negative price for a positive payoff security gives arbitrage).

Here there is no risk-neutral probability: the equations (2.5) have the unique solution $q_1 = 2$, $q_2 = -0.83$ which does not yield a probability measure.

Exercise 2.26 Consider a trinomial model for stock prices with $S(0) = 120$ and $S(1) = 135, 125, 115$, respectively. Assume that $R = 10\%$. Consider a call with strike 120 as the second security. Show that $C(0) = 120/11$ allows arbitrage and that there is a unique degenerate probability which makes discounted stock and call prices a martingale. Carry out the same analysis for $C(0) = 255/12$ and draw a conclusion about admissible call prices.

Exercise 2.27 If the returns on stocks are $5\%, 8\%, -20\%$ on stock 1 and $-5\%, 10\%, a\%$ on stock 2, find a so that there exists a risk-neutral probability, where $R = 5\%$.

Exercise 2.28 Find the price of a **basket option** (where the strike is compared with the sum of two stock prices) with payoff $H(1) = \max\{(S_1(1) + S_2(1) - X), 0\}$ where $S_1(0) = 100$, $S_2(0) = 50$, $A(0) = 1$, $X = 150$, the returns are $20\%, 5\%, -20\%$ for stock 1 and $-10\%, 8\%, 2\%$ for stock 2, and $R = 5\%$. Use replication as well as a risk-neutral probability and compare the prices obtained.

To price options we need both conditions: we need no-arbitrage to have replication, and completeness in order to obtain a unique price. This leads to the second fundamental theorem.

Theorem 2.32

A market model is arbitrage-free and complete if and only if there exists a unique risk-neutral probability Q.

As with the first fundamental theorem, this result will be formulated and proved in a more general setting in the next section. Our two simple examples (binomial and trinomial models) serve to illustrate the main features of the general theory we now proceed to develop.

2.6   A general single-step model

Assume given a riskless asset A with $A(0) = 1$ (we keep this assumption throughout this section to simplify notation), accruing interest at rate R, together with an arbitrary finite number of assets with prices $S_1(n), \ldots, S_d(n)$, which we consider at times $n = 0, 1$. We assume that for $i = 1, \ldots, d$ the prices $S_i(0)$ are known (non-random) and that at time 1 each $S_i(1)$ is a (positive) random variable defined on a finite sample space $\Omega = \{\omega_1, \ldots, \omega_M\}$, with a probability measure P defined on all the subsets of Ω by the formula

$$P(A) = \sum_{\omega \in A} P(\omega)$$

where $P(\omega_j) = p_j \in (0, 1)$ for $j = 1, \ldots, M$, and $\sum_{j=1}^{M} p_j = 1$. A random variable is now a function

$$X: \{\omega_1, \ldots, \omega_M\} \to \mathbb{R}$$

with expectation given by

$$\mathbb{E}(X) = \sum_{j=1}^{M} p_j X(\omega_j).$$

The random vector of prices $(S_1(1), \ldots, S_d(1))$ is built of d random variables, each taking at most M different values. In fact, we shall assume that altogether M different values appear at time 1. This ensures that all M elements of Ω are 'needed', since if the random variables $S_i(1)$, $i \leq d$, had fewer values than there are elements of the domain Ω, this would mean that for some ω_1, ω_2 all stock prices are the same and so some of the ω's were redundant and could be removed from Ω. As a consequence of this natural non-degeneracy assumption, in the same way as in the binomial or trinomial model, any random variable $X: \Omega \to \mathbb{R}$ can be written in the form $X = h(S_1(1), \ldots, S_d(1))$ for some function $h: \mathbb{R}^d \to \mathbb{R}$.

These data constitute a **finite single-step market model**. The notion of a portfolio must be adjusted to incorporate d stocks: it is a $(d + 1)$-vector

$(\mathbf{x}, y) = (x_1, \ldots, x_d, y)$ whose coordinates indicate the stock holdings and risk-free investment respectively. The **initial value** of the portfolio $(\mathbf{x}, y)$ is $V_{(\mathbf{x},y)}(0) = \sum_{i=1}^{d} x_i S_i(0) + yA(0)$, while its **final value** is the random variable

$$V_{(\mathbf{x},y)}(1) = \sum_{i=1}^{d} x_i S_i(1) + yA(1).$$

Note that fixing the initial value $V(0)$ and the vector $\mathbf{x}$ of stock holdings of a portfolio automatically determines the bond holding y. This is true, in particular, for arbitrage opportunities: recall that a portfolio is an **arbitrage opportunity** if $V(0) = 0$, $V(1) \geq 0$, and $V(1) > 0$ with a positive probability, that is, in our setting, if $V(1, \omega)$ is positive for at least one $\omega \in \Omega$.

The first fundamental theorem of mathematical finance, which we now formulate and prove in this general setting, gives an equivalent condition for the absence of arbitrage.

First fundamental theorem

We consider a simple version of this key result, applicable to the single-step model. The general multi-step case will be considered in the next chapter. First we note what is meant by a risk-neutral probability measure in this context:

Definition 2.33
The sequence $Q = \{q_1, \ldots, q_M\}$ of positive numbers is a **risk-neutral** probability measure for $\Omega = \{\omega_1, \ldots, \omega_M\}$ and stock prices $\{(S_i(0), S_i(1)) : i = 1, \ldots, d\}$ if $\sum_{j=1}^{M} q_j = 1$ and $\mathbb{E}_Q(S_i(1)) = (1 + R)S_i(0)$ for all i, where $\mathbb{E}_Q$ denotes the expectation with respect to the probability $Q(\omega_j) = q_j > 0$ for $j \leq M$, and R denotes the riskless interest rate. Q is often called a (single-step) **martingale probability** for the stock price processes $\{S_i : i = 1, \ldots, d\}$.

Theorem 2.34
In a finite single-step market model there is no arbitrage if and only if there exists a risk-neutral probability measure.

Proof Recall that we assume $A(0) = 1$. First suppose that the model allows risk-neutral probabilities. Consider any portfolio with $V(0) = 0$. Assume that $V(1) \geq 0$ (otherwise this portfolio is not an arbitrage

opportunity). Compute

$$
\begin{aligned}
\mathbb{E}_Q(V(1)) &= \sum_{j=1}^{M}\left(\sum_{i=1}^{d} x_i S_i(1,\omega_j)\right)q_j + y(1+R) \\
&= \sum_{i=1}^{d} x_i\left(\sum_{j=1}^{M} S_i(1,\omega_j)q_j\right) + y(1+R) \\
&= \sum_{i=1}^{d} x_i \mathbb{E}_Q(S_i(1)) + y(1+R) \\
&= (1+R)\sum_{i=1}^{d} x_i S_i(0) + y(1+R) \\
&= (1+R)V(0) = 0.
\end{aligned}
$$

This implies that $V(1) = 0$ for all ω since zero expectation of a non-negative random variable forces this random variable to be identically zero, hence there are no arbitrage opportunities.

For the converse implication, assume that the pricing model does not allow arbitrage. Define the **discounted gains** of the portfolio

$$
(\mathbf{x}, y) = (x_1, x_2, \ldots, x_d, y)
$$

as the random variable $G_{\mathbf{x}}$ with values

$$
G_{\mathbf{x}}(\omega) = \sum_{i=1}^{d} x_i\left[\frac{S_i(1,\omega)}{1+R} - S_i(0)\right]
$$

for $\omega \in \Omega$. Note that y does not appear, since the discounted gains of A are zero by definition. $G_{\mathbf{x}}$ is well-defined for any vector $\mathbf{x}$ in $\mathbb{R}^d$.

The set

$$
W = \left\{G_{\mathbf{x}}\colon \Omega \to \mathbb{R} : G_{\mathbf{x}}(\omega) = \sum_{i=1}^{d} x_i\left[\frac{S_i(1,\omega)}{1+R} - S_i(0)\right], \mathbf{x} = (x_i)_{i\le d} \in \mathbb{R}^d\right\}
$$

is a vector space, as it is built of discounted portfolio gains. It can be identified with a subspace of $\mathbb{R}^M$, writing $G_{\mathbf{x}} = (G_{\mathbf{x}}(\omega_j))_{j\le M}$, because $\Omega = \{\omega_1, \ldots, \omega_M\}$ has M elements.

We verify the following property of the elements of W: if $G_{\mathbf{x}}(\omega) \ge 0$ for all ω then $G_{\mathbf{x}}(\omega) = 0$ for all ω. To see this, take $\mathbf{x} = (x_i)_{i\le d}$ such that $G_{\mathbf{x}}(\omega) \ge 0$ for all ω. Ensure that the portfolio $(\mathbf{x}, y)$ has zero initial wealth $V(0) = 0$ by supplementing the x_i by a suitable y. The discounted final

value of this portfolio is

$$\tilde{V}_{(x,y)}(1) = \frac{1}{1+R} \sum_{i=1}^{d} x_i S_i(1) + y$$

$$= \frac{1}{1+R} \sum_{i=1}^{d} x_i S_i(1) + y - V(0)$$

$$= \sum_{i=1}^{d} x_i \left[\frac{S_i(1)}{1+R} - S_i(0) \right]$$

$$= G_x \geq 0$$

hence to avoid arbitrage $\tilde{V}_{(x,y)}(1) = G_x$ must be zero.

The risk-neutral probabilities we seek belong to the following subset of $\mathbb{R}^M$:

$$A = \left\{ Q = (q_1, \ldots, q_M) : \sum_{j=1}^{M} q_j = 1, q_j \geq 0 \right\}.$$

We shall construct a vector Q in A with positive coordinates, and orthogonal to the subspace W. The coordinates of such a vector give the required probabilities q_j, since orthogonality means that the Euclidean inner product of $(q_1, \ldots, q_M)$ and $(G_x(\omega_1), \ldots, G_x(\omega_M))$ vanishes for each G_x in W, that is, with $\mathbb{E}_Q$ as in the definition of risk-neutrality,

$$\mathbb{E}_Q(G_x) = \sum_{j=1}^{M} q_j G_x(\omega_j) = 0$$

for all G_x. But if for $i \leq d$ we take $x_i = 1$ and $x_k = 0$, $k \neq i$, then $G_x = \frac{S_i(1)}{1+R} - S_i(0)$ so that $\mathbb{E}_Q(S_i(1)) = S(0)(1 + R)$ for all $i = 1, \ldots, d$.

The existence of $(q_1, \ldots, q_M)$ follows from the following lemma which we shall also use later, when the multi-step version of the theorem will be presented.

Lemma 2.35
Suppose $A \subset \mathbb{R}^n$ is convex and compact, and W is a vector subspace of $\mathbb{R}^n$ disjoint from A. Then there exists $z \in \mathbb{R}^n$ such that $\langle z, a \rangle > 0$ for all $a \in A$, and $\langle z, w \rangle = 0$ for all $w \in W$, where $\langle x, y \rangle = \sum_{i=1}^{n} x_i y_i$ is the Euclidean inner product in $\mathbb{R}^n$.

Proof See page 45.   □

To see that this is sufficient to prove the theorem with $n = M$ and A, W as above, note that A is obviously convex. It is compact, as it is closed

and bounded (Heine–Borel theorem!). Since $G_x \geq 0$ implies $G_x = 0$, it follows that $A \cap W = \emptyset$. Now take $(a_1, ..., a_M)$ in A with $a_j = 1$ for some j (and so with the remaining coordinates necessarily zero) hence the lemma, applied to $\mathbb{R}^M$, provides $(z_1, ..., z_M)$ with $z_j > 0$ for all $j = 1, \ldots, M$ and $\sum_{j=1}^{M} z_j G_x(\omega_j) = 0$ for all G_x in W. So we need only take

$$q_j = \frac{1}{\sum_{i=1}^{M} z_i} z_j$$

for $j \leq M$ to ensure that $\sum_{j=1}^{M} q_j = 1$, while all $q_j > 0$ and

$$\sum_{j=1}^{M} q_j G_x(\omega_j) = 0$$

for all G_x in W. This completes the proof of the theorem.   □

Remark 2.36
We have shown that for finite single-step models the existence of a risk-neutral probability assignment or martingale probability is equivalent to the requirement that the model does not allow arbitrage. We shall show in Chapter 3 that this remains true for multi-step finite market models in general. Our proof there will depend heavily on the single-step case, and crucially on the finiteness of the market model, that is, finiteness of the sample space Ω.

Next we turn our attention to the question of completeness.

Second fundamental theorem

The trinomial model is an example of an incomplete market model, the defining feature being the lack of replicating portfolios for some derivative securities. The binomial model, on the other hand, allows for such a replication of all claims and is an example of a complete market model. We re-state the definition more generally. Recall that our market model contains d risky securities, whose prices we denote, for ease of notation, as a random vector $\mathbf{S}(1) = (S_1(1), \ldots, S_d(1))$. The value at 1 of the portfolio $(\mathbf{x}, y)$ is the random variable $V_{(\mathbf{x},y)}(1) = \langle \mathbf{x}, \mathbf{S}(1) \rangle + yA(1)$, where $\langle ., . \rangle$ denotes the inner product in $\mathbb{R}^d$.

Definition 2.37
An arbitrage-free market model is **complete** if for each derivative security $H = h(\mathbf{S}(1))$ there exists a replicating portfolio.

Any random variable H is a derivative security in our market model, since its value is completely determined by the price vector $\mathbf{S}(1)$ and it can be written in the form $H = h(\mathbf{S}(1))$ for some $h\colon \mathbb{R}^d \to \mathbb{R}$, which is a consequence of the non-degeneracy assumption made at the beginning of this section. In particular, for any $\omega \in \Omega$, $\mathbf{1}_{\{\omega\}}$ is a derivative security. We now show that in a complete market model all risk-neutral probabilities coincide.

Theorem 2.38

An arbitrage-free market model is complete if and only if there is exactly one risk-neutral probability.

Proof No arbitrage implies the existence of a martingale probability, so we need to show that we cannot have more than one such probability in a complete market. Suppose we have two martingale probabilities $Q_1 \neq Q_2$. For any $\omega \in \Omega$ the random variable $\mathbf{1}_{\{\omega\}}$ is a derivative security. By completeness of the market model there exists a replicating portfolio, given by $(\mathbf{x}, y)$ such that

$$\langle \mathbf{x}, \mathbf{S}(1)\rangle + y(1 + R) = \mathbf{1}_{\{\omega\}}.$$

Take the expectation with respect to Q_k, $k = 1, 2$:

$$\mathbb{E}_{Q_k}(\langle \mathbf{x}, \mathbf{S}(1)\rangle + y(1 + R)) = \mathbb{E}_{Q_k}(\mathbf{1}_{\{\omega\}}) = Q_i(\omega)$$

and note that the left-hand side is independent of k, since

$$\mathbb{E}_{Q_k}(\langle \mathbf{x}, \mathbf{S}(1)\rangle + y(1 + R)) = \langle \mathbf{x}, \mathbb{E}_{Q_k}(\mathbf{S}(1))\rangle + y(1 + R)$$
$$= \langle \mathbf{x}, \mathbf{S}(0)\rangle(1 + R) + y(1 + R)$$

so that

$$Q_1(\omega) = Q_2(\omega).$$

But $\omega \in \Omega$ was arbitrary, so the probabilities Q_1, Q_2 coincide..

For the converse implication, assume Q is the unique martingale probability and suppose there is a derivative D, which cannot be replicated. Our goal will be to construct a martingale probability Q_1 different from Q.

Consider the set of values at time 1 of all portfolios: $W = \{V_{(\mathbf{x},y)}(1) : (\mathbf{x}, y) \in \mathbb{R}^{d+1}\}$. Since none replicates D, we conclude that $D \notin W$. We treat W as a vector subspace of $\mathbb{R}^M$ by identifying $\mathbb{R}^M$ with the set of all random variables on $\Omega = \{\omega_1, \dots, \omega_M\}$. The subspace W contains the vector $\mathbf{1} = (1, \dots, 1)$ because if $\mathbf{x} = \mathbf{0}$ and $y = \frac{1}{1+R}$ then $V_{(\mathbf{x},y)}(1) = 1$ for all scenarios. Now equip $\mathbb{R}^M$ with the inner product $\langle \mathbf{w}, \mathbf{v}\rangle_Q = \sum_{j=1}^{M} w_j v_j Q(\omega_j)$ and use

the following version of Lemma 2.35 with the subspace W and the compact convex set $A = \{D\}$.

Lemma 2.39

Suppose $A \subset \mathbb{R}^n$ is convex and compact, and W is a vector subspace of $\mathbb{R}^n$ disjoint from A. Then there exists $z \in \mathbb{R}^n$ such that $\langle z, a \rangle_Q > 0$ for all $a \in A$, and $\langle z, w \rangle_Q = 0$ for all $w \in W$, where $\langle x, y \rangle_Q = \sum_{i=1} x_i y_i q_i$, $q_i > 0$, is an inner product in $\mathbb{R}^n$.

Proof   See page 47.   □

From the lemma we obtain an $\mathbb{R}^M$-vector $Z = (z_1, \ldots, z_M)$ such that $\langle Z, D \rangle_Q > 0$ and $\langle Z, V \rangle_Q = 0$ for $V \in W$. The inequality implies that $Z \neq \mathbf{0}$, while, taking $V = \mathbf{1}$ in the identity, we have $\langle Z, \mathbf{1} \rangle_Q = \sum_{j=1}^M z_j Q(\omega_j) = 0$ hence $\mathbb{E}_Q(Z) = 0$, where the expectation is taken under Q.

Now we define a new measure, which will turn out to be a martingale probability different from Q

$$Q_1(\omega_j) = \left(1 + \frac{z_j}{2a}\right) Q(\omega_j)$$

where $a = \max_{\omega_j \in \Omega} |z_j| > 0$. This is a probability measure since

$$\sum_{j=1}^M Q_1(\omega_j) = \sum_{j=1}^M Q(\omega_j) + \sum_{j=1}^M \frac{z_j}{2a} Q(\omega_j)$$

$$= 1 + \frac{1}{2a} \mathbb{E}_Q(Z) = 1.$$

Clearly $-a \leq z_j$ for all j, so the number $1 + z_j/2a$ is always positive and for at least one coordinate it is different from 1 since Z is non-zero, thus $Q_1 \neq Q$. Finally, we check the martingale property of each S_i (for $i \leq d$) under Q_1:

$$\mathbb{E}_{Q_1}(S_i(1)) = \sum_{j=1}^M S_i(1, \omega_j)(1 + \frac{z_j}{2a}) Q(\omega_j)$$

$$= \mathbb{E}_Q(S_i(1)) + \frac{1}{2a} \sum_{j=1}^M z_j S_i(1, \omega_j) Q(\omega_j)$$

$$= S_i(0)(1 + R).$$

The final identity follows because $S_i(1)$ belongs to W (take $x_i = 1, x_k = 0$ for $k \neq i, y = 0$) so that, with $V = (v_j)_{j \leq M}$ where $v_j = S_i(1, \omega_j)$, the last term above is

$$\frac{1}{2a} \langle Z, V \rangle_Q = 0.$$

□

We can now apply the fundamental theorems to option pricing in complete models satisfying the No Arbitrage Principle. Suppose the replicating portfolio is $(\mathbf{x}, y) = (x_1, \dots, x_d, y)$

$$V_{(\mathbf{x},y)}(1) = H(1), \quad \text{so that} \quad H(0) = V_{(\mathbf{x},y)}(0)$$

since otherwise we have an arbitrage opportunity. The expectation with respect to the unique risk-neutral probability gives

$$\mathbb{E}_Q(V_{(\mathbf{x},y)}(1)) = \mathbb{E}_Q(\langle \mathbf{x}, \mathbf{S}(1) \rangle + y(1 + R))$$

$$= \sum_{i=1}^{d} x_i \mathbb{E}_Q(S_i(1)) + y(1 + R)$$

$$= (1 + R)\left(\sum_{i=1}^{d} x_i S_i(0) + y \right)$$

$$= (1 + R)V_{(\mathbf{x},y)}(0) = (1 + R)H(0)$$

where we have used the martingale property of all stock prices. Since we have replication we obtain

$$H(0) = \frac{1}{1 + R}\mathbb{E}_Q(H(1)).$$

Finally we note that the sub- and super-replicating prices coincide in complete models.

Theorem 2.40
Completeness implies $H^{\text{sub}} = H^{\text{super}} = H$, say.

Proof If $(\mathbf{x}, y) = (x_1, \dots, x_d, y)$ is a replicating portfolio, $V_{(\mathbf{x},y)}(1) = H(1)$ and $(\overline{\mathbf{x}}, \overline{y})$ is any super-replicating portfolio, $V_{(\overline{\mathbf{x}},\overline{y})}(1) \geq H(1)$, then

$$V_{(\overline{\mathbf{x}},\overline{y})}(1) \geq V_{(\mathbf{x},y)}(1).$$

The No Arbitrage Principle implies

$$V_{(\overline{\mathbf{x}},\overline{y})}(0) \geq V_{(\mathbf{x},y)}(0)$$

so taking the infimum over super-replicating portfolios we have

$$\inf_{(\overline{\mathbf{x}},\overline{y})}\{V_{(\overline{\mathbf{x}},\overline{y})}(0)\} \geq V_{(\mathbf{x},y)}(0).$$

But the replicating price belongs to the set of all super-replicating prices

$$V_{(\mathbf{x},y)}(0) \in \{V_{(\overline{\mathbf{x}},\overline{y})}(0) : (\overline{\mathbf{x}}, \overline{y}) \text{ super-replicating}\}$$

so the infimum is attained and

$$\inf_{(\bar{x},\bar{y})}\{V_{(\bar{x},\bar{y})}(0)\} = V_{(x,y)}(0).$$

The argument for sub-replicating portfolios is similar and leads to

$$V_{(x,y)}(0) = \sup_{(\underline{x},\underline{y})}\{V_{(\underline{x},\underline{y})}(0)\},$$

where the supremum is taken over all sub-replicating portfolios.   □

2.7   General properties of derivative prices

Forward contracts

The simplest example of a derivative is a **forward** contract. This contract is a binding agreement between two parties to buy or sell the underlying asset at a given future time for a specified delivery price K. Again, a party committed to buying the asset holds a **long** position, the seller holds a **short** position. The payoff at time 1 for the long position is

$$H_{\mathrm{lf}}(1) = S(1) - K$$

and brings profit if $S(1) > K$. For the short position the payoff is $H_{\mathrm{sf}}(1) = K - S(1)$.

In a complete arbitrage-free model the price of such a contract can be easily computed:

$$H_{\mathrm{lf}}(0) = \mathbb{E}_Q(\tilde{H}_{\mathrm{lf}}(1)) = \mathbb{E}_Q(\tilde{S}(1) - \tilde{K}) = S(0) - K(1+R)^{-1}.$$

However, this formula can be proved without referring to any model.

Proposition 2.41
The No Arbitrage Principle implies that the price of a long forward contract with delivery price K is $H_{\mathrm{lf}}(0) = S(0) - K(1+R)^{-1}$.

Proof   Suppose $H_{\mathrm{lf}}(0) < S(0) - K(1+R)^{-1}$. Take $z = 1$, $x = -1$ and y such that $V_{(x,y,z)}(0) = 0$, that is $y = \frac{S(0)-H_{\mathrm{lf}}(0)}{A(0)}$. The terminal value of the portfolio is a positive constant, $V_{(x,y,z)}(1) = -S(1) + [S(0) - H_{\mathrm{lf}}(0)](1+R) + [S(1) - K] > 0$, which contradicts the No Arbitrage Principle. The reverse inequality can be proved similarly.   □

If the value of the forward contract is zero, then the corresponding delivery price is called the **forward price**; it is denoted $F(0,1)$ and given

by
$$F(0, 1) = S(0)(1 + R).$$

Call-put parity

Comparing the payoffs of call, put and forward contract we observe that

$$C(1) - P(1) = H_{\text{lf}}(1)$$

since $(x - K)^+ - (K - x)^+ = x - K$. Dividing both sides by $1 + R$ and taking the expectation with respect to the risk-neutral probability (provided we have one at our disposal) we get the following relation.

Theorem 2.42 Call-put parity
If $C(0)$ and $P(0)$ denote (respectively) the call and put prices on a stock S with strike price K then

$$C(0) - P(0) = S(0) - K(1 + R)^{-1}.$$

With the experience we have gathered, it is no surprise that such a relationship can be proved independently of any model. We begin with a general fact.

Proposition 2.43
Suppose given any two derivative securities H, H'. Then $H(1) \geq H'(1)$ implies $H(0) \geq H'(0)$.

Proof If $H(0) < H'(0)$, buy H, sell H', the difference is the arbitrage profit (more precisely, take $x = 0$, $y = \frac{H'(0)-H(0)}{A(0)}$, $z_H = 1$, $z_{H'} = -1$ and see that this is an arbitrage). □

Corollary 2.44 Law of one price
If $H(1) = H'(1)$ then $H(0) = H'(0)$.

Now the call-put parity relation immediately follows from the relation between the payoffs.

Arbitrage bounds on option prices

We would like to discuss the dependence of option price on today's value of the underlying stock. This is quite a natural idea but it turns out to be a bit awkward. The point is that $S(0)$ is a known quantity, so we cannot play with it. To discuss the call price as a function of $S(0)$, denoted S in what follows, we must allow some scope for changing it.

A number of explanations, none rigorous, can be put forward, including:

- consider a parallel world where an identical company has a different value,
- allow jumps of stock prices so that at a certain time we may record two values,
- imagine a derivative representing aS and treat it as new underlying S',
- allow a time change so that the new price is the stock price after a short while. This is probably the most plausible story, but not allowed in our single-step set-up, where nothing happens in the interim.

Anyway, with these flimsy excuses we shall nevertheless consider the call price as a function of the current stock price using the notation $C(S)$.

Proposition 2.45
The function $C(S)$ satisfies

$$\max\{0, S - K(1 + R)^{-1}\} \le C(S) \le S.$$

Proof We use call-put parity: $C(S) - P(S) = S - K(1+R)^{-1}$, and $P(S) \ge 0$, so

$$C(S) \ge S - K(1 + R)^{-1}.$$

If $C(S) > S$ then we can sell the call and buy the stock. At exercise, the call payoff is less than $S(1)$. This proves the second bound. □

Exercise 2.29 Show that $S' < S$ implies $C(S) - C(S') \le S - S'$ and $P(S') - P(S) \le S - S'$.

Exercise 2.30 Prove that the call price $C(S)$ is a convex function of the stock price S: in particular, show that

$$C\left(\frac{S' + S''}{2}\right) \le \frac{C(S') + C(S'')}{2}.$$

Employing call-put parity, show that the same is true for the put.

Similar properties can be derived for the dependence of the call and put prices on the strike, K. They are easier to formulate since options with different strike prices are quoted on the exchanges. To emphasise the dependence of the call price on the strike we use the notation $C = C(K)$.

Proposition 2.46

The function $C(K)$ is decreasing, i.e., $K' \leq K$ implies $C(K') \geq C(K)$. The function $P(K)$ is increasing: $K' \leq K$ implies $P(K') \leq P(K)$.

Proof If $K' \leq K$ then $(S(1) - K')^+ \geq (S(1) - K)^+$, and also $(K' - S(1))^+ \leq (K - S(1))^+$. Inequalities of payoffs imply inequalities for prices as proved in Proposition 2.43 □

Exercise 2.31 Show that if $K' < K$ then

$$C(K') - C(K) \leq (1 + R)^{-1}(K - K'),$$
$$P(K) - P(K') \leq (1 + R)^{-1}(K - K').$$

Exercise 2.32 Show that the call price is a convex function of the strike price.

2.8 Proofs

Lemma 2.35

Suppose $A \subset \mathbb{R}^n$ is convex and compact, and W is a vector subspace of $\mathbb{R}^n$ disjoint from A. Then there exists $z \in \mathbb{R}^n$ such that $\langle z, a \rangle > 0$ for all $a \in A$, and $\langle z, w \rangle = 0$ for all $w \in W$, where $\langle x, y \rangle = \sum_{i=1}^{n} x_i y_i$ is the Euclidean inner product in $\mathbb{R}^n$.

Proof Consider the set

$$A - W = \{a - w : a \in A, w \in W\}.$$

Since A and W are disjoint, $0 \notin A - W$.

Next, we note that $A - W$ is convex since both A and W are. In more detail, if $x, y \in A - W$, $x = a - v$, $y = b - w$, then with $\alpha \in [0, 1]$, $\alpha x + (1 - \alpha)y = [\alpha a + (1 - \alpha)b] - [\alpha v + (1 - \alpha)w] \in A - W$. Thus $A - W$ is convex.

Consider the set $B = \{|x| : x \in A - W\}$. We will show that it is closed and to this end consider a convergent sequence $b_n \in B$, $b_n \to b$. Then there exists $x_n \in A - W$ such that $|x_n| = b_n$, and we can write $x_n = a_n - w_n$ for some $a_n \in A$, $w_n \in W$. The sequence a_n has a convergent subsequence $a_{n_k} \to a$, since A is compact. The sequence w_{n_k} is bounded since otherwise $|a_{n_k} - w_{n_k}| = b_{n_k}$ would go to infinity. So selecting a further subsequence

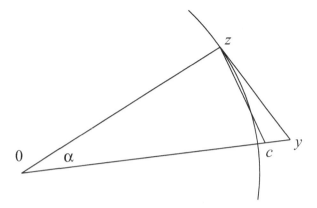

Figure 2.2

gives a convergent sequence $w_{n_{k_m}} \to w$. Now by continuity of $x \mapsto |x|$, we have $|a - w| = b$ so $b \in B$. (An alternative is to consider the intersection of $A - W$ with a closed ball with centre at the origin, large enough for this intersection to be non-empty. The intersection is compact, so its image under the continuous mapping $x \mapsto |x|$ is closed.)

Take z to be the element of $A - W$ closest to 0, so that for any other element c of $A - W$ we have $|c| \geq |z| > 0$ (recall that $0 \notin A - W$). The existence of z follows from the fact that the set $B = \{|x| : x \in A - W\}$ is closed, does not contain 0, and so has the smallest positive element, which is the Euclidean norm of some element of $A - W$.

Consider the triangle (in R^n) with vertices $0, z, c$. We shall prove that $\langle z, c \rangle \geq \langle z, z \rangle = |z|^2 > 0$. The idea is best explained by a figure. We have

$$\langle z, c \rangle = |z|\,|c|\cos\alpha = |z|\,|c|\frac{|z|}{|y|} = |z|^2\frac{|c|}{|y|}$$

so it is sufficient to show that $|c| \geq |y|$. Suppose, $|c| < |y|$ (see Figure 2.2). The line segment joining c and z is contained in the convex set $A - W$. But the line intersects the interior of a ball with the centre at 0 and radius $|z|$. So this segment contains a point with distance to 0 strictly smaller than $|z|$ – a contradiction with the definition of z.

This gives $\langle z, a - w \rangle = \langle z, a \rangle - \langle z, w \rangle \geq \langle z, z \rangle$ for each $w \in W$. However, W is a vector space, so $nw \in W$ for each n, which makes the inequality impossible unless $\langle z, w \rangle = 0$. This in turn yields $\langle z, a \rangle \geq \langle z, z \rangle > 0$ so both claims are proved.   □

Lemma 2.39

Suppose $A \subset \mathbb{R}^n$ is convex and compact, and W is a vector subspace of $\mathbb{R}^n$ disjoint from A. Then there exists $z' \in \mathbb{R}^n$ such that $\langle z', a \rangle_Q > 0$ for all $a \in A$, and $\langle z', w \rangle_Q = 0$ for all $w \in W$, where

$$\langle x, y \rangle_Q = \sum_{i=1} x_i y_i q_i,$$

$q_i > 0$, is an inner product in $\mathbb{R}^n$.

Proof By Lemma 2.35 we have $z \in \mathbb{R}^n$ with $\sum_{i=1}^{n} z_i a_i > 0$, $\sum_{i=1}^{n} z_i w_i = 0$ for $a = (a_1, \ldots, a_n) \in A$, $w = (w_1, \ldots, w_n) \in W$. Take $z_i' = z_i / q_i$ which satisfies the claims since $\sum_{i=1} z_i' y_i q_i = \sum_{i=1} z_i y_i$ for any y_i. $\square$

3

Multi-step binomial model

Having described single-step pricing models rather fully, we are ready to consider models with a finite number of consecutive trading dates. We shall see that these models behave essentially as a succession of one-step models, so that our earlier analysis can be applied repeatedly to yield explicit pricing formulae.

For a simple binomial model we now describe how the use of risk-neutral probabilities implies the martingale property of discounted stock prices and thus of the discounted value process of any self-financing strategy. In this model pricing techniques for European options using replicating portfolios or risk-neutral probabilities are compared and an explicit pricing formula for the European call is then derived.

3.1 Two-step example

Most of the essential features of a general multi-step model can be seen in a simple example with two time steps, where we avoid cumbersome notation related to a general case. Here we take time to be 0, T, $2T$, and we simplify the notation by just specifying the number of a step, ignoring its length. We wish to build a model of stock prices with three ingredients

$S(0)$, $S(1)$, $S(2)$, where $S(0)$ is a given number and the remaining quantities are random variables. The construction consists of two repetitions of the single-step dynamics. In the single-step case the core of the construction was the model of the rate of return with two possible values, which can be thought of as related to a single toss of a coin. Intuitively, for many steps we can use more coins, or toss one coin repeatedly. We write the results obtained in a two-step experiment as a pair built of symbols u and d. This gives the appropriate sample space as

$$\Omega = \{uu, ud, du, dd\}.$$

The probability on Ω will be defined by multiplying probabilities for single coin tosses. Denoting the probability of an up movement in each single step by p we have

$$P(uu) = p^2,$$
$$P(ud) = P(du) = p(1 - p),$$
$$P(dd) = (1 - p)^2,$$

using the simplified notation $P(\omega)$ rather than $P(\{\omega\})$. Given the probabilities of single-element sets we can find a probability of any subset of Ω by the additivity principle:

$$P(A) = \sum_{\omega \in A} P(\omega).$$

Next we define the returns K_1, K_2 as random variables on Ω defined for $n = 1, 2$ by

$$K_n = \begin{cases} U & \text{with probability } p, \\ D & \text{with probability } 1 - p. \end{cases}$$

The value of K_n is assumed to depend only on the nth element of ω and it acts in the same way as in the single-step binomial model, with K_1 determined by the first step, K_2 by the second. So

$$K_1(uu) = K_1(ud) = U,$$
$$K_1(du) = K_1(dd) = D,$$
$$K_2(uu) = K_2(du) = U,$$
$$K_2(ud) = K_2(dd) = D.$$

Observe that for all real numbers x_1, x_2 we have

$$P(K_1 = x_1 \text{ and } K_2 = x_2) = P(K_1 = x_1) \times P(K_2 = x_2)$$

written more formally as

$$P(\{\omega : K_1(\omega) = x_1\} \cap \{\omega : K_2(\omega) = x_2\})$$
$$= P(\{\omega : K_1(\omega) = x_1\}) \times P(\{\omega : K_2(\omega) = x_2\}) \quad (3.1)$$

and we say that K_1, K_2 are **independent**.

The stock prices are defined step by step

$$S(1) = S(0)(1 + K_1),$$
$$S(2) = S(1)(1 + K_2) = S(0)(1 + K_1)(1 + K_2).$$

We introduce a convenient self-explanatory notation where a superscript determines both the number of steps and the position on the tree:

$$S(1) = \begin{cases} S^u = S(0)(1 + U), \\ S^d = S(0)(1 + D), \end{cases}$$

$$S(2) = \begin{cases} S^{uu} = S(0)(1 + U)^2, \\ S^{ud} = S^{du} = S(0)(1 + U)(1 + D), \\ S^{dd} = S(0)(1 + D)^2. \end{cases}$$

Example 3.1
Let $U = 20\%$, $D = -10\%$, $p = 0.6$ and then we have a concrete **recombining** (i.e. $S^{ud} = S^{du}$) tree of prices:

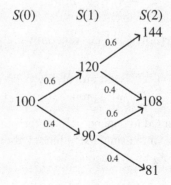

The market is completed by assuming a risk-free asset, represented by the money market account, and determined by $A(0) = 100$, and riskless return $R = 5\%$. We have

$$A(n) = A(0)(1 + R)^n, \quad n = 1, 2,$$

by a straightforward extension of the familiar single-step scheme.

Trading strategies

In the above example, suppose we have at our disposal the sum of 50 and wish to invest in the market buying one share of stock. For the first portfolio the stock and risk-free positions will be denoted $x(1)$ and $y(1)$ respectively. This is slightly surprising since one would expect to indicate time by 0 here, as this is the moment we are designing this portfolio; however, this is an established notational tradition justified by the fact that we will hold this portfolio until the next step, upon which we focus our attention.

Taking $x(1) = 1$, with $V(0) = 50$, we have a short risk-free position

$$y(1) = \frac{V(0) - x(1)S(0)}{A(0)} = \frac{50 - 1 \times 100}{100} = -0.5.$$

At time 1 we consider the two possible outcomes of the first step:

Case 1: 'up'

The value of our portfolio is now

$$V^u = x(1)S^u + y(1)A(0)(1 + R) = 67.5.$$

The next portfolio is denoted $(x^u(2), y^u(2))$ and we decide to decrease our stock position to 0.8 which determines the risk-free component since we assume no inflow or outflow of funds, so

$$67.5 = 0.8 \times 120 + y^u(2) \times 105$$

to give $y^u(2) = -0.285$. We can find the final values of our investment

$$V^{uu} = 0.8S^{uu} + (-0.285)A(0)(1 + R)^2 = 85.275,$$
$$V^{ud} = 0.8S^{ud} + (-0.285)A(0)(1 + R)^2 = 56.475.$$

Case 2: 'down'

It is the stock that determines the value:

$$V^d = x(1)S^d + y(1)A(0)(1 + R) = 37.5.$$

With cheap stock we decide to buy more so we set $x^d(2) = 1.2$. This implies

$$37.5 = 0.8 \times 90 + y^d(2) \times 105$$

with $y^d(2) = -0.671$. The final values are

$$V^{du} = 1.2 \times S^{du} + (-0.671) \times A(0)(1 + R)^2 = 55.575,$$
$$V^{dd} = 1.2 \times S^{dd} + (-0.671) \times A(0)(1 + R)^2 = 23.175.$$

Note that the tree of portfolio values is not recombining: $V^{ud} \neq V^{du}$. In general, the value of a strategy is a process given by

$$V_{(x,y)}(0) = x(1)S(0) + y(1)A(0),$$
$$V_{(x,y)}(1) = x(1)S(1) + y(1)A(1),$$
$$V_{(x,y)}(2) = x(2)S(2) + y(2)A(2),$$

with the self-financing condition

$$V_{(x,y)}(1) = x(2)S(1) + y(2)A(1)$$

representing the fact that at the rebalancing moment $n = 1$ when $(x(2), y(2))$ are selected, we only use the funds available then, and we use them all.

Pricing

As in the single-step model the basis for pricing is the No Arbitrage Principle which takes the following form:

Assumption 3.2

There is no arbitrage on the underlying market, where an arbitrage is a strategy $(x(n), y(n))$, $n = 1, 2$, with $V(0) = 0$, non-negative future values $V_{(x,y)}(n) \geq 0$, $n = 1, 2$, with strict inequality for at least one time instant and one $\omega \in \Omega$.

A derivative security of European type has payoff of the form $H = h(S(2))$ for some real-valued function h defined on $[0, \infty)$. Such a security is called **path-independent**; the **path-dependent** version has payoff $H = h(S(1), S(2))$ for some $h: [0, \infty) \times [0, \infty) \to \mathbb{R}$. As for the single-step model, we now formulate the version of the No Arbitrage Principle for the extended market, which allows us to determine the prices of such a security:

Assumption 3.3

The no-arbitrage prices of a security with payoff H form a sequence $H(n)$, $n = 0, 1, 2$, such that $H(2) = H$ and there is no abitrage in the extended market. Thus we assume that there is no strategy $(x(n), y(n), z(n))$, $n = 1, 2$, with

$$V_{(x,y,z)}(0) = x(1)S(0) + y(1)A(0) + z(1)H(0) = 0,$$

$$V_{(x,y,z)}(n) = x(n)S(n) + y(n)A(n) + z(n)H(n) \geq 0,$$

with strict inequality for at least one n and one ω.

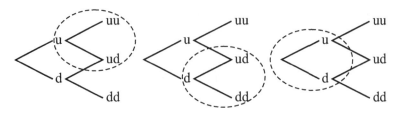

Figure 3.1

Example 3.4

Let $S(0) = 100$, $U = 20\%$, $D = -10\%$, $R = 5\%$. Consider a call with exercise price $K = 100$ at time 2. The payoff of the option is

$$C(2) = \begin{cases} (S(0)(1+U)^2 - K)^+ = 44 & \text{if } \omega = uu, \\ (S(0)(1+U)(1+D) - K)^+ = 8 & \text{if } \omega = ud \text{ or } \omega = du, \\ (S(0)(1+D)^2 - K)^+ = 0 & \text{if } \omega = dd. \end{cases}$$

We move backwards in time and so we compute the prices $C(1)$ in both cases first, and finally $C(0)$, following the scheme depicted in Figure 3.1.

For $C(1)$ in the 'up' case we have the system

$$V^{uu} = x^u(2)S^{uu} + y^u(2)A(0)(1+R)^2 = 44,$$
$$V^{ud} = x^u(2)S^{ud} + y^u(2)A(0)(1+R)^2 = 8,$$

with solution

$$x^u(2) = 1,$$
$$y^u(2) = -0.907,$$

and in the 'down' case we solve

$$V^{du} = x^d(2)S^{du} + y^d(2)A(0)(1+R)^2 = 8,$$
$$V^{dd} = x^d(2)S^{dd} + y^d(2)A(0)(1+R)^2 = 0,$$

to find

$$x^u(2) = 0.296,$$
$$y^u(2) = -0.218.$$

We can now build the random variable $C(1)$ by writing

$$C^u = x^u(2)S^u + y^u(2)A(0)(1+R) = 24.762,$$
$$C^d = x^d(2)S^d + y^d(2)A(0)(1+R) = 3.810,$$

and by replication

$$V^u = x(1)S^u + y(1)A(0)(1 + R) = 24.762,$$
$$V^d = x(1)S^d + y(1)A(0)(1 + R) = 3.810,$$

we find

$$x(1) = 0.698,$$
$$y(1) = -0.562,$$

resulting in

$$C(0) = x(1)S(0) + y(1)A(0) = 13.605.$$

It remains to check that the procedure agrees with the No Arbitrage Principle but this just requires a moment of reflection. Suppose that $C(0) <$ 13.605 (bearing in mind the rounding error), in which case we buy the option and sell the strategy investing the difference risk free. Replication at the exercise time ensures that the value of the strategy will cancel with the option payoff and a profit will remain. For the opposite inequality we take the opposite action. If the option price and replicating strategy differ at time 1 at some node, u or d, we do nothing at time 0 and perform the above actions at time 1 instead.

Note that the values of the strategy constructed above form a recombining tree, but this does not have to be the case if the payoffs of the derivative security for ud and du are different.

Exercise 3.1   Find the tree of the values of the derivatives with the following payoffs: $H_1 = (\max\{S(n) : n = 0, 1, 2\} - 100)^+$, $H_2 = \left(\frac{S(0)+S(1)+S(3)}{3} - 100\right)^+$. (Note that these are path-dependent derivatives.)

Recall that in the single-step model a convenient alternative was to use risk-neutral probabilities to compute the price of a derivative security. This can be easily done numerically at each step of the above procedure, but our goal is to give the story extra flavour by developing some theory which can be generalised to more general settings.

3.2 Partitions and information

For our next topic it is better to extend the time scale to three steps. This gives the appropriate sample space as

$$\Omega = \{uuu, uud, udu, udd, duu, dud, ddu, ddd\}.$$

The probability will be defined as before, so

$$P(uuu) = p^3,$$
$$P(uud) = P(udu) = P(duu) = p^2(1 - p),$$
$$P(udd) = P(dud) = P(ddu) = p(1 - p)^2,$$
$$P(ddd) = (1 - p)^3.$$

We have to modify the definition of K_1, K_2 and add the third return K_3 with value U for triples ending with u and D otherwise, so that K_n depends only on the nth element of ω, just as in the single-step binomial model. However, the notion of independence is now somewhat more involved, as clarified by the following exercise.

Exercise 3.2 Prove that K_1, K_2, K_3 are independent, which by definition means that for each pair we have condition (3.1) and also

$$P\left(\bigcap_{k=1}^{3}\{\omega : K_i = x_i\}\right) = \prod_{k=1}^{3} P(\{\omega : K_i = x_i\}).$$

The third stock price takes the form

$$S(3) = S(2)(1 + K_3) = \begin{cases} S^{uuu} = S(0)(1 + U)^3, \\ S^{uud} = S^{udu} = S^{duu} = S(0)(1 + U)^2(1 + D), \\ S^{ddu} = S^{dud} = S^{udd} = S(0)(1 + U)(1 + D)^2, \\ S^{ddd} = S(0)(1 + D)^3. \end{cases}$$

Within the numerical scheme of the previous section we have the complete picture

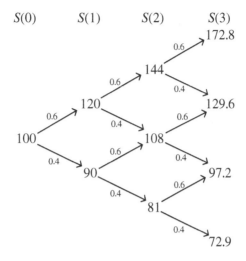

Consider the following random variable

$$H = (S(3) - 100)^+$$

which is nothing but a call payoff with strike $K = 100$.

If we own such a security we might be interested in the expected payoff so we compute

$$\mathbb{E}(H) = 72.8 \times P(\{uuu\}) + 29.6 \times P(\{uud, udu, duu\})$$
$$+ 0 \times P(\{udd, dud, ddu\}) + 0 \times P(\{ddd\})$$
$$= 28.512.$$

Exercise 3.3   Extend the pricing scheme of the previous section to find the option price and observe that it is not equal to the expectation computed above.

Next we analyse the future possible developments and their impact on our views. It is important to emphasise that we are now performing a 'what if' analysis. We do not travel in time but consider hypothetically all possible future turns of events with the purpose of revising our point of view and possibly responding with some appropriate action.

Position at step 1

Case 'up'

Let us prepare ourselves for the case of an increase in the stock price after one step. This means that the collection of all scenarios available

will be reduced to the triples beginning with u, which we denote by $B_u = \{uuu, uud, udu, udd\}$. Knowledge that the first step is 'up' means that this set will play the role of Ω and a probability is produced by adjusting the original probabilities to ensure that the new probability of B_u is 1. For $\omega \in B_u$ we put

$$P_u(\omega) = \frac{P(\omega)}{P(B_u)}.$$

Observe that u is the first element of each $\omega \in B_u$ and according to the definition of P, we have $P(B_u) = p$ and this is the first factor producing $P(\omega)$, so it will cancel. For instance

$$P_u(udu) = \frac{P(udu)}{P(B_u)} = \frac{p(1-p)p}{p} = (1-p)p.$$

Of course $P_u(B_u) = \frac{1}{P(B_u)} \sum_{\omega \in B_u} P(\omega) = 1$. Observe that for $A \subseteq B_u$,

$$P_u(A) = \frac{P(A \cap B_u)}{P(B_u)} = P(A|B_u)$$

so P_u is what is called, quite generally, the **conditional probability** $P(\cdot|B_u)$, considered for subsets of B_u.

Next we compute the expectation of H in this new probability space. We consider values of H corresponding to all four elements of B_u, and use a natural version of the, by now familiar, formula for the expectation:

$$\sum_{\omega \in B_u} H(\omega)P_u(\omega) = 72.8 \times 0.6^2 + 29.6 \times 2 \times 0.6 \times 0.4 + 0 \times 0.4^2 = 40.416$$

which would be good news for the option holder.

We introduce the following two alternative notations for this (conditional) expectation:

$$\mathbb{E}(H|B_u) = \mathbb{E}(H|S(1) = 120) = 40.416.$$

Case 'down'

In the case of a down move at the first step we introduce, similarly, the set B_d of all still remaining scenarios (all those beginning with a d) and the adjusted probabilities for $\omega \in B_d$:

$$P_d(\omega) = \frac{P(\omega)}{P(B_d)}.$$

Clearly, the expectation of H in this situation is

$$\mathbb{E}(H|B_d) = \mathbb{E}(H|S(1) = 90) = 29.6 \times p^2 = 10.656,$$

a bit disappointing for anyone who owns such a security

The two cases considered decompose all scenarios into two groups. Mathematically, we have a so-called partition of Ω, meaning that $\Omega = B_u \cup B_d$, and the components are disjoint, which motivates the following general definition.

Definition 3.5
A family $\mathcal{P} = \{B_i\}$ of subsets of Ω is a **partition** of Ω if $B_i \cap B_j = \emptyset$ for $i \neq j$ and $\Omega = \bigcup B_i$.

The partition defined at the first step will be denoted

$$\mathcal{P}_1 = \{B_u, B_d\}.$$

We put together these two cases defining a random variable with two competing notations, equivalent since the partition $\mathcal{P}_1$ is fully determined by $S(1)$,

$$\mathbb{E}(H|\mathcal{P}_1)(\omega) = \mathbb{E}(H|S(1))(\omega) = \begin{cases} 40.416 \text{ if } \omega \in B_u, \\ 10.656 \text{ if } \omega \in B_d. \end{cases}$$

Position at step 2
Consider all possible price movements in the first two steps. There are four cases, which can be described by specifying a partition

$$\mathcal{P}_2 = \{B_{uu}, B_{ud}, B_{du}, B_{dd}\}$$

of Ω into four disjoint sets of paths:

$$B_{uu} = \{uuu, uud\},$$
$$B_{ud} = \{udu, udd\},$$
$$B_{du} = \{duu, dud\},$$
$$B_{dd} = \{ddu, ddd\}.$$

Each of these is equipped with probabilities defined as before. Observe the effect of the cancellation mentioned above and notice for example that $P(B_{ud}) = p(1 - p)$ so $P_{ud}(udu) = p$, $P_{ud}(udd) = 1 - p$ and in each case we have a well-known single-step binomial tree.

As before, we compute the expected value of H in each case. Clearly

$$\mathbb{E}(H|B_{uu}) = 55.52,$$
$$\mathbb{E}(H|B_{ud}) = 17.76,$$
$$\mathbb{E}(H|B_{du}) = 17.76,$$
$$\mathbb{E}(H|B_{dd}) = 0,$$

hence

$$\mathbb{E}(H|\mathcal{P}_2)(\omega) = \begin{cases} 55.52 \text{ if } \omega \in B_{uu}, \\ 17.76 \text{ if } \omega \in B_{ud} \cup B_{du}, \\ 0 \text{ if } \omega \in B_{dd}. \end{cases}$$

Remark 3.6

We can see that for the middle prices we get the same value on each of the two corresponding sets and so we could employ the alternative, more intuitive notation $\mathbb{E}(H|S(2))$. To this end, note that the partition generated by the values of $S(2)$ is different from the partition related to the history of the movements over the first two steps, introduced above. The partition generated by $S(2)$ consists of just three elements: B_{uu}, $B_{ud} \cup B_{du}$, B_{dd}, and the random variable $\mathbb{E}(H|S(2))$ takes three values. The fact that the values $\mathbb{E}(H|B_{ud})$, $\mathbb{E}(H|B_{du})$ coincide gives the equivalence of these two approaches in this instance, but this does not have to be the case in general.

The actual values of $S(2)$ are irrelevant for defining the conditional expectation since they do not appear in the computations. What matters is the partition related to these values, which just play the discerning or differentiating role.

Position at step 3

Given the knowledge of all three steps we will know the actual payoff. The above analysis can formally be performed for the partition

$$\mathcal{P}_3 = \{B_{uuu}, \ldots, B_{ddd}\}$$

of Ω into single-element parts with no randomness and obvious conclusion that

$$\mathbb{E}(H|\mathcal{P}_3) = H.$$

We are in a position to give a general definition.

Definition 3.7

For any random variable X and any event B such that $P(B) \neq 0$ the **conditional expectation** of X given B is defined by

$$\mathbb{E}(X|B) = \sum_{\omega \in \Omega} X(\omega)P(\omega|B)$$

where $P(\omega|B) = \frac{1}{P(B)}P(\omega)$ for $\omega \in B$ and $P(\omega|B) = 0$ otherwise. Given a partition $\mathcal{P} = \{B_i\}$, the above definition applied to each B_i gives a function defined for each ω in Ω, constant on each B_i,

$$\mathbb{E}(X|\mathcal{P}): \Omega \rightarrow \mathbb{R}$$

by assigning

$$B_i \ni \omega \to \mathbb{E}(X|B_i).$$

This random variable is called the **conditional expectation** of X with respect to the partition $\{B_i\}$.

   Properties of $\mathbb{E}(X|\mathcal{P})$ are discussed in a general setting in the next chapter. Here we continue the analysis of binomial trees.

3.3 Martingale properties

In the single-step model, a martingale was simply a process with constant expectation. With many steps this notion is more sophisticated and we begin with an example.

Discounted stock prices

We work with the three-steps case as in the previous section, and introduce **discounted stock prices** writing

$$\widetilde{S}(n) = S(n)(1 + R)^{-n}.$$

Recall that in the single-step model we changed the probability to $q = \frac{R-D}{U-D}$ and obtained, for the probability $Q = \{q, 1 - q\}$ defined on $\{u, d\}$, that

$$\mathbb{E}_Q(\tilde{S}(1)) = q\frac{S^u}{1 + R} + (1 - q)\frac{S^d}{1 + R} = S(0).$$

In the three-step model the probability Q is defined on subsets of $\Omega = \{u, d\}^3$ in the same way as P was defined by means of p. For example, $Q(udu) = q^2(1 - q)$ and then $Q(\{\omega : S(1)(\omega) = S^u\}) = Q(B_u) = q$. Taking a trivial partition $\mathcal{P}_0 = \{\Omega\}$ and noting that conditional expectation with respect to $\mathcal{P}_0$ coincides with the expectation we have

$$\mathbb{E}_Q(X|\mathcal{P}_0) = \mathbb{E}_Q(X|\Omega) = \frac{1}{P(\Omega)}(qX^u + (1 - q)X^d) = \mathbb{E}_Q(X)$$

for any random variable, we can write the above relation in a fancy way

$$\mathbb{E}_Q(\tilde{S}(1)|\mathcal{P}_0) = S(0).$$

Next, we compute $\mathbb{E}_Q(\tilde{S}(2)|\mathcal{P}_1)$ which requires finding $\mathbb{E}_Q(\tilde{S}(2)|B_u)$ and $\mathbb{E}_Q(\tilde{S}(2)|B_d)$. Now

$$\mathbb{E}_Q(\tilde{S}(2)|B_u) = \frac{1}{Q(B_u)} \frac{1}{(1+R)^2} (q^2 S^{uu} + q(1-q)S^{ud})$$

$$= \frac{1}{(1+R)^2} (qS^u(1+U) + (1-q)S^u(1+D)) \text{ (since } Q(B_u) = q)$$

$$= \frac{1}{(1+R)^2} S^u(1+R) \text{ (since } qU + (1-q)D = R)$$

$$= \frac{1}{1+R} S^u,$$

and similarly

$$\mathbb{E}_Q(\tilde{S}(2)|B_d) = \frac{1}{1+R} S^d.$$

Putting these together we have

$$\mathbb{E}_Q(\tilde{S}(2)|\mathcal{P}_1) = \tilde{S}(1).$$

The final step is to find $\mathbb{E}_Q(\tilde{S}(3)|\mathcal{P}_2)$; we just consider one of the four cases in detail

$$\mathbb{E}_Q(\tilde{S}(3)|B_{uu}) = \frac{1}{Q(B_{uu})} \frac{1}{(1+R)^3} (q^3 S^{uuu} + q^2(1-q)S^{uud})$$

$$= \frac{1}{(1+R)^3} (qS^{uu}(1+U) + (1-q)S^{uu}(1+D))$$

$$\text{(since } Q(B_{uu}) = q^2)$$

$$= \frac{1}{(1+R)^3} S^{uu}(1+R) \text{ (since } qU + (1-q)D = R)$$

$$= \frac{1}{(1+R)^2} S^{uu},$$

with the conclusion

$$\mathbb{E}_Q(\tilde{S}(3)|\mathcal{P}_2) = \tilde{S}(3).$$

We are ready for a general definition.

Definition 3.8
A sequence $(M(n))_{n \leq N}$ of random variables defined on Ω is a **martingale** for the filtration $(\mathcal{P}_n)_{n \leq N}$ and probability P if

$$\mathbb{E}_P(M(n)|\mathcal{P}_{n-1}) = M(n-1).$$

So the discounted stock prices follow a martingale with respect to Q for $n = 0, 1, 2, 3$ and later we will see that of course this is true for any number of steps.

Exercise 3.4   Illustrate the martingale property of stock prices under the risk-neutral probability by numerical computations.

Strategies and pricing

Suppose that we invest $V(0)$, choosing the stock positions $x(n)$, $n = 1, 2, 3$ with $x(1)$ decided at time 0, so constant, $x(2)$ decided at time 1, thus being a random variable with two values $x^u(2)$, $x^d(2)$, and $x(3)$ decided at time 2 on the basis of the information provided by the stock prices. The risk-free position is chosen according to the self-financing principle

$$y(1) = \frac{V(0) - x(1)S(0)}{A(0)},$$

$$y(2) = \frac{V_{(x,y)}(1) - x(2)S(1)}{A(1)},$$

$$y(3) = \frac{V_{(x,y)}(2) - x(3)S(2)}{A(2)},$$

where we should remember that the last two lines represent equalities between random variables.

We will show that the discounted strategy values have the martingale property. First

$$\mathbb{E}_Q(\tilde{V}_{(x,y)}(1)|\mathcal{P}_0) = \frac{1}{1+R}\Big(q\,[x(1)S^u + y(1)A(1)]$$
$$+ (1-q)\big[x(1)S^d + y(1)A(1)\big]\Big)$$
$$= \frac{1}{1+R}x(1)[qS(0)(1+U) + (1-q)S(0)(1+D)]$$
$$+ y(1)A(0)$$
$$= x(1)S(0) + y(1)A(0)$$
$$= V(0).$$

Next, to find $\mathbb{E}_Q(\tilde{V}_{(x,y)}(2)|\mathcal{P}_1)$ we compute

$$\mathbb{E}_Q(\tilde{V}_{(x,y)}(2)|B_u) = \frac{1}{(1+R)^2} \frac{1}{P(B_u)} \big(q^2\left[x^u(2)S^{uu} + y^u(2)A(2)\right]$$

$$+ q(1-q)[x^u(2)S^{ud} + y^u(2)A(2)]\big)(\text{since } P(B_u) = q)$$

$$= \frac{1}{(1+R)^2}x^u(2)[qS^{uu} + (1-q)S^{ud}] + \frac{1}{1+R}y^u(2)A(1)$$

$$= \frac{1}{(1+R)^2}x^u(2)S^u(1+R) + \frac{1}{1+R}y^u(2)A(1)$$

$$= \frac{1}{1+R}(x^u(2)S^u + y^u(2)A(1))$$

$$= \tilde{V}^u(1)$$

having inserted $y(2)$. In addition to the single-step martingale property, the key points here are that $x^u(2)$ is constant on B_u, with the same value in each of the two cases, and the self-financing property, as captured by the form of the risk-free component.

Clearly, similar analyses can be performed for B_d and in all cases at time 2 and so, for $n = 0, 1, 2$ we have shown that

$$\mathbb{E}_Q(\tilde{V}_{(x,y)}(n+1)|\mathcal{P}_n) = \tilde{V}_{(x,y)}(n).$$

As an immediate consequence we have the martingale property of the process of option prices since they are values of the replicating strategy.

Exercise 3.5 Take $N = 3$ and let $S(0) = 100$, $U = 20\%$, $D = -10\%$, $R = 5\%$. Consider a call with exercise price $K = 100$ at time 3 and find the process $C(n)$.

Exercise 3.6 Consider the filtration generated by the sequence $C(n)$, $n = 0, 1, 2$. Find the parameters so that it is identical to the filtration generated by the stock prices. Can we have a constant filtration $\mathcal{P}_0 = \mathcal{P}_1 = \mathcal{P}_2$?

The final property of the discounted value process we shall need is that for $n = 0, 1, 2, 3$,

$$\mathbb{E}_Q(\tilde{V}_{(x,y)}(n)) = V(0).$$

This will imply, in particular, that

$$C(0) = \frac{1}{(1+R)^3} \mathbb{E}_Q((S(3) - K)^+).$$

We already have this result for $n = 1$, and we only analyse the case $n = 2$ to see the general pattern, leaving the rest to the reader:

$$\mathbb{E}_Q(\tilde{V}_{(x,y)}(2)) = \frac{1}{(1+R)^2}[q^2V^{uu} + q(1-q)V^{ud} + (1-q)qV^{du} + (1-q)^2V^{dd}]$$

$$= \frac{1}{(1+R)^2}[q(qV^{uu} + (1-q)V^{ud}) + (1-q)(qV^{du} + (1-q)V^{dd})]$$

and here

$$qV^{uu} + (1-q)V^{ud} = qx^u(2)S^{uu} + qy^u(2)A(2) + (1-q)x^u(2)S^{ud}$$
$$+ (1-q)y^u(2)A(2)$$
$$= x^u(2)[qS^{uu} + (1-q)S^{ud}] + y^u(2)A(2)$$
$$= x^u(2)S^u(1+R) + y^u(2)A(1)(1+R)$$
$$= V^u(1+R) \text{ (by the self-financing property)},$$
$$qV^{du} + (1-q)V^{dd} = V^d(1+R) \text{ (similarly)}$$

so that

$$\mathbb{E}_Q(\tilde{V}_{(x,y)}(2)) = \frac{1}{1+R}[qV^u + (1-q)V^d]$$
$$= \mathbb{E}_Q(\tilde{V}_{(x,y)}(1))$$
$$= V(0).$$

3.4   The Cox–Ross–Rubinstein model

We generalise the above analysis by extending the scheme to N steps. We assume that trading occurs at finitely many specified dates. Denote the time interval between trading dates by h, so that trading occurs at times $t = nh$, $n = 1, 2, \ldots, N$.

We introduce the sample space for the N-step model exactly as was done for $n = 2, 3$. Namely, we set $\Omega = \{u, d\}^N$, and, in keeping with the above cases, for ω in Ω the probability will take the form

$$P(\omega) = p^k(1-p)^{N-k}.$$

Each ω in Ω (called a **path**) is a sequence of length N consisting of u's and d's. All paths ω with k occurrences of u have the above probability, and the probability of this set of paths is $\binom{N}{k}p^k(1-p)^{N-k}$.

For $n \leq N$ the binomial splittings induce a partition of Ω into 2^n disjoint sets: $\mathcal{P}_n = \{B_{\mathrm{uu...u}}, ..., B_{\mathrm{dd...d}}\}$, where each set in the partition has an n-tuple subscript consisting of u's and d's, so that in each set all paths ω have their first n entries in common. We see (as is obvious in the earlier examples) that for $n \leq N$, each set in the partition $\mathcal{P}_n$ is a (disjoint) union of two sets in $\mathcal{P}_{n+1}$ – just as for $N = 3$, $B_{\mathrm{u}} = B_{\mathrm{uu}} \cup B_{\mathrm{ud}}$. More generally, we say that a sequence of partitions $(\mathcal{P}_n)_{n\leq N}$ is **refining** if, for each $n \leq N$, $\mathcal{P}_n$ is a finite union of sets in $\mathcal{P}_{n+1}$.

Fix two numbers $-1 < D < U$ to represent the random returns in each step defined by

$$K_n = \begin{cases} U \text{ with probability } p, \\ D \text{ with probability } 1-p. \end{cases}$$

Again, K_n acts only on the nth entry of the sequence defining the path ω. We note that these returns are independent, in the sense described in the next remark.

Remark 3.9

The random variables $\{K_n : n = 1, 2, \ldots, N\}$ defined on $\Omega = \{\mathrm{u}, \mathrm{d}\}^N$ are **independent**. By this we mean that for any subset $\{i_1, \ldots, i_k\}$ of indices from $\{1, \ldots, N\}$ and any real $x_1, \ldots, x_k$, we have

$$P\left(\bigcap_{j=1}^{k}\{K_{i_j} = x_j\}\right) = \prod_{j=1}^{k} P(K_{i_j} = x_j).$$

This is again easy to see from the definition of the K_n (see also Exercise 3.2).

Assume that $S(0)$ is given, while

$$S(n) = S(n-1)(1 + K_n).$$

which means that the stock prices follow a **recombining binomial tree**.

In addition to holding stock we can invest in a money market account, which we take as a security manufactured by a series of single risk-free deposits, with return R per period, assumed constant throughout. So we have a sequence of numbers, known in advance, with $A(0)$ given (we will frequently take $A(0) = 1$ for simplicity), and

$$A(n) = A(n-1)(1 + R)$$

for $n = 1, \ldots, N$. To avoid arbitrage we assume that $D < R < U$, as we did in the single-step case.

The key property observed for a three-step model can be easily extended.

Theorem 3.10

The sequence of discounted stock prices in the binomial model is a martingale with respect to the filtration $\mathcal{P}_n$ and probability Q.

Proof The key argument, repeated in each case above, is concerned with examining the two next step prices at each node and computing their expectation exactly as for a single step. This can be summarised in the following way: for $B \in \mathcal{P}_n$ at $n = 0, 1, 2, \ldots, N - 1$,

$$Q(S(n + 1) = S(n)(1 + U)|B) = q,$$
$$Q(S(n + 1) = S(n)(1 + D)|B) = 1 - q,$$

and since $q = \frac{R-D}{U-D}$, and hence $1 - q = \frac{U-R}{U-D}$ we obtain

$$\mathbb{E}_Q(S(n + 1)|\mathcal{P}_n) = S(n)(1 + U)\frac{R - D}{U - D} + S(n)(1 + D)\frac{U - R}{U - D}$$
$$= S(n)(1 + R)$$

which gives the result upon discounting. $\qquad\qquad\square$

The above observations lead us to the following theorem

Theorem 3.11

In the binomial model the discounted prices of a derivative security with given payoff $H(N)$ are given, under the martingale probability, by the recursive relations

$$\tilde{H}(n - 1) = \mathbb{E}_Q(\tilde{H}(n)|\mathcal{P}_{n-1})$$

for $n = 1, 2, \ldots, N$. In particular, the initial price is given by

$$H(0) = (1 + R)^{-N}\mathbb{E}_Q(H(N)).$$

Proof In the binomial model we can replicate the final payoff by a series of steps, moving backwards in time. The values of such a strategy clearly give no-arbitrage prices at any time and any position of the tree. For, if the price $H(n)$ were different from $V(n)$ at some ω, we would construct an arbitrage by doing nothing till n (taking $x(k) = 0$, $y(k) = 0$ for $k < n$), and at time n by shorting the expensive and buying the cheap security. Holding this till maturity we would maintain the difference since, at maturity, replication ensures that we would break even. (Strictly speaking, the surplus should be invested in the money market account.)

A replicating strategy is self-financing by its very construction. To see that it is 'predictable', note that the number $x(1)$ computed at time 0 is the fraction

$$x(1) = \frac{H^u - H^d}{S^u - S^d}.$$

So $x(1)$ is a deterministic number. Then, by induction, $x(n+1)$ will involve all the values of H and S at time $n+1$ and so it will only depend on the position on the tree at time n when the computation is performed. This means that $x(n+1)$ will depend on n first elements of the N-tuple ω and so it will be known at time n.

Finally, we know that $\widetilde{V}(n)$ and so $\widetilde{H}(n)$ must be a martingale under Q and the claim follows from the martingale condition

$$\mathbb{E}_Q(\widetilde{V}(n)|\mathcal{P}_{n-1}) = \widetilde{V}(n-1)$$

after multiplying both sides by $(1 + R)^{n-1}$. □

If the random variable $H(N)$ has the following form

$$H(N) = h(S(N))$$

then we may write

$$H(N) = h(S(0)(1 + U)^Y(1 + D)^{N-Y})$$

where Y is a random variable giving the number of upward movements in N steps. Hence

$$H(0) = (1 + R)^{-N} \sum_{k=0}^{N} \binom{N}{k} q^k (1 - q)^{N-k} h\left(S(0)(1 + U)^k(1 + D)^{N-k}\right).$$

Example 3.12 The CRR formula
In particular, for the European call option with strike K this summation begins at the first integer at which the payoff is non-zero

$$H(0) = (1 + R)^{-N} \sum_{k=l}^{N} \binom{N}{k} q^k (1 - q)^{N-k} (S(0)(1 + U)^k(1 + D)^{N-k} - K)$$

where

$$l = \min\{k : S(0)(1 + U)^k(1 + D)^{N-k} > K\}.$$

This formula can be given a concise form. First recognise two terms on the right

$$H(0) = (1 + R)^{-N}S(0) \sum_{k=l}^{N} \binom{N}{k} q^k(1 - q)^{N-k}(1 + U)^k(1 + D)^{N-k}$$

$$- (1 + R)^{-N}K \sum_{k=l}^{N} \binom{N}{k} q^k(1 - q)^{N-k}.$$

The second term can be written as

$$-(1 + R)^{-N}K(1 - F_q(l - 1))$$

where F_q is the cumulative distribution function of the binomial distribution,

$$F_q(n) = \sum_{k=0}^{n} \binom{N}{k} q^k(1 - q)^{N-k}.$$

The first term can be rearranged as

$$S(0) \sum_{k=l}^{N} \binom{N}{k} \left(q\frac{1 + U}{1 + R}\right)^k \left((1 - q)\frac{1 + D}{1 + R}\right)^{N-k}.$$

Write

$$q_1 = q\frac{1 + U}{1 + R}$$

so that

$$1 - q_1 = \frac{1 + R - q - qU}{1 + R} = \frac{(1 - q) + (R - qU)}{1 + R}$$

and, since $qU + (1 - q)D = R$, we have

$$1 - q_1 = (1 - q)\frac{1 + D}{1 + R}.$$

The first term above then takes the form

$$S(0) \sum_{k=l}^{N} \binom{N}{k} q_1^k(1 - q_1)^{N-k} = S(0)(1 - F_{q_1}(l - 1))$$

using the distribution function again. Finally

$$C(0) = S(0)(1 - F_{q_1}(l - 1)) - (1 + R)^{-N}K(1 - F_q(l - 1)).$$

This is the **Cox–Ross–Rubinstein** (CRR) formula for the initial price of a European call option. (Many texts prefer to state this formula in terms of

the **complementary** binomial distribution Ψ, where

$$\Psi(l, N, r) = 1 - F_r(l-1) = \sum_{k=l}^{N} \binom{N}{k} r^k (1-r)^{N-k}$$

for $0 < r < 1$.)

The coefficient at $S(0)$ has a clear meaning: it is the probability that the option will be exercised, computed by means of the modified martingale probability q_1.

In the second term the exercise price is discounted, which is logical since the exercise price K is valid at time N, but the formula is concerned with the current prices. The coefficient at the discounted K gives the martingale probability that the option will be exercised.

The next three exercises illustrate further applications of the above analysis.

Asian options come in many varieties. The guiding principle is that the payoff should represent an averaging of the prices of the underlying up to the trading horizon N. Such options are popular on commodities markets, for example, in guarding against price manipulation near the trading horizon. We consider an example of a **fixed strike** option where the underlying is given as the arithmetic average, $A(N) = \frac{1}{N} \sum_{k=0}^{N} S(k)$, of the asset values, so that the payoff takes the form $H(N) = \max(A(N) - K, 0)$.

Exercise 3.7   Find the process of prices of the Asian option with payoff $H(5) = \max\{\frac{1}{6} \sum_{k=0}^{5} S(k) - K, 0\}$ where $S(0) = 60, U = 12\%$, $U = -6\%, R = 4\%, K = 62$.

Exercise 3.8   A popular combination of a call and a put is a **bottom straddle**, which involves buying both options with the same strike price K and expiry N. Verify that the payoff function is given by $H(N) = |S(N) - K|$. With the data from the previous exercise, compute the prices and values of the hedging strategy for a straddle with expiry $N = 5$, that is, consider $H(5) = |S(5) - K|$. Find the prices of the security with payoff $H(5) = 1$ if $S(5) \geq K$ and $H(5) = 0$ otherwise.

Exercise 3.9   A financial advisor selects a stock and receives a bonus of 100 for each up move of stock prices payable at time 5. Find the process of values of this bonus regarded as a derivative (use the same parameters as in the previous exercises).

3.5   Delta hedging

Let us put ourselves in a position of an option writer who has sold a call with exercise time $N = 3$ for the no-arbitrage price resulting from the binomial model with $U = 20\%, D = -10\%, S(0) = 100$ with $R = 10\%$, with an exercise price of $K = 105$. The price can be easily computed using the CRR formula: $C(0) = 23.31$.

We are exposed to some risk. For instance, if the stock keeps going up in each period, we will have to pay the holder of the option the sum of 67.80. Of course, if the stock goes down we will keep the price we have cashed. To make our position safe we embark on **hedging**, which boils down to replicating the option by means of a suitable strategy.

However, we do not have to construct the whole tree of replicating portfolios by working backwards from the payoff. This would be simple in the case considered here, but for large trees, with many time instants, it could become unduly complicated. Instead, we work step-by-step from the beginning, following the path of actual stock changes and not bothering to analyse all scenarios.

Our first portfolio requires finding the call prices at time 1 for which we again use the CRR formula:

$$C(1) = \left\{ \begin{array}{c} 33.94 \\ 9.04 \end{array} \right.$$

and then computing the **delta coefficient**, (i.e. the ratio of one-step price changes in option and stock) which, as we have seen, gives our stock position $x(1)$:

$$x(1) = \frac{33.94 - 9.04}{120 - 90} = 0.83$$

meaning that we have to buy this fraction of a share. This enables us to complete the portfolio by taking

$$y(1) = 23.31 - 0.83 \times 100 = -59.70$$

which means borrowing this money to have zero initial balance.

Now suppose the stock goes up. The new delta based on two option prices at time 2 is

$$x^u(2) = \frac{48.55 - 14.91}{144 - 108} = 0.93$$

which means we have to purchase more stock (where we use our convention exceptionally adding the time for greater clarity). Our money market position also includes the interest added to the debt

$$y^u(2) = y(1)(1 + r) + (x^u(2) - x(1)) \times S^u(1) = -78.18.$$

Next, suppose the stock goes down, and we have

$$x^{ud}(3) = \frac{24.60 - 0}{129.60 - 97.20} = 0.76$$

meaning that it is time to sell the fraction $0.93 - 0.76 = 0.17$ of a share with result that that our money market position becomes

$$y^{ud}(3) = -67.09.$$

At the next instant the option will be exercised.

Suppose the stock goes up and $S^{udu} = 129.60$. We owe the option holder the sum $129.60 - 105 = 24.60$. We owe the bank (negative money market position) $67.09 \times (1 + 10\%) = 73.80$. So together we have to pay 98.40. We own 0.76 of a share worth 129.60, which we sell and get $0.76 \times 129.60 = 98.40$ as required.

It is easy to see that following any other path and performing the required activities similarly we will end up with zero, which is no surprise since pricing was based on replication, and here we have just tested the scheme.

Exercise 3.10 Build a modification of the above computations where the shares are not divisible, that is, the stock position must be an integer, but you have sold and will hedge a package of 10 options. How will the results influence the initial price?

Remark 3.13

It is worth noting that the stock holding $x(1)$ is not the coefficient at $S(0)$ in the CRR formula.

4

Multi-step general models

Building on our experience with binomial models, we now formulate a general market model with finite sample space and finitely many discrete time steps. Beginning with a single-stock model, we review the definitions of basic concepts encountered for binomial models, such as partitions of the sample space, conditional expectations with respect to partitions or random variables, filtrations and martingales, and derive some of their properties. We then describe self-financing, predictable trading strategies and formulate the No Arbitrage Principle for general finite models. Finally, moving to a multi-stock model, the two Fundamental Theorems of Asset Pricing, describing absence of arbitrage and market completeness in terms of existence and uniqueness of the risk-neutral probabilities, are proved for finite multi-step models.

4.1 Partitions and conditioning

Assume given a finite sample space $\Omega = \{\omega_1, \omega_2, \ldots, \omega_M\}$, which remains fixed throughout this chapter. Fix a probability P on Ω with $P(\{\omega\}) > 0$

for all ω in Ω. We again write $P(\omega)$ for ease of notation. The additivity principle shows that $P(A) = \sum_{\omega \in A} P(\omega)$ for any $A \subset \Omega$, and we insist that $P(\Omega) = 1$. For any non-empty $B \subset \Omega$, define a new probability $P_B(\omega) = P(\omega)/P(B)$ if $\omega \in B$ and 0 otherwise. Thus $P_B(B) = 1$, and for any $A \subset \Omega$, $P_B(A) = P(A \cap B)/P(B)$. We call this the **conditional probability** of A given B.

As in Definition 3.7, for any random variable X and any non-empty event $B \subset \Omega$ the **conditional expectation** of X given B is defined by $\mathbb{E}(X|B) = \sum_{\omega \in \Omega} X(\omega)P_B(\omega)$.

Let $\mathbf{1}_B$ be the indicator of the set B. We have

$$
\begin{aligned}
\sum_{\omega \in \Omega} X(\omega)P_B(\omega) &= \sum_{\omega \in \Omega} X(\omega)\frac{P(\{\omega\} \cap B)}{P(B)} \\
&= \frac{1}{P(B)} \sum_{\omega \in B} X(\omega)P(\omega) \\
&= \frac{1}{P(B)} \sum_{\omega \in \Omega} X(\omega)\mathbf{1}_B(\omega)P(\omega) \\
&= \frac{1}{P(B)}\mathbb{E}(\mathbf{1}_B X)
\end{aligned}
$$

so that

$$
\mathbb{E}(X|B) = \frac{1}{P(B)}\mathbb{E}(\mathbf{1}_B X). \tag{4.1}
$$

Recall Definition 3.5: a **partition** of Ω is a finite, pairwise disjoint sequence $\mathcal{P} = \{B_i : i \leq k\}$ of subsets of Ω whose union is Ω. Applying the above construction to each B_i gives a random variable $\mathbb{E}(X|\mathcal{P}): \Omega \to \mathbb{R}$, with constant value $\mathbb{E}(X|B_i)$ at $\omega \in B_i$ for each $i \leq k$. $\mathbb{E}(X|\mathcal{P})$ is the **conditional expectation** of X with respect to the partition $\mathcal{P}$.

Applying (4.1), for $\omega \in B_i$ we get for each $i \leq k$,

$$
\mathbb{E}(X|\mathcal{P})(\omega) = \frac{1}{P(B_i)}\mathbb{E}(\mathbf{1}_{B_i} X),
$$

so glueing these together we have

$$
\mathbb{E}(X|\mathcal{P}) = \sum_{i=1}^{k} \mathbf{1}_{B_i} \frac{1}{P(B_i)}\mathbb{E}(\mathbf{1}_{B_i} X). \tag{4.2}
$$

Remark 4.1

A partition $\mathcal{P}$ can be expanded to a **field** $\mathcal{F}$ by forming all possible (finite!) unions of elements of $\mathcal{P}$ and adding the empty set:

$$\mathcal{F} = \{\emptyset\} \cup \left\{ \bigcup B_j : \{B_1, B_2, \ldots\} \subset \mathcal{P} \right\}.$$

This procedure can be reversed. The minimal non-empty elements of a field $\mathcal{F}$ are its **atoms**, which together form a partition of Ω, yielding the original field by the above expansion.

Example 4.2

If X is an arbitrary random variable on Ω and Y is a random variable with possible values $y_1, y_2, \ldots, y_k$, then the conditional expectation $\mathbb{E}(X|Y)$ of X given Y is the conditional expectation of X with respect to the partition $\mathcal{P} = \{B_i\}_{i \leq k}$ where $B_i = \{\omega : Y(\omega) = y_i\}$ so that we can write

$$\mathbb{E}(X|Y) = \mathbb{E}(X|Y = y_i) \quad \text{if } Y = y_i$$

for $i = 1, 2, \ldots, k$.

Observe that if Y is constant on a subset of Ω, then $\mathbb{E}(X|Y)$ is also constant on that subset, and that the values of $\mathbb{E}(X|Y)$ depend on the subsets on which Y is constant, and not on the actual values of Y. For random variables Y and W defining the same partition, we shall always have the same conditional expectations

$$\mathbb{E}(X|Y) = \mathbb{E}(X|W).$$

For random variables V and Z defining different partitions, in general we have

$$\mathbb{E}(X|V) \neq \mathbb{E}(X|Z).$$

4.2 Properties of conditional expectation

First, note that taking the conditional expectation is a linear operation: for any random variables X_1, X_2, Y and any numbers $a, b \in \mathbb{R}$ we have

$$\mathbb{E}(aX_1 + bX_2|Y) = a\mathbb{E}(X_1|Y) + b\mathbb{E}(X_2|Y).$$

This is evident from the definition and the linearity of the usual expectation:

$$LHS = \sum_{\omega \in \Omega} (aX_1(\omega) + bX_2(\omega))P_B(\omega)$$

$$= a \sum_{\omega \in \Omega} X_1(\omega)P_B(\omega) + b \sum_{\omega \in \Omega} X_2(\omega)P_B(\omega) = RHS.$$

Proposition 4.3

The expectation of the conditional expectation is the same as the expectation

$$\mathbb{E}(\mathbb{E}(X|Y)) = \mathbb{E}(X). \tag{4.3}$$

Proof   Denoting $B_n = \{\omega : Y(\omega) = y_n\}$, we have

$$\mathbb{E}(\mathbb{E}(X|Y)) = \sum \mathbb{E}(X|B_n)P(B_n) \text{ (definition of expectation)}$$

$$= \sum_n \frac{1}{P(B_n)}\mathbb{E}(X\mathbf{1}_{B_n})P(B_n)$$

$$\quad \text{(definition of conditional expectation)}$$

$$= \sum_n \mathbb{E}(X\mathbf{1}_{B_n})$$

$$= \mathbb{E}(X\sum_n \mathbf{1}_{B_n}) \text{ (additivity of expectation)}$$

$$= \mathbb{E}(X) \ (B_n \text{ is a partition so } \sum_n \mathbf{1}_{B_n} = 1)$$

as required. $\square$

   This result can be interpreted as follows: the average of averages is the same as the overall average.

   Property (4.3) can be generalised. First consider an example, using the random variables $S(1)$ and $S(2)$ specified for the first two stock prices by the non-recombining binomial model. The partition $\mathcal{P}_1$ defined by $S(1)$ consists of two sets B_u, B_d, and the partition $\mathcal{P}_2$ determined by $S(2)$ of four B_{uu}, B_{ud}, B_{du}, B_{dd} (as defined in the previous chapter). Notice that $B_u = B_{uu} \cup B_{ud}$, $B_d = B_{du} \cup B_{dd}$. We say that $\mathcal{P}_2$ is finer than $\mathcal{P}_1$. In practice this means that $S(2)$ carries more information than $S(1)$, that is, if the value of $S(2)$ becomes known, then we also know the value of $S(1)$.

Definition 4.4

Given two partitions $\mathcal{P}_1$, $\mathcal{P}_2$, we say $\mathcal{P}_2$ is **finer** than $\mathcal{P}_1$ if each element of $\mathcal{P}_1$ can be represented as a union of some elements of $\mathcal{P}_2$. Equivalently, we say that $\mathcal{P}_1$ is **coarser** than $\mathcal{P}_2$.

Remark 4.5

If the tree is recombining, the partition defined by $S(2)$ is not finer than the partition generated by $S(1)$. The middle value of $S(2)$ does not give us the information about the first price since we can arrive there from the up as well as from the down state. A remedy is to define the partition $\mathcal{P}_2$ in a different way by composing it of the sets on which **both** $S(1)$ and $S(2)$ are

constant. Then $\mathcal{P}_2$ is finer than $\mathcal{P}_1$ and taking $\mathcal{P}_3$ defined by $S(1)$, $S(2)$ and $S(3)$ we see that $\mathcal{P}_3$ is finer than $\mathcal{P}_2$.

Proposition 4.6
Consider discrete random variables Y, Z and suppose that Y defines a finer partition than Z. Then the following formula holds

$$\mathbb{E}(\mathbb{E}(X|Y)|Z) = \mathbb{E}(X|Z). \tag{4.4}$$

This is often known as the **tower property** *or the iterated expectations property.*

Proof   It is sufficient to note that the argument used in the previous proposition applies to each set $\{Z = z_i\}$. More specifically, write $C_j = \{Z = z_j\}$, $B_i = \{Y = y_i\}$. The partition $\{B_i\}_i$ is finer, so for each j we can find a collection I_j of indices such that $C_j = \bigcup_{i \in I_j} B_i$. For $\omega \in C_j$

$$\mathbb{E}(\mathbb{E}(X|Y)|Z)(\omega) = \frac{1}{P(C_j)}\mathbb{E}(\mathbb{E}(X|Y)\mathbf{1}_{C_j}) \quad \text{(by (4.1))}$$

$$= \frac{1}{P(C_j)}\mathbb{E}\left(\sum_{i \in I_j}\mathbf{1}_{B_i}\frac{1}{P(B_i)}\mathbb{E}(\mathbf{1}_{B_i}X)\mathbf{1}_{C_j}\right)$$

$$\text{(by (4.2))}$$

$$= \frac{1}{P(C_j)}\mathbb{E}\left(\sum_{i \in I_j}\mathbf{1}_{B_i}\frac{1}{P(B_i)}\mathbb{E}(\mathbf{1}_{B_i}X)\right)$$

since $B_i \subset C_j$ so $\mathbf{1}_{B_i}\mathbf{1}_{C_j} = \mathbf{1}_{B_i}$. Next by linearity of expectation we further have

$$= \frac{1}{P(C_j)}\sum_{i \in I_j}\frac{1}{P(B_i)}\mathbb{E}(\mathbf{1}_{B_i}X)\mathbb{E}(\mathbf{1}_{B_i})$$

$$= \frac{1}{P(C_j)}\sum_{i \in I_j}\frac{1}{P(B_i)}\mathbb{E}(\mathbf{1}_{B_i}X)P(B_i) \quad \text{(since } \mathbb{E}(\mathbf{1}_{B_i}) = P(B_i))$$

$$= \frac{1}{P(C_j)}\sum_{i \in I_j}\mathbb{E}(\mathbf{1}_{B_i}X)$$

$$= \frac{1}{P(C_j)}\mathbb{E}(\mathbf{1}_{C_j}X) \quad \text{(since } \mathbf{1}_{C_j} = \sum_{i \in I_j}\mathbf{1}_{B_i})$$

$$= \mathbb{E}(X|Z)(\omega) \quad \text{as claimed.}$$

$\square$

Proposition 4.7

Assume that the partition defined by Y is finer than that defined by Z. In this case the following formula holds

$$\mathbb{E}(ZX|Y) = Z\mathbb{E}(X|Y). \tag{4.5}$$

This is often referred to as '**taking out what is known**'.

Proof Fix an element B of the partition generated by Y and notice that Z is constant on B taking value z, say. Then

$$\mathbb{E}(ZX|B) = \sum_{\omega \in B} Z(\omega)X(\omega)P_B(\omega)$$

$$= \sum_{\omega \in B} zX(\omega)P_B(\omega)$$

$$= z \sum_{\omega \in B} X(\omega)P_B(\omega)$$

$$= z\mathbb{E}(X|B)$$

so the result holds on B. By glueing together the formulae obtained for every such B, we have proved our assertion. $\qquad\square$

The intuition behind this result is that once the value of Y becomes known, we will also know the value of Z and therefore can treat it as if it were a number, rather than a random variable, moving it out in front of the expectation. In particular, for $X \equiv 1$, we get $\mathbb{E}(Z|Y) = Z$.

The final property extends the familiar feature of independent events, namely, the fact that the conditional probability of an event A is not sensitive with respect to B independent of A, specifically, $P_B(A) = P(A)$ as we noticed before.

Proposition 4.8

If Y and Z are independent random variables, then

$$\mathbb{E}(Y|Z) = \mathbb{E}(Y) \quad and \quad \mathbb{E}(Z|Y) = \mathbb{E}(Z).$$

Proof Take an element B of the partition generated by Z, and assume that on the set B the random variable Y takes values $y_1, \ldots, y_k$. Then

$$\mathbb{E}(Y|Z) = \sum_{i=1}^{k} y_i P_B(Y = y_i)$$

$$= \sum_{i=1}^{k} y_i P(Y = y_i) \quad \text{(by independence)}$$

$$= \mathbb{E}(Y)$$

with the same proof for the second identity. $\qquad\square$

4.3 Filtrations and martingales

Example 4.2 suggests a formal definition:

Definition 4.9

Let X be a random variable defined on $\Omega = \{\omega_1, \ldots, \omega_M\}$, taking distinct values $\{x_1, \ldots, x_k\}$. The partition determined by X is the family of sets $\mathcal{P}_X = \{B_i\}_{i=1}^k$ defined by

$$B_i = \{\omega : X(\omega) = x_i\}.$$

The idea is that we decompose the set Ω into pairwise disjoint parts on which X is constant.

Consider two random variables, X, Y, where X takes values $\{x_1, \ldots, x_k\}$ and Y takes values $\{y_1, \ldots, y_l\}$. First construct the partition $\mathcal{P}_X$ defined by X, then decompose each element B_i according to the values taken by Y on B_i:

$$B_i = \bigcup_{j=1}^l B_{ij}, \quad B_{ij} = \{\omega \in B_i : Y(\omega) = y_j\}.$$

This defines a partition of Ω, denoted by $\mathcal{P}_{XY} = \{B_{ij}\}$, which is finer than $\mathcal{P}_X$. We can proceed in this way introducing consecutively additional random variables.

To summarise, let $X_1, \ldots, X_n$ be a sequence of random variables and denote the partition defined by $X_1, \ldots, X_k$ by $\mathcal{P}_k$. We have a sequence of partitions with $\mathcal{P}_{k+1}$ finer than $\mathcal{P}_k$. Such a sequence is called **filtration**.

If the sequence of partitions $\mathcal{P}_n$ forms a filtration, the tower property has the following consequence: for $n < m$

$$\mathbb{E}(\mathbb{E}(X|\mathcal{P}_m)|\mathcal{P}_n) = \mathbb{E}(X|\mathcal{P}_n)$$

so if we denote $Y(n) = \mathbb{E}(X|\mathcal{P}_n)$ we have

$$\mathbb{E}(Y(m)|\mathcal{P}_n) = Y(n).$$

This sequence gives an example of a martingale, generalising what we observed in the binomial setting. Since the properties of conditional expectation we have derived hold in general, we continue to describe an arbitrary sequence $M(n)$ of random variables defined on Ω. In applications this role will usually be played by the stock prices $S(n)$ or by the value process $V(n)$ of a given trading strategy. In our applications the time horizon N (and hence the length of any such sequence) will remain finite.

Definition 4.10

A sequence $M(n)$ of random variables is a **martingale** with respect to the filtration $\{\mathcal{P}_n\}$ if for all $n < m$

$$\mathbb{E}(M(m)|\mathcal{P}_n) = M(n).$$

In terms of 'information' carried by a filtration, this property can be read as follows: given some (partial) information, the expected value of some quantity (price) in the future is the value of the quantity at that time. In other words, the values $M(n)$ encapsulate all the predictive power of the information available at time n.

If $M(n)$ is a martingale with respect to $\mathcal{P}_n$ then by definition $\mathcal{P}_{M(n)}$ is a subpartition of P_n since $M(n)$ is the conditional expectation with respect to $\mathcal{P}_n$. We then say that $M(n)$ is $\mathcal{P}_n$-**measurable.**

Proposition 4.11

If $\mathbb{E}(M(n+1)|\mathcal{P}_n) = M(n)$ *then* M *is a martingale.*

Proof   This follows from the tower property. Let $m > n$,

$$\mathbb{E}(M(m)|\mathcal{P}_n) = \mathbb{E}(\mathbb{E}(M(m)|\mathcal{P}_{m-1})|\mathcal{P}_n)$$
$$= \mathbb{E}(M(m-1)|\mathcal{P}_n)$$
$$= \dots$$
$$= M(n)$$

after $m - n$ steps. $\qquad\square$

Exercise 4.1   Show that if $M(n)$ is $\mathcal{P}_n$-measurable, and $\mathbb{E}(M(n+1) - M(n)|\mathcal{P}_n) = 0$ then M is a martingale.

We formalise the important example given above.

Proposition 4.12

Let X *be a random variable and let* $\mathcal{P}_0, \mathcal{P}_1, \mathcal{P}_2, \dots$ *be a filtration. Then the sequence*

$$\mathbb{E}(X|\mathcal{P}_0), \mathbb{E}(X|\mathcal{P}_1), \mathbb{E}(X|\mathcal{P}_2), \dots$$

is a martingale.

Proof   For the sequence $\mathbb{E}(X|\mathcal{P}_n)$ to be a martingale, it must satisfy the condition

$$\mathbb{E}(\mathbb{E}(X|\mathcal{P}_m)|\mathcal{P}_n) = \mathbb{E}(X|\mathcal{P}_n),$$

for $n < m$, which holds by the tower property because partition $\mathcal{P}_m$ is finer than partition $\mathcal{P}_n$. □

A martingale is a mathematical model of a fair game of chance: On average we expect our wealth to remain the same after each round of the game as the following proposition shows. It says that constant expectation is a necessary condition for a martingale.

Proposition 4.13
If $(M(n))_{n\geq0}$ is a martingale (with respect to a filtration $(\mathcal{P}_n)_{n\geq0}$, then

$$\mathbb{E}(M(0)) = \mathbb{E}(M(1)) = \mathbb{E}(M(2)) = \cdots.$$

Proof If $M(0), M(1), M(2), \ldots$ is a martingale, then $M(n) = \mathbb{E}(M(n + 1)|\mathcal{P}_n)$ for each n. Applying expectation to both sides of this equality we have

$$\mathbb{E}(M(n)) = \mathbb{E}(\mathbb{E}(M(n + 1)|\mathcal{P}_n)) = \mathbb{E}(M(n + 1))$$

for each n, as required. □

Exercise 4.2   Give an example showing that the reverse implication does not hold, i.e. $\mathbb{E}(M(0)) = \mathbb{E}(M(1)) = \mathbb{E}(M(2))$ does not necessarily mean that $M(0), M(1), M(2)$ is a martingale.

Definition 4.14
We say that a sequence $M(0), M(1), M(2), \ldots$ of random variables is a **submartingale** (respectively, a **supermartingale**) with respect to a filtration $\mathcal{P}_0, \mathcal{P}_1, \mathcal{P}_2, \ldots$ if the partition of $M(n)$ is coarser than $\mathcal{P}_n$ and

$$\mathbb{E}(M(n + 1)|\mathcal{P}_n) \geq M(n) \quad (\text{respectively, } \leq M(n))$$

for each $n = 0, 1, 2, \ldots$

The condition that the partition of $M(n)$ should be coarser than $\mathcal{P}_n$, i.e., that $M(n)$ is **measurable** with respect to $\mathcal{P}_n$, simply means that $M(n)$ is known at time n, since $\mathcal{P}_n$ contains each set on which $M(n)$ is constant. The partition $\mathcal{P}_n$ represents our knowledge at time n and if $\mathcal{P}_n$ is known, then $M(n)$ is known. In defining martingales we did not need to state explicitly the condition that the partition of $M(n)$ should be coarser than $\mathcal{P}_n$ because it follows directly from the identity $\mathbb{E}(M(n + 1)|\mathcal{P}_n) = M(n)$.

Definition 4.15

We can also define an increasing sequence of fields $(\mathcal{F}_n)_{n \leq N}$, again called a **filtration**, where $\mathcal{F}_0 = \{\varnothing, \Omega\}$ and for $n \geq 1$, $\mathcal{F}_n$ is generated by the first n elements of the sequence, i.e. by $M(1), \ldots, M(n)$. The field generated by a single random variable X is of the form $\mathcal{F}_X = \{X^{-1}(B) : B \subset \mathbb{R}, B \text{ a}$ Borel set$\}$ and we take $\mathcal{F}_n$ to be the smallest field containing $\mathcal{F}_{M(k)}$ for all $k = 1, \ldots, n$. In this way we ensure that $(M(n))_{n \leq N}$ is **adapted** to $(\mathcal{F}_n)_{n \leq N}$, which means that for all n, $M(n)$ is $\mathcal{F}_n$-measurable.

In applications, where the sequence in question is usually a sequence $\{S(n) : n = 0, 1, \ldots, N\}$ of stock prices, it will be convenient to assume that $\mathcal{F}_N = \mathcal{F}$. The latter is 2^Ω, so to ensure equality we have to reduce Ω if the atoms of $\mathcal{F}_N$ are not single-element sets by picking one element in each to form the new sample space, again denoted by Ω for simplicity.

4.4 Trading strategies and arbitrage

We return to the special case where the martingales we seek are related to stock prices. So assume that a sequence $S(0), S(1), \ldots, S(n)$ of stock prices is given, where n runs through the trading dates in some pricing model with horizon N. By a (trading) **strategy** we mean a series of portfolios, as discussed in the single-period case. At each step our decision on how to adjust the previous portfolio depends on the information available at this time and such a strategy is a collection of random variables.

We are ready for general definitions.

Definition 4.16

A **strategy** is a sequence of pairs of random variables showing, for $n = 1, 2, \ldots, N$, the number of shares $x(n)$ of stock and the number $y(n)$ of money market account units chosen at time $n - 1$ and held until time n, and such that $(x(n), y(n))$ is $\mathcal{F}_{n-1}$-measurable. In general, a sequence of random variables satisfying this measurability requirement is called **predictable**.

Definition 4.17

The **value process** of a strategy is a sequence defined for $n = 1, \ldots, N$ by

$$V_{(x,y)}(n) = x(n)S(n) + y(n)A(n)$$

together with the initial investment

$$V_{(x,y)}(0) = x(1)S(0) + y(1)A(0).$$

The next definition summarises the requirement that the funds available at a given time are used for building the next portfolio, that is, no inflows or outflows of funds are allowed.

Definition 4.18
A strategy is **self-financing** if

$$V_{(x,y)}(n) = x(n+1)S(n) + y(n+1)A(n)$$

for all $n = 1, \ldots, N-1$.

For any sequence $X(n)$ denote by $\Delta X(n)$ the increment $X(n) - X(n-1)$ for $n = 1, \ldots, N$. We can write the self-financing condition in a form which will be useful later:

$$\Delta V_{(x,y)}(n) = x(n)\Delta S(n) + y(n)\Delta A(n).$$

This is immediate since the strategy $(x(n), y(n))$ is self-financing iff $V_{(x,y)}(n-1) = x(n)S(n-1) + y(n)A(n-1)$.

We have seen that, given the initial wealth, all that matters are the decisions concerning the numbers of shares held, with the money market position following as a consequence. And so,

$$y(1) = \frac{1}{A(0)}(V_{(x,y)}(0) - x(1)S(0))$$

and completing the picture with the induction step

$$y(n+1) = \frac{1}{A(n)}(V_{(x,y)}(n) - x(n+1)S(n))$$

we have proved the following result.

Proposition 4.19
Given a predictable sequence $x(n)$ and initial wealth $V(0)$ there exists a unique predictable sequence $y(n)$ such that the strategy $(x(n), y(n))$ is self-financing and $V(0)$ is its initial value.

Proof   All that remains is to observe that $y(n+1)$ is $\mathcal{F}_n$-measurable since all the ingredients on the right are.   □

Exercise 4.3   Prove a version of the previous proposition, where $V(0)$ and predictable $y(n)$ are given and $x(n)$ has to be constructed so that the strategy is self-financing.

Exercise 4.4 Give an example where the values of a strategy become negative. Find conditions on the sequence $x(n)$ so that $V_{(x,y)}(n) \geq 0$ for all n.

Exercise 4.5 Find a condition on $x(n)$ so that $y(n) \geq 0$ (no risk-free borrowing) and the strategy is self-financing.

Next, we focus on a key property of the discounted values of a strategy. For the multi-step binomial model we described in the previous chapter how to construct a probability Q on the sample space Ω built for that model such that the discounted stock prices form a Q-martingale. This provides the basis for the assumption made in the following theorem. In the next section we will show that this assumption is equivalent to the No Arbitrage Principle for general finite models.

Theorem 4.20
Suppose that there exists a probability Q such that $\mathbb{E}_Q(\tilde{S}(n+1)|\mathcal{F}_n) = \tilde{S}(n)$ for all $n \geq 0$. Then the discounted values of a self-financing strategy form a martingale with respect to Q.

Proof Recall that by definition $\widetilde{V}_{(x,y)}(n) = (1+R)^{-n}V_{(x,y)}(n)$. Next, with $A(0) = 1$ for simplicity, $A(n) = (1+R)^n$ so $\tilde{A}(n) = 1$, and we also know that $\tilde{S}(n)$ is a martingale, that is, $\mathbb{E}_Q(\tilde{S}(n+1)|\mathcal{F}_n) = \tilde{S}(n)$. We can proceed with the verification of the claim:

$$\mathbb{E}_Q(\widetilde{V}_{(x,y)}(n+1)|\mathcal{F}_n) = \mathbb{E}_Q(x(n+1)\tilde{S}(n+1) + y(n+1)\tilde{A}(n+1)|\mathcal{F}_n)$$

$$\text{(definition of the value of a strategy)}$$

$$= x(n+1)\mathbb{E}_Q(\tilde{S}(n+1))|\mathcal{F}_n) + y(n+1)$$

$$\text{(predictability of the strategy)}$$

$$= x(n+1)\tilde{S}(n) + y(n+1)$$

$$\text{(since } \tilde{S}(n) \text{ is a martingale)}$$

$$= (1+R)^{-n}(x(n+1)S(n) + y(n+1)A(n))$$

$$= (1+R)^{-n}(x(n)S(n) + y(n)A(n))$$

$$\text{(self-financing condition)}$$

$$= \widetilde{V}_{(x,y)}(n).$$

$\square$

Let us emphasise that this result does not use the particular form of the model of stock prices. We only used the martingale property of the discounted prices together with the self-financing and predictability conditions.

We conclude the section by giving a multi-step version of the No Arbitrage Principle. First we define what is meant by arbitrage opportunities in our multi-step single-stock model based on the finite sample space Ω.

Definition 4.21
A strategy $(x(n), y(n))$ is an **arbitrage opportunity** if

$$V_{(x,y)}(0) = 0, \quad V_{(x,y)}(n) \geq 0$$

for all n and for some n there is an ω in Ω such that

$$V_{(x,y)}(n, \omega) > 0.$$

Assumption 4.22 No Arbitrage Principle
We assume that arbitrage opportunities do not exist in the market model.

Remark 4.23
As we have seen before, for extended markets the definition of arbitrage strategy has to be modified to include positions in the relevant derivative securities.

The next proposition provides an apparently weaker, but in fact equivalent, version of the notion of arbitrage which is useful in some applications.

Proposition 4.24
If a market model admits a predictable, self-financing strategy $(x(n), y(n))$ with $V_{(x,y)}(0) = 0$, $V_{(x,y)}(N) \geq 0$ and $V_{(x,y)}(N, \omega) > 0$ for some $\omega \in \Omega$, then it also admits an arbitrage opportunity (as in Definition 4.21).

Proof Suppose we have a strategy $(x(n), y(n))$ satisfying the assumption of the proposition, and suppose that it does not satisfy Definition 4.21 so its value is negative at some times for some ω. Then there is a last trading date $m < N$ at which there is an $\omega_0 \in \Omega$ such that $V_{(x,y)}(m, \omega_0) < 0$. On this ω_0 the strategy $(x(n), y(n))$ generates some profit at time $m + 1$ since the value becomes non-negative after being negative at m. We shall exploit this to construct an arbitrage in the sense of Definition 4.21.

To construct $(x^*(n), y^*(n))$ we 'do nothing' outside ω_0:

$$x^*(n, \omega) = y^*(n, \omega) = 0 \text{ for all } n \leq N, \omega \neq \omega_0.$$

We also take no action on ω_0 for all trading dates up to m:

$$x^*(n, \omega_0) = y^*(n, \omega_0) = 0 \text{ for all } n \leq m.$$

Of course, $V_{(x^*,y^*)}(n) = 0$ for all $n \leq m$. At the next step we employ the original strategy

$$x^*(m+1, \omega_0) = x(m+1, \omega_0).$$

Clearly, the process $x^*(n), n \leq m+1$ is predictable since $x(m+1)$ is $\mathcal{F}_m$-measurable. We know (Proposition 4.19) that there exists a unique predictable sequence $y^*(n)$ such that $(x^*(n), y^*(n))$ is self-financing. Using the explicit expression found in the proof of Proposition 4.19 we have

$$y^*(n) = \frac{1}{A(n-1)}(V_{(x^*,y^*)}(n-1) - x^*(n)S(n-1)), \quad n \geq 1,$$

so $y^*(n) = 0$ for $n \leq m$. Next,

$$y^*(m+1) = \frac{1}{A(m)}(V_{(x^*,y^*)}(m) - x^*(m+1)S(m))$$

$$= -x(m+1)\frac{1}{A(m)}S(m)$$

so the value process satisfies

$$V_{(x^*,y^*)}(m+1) = x(m+1)S(m+1)$$

$$- x(m+1)\frac{1}{A(m)}S(m)A(m+1)$$

$$= V_{(x,y)}(m+1) - y(m+1)A(m+1)$$

$$- x(m+1)\frac{1}{A(m)}S(m)A(m+1).$$

Inserting the form of y

$$y(m+1) = \frac{1}{A(m)}(V_{(x,y)}(m) - x(m+1)S(m))$$

we further obtain

$$V_{(x^*,y^*)}(m+1) = V_{(x,y)}(m+1)$$

$$- \frac{1}{A(m)}(V_{(x,y)}(m) - x(m+1)S(m))A(m+1)$$

$$- x(m+1)\frac{1}{A(m)}S(m)A(m+1)$$

$$= V_{(x,y)}(m+1)$$

$$- (V_{(x,y)}(m) - x(m+1)S(m))(1+R)$$

$$- x(m+1)S(m)(1+R)$$

$$= V_{(x,y)}(m+1) - V_{(x,y)}(m)(1+R) > 0$$

since $V_{(x,y)}(m + 1) \geq 0$, $V_{(x,y)}(m) < 0$ by the definition of m (all this is considered at ω_0, which we omit to keep the notation clear). So we have found an instant $m + 1$ and an $\omega = \omega_0$ where the value is strictly positive. It remains to make sure that $V_{(x^*,y^*)}(n) \geq 0$ for the remaining instants $n > m + 1$. This can be easily accomplished by immediately putting all the money in the risk-free money market account: for $n \geq m + 2$ the stock and bond positions are constant

$$x^*(n, \omega_0) = 0,$$

$$y^*(n, \omega_0) = \frac{1}{A(m + 1)} V_{(x^*,y^*)}(m + 1),$$

and

$$V_{(x^*,y^*)}(m + 1 + k) = V_{(x^*,y^*)}(m + 1)(1 + R)^k > 0$$

which is more than we need to prove that we have constructed an arbitrage opportunity in the sense of Definition 4.21.   □

4.5   A general multi-step model

The multi-step models we have discussed so far all involve a market with a single underlying stock. We now analyse derivative securities defined on an underlying market containing several risky assets (stocks) and a single money market account. As we saw for trinomial models, where market completeness requires two underlying stocks, pricing and hedging derivatives in such a model proceeds much as in the single-stock case, and it is often useful to treat the vector of stock prices as a single entity. With this proviso, much of theory we have developed so far will generalise to this more general setting quite simply, and we begin by reviewing the main concepts.

We still assume that time runs in a discrete way, just as in the binomial model. With h being the length of the time step we use $n = 0, 1, \ldots, N$ to indicate the time instant nh. The basic market consists of the money market account and d risky assets (stocks) with prices $S_1(n), \ldots, S_d(n)$, which comprise the components of the $\mathbb{R}^d$-valued function $\mathbf{S}(n)$ and are discrete strictly positive random variables defined on the finite sample space $\Omega = \{\omega_1, \ldots, \omega_M\}$. The dynamics of the single risk-free asset (the money market account) are again determined by the risk-free rate R, which is assumed constant, so $A(n) = A(0)(1 + R)^n$. A **portfolio** is the vector

$(\mathbf{x}, y) = (x_1, \ldots, x_d, y)$ with coordinates representing positions in the corresponding securities. A **strategy** is a sequence of portfolios

$$(\mathbf{x}(n), y(n)) = (x_1(n), \ldots, x_d(n), y(n)), \ n = 1, \ldots, N.$$

These are $\mathbb{R}^{d+1}$-valued functions (i.e. random vectors), except for the initial portfolio, which is determined at time 0 and so is deterministic. We shall write $(\mathbf{x}, y)$ for this sequence.

Later, this market will be extended by adding derivative securities and the portfolio vectors will contain additional coordinates z_k, reflecting positions in these assets.

The **value** of a strategy at time n is

$$V_{(\mathbf{x},y)}(n) = \sum_{j=1}^{d} x_j(n) S_j(n) + y(n) A(n), \ \text{for } n = 1, 2, \ldots, N,$$

$$V_{(\mathbf{x},y)}(0) = \sum_{j=1}^{d} x_j(1) S_j(0) + y(1) A(0).$$

We shall again assume throughout that the strategies we consider are **predictable**, so the random vectors $(\mathbf{x}(n+1), y(n+1))$ are $\mathcal{F}_n$-measurable. This condition reflects the convention that the portfolio at time $n + 1$ is constructed at time n using the funds and the information about stock prices available at that time.

The key ideas developed for the single-stock model also apply in this more general model. A strategy is **self-financing** if

$$V_{(\mathbf{x},y)}(n) = \sum_{j=1}^{d} x_j(n+1) S_j(n) + y(n+1) A(n) \ \text{for } n = 0, 1, \ldots, N-1.$$

We state the version of the No Arbitrage Principle which applies in the model as follows:

Definition 4.25
A strategy $(\mathbf{x}, y)$ is an **arbitrage opportunity** in the underlying market if its value process satisfies $V_{(\mathbf{x},y)}(0) = 0$, $V_{(\mathbf{x},y)}(n) \geq 0$ for all n and for some n there is an ω such that $V_{(\mathbf{x},y)}(n, \omega) > 0$. For the market extended by adding some derivative securities the definition is similar.

The construction given for the single-stock model in Proposition 4.24 also applies in the multi-stock setting: the only change is to replace the stock holdings $x(n)$ by the vector $\mathbf{x}(n)$.

Assumption 4.26 No Arbitrage Principle
Arbitrage opportunities do not exist in any market model.

In the First Fundamental Theorem below we shall prove that this is equivalent to the existence of a martingale probability; that is a probability Q with $Q(\omega) > 0$ for all ω in Ω and such that for each $j = 1, \ldots, d$, the discounted stock price process $\{\widetilde{S}_j(n) : n = 0, 1, \ldots, N\}$ is a Q-martingale.

The following definition is both intuitive and useful.

Definition 4.27
The **gains process** $G_{(\mathbf{x},y)} = (G_{(\mathbf{x},y)}(n))_{n \leq N}$ generated by the strategy $(\mathbf{x}, y)$ is defined by

$$G_{(\mathbf{x},y)}(0) = 0,$$

$$G_{(\mathbf{x},y)}(n) = \sum_{k=1}^{n} \left(\sum_{j=1}^{d} x_j(k)\Delta S_j(k) + y(k)\Delta A(k) \right) \text{ for } n = 1, \ldots, N.$$

It follows immediately that the strategy $(\mathbf{x}, y)$ is self-financing if and only if $\Delta V_{(\mathbf{x},y)}(n) = \Delta G_{(\mathbf{x},y)}(n)$ for $n \geq 1$. Since $V_{(\mathbf{x},y)}(n) = V_{(\mathbf{x},y)}(0) + \sum_{i=1}^{n} \Delta V_{(\mathbf{x},y)}(i)$ is a telescoping sum, and similarly for G, the strategy is self-financing if and only if

$$V_{(\mathbf{x},y)}(n) = V_{(\mathbf{x},y)}(0) + G_{(\mathbf{x},y)}(n) \text{ for } n = 0, 1, \ldots, N.$$

In self-financing and predictable strategies the risk-free position is a secondary variable as the following theorem shows.

Theorem 4.28
Given $V(0)$ and a predictable sequence $\mathbf{x} = (x_1(n), \ldots, x_d(n))$ there exists a unique predictable sequence $y(n)$ such that
- $V_{(\mathbf{x},y)}(0) = V(0)$,
- *the strategy $(\mathbf{x}, y)$ is self-financing.*

Proof This is proved by induction. First, let

$$y(1) = \frac{V(0) - x_1(1)S_1(0) - \cdots - x_d(1)S_d(0)}{A(0)},$$

which ensures that $V_{(\mathbf{x},y)}(0) = V(0)$. Thus $y(1)$ is non-random, as is necessary for $y(n)$ to be predictable. By definition, we have therefore determined $V_{(\mathbf{x},y)}(1)$ uniquely, and the initial induction step is complete.

$$V_{(\mathbf{x},y)}(1) = x_1(1)S_1(1) + \cdots + x_d(1)S_d(1) + y(1)A(1).$$

Next, for the induction step, assume that $y(n)$ is known; thus so is $V_{(\mathbf{x},y)}(n)$. We again define the next term in such a way that the self-financing condition is guaranteed:

$$y(n+1) = \frac{V_{(\mathbf{x},y)}(n) - x_1(n+1)S_1(n) - \cdots - x_d(n+1)S_d(n)}{A(n)}.$$

Then $y(n+1)$ is $\mathcal{F}_n$-measurable since for $j = 1, 2, \ldots, d$ both the $x_j(n+1)$ and $S_j(n)$ are; the former by hypothesis, the latter by definition of the $\mathcal{F}_n$. This completes the induction step. $\qquad\square$

Recall the definition of **discounted prices**; in fact, for any asset X we set

$$\widetilde{X}(i) = \frac{X(i)}{(1+R)^i}.$$

Then the successive differences are

$$\Delta\widetilde{X}(i) = \frac{X(i)}{(1+R)^i} - \frac{X(i-1)}{(1+R)^{i-1}}$$

which is **not** the same as

$$\widetilde{\Delta X}(i) = \Delta X(i)(1+R)^{-i} = \frac{X(i)}{(1+R)^i} - \frac{X(i-1)}{(1+R)^i}.$$

In particular we obtain

$$\widetilde{A}(i) = \frac{A(i)}{(1+R)^i} = A(0), \text{ hence } \Delta\widetilde{A}(i) = 0.$$

The **discounted gains process** will be denoted by

$$\widetilde{G}_{\mathbf{x}}(n) = \sum_{i=1}^{n}\sum_{j=1}^{d} x_j(i)\Delta\widetilde{S}_j(i) = \sum_{i=1}^{n}\langle \mathbf{x}(i), \Delta\widetilde{\mathbf{S}}(i)\rangle,$$

where we use the notation $\langle \mathbf{a}, \mathbf{b}\rangle = \sum_{j=1}^{d} a_j b_j$ for the usual inner product of vectors in $\mathbb{R}^d$. The vector $\Delta\widetilde{\mathbf{S}}(i)$ has the discounted price increments $\Delta\widetilde{S}_j(i)$ as its components. As the discounted increment in A is zero, there is now no dependence on y, only on $\mathbf{x}$.

We now verify that for self-financing strategies the sum of the initial investment and discounted gains gives the discounted value process.

Theorem 4.29

If a strategy $(\mathbf{x}, y)$ is self-financing then

$$\widetilde{V}_{(\mathbf{x},y)}(n) = V_{(\mathbf{x},y)}(0) + \widetilde{G}_{\mathbf{x}}(n).$$

Proof Fix $n \leq N$ and suppose $(x_1(n), \ldots, x_d(n), y(n))$ is self-financing. We write

$$\widetilde{V}_{(\mathbf{x},y)}(i+1) = \frac{1}{(1+R)^{i+1}}(\langle \mathbf{x}(i+1), \mathbf{S}(i+1)\rangle + y(i+1)A(i+1))$$
$$= \langle \mathbf{x}(i+1), \widetilde{\mathbf{S}}(i+1)\rangle + y(i+1)A(0),$$

and similarly

$$\widetilde{V}_{(\mathbf{x},y)}(i) = \frac{1}{(1+R)^{i}}(\langle \mathbf{x}(i+1), \mathbf{S}(i)\rangle + y(i+1)A(i))$$
$$= \langle \mathbf{x}(i+1), \widetilde{\mathbf{S}}(i)\rangle + y(i+1)A(0).$$

Subtracting gives, for each $i = 0, 1, \ldots, n-1$

$$\Delta\widetilde{V}_{(\mathbf{x},y)}(i+1) = \widetilde{V}_{(\mathbf{x},y)}(i+1) - \widetilde{V}_{(\mathbf{x},y)}(i) = \langle \mathbf{x}(i+1), \Delta\widetilde{\mathbf{S}}(i+1)\rangle$$
$$= \Delta\widetilde{G}_{\mathbf{x}}(i+1),$$

so that with $k = i + 1$ we obtain

$$\widetilde{V}_{(\mathbf{x},y)}(n) - V_{(\mathbf{x},y)}(0) = \sum_{k=1}^{n} \Delta\widetilde{V}_{(\mathbf{x},y)}(k) = \sum_{k=1}^{n} \Delta\widetilde{G}_{\mathbf{x}}(k) = \widetilde{G}_{\mathbf{x}}(n).$$

□

A strictly positive price process is often called a **numeraire**, i.e. a benchmark security against which the price changes of other securities can be compared.

Exercise 4.6 Given an $\mathcal{F}_n$-adapted sequence of d-vectors with $Z_j(n) > 0$ for all $n = 0, 1, \ldots, N$, $j = 0, 1, \ldots, d$ with $(\mathbf{x}, y)$ and $(\mathbf{S}, A)$ as above, show that the strategy $(\mathbf{x},y)$ is self-financing for the price process $(\mathbf{S}, A)$ if and only if it is self-financing for the price process $(Z_1 S_1, \ldots, Z_d S_d, Z_0 A)$.

The exercise verifies that the self-financing property of trading strategies is **invariant** under a change of numeraire.

Exercise 4.7 Explain why the result of the previous exercise shows that the converse of Theorem 4.29 also holds.

To discuss martingale properties in general we introduce a filtration of fields $\mathcal{F}_n$ as before. Then we have the familiar definition:

Definition 4.30

A probability Q is **risk-neutral** (or a **martingale probability**) if the discounted stock prices are martingales

$$\mathbb{E}_Q(\widetilde{S}_j(n+1)|\mathcal{F}_n) = \widetilde{S}_j(n) \quad \text{all } j,$$

where for each n, $\mathcal{F}_n$ is generated by $S_j(k)$, $k \leq n$, $j = 1, \ldots, d$ (i.e. the smallest field for which all $S_j(k)$, $k \leq n$, are measurable).

We proved that if a predictable strategy $(\mathbf{x}, y)$ is self-financing, then

$$\widetilde{V}_{(\mathbf{x},y)}(n) = V_{(\mathbf{x},y)}(0) + \widetilde{G}_\mathbf{x}(n).$$

We shall prove that under a risk-neutral probability $\widetilde{V}_{(\mathbf{x},y)}(n)$ is a martingale as well, thus generalising Theorem 4.20. To this end we formulate the appropriate theorem using general notation since it can be used in various applications.

Theorem 4.31

If $M_j(n)$ are martingales and the processes $H_j(n)$ are predictable, $j = 1, \ldots, d$, then the process $X(n)$ defined by

$$X(n) = X(0) + \sum_{k=1}^{n} \sum_{j=1}^{d} H_j(k)\Delta M_j(k) = X(0) + \sum_{k=1}^{n} \langle \mathbf{H}(k), \Delta \mathbf{M}(k) \rangle$$

is a martingale, where $X(0) = x_0$ is an arbitrary real number.

This right-hand side of the above equation is sometimes called a **martingale transform** or **discrete stochastic integral**.

Proof See page 108. □

We will also need the following result.

Theorem 4.32

For $M(n)$ to be a martingale it is sufficient that for each predictable process $H(n)$

$$\mathbb{E}\left(\sum_{n=1}^{N} H(n)\Delta M(n))\right) = 0.$$

Proof See page 109. □

4.6   The Fundamental Theorems of Asset Pricing

We remain with the multi-step, multi-stock model described above, and prove the two key results for arbitrage (or risk-neutral) pricing of European derivative securities in a discrete-time setting, linking the absence of arbitrage to the existence and uniqueness of risk-neutral probabilities.

We begin by distinguishing between two basic types of European derivative securities, examples of which we have already encountered in various exercises.

Definition 4.33

A **European derivative security** confers the right to obtain at time N a payoff $H(N)$ of a form specified at the initial trading date 0. We say that H is

- **path independent** if $H(N) = h(\mathbf{S}(N))$ for some $h \colon \mathbb{R}^d \to \mathbb{R}$,
- **path dependent** if $H(N) = h(\mathbf{S}(0), \mathbf{S}(1), \ldots, \mathbf{S}(N))$, where the market model has time set $\mathbb{T} = 0, 1, \ldots, N$, and $h \colon \mathbb{R}^{(N+1)d} \to \mathbb{R}$.
  (We need not impose any regularity on h since $\mathcal{F} = 2^\Omega$.)

Call and put options are clearly path independent.

Throughout this section we assume that the filtration $(\mathcal{F}_n)_{n \leq N}$ generated by the stock prices satisfies $\mathcal{F}_N = \mathcal{F} = 2^\Omega$. We say that two probabilities P_1, P_2 are **equivalent** (written as $P_1 \sim P_2$) if they have the same sets of probability zero. Recall that the sample space $\Omega = \{\omega_1, \ldots, \omega_M\}$ is finite, we assume that P is defined on $\mathcal{F} = 2^\Omega$, and that we take $P(\omega) > 0$ for all ω. So in our setting, to ensure the equivalence $P \sim Q$, any risk-neutral probability must have $Q(\omega) > 0$ for all ω. It is worth mentioning that Q is defined on the field 2^Ω due to the standing assumption that $\mathcal{F}_N = \mathcal{F}$.

First Fundamental Theorem

Theorem 4.34

Absence of arbitrage is equivalent to the existence of a risk-neutral probability Q equivalent to P, such that all discounted price processes $\widetilde{S}_j(n)$, $j = 1, \ldots, d$, are martingales with respect to Q.

Proof   Assume first the existence of a risk-neutral probability Q. Take any predictable strategy $(\mathbf{x}, y)$ and note that its discounted value process $\widetilde{V}_{(\mathbf{x}, y)}(n)$ is a martingale.

Suppose $V(0) = 0$, $V_{(x,y)}(n) \geq 0$ which are necessary conditions for an arbitrage. Then by the martingale property of $\widetilde{V}$ under Q,

$$\mathbb{E}_Q(\widetilde{V}_{(x,y)}(n)) = \mathbb{E}_Q(\widetilde{V}_{(x,y)}(0)) = \mathbb{E}_Q(V_{(x,y)}(0)) = 0$$

so after multiplying both sides by $(1 + R)^n$

$$\mathbb{E}_Q(V_{(x,y)}(n)) = \sum_{\omega \in \Omega} Q(\omega) V_{(x,y)}(n, \omega) = 0.$$

Since all terms are non-negative, $Q(\omega)V_{(x,y)}(n, \omega) = 0$ for all n but $Q(\omega) > 0$, so $V_{(x,y)}(n, \omega) = 0$ for each $\omega \in \Omega$, and this shows that it is impossible to construct an arbitrage.

For the converse implication assume the absence of arbitrage. Let the sequence $\mathbf{x} = \{(x_1(n), \ldots, x_d(n)) : n = 1, \ldots, N\}$ be predictable. The probability space $\Omega = \{\omega_1, \ldots, \omega_M\}$ is finite so a random variable can be regarded as an element of the Euclidean vector space $\mathbb{R}^M$. This means that the discounted gains process $\widetilde{G}_\mathbf{x}$ has the form, for each n,

$$\widetilde{G}_\mathbf{x}(n) = (\widetilde{G}_\mathbf{x}(n, \omega_1), \ldots, \widetilde{G}_\mathbf{x}(n, \omega_M)) \in \mathbb{R}^M$$

and so

$$W = \{\widetilde{G}_\mathbf{x}(N) : \mathbf{x} \text{ predictable}\} \subset \mathbb{R}^M.$$

W is a subspace of $\mathbb{R}^M$, since it is clearly closed under linear combinations.

We shall show that if $\widetilde{G}_\mathbf{x}(N, \omega) \geq 0$ for all ω, then $\widetilde{G}_\mathbf{x}(N, \omega) = 0$ for all ω. Take $V(0) = 0$ and complete $\mathbf{x}$ with $y(n)$ so that $(\mathbf{x}, y)$ is a self-financing predictable strategy. Recall that in general $\widetilde{V}_{(x,y)}(n) = V(0) + \widetilde{G}_\mathbf{x}(n)$, and so by Proposition 4.24 we see that $\widetilde{G}_\mathbf{x}(N, \omega) = 0$ for all ω.

To conclude the proof of the theorem, recall that we are working under the No Arbitrage Principle and that we have identified $W = \{\widetilde{G}_\mathbf{x}(N) : \mathbf{x}$ predictable$\}$ as a subspace of $\mathbb{R}^M$. We apply the Separation Lemma (Lemma 2.35), which says that if $A \subset \mathbb{R}^M$ is convex and compact and W is a vector subspace of $\mathbb{R}^M$ disjoint from A, then there exists $\mathbf{z} = (z_i)_{i \leq M} \in \mathbb{R}^M$ such that $\langle \mathbf{z}, \mathbf{a} \rangle > 0$ for all $\mathbf{a} \in A$, and $\langle \mathbf{z}, \mathbf{w} \rangle = 0$ for all $\mathbf{w} \in W$ (with $\langle \cdot, \cdot \rangle$ denoting the Euclidean inner product in $\mathbb{R}^M$). For our application we take:

$$A = \left\{ \mathbf{a} = (q_1, \ldots, q_M) : \sum_{i=1}^M q_i = 1, q_i \geq 0 \right\},$$

and the above W.

Define

$$Q(\omega_i) = \frac{z_i}{\sum_{i=1}^M z_i} > 0$$

and using the definition of the inner product in $\mathbb{R}^M$ we obtain

$$\langle \mathbf{z}, \mathbf{w} \rangle = \sum_{i=1}^{M} z_i \widetilde{G}_{\mathbf{x}}(N, \omega_i) = 0$$

so

$$\sum_{i=1}^{M} Q(\omega_i) \widetilde{G}_{\mathbf{x}}(N, \omega_i) = \mathbb{E}_Q(\widetilde{G}_{\mathbf{x}}(N)) = 0.$$

But the stock holdings $\mathbf{x}$ were taken as an arbitrary predictable (vector) process, and we may, for example, fix $j \leq d$ and take $\mathbf{x}(n) = (0, \ldots, 0, x_j(n), 0 \ldots, 0)$ for $n \leq N$, where the real-valued process $x_j(n)$ is predictable. The above identity reduces to

$$\mathbb{E}_Q\left(\sum_{i=1}^{N} x_j(i) \Delta \widetilde{S}_j(i) \right) = 0.$$

By Theorem 4.32 the $\widetilde{S}_j(n)$ are martingales for $j = 1, \ldots d$, since the $x_j(n)$ are arbitrary predictable sequences. □

Remark 4.35

The First Fundamental Theorem therefore describes the 'economic' no-arbitrage axiom in purely mathematical terms, namely the existence of an equivalent martingale measure. Our proof contains the crucial additional assumption that the sample space Ω has finitely many elements (and we can therefore give each of them positive probabilities). This naturally begs the question whether this restriction can be removed. In discrete-time models this does turn out to be the case, although the proof uses considerably more advanced concepts in functional analysis which are beyond our scope.[1]

Even in the relatively simple setting of finite market models, the above theorem does not tell us whether the risk-neutral probability Q is unique. In fact, we have already seen in the one-step trinomial model that this need not be the case. Our next result characterises the pricing models with unique risk-neutral probabilities.

Second Fundamental Theorem

We formulate the main principle of pricing by arbitrage. It is based on the No Arbitrage Principle but takes into account the fact that the notion of

---

[1] See R. J. Elliott and P. E. Kopp, *Mathematics of Financial Markets*, Springer 2005.

arbitrage is relative to the market since the notion of portfolio depends on the choice of the securities traded.

Definition 4.36

The **payoff** of a derivative security is any random variable H measurable with respect to the field $\mathcal{F}_N$ generated by the underlying securities prices up to time N. The **prices** of H form a sequence $H(n)$ such that $H(N) = H$ and the market extended by H is free of arbitrage. (Recall that we assume $\mathcal{F}_N = 2^\Omega$ by adjusting Ω if necessary.)

The **basic market** of underlying securities consists of d stocks and the risk-free asset. The **extended market** includes some specified additional securities.

Definition 4.37

A derivative security can be **replicated** if there exists a self-financing predictable strategy $(\mathbf{x}, y)$ such that

$$H(N) = V_{(\mathbf{x}, y)}(N).$$

Definition 4.38

The market is **complete** if every derivative security can be replicated.

As we shall see, completeness and lack of arbitrage are crucial conditions for satisfactory pricing. We have exactly the same result as in the single-step case.

Theorem 4.39

An arbitrage-free market model is complete if and only if there is exactly one risk-neutral probability $Q \sim P$.

Proof This proof is very similar to the proof for the single-period case given earlier. As in the First Fundamental Theorem we shall make crucial use of the finiteness of Ω.

First, assume the No Arbitrage Principle and completeness. A risk-neutral probability exists by the First Fundamental Theorem so all we have to do is to prove uniqueness.

Suppose we have two risk-neutral probabilities $Q_1 \neq Q_2$. Fix A in $\mathcal{F}_N$ and define a special derivative security with the payoff

$$H(N) = \mathbf{1}_A.$$

By completeness, there exists a self-financing predictable strategy $(\mathbf{x}, y)$ such that

$$V_{(\mathbf{x}, y)}(N) = \mathbf{1}_A.$$

Taking expectations with respect to each risk-neutral measure we see that

$$\mathbb{E}_{Q_i}(V_{(\mathbf{x},y)}(N)) = \mathbb{E}_{Q_i}(\mathbf{1}_A) = Q_i(A) \quad i = 1, 2.$$

But the discounted values form a martingale, so the expectation is constant in time

$$(1 + R)^{-N}\mathbb{E}_{Q_i}(V_{(\mathbf{x},y)}(N)) = \mathbb{E}_{Q_i}(\widetilde{V}_{(\mathbf{x},y)}(N)) = V_{(\mathbf{x},y)}(0).$$

The right-hand side does not depend on i so $Q_1(A) = Q_2(A)$ (both are equal to $V_{(\mathbf{x},y)}(0)(1 + R)^N$). Hence $Q_1 = Q_2$, as $A \in \mathcal{F}_N$ was arbitrary.

For the converse implication assume that there exists a unique risk-neutral probability $Q \sim P$. The No Arbitrage Principle applies, by the First Fundamental Theorem. To prove completeness, we suppose that a certain derivative security with payoff $H(N)$ cannot be replicated, and show that this allows us to construct another risk-neutral probability, which is a contradiction. Consider the set of real random variables defined on Ω by

$$W = \{V_{(\mathbf{x},y)}(N) : (\mathbf{x}, y) \text{ self-financing, predictable}\}.$$

This is a vector subspace of $\mathbb{R}^M$ with $H(N) \notin W$. Investing risk free we can obtain a deterministic final value so $\mathbf{1} = (1, \ldots, 1) \in W$.

Equip $\mathbb{R}^M$ with the inner product

$$\langle \mathbf{z}, \mathbf{w} \rangle_Q = \sum_{i=1}^{M} z_i w_i Q(\omega_i).$$

By Lemma 2.39 with $A = \{H(N)\}$ there exists $\mathbf{z}$ such that $\mathbf{z} \neq \mathbf{0}$, $\mathbb{E}_Q(\mathbf{z}) = 0$, since $\mathbf{1} \in W$. Write $a = \max_{i=1,\ldots,M} |z_i| < \infty$, and define a new probability

$$Q_1(\omega_i) = \left(1 + \frac{z_i}{2a}\right) Q(\omega_i), \text{ for } i = 1, \ldots, M.$$

We proved (see the proof of the single-period Second Fundamental Theorem) that
1. Q_1 is a probability equivalent to P: $Q_1(\omega_i) > 0$.
2. Q_1 is different from Q.
We shall see that
3. Q_1 is risk neutral.
To this end take a predictable sequence $\mathbf{x}(n)$, and use it to create a self-financing strategy $(\mathbf{x},y)$ with initial value $V(0) = 0$. We use the fact that the

discounted values are Q-martingales so the expectation is constant in time:

$$\mathbb{E}_{Q_1}(\widetilde{V}_{(\mathbf{x},y)}(N)) = \sum_{i=1}^{M} Q(\omega_i)(1 + \frac{z_i}{2a})\widetilde{V}_{(\mathbf{x},y)}(N)$$

$$= \sum_{i=1}^{M} Q(\omega_i)\widetilde{V}_{(\mathbf{x},y)}(N) + \frac{1}{2a(1 + R)^N} \sum_{i=1}^{M} z_i V_{(\mathbf{x},y)}(N)Q(\omega_i)$$

$$= \mathbb{E}_Q(\widetilde{V}_{(\mathbf{x},y)}(N)) + \frac{1}{2a(1 + R)^N} \langle \mathbf{z}, V_{(\mathbf{x},y)}(N) \rangle_Q$$

$$= V(0) + \frac{1}{2a(1 + R)^N} \langle \mathbf{z}, V_{(\mathbf{x},y)}(N) \rangle_Q$$

$$= 0,$$

since $\langle \mathbf{z}, \mathbf{w} \rangle = 0$ for $\mathbf{w} \in W$. Since $\mathbf{x}(n)$ was arbitrary, Theorem 4.32 shows that Q_1 is risk neutral. Conditions 1,2,3 give a contradiction with the uniqueness of the risk-neutral probability. So every derivative security can be replicated, i.e. the model is complete. □

Consequences for option pricing

We give a summary of the consequences of the Fundamental Theorems.

Theorem 4.40
If the underlying market (d stocks and money market) does not admit arbitrage and a derivative security with payoff H(N) is replicable by a strategy (x, y) then for the extended market to be arbitrage-free, we must have

$$H(n) = V_{(\mathbf{x},y)}(n).$$

To see this, note that if we had an inequality at any time, an arbitrage could be constructed. The investment would be started at that time, the option sold and the portfolio bought (or vice versa). The profit would be maintained since at the final moment the option payoff is identical to the portfolio value.

Then, employing the fact that the stock prices and also the values of strategies are martingales with respect to the unique risk-neutral probability, we obtain

$$\widetilde{V}_{(\mathbf{x},y)}(n) = \mathbb{E}_Q(\widetilde{V}_{(\mathbf{x},y)}(N)|\mathcal{F}_n)$$

$$= \mathbb{E}_Q(\widetilde{H}(N)|\mathcal{F}_n)$$

inserting the payoff as a result of the replication assumption. By definition

$$\widetilde{V}_{(x,y)}(n) = \widetilde{H}(n) = (1 + R)^{-n} H(n)$$

so

$$H(n) = \frac{1}{(1 + R)^{N-n}} \mathbb{E}_Q(H(N)|\mathcal{F}_n).$$

In particular (for $n = 0$)

$$H(0) = (1 + R)^{-N} \mathbb{E}_Q(H(N)).$$

4.7 Selecting and calibrating a pricing model

In view of the Second Fundamental Theorem, a desirable model is a complete one. So if we wish to consider just one stock a natural choice is the binomial model. However, any pricing model has no relevance unless we can relate it clearly to real market data.

We face the crucial task of choosing the parameters of our pricing model so that our mathematical creation resembles the real world. The available historical data are typically the source of inspiration for this. From past stock prices we can compute characteristics such as average return or sample variance of return and then make the brave assumption that these past numbers reflect the future. This is of course problematic and a serious analysis of the whole issue is beyond our scope, so we shall confine ourselves to brief remarks.

In our simple binomial model, where the returns have identical distributions, the task is to find p, U, D. Assume that the average past return is μ and the variance of the return is σ^2. Then we can fit the parameters to the data by solving two equations

$$pU + (1 - p)D = \mu,$$
$$(U - D)^2 p(1 - p) = \sigma^2.$$

Remember, however, that the reliability of μ obtained from historical data is questionable. Here we have too much flexibility, since there are two equations in three variables. We could try to compute some further moments of returns or we can make further simplifying assumptions. A widely used simplification is to take $D = 1/U$, for example $U = e^a$, $D = e^{-a}$ for some a. Another possibility is to take $p = 0.5$ which reflects the observed irrelevance of p for pricing, but in calibration the choice of p is relevant since this parameter interplays with the returns.

Further ad hoc choices are concerned with risk-neutral probability q. We could require $q = 0.5$, for simplicity, meaning that $\frac{U+D}{2} = R$, and fit the variance to the risk-neutral probabilities by letting $q(1 - q)(U - D)^2 = \sigma^2$. The source of inspiration here is the fact that in the popular continuous-time Black–Scholes model (see [BSM] in the current series) the coefficient responsible for the variance does not change if we move to the risk-neutral probability.

Suppose the binomial model has been constructed. Now we are in a position to find unique no-arbitrage prices of all derivative securities. However, suppose that an option is traded, the price is given by the market and does not agree with the theoretical findings of our model. This means that arbitrage is available in our model but not necessarily in reality! If the option price is reliable, for instance if this security is liquid with a substantial volume of trading, we must conclude that our model is wrong. We could rectify the situation by extending to a trinomial model, taking the option as an additional security. Our model is now free of arbitrage and complete. However, we may need to expand it further if other option prices are given (for instance calls with various strikes) and do not agree with the new model's predictions.

Of course, serious pricing requires a multi-step model. This gives yet another way of adding flexibility to the modelling, by allowing single-step returns to have various distributions. We do not pursue this here since serious technical complications emerge but this line of reasoning will be needed when we discuss random interest rates.

This discussion illustrates the fundamental issue that market data cannot be ignored and perhaps we should reconsider the whole approach to model building, focussing instead on the information provided by current market prices. Options are related to future stock prices, so their prices reflect the market view on the future stock evolution, and 'the market is always right'. In particular, in a trinomial incomplete model the market 'chooses' the unique risk-neutral probability by providing the price of an option.

In line with this observation we could seek conditions to determine the model parameters by means of the pricing formulae of the form: $H(0) = \mathbb{E}_Q(\tilde{H}(1))$, which, if the shape of $H(1)$ is known, involve only the returns U and D.

Exercise 4.8 Build a binomial model with $S(0) = 100$, $R = 10\%$ if calls with strikes 100 and 105 have prices 10 and 8, respectively.

One more issue related to calibration is the choice of the length of the time step. Taking h small has the advantage of being close to the real world, where price changes are frequent. For small h, the size of the price change also has to be small. In reality stock prices behave in a manner resembling a binomial tree with changes given by a prescribed small amount d (a **tick**). But a model with changes of the type $S(n+1) = S(n) \pm d$ cannot be realistic since after some steps the prices might become negative. So the tick size must be reduced when the price drops considerably and so a proportional pricing model with multiplicative price changes seems to be more reasonable.

The size of h corresponds to the number of steps. If a typical option is issued with three months to exercise, daily changes would mean the size of Ω is of the order of 2^{60} which makes computations impossible. And one must not forget that in reality changes are made much more frequently than on a daily basis. A way forward, therefore, is to develop a continuous-time approach. This is delayed until volume [BSM] in this series, as it requires substantial mathematical preparation, provided in [PF] and [SCF].

4.8   More examples of derivatives

In this concluding section we use the general theory developed above to investigate simple properties of forwards and futures, and provide a brief glimpse of the variety of derivatives that can be built from the basic building blocks we have analysed. We begin by observing that call-put parity has a natural counterpart in multi-step models.

Call-put parity

In a complete arbitrage-free model we may proceed as in Section 2.7 and consider the relation between the discounted payoffs of call and put options

$$\tilde{C}(N) - \tilde{P}(N) = \tilde{S}(N) - K(1+R)^{-N}.$$

Taking conditional expectations on both sides we have

$$\mathbb{E}_Q(\tilde{C}(N)|\mathcal{F}_n) - \mathbb{E}_Q(\tilde{P}(N)|\mathcal{F}_n) = \mathbb{E}_Q(\tilde{S}(N)|\mathcal{F}_n) - K(1+R)^{-N}$$

which yields $\tilde{C}(n) - \tilde{P}(n) = \tilde{S}(n) - K(1+R)^{-N}$, thus generalising Theorem 2.42.

Theorem 4.41 Call-put parity

For any $n \in \{0, \ldots, N\}$ we have the following relation between the call and put values

$$C(n) - P(n) = S(n) - K(1 + R)^{-(N-n)}.$$

This theorem does not in fact require using any particular model and can be justified directly by the No Arbitrage Principle. To this end, we need only generalise the Law of One Price (Corollary 2.44).

Theorem 4.42 The law of one price

If H, H' are two European path-independent derivative securities with the same payoff

$$H(N) = H'(N)$$

then for each $n \leq N$ their values agree:

$$H(n) = H'(n).$$

Proof This is routine: if for one ω_0, at some time n_0 we have $H(n_0, \omega_0) < H'(n_0, \omega_0)$, say, then we do nothing up to time n_0, take $z_H(n_0, \omega_0) = 1$, $z_{H'}(n_0, \omega_0) = -1$, $y(n_0, \omega_0) = H'(n_0, \omega_0) - H(n_0, \omega_0)$ to obtain an arbitrage opportunity. □

Forwards and futures

Recall that a forward contract (long position) with delivery price K is a derivative security with payoff $H(N) = S(N) - K$. Then, in a complete model free of arbitrage

$$H(n) = (1 + R)^{-(N-n)} \mathbb{E}_Q(S(N) - K) = S(n) - K(1 + R)^{-(N-n)}.$$

As in Chapter 2, we can give a model-independent proof of this formula.

Proposition 4.43

The time n value of a forward contract initiated at time 0 with delivery price K is $H(n) = S(n) - K(1 + R)^{-(N-n)}$.

Proof We build a portfolio such that at time N, $V_{(x,y,z)}(N) = S(N) - K$ taking $x(n) = 1$, $y(n) = -\frac{1}{A(0)}K(1 + R)^{-N}$. Hence by no arbitrage at each time n we must have $V_{(x,y)}(n) = H(n)$ by a straightforward argument. At time n, $V_{(x,y)}(n) = S(n) + y(n)A(n) = S(n) - K(1 + R)^{-(N-n)}$, which completes the proof. □

Generally, we define the **forward price** $F(n, N)$ as the delivery price that gives zero value to a contract entered into at time n, with delivery at time N.

Corollary 4.44
No-arbitrage implies that the forward price at time $n < N$ is

$$F(n, N) = S(n)(1 + R)^{N-n}.$$

Proof   From $H(n) = 0$ we get the result at once.   □

In particular $F(0, N) = S(0)(1 + R)^N$ (as we observed in Chapter 2 for $N = 1$).

Exercise 4.9   Suppose that you have entered a long forward contract with forward price $F(0, 2) = 124.75$. At time 1 you would like to close this position. How much money would you have to pay (or receive) if $S(1) = 120$ and $R = 9\%$?

In addition to stock prices markets also quote so-called **futures prices**. The principal difference between them and forwards is that futures are quoted on an exchange, whereas forwards are traded 'over-the-counter' (OTC), by mutual agreement between the two parties concerned. The exchange seeks to minimise the risk of default, so investors are required to hold a **margin account** with the exchange, whose funds can be adjusted daily to reflect the fluctuations in futures prices.

We restrict our attention to discrete-time situations. Use $f(n, N)$ to denote the futures price of a commodity, which is established at time n when the contract is initiated. This provides a series of derivative securities with underlying asset $S(n)$ defined by means of the following axioms:

- $f(N, N) = S(N)$.
- $f(n, N)$ is $\mathcal{F}_n$-measurable, where $\mathcal{F}_n$ is the field generated by the stock prices $S(1), \ldots, S(n)$.
- At time n a long futures position generates the cash flow

$$f(n, N) - f(n - 1, N), \quad n = 1, \ldots, N.$$

- A time n a short futures position generates the cash flow

$$f(n - 1, N) - f(n, N), \quad n = 1, \ldots, N.$$

- It costs nothing to enter any futures position at any time.

The cash flows generated in the margin accounts by changes in the futures position are called **marking-to-market**. If we neglect the time value of money then the holder of the long futures position has the total cash flow

$$\sum_{n=0}^{N}[f(n,N) - f(n-1,N)] = f(N,N) - f(0,N) = S(N) - f(0,N), \quad (4.6)$$

which looks very similar to the long forward payoff. The only difference, $f(0,N)$ in place of $F(0,N)$, is irrelevant if the risk-free returns are known for the future periods, as is shown in the next result. Again we require extended strategies, this time involving either forwards or futures as the derivative security. Our no-arbitrage assumption remains in place for both cases.

Theorem 4.45
If the interest rate is constant, then $f(0,N) = F(0,N)$.

Proof We restrict to the special case $N = 2$. One forward contract gives the payoff $S(2) - F(0,2)$. We will design a futures-based strategy with zero cost, which will generate the sum $f(0,2) - S(2)$. Since the combined balance is $f(0,2) - F(0,2)$, which is a deterministic quantity produced at zero cost, it must be zero.

To build the required strategy we write (as in (4.6))

$$f(0,2) - S(2) = f(0,2) - f(2,2)$$
$$= (f(0,2) - f(1,2)) + (f(1,2) - f(2,2))$$

and then replicate each bracketed term on the right.

The latter is the futures short position cash flow at time 2, so to generate it we have to open this contract at time 1.

The former after discounting becomes $\frac{1}{1+R}(f(0,2) - f(1,2))$, which is the payoff at time 1 of the fraction $\frac{1}{1+R}$ of the short futures position opened at time 0. If we open such a fraction (for free), and invest the proceeds obtained at time 1 (or borrow rather than invest if the amount is negative) risk free, this will give us $f(0,2) - f(1,2)$ at time 2 as required.

More formally, at time 0 we take
$x(1) = 0, y(1) = 0,$
$z_{\text{forward}}(1) = 1, z_{\text{futures}}(1) = -\frac{1}{1+R},$
which is free, and at time 1, at zero cost, we change this to
$x(2) = 0, y(2) = \frac{1}{1+R}(f(0,2) - f(1,2)),$
$z_{\text{forward}}(2) = 1, z_{\text{futures}}(2) = -1.$

(The key point is the knowledge of the future interest rate for the period starting at time 1 which allows us to figure out the size of the initial futures position.)   □

Exercise 4.10   Suppose that the stock prices on consecutive days are 100, 100.33, 100.33, 100.15, 99, 101. Find the cash flow of the long futures position if the annual risk-free rate is 9%.

Complex derivatives

Call and put options are often called (plain) **vanilla** options, as they have no special features and are regarded by market traders as very familiar. More complex options are often called **exotic**, although this terminology is not used with much precision.

Vanillas can be combined in various ways to form trading strategies whose payoffs are suited to investors' various perceived needs. We offer some simple examples, reflecting different investment needs:

Example 4.46

To construct a **covered call** we write a call, strike K, (receiving the call premium $C(0)$) and hold one share in the stock. The initial value of this position is $S(0) - C(0) > 0$ (else the buyer of the call might just as well buy the share to begin with!) and we are 'covered' against having to relinquish our share for K at time N: our final position is $C(0) - S(0) + \min(S(N), K)$, which is positive: by parity, and as $P(0) > 0$ and $(1 + R)^{-N} \leq 1$ we obtain

$$C(0) > S(0) - (1 + R)^{-N}K \geq S(0) - K. \tag{4.7}$$

Note, however, that our profit is capped at $C(0) - S(0) + K$, whereas for the call holder (who has invested only the call premium) the potential profit $S(N) - K - C(0)$ is unbounded above.

Exercise 4.11   Conduct a similar analysis of the **protective put**, which consists of long positions (of one unit each) in the underlying stock and a put option on the stock.

Example 4.47

Spreads are portfolios using options of the same type, some in long and some in short positions. A popular example is the **butterfly spread**, which is designed for investors who believe that large fluctuations in the price of the underlying stock are unlikely in $[0, N]$. One buys calls with strikes K_1 and $K_3 > K_1$ and at the same time sells two calls at strike $K_2 = \frac{1}{2}(K_1 + K_3)$. The initial outlay is thus $I(0) = C_1(0) + C_3(0) - 2C_2(0)$, which is positive, as the call price is a convex function of the strike. The payoff is 0 outside the strike interval $(K_1, K_3]$, $S(N) - K_1$ on $(K_1, K_2]$ and $K_3 - S(N)$ on $(K_2, K_3]$. An investor who believes that the stock price will not vary much from X_2 is thus likely to profit from this position and is well protected against large unforeseen price changes.

Example 4.48

As we saw in Exercise 3.8, the bottom **straddle** consists of long positions in both a call and a put with common strike K and expiry date N. This is a simple example of a **combination**, using options of different types on the same underlying. We buy a call and a put, both with strike K and expiry N. The payoff is $|S(N) - K|$, against an initial outlay of $C(0) + P(0)$. Thus the holder will lose money if the price of the stock stays close to K but can gain substantially if the final price differs significantly from K. This investment thus suits an investor who expects large price changes, by taking options with strike close to $S(0)$.

Path-dependent options

Recall, that a European derivative security H is path dependent if $H(N) = h(S(0), S(1), \ldots, S(N))$, where $h: \mathbb{R}^{N+1} \to \mathbb{R}$ is Borel-measurable. We shall consider some common path-dependent options below.

Example 4.49

Barrier options are instruments that are designed to hedge against movements in the stock price crossing a given level, seen as a 'barrier' Y say. If the stock price reaches (or crosses) Y, a **knock-out** barrier option becomes

worthless: if $S(n)$ reaches Y from below we call it **up-and-out**, otherwise **down-and-out**. On the other hand, a **knock-in** option only comes into existence once the barrier is reached, although the option premium has been paid at the outset. For a single barrier Y we can devise eight European-style barrier options by using the terms call and put, up and down, in and out in combination. In addition, one can develop two-sided barrier options, using both an upper and a lower barrier, with different outcomes depending on whether activation (or deactivation) occurs when either or both barriers are breached.

The somewhat lengthy computation of closed-form formulae giving rational prices for the different option premia (within the standard Black–Scholes model setting) is now part of the standard literature. Fortunately there are again some shortcuts: in each case the sum of the payoffs of an in-option and an out-option with the same strike, expiry and barrier is obviously the same as that of the ordinary option of that type, since only one of the barrier options survives and then has the same payoff as the standard option.

Further complications for computation can arise in practice, where the option holder may be given a **rebate** when the option is knocked out, or, as for **Parisian** options, the option is knocked out only once the barrier has been breached for a specified length of time. Barrier options are attractive to a buyer seeking to minimise the cost of option premia by excluding scenarios she considers unlikely, while accepting the risk that they may occur. For example, a down-and-out call should be cheaper than an ordinary one, since the option is knocked out if $S(n)$ reaches Y from above, irrespective of whether the stock price recovers to above Y by time N. The writer of an up-and out call, on the other hand, limits her potential liabilities in the event that the stock rises sharply.

Example 4.50
Lookback options come in several guises, using the maximum M_{lb} or minimum m_{lb} of the underlying stock price over a preset 'lookback period' within $\mathbb{T}$. We have the **floating strike** variety, where the strike becomes a random variable. Thus the lookback call allows one to buy the stock at the minimum value achieved in the lookback period, hence the payoff is

$(S(N)-m_{lb})^+$. For the put the holder uses the maximum instead, with payoff $(M_{lb}-S(N))^+$. There are also **fixed strike** versions, with payoffs $(M_{lb}-K)^+$ and $(K-m_{lb})^+$, and even **partial lookbacks**, using a preset fraction λM_{lb} or λm_{lb} instead. Clearly all these are designed to 'eliminate regret' over lost opportunities, and their premia will reflect this.

Example 4.51

The **Asian call** option, in a model with time set $\mathbb{T} = \{0, 1, 2, \dots, N\}$, has payoff $H(N) = (A(N) - K)^+$, where $A(N)$ is either the arithmetic average $\frac{1}{N}\sum_{i=1}^{N} S(i)$ or the geometric average $[\prod_{i=1}^{N} S(i)]^{1/n}$ of the stock prices, together with a **fixed strike** K. Clearly these are path-dependent options. They are usually traded as of European type, to avoid early exercise occurring before the averaging period is completed, thus losing the protection it can provide.

To see why one may wish to use such options in certain situations, consider a fixed strike $K = 1.5$, $N = 6$ and $A(N)$ as the arithmetic average. Suppose that the price evolution of the underlying S is given by

n	1	2	3	4	5	6
$S(n)$	1.5	1.6	1.7	1.8	1.6	1.4

Then $H(6) = 0.1$, whereas for a European call $C(6) = 0$. The Asian option may be preferred by a company which regularly buys some asset and wants to hedge against high prices, for example, to guard against price spikes near the trading horizon. It can buy a series of vanilla call options with different maturities or a single Asian call on the average price. The latter is usually satisfactory from the point of view of securing the company's business.

Pricing formulae have been extended to cover many other exotic options, including choosers, where the option holder can decide at an intermediate time $0 < N_1 < N$ whether he wishes to treat his option as a put or a call, and compound options, where the underlying is not a stock but an option with earlier expiry. Methods for determining rational prices and market applications for such derivatives can be developed in various model settings.

4.9   Proofs

Theorem 4.31

If $M_j(n)$ are martingales and the processes $H_j(n)$ are predictable, $j =$
$1,\ldots,d$, then the process $X(n)$ defined by

$$X(n) = X(0) + \sum_{k=1}^{n}\sum_{j=1}^{d} H_j(k)\Delta M_j(k) = X(0) + \sum_{k=1}^{n}\langle \mathbf{H}(k), \Delta\mathbf{M}(k)\rangle$$

is a martingale, where $X(0) = x_0$ is an arbitrary real number.

Proof   First note

$$X(n+1) - X(n) = \sum_{j=1}^{d} H_j(n+1)\Delta M_j(n+1)$$

$$= \sum_{j=1}^{d} H_j(n+1)\big[M_j(n+1) - M_j(n)\big].$$

The theorem is formulated for any probability space hence we use the general symbol for expectation. We take the conditional expectation of the above equality to get

$$\mathbb{E}(X(n+1) - X(n)|\mathcal{F}_n)$$

$$= \mathbb{E}\left(\sum_{j=1}^{d} H_j(n+1)\big[M_j(n+1) - M_j(n)\big]\Big|\mathcal{F}_n\right)$$

$$= \sum_{j=1}^{d}\mathbb{E}\left(H_j(n+1)\big[M_j(n+1) - M_j(n)\big]\Big|\mathcal{F}_n\right)$$

$$= \sum_{j=1}^{d} H_j(n+1)\mathbb{E}(M_j(n+1) - M_j(n)|\mathcal{F}_n)$$

$$= 0$$

where we used the property of conditional expectations called 'taking out what is known' – the process H is predictable so the value at time $n+1$ is measurable with respect to $\mathcal{F}_n$. The final result: $\mathbb{E}(X(n+1) - X(n)|\mathcal{F}_n) = 0$ proves that X is a martingale   □

Theorem 4.32

For $M(n)$ to be a martingale it is sufficient that for each predictable process $H(n)$

$$\mathbb{E}\left(\sum_{n=1}^{N} H(n)\Delta M(n))\right) = 0.$$

Proof We will show

$$\mathbb{E}(M(k+1)|\mathcal{F}_k) = M(k).$$

Take $A \in \mathcal{F}_k$ and write

$$H(n) = \begin{cases} \mathbf{1}_A & \text{for } n = k+1, \\ 0 & \text{otherwise,} \end{cases}$$

and then the sum reduces to just one term

$$\sum_{n=1}^{N} H(n)\Delta M(n) = \mathbf{1}_A \Delta M(k+1).$$

By the assumption

$$\mathbb{E}\left(\sum_{n=1}^{N} H(n)\Delta M(n)\right) = \mathbb{E}(\mathbf{1}_A \Delta M(k+1))$$

$$= \mathbb{E}(\mathbf{1}_A[M(k+1) - M(k)]) = 0,$$

so the definition of conditional expectation completes the proof. □

5

American options

As we recall, a European option confers the right to a random payoff at a prescribed time N in the future. In contrast, **American** derivative securities allow the holder to exercise the corresponding right at any time $n \leq N$, so for an American call we can obtain on demand the payoff $(S(n) - K)^+$ at any time $n \leq N$. When exercised, such an option is terminated. The payoff depends on the values of $S(n)$ for all n up to the moment of exercise, hence a representation of the payoff similar to that of the European case is not possible in general. Even in the simple binomial setting, a direct analogue of the CRR formula is not possible, as the payoff depends on the holder's choice of exercise date. This requires (random) stopping times to describe optimal exercise of the option.

We discuss optimal stopping times in a general discrete-time model with finitely many trading dates, where we assume that we are given a finite probability space $(\Omega, \mathcal{F}, P)$ equipped with a filtration of fields $\mathcal{F}_n$ (see Definition 4.15) generated by some process $S(n)$ representing the underlying security. We illustrate the resulting pricing techniques for single-stock models numerically throughout in a binomial example where, as usual, the space Ω is taken in the form $\{u, d\}^N$, that is, an element ω is a N-tuple built of symbols u, d corresponding to the returns U, D of the price.

0	1	2	3	4	5
stock prices					201
				175	
			152		157
		132		137	
	115		119		123
100		104		107	
	90		93		96.4
		81		84	
			73		75.5
				66	
					59

Figure 5.1

5.1 Pricing

First consider a binomial model and assume that the option holder's choice of exercise date is made in order to maximise the amount received. At each time she faces the choice between exercising immediately and postponing this till later. The sum of money given by the payoff can readily be seen at each time, in each scenario, being a known function of the current stock price. Valuing the alternative poses a problem and depends on assumptions about the future behaviour of the stock. This makes it natural to seek to solve the pricing problem by means of backward induction, while taking into account, at each node of the binomial tree, the additional choice of whether to exercise or not. The method is best illustrated through an example which is sufficiently complex to reveal the various possible scenarios while remaining very simple computationally.

Thus, all notions and theorems in this chapter will be illustrated by a concrete example of a single-stock model in a 5-step binomial tree. We begin with the specification of the dynamics of the underlying security. The initial price is $S(0) = 100$, the returns are $U = 15\%$, $D = -10\%$, so the tree of the prices is as shown in Figure 5.1. Consider a put option with expiry date $N = 5$ and exercise price $K = 100$. Since the American option can be exercised at any time prior to the expiry, it is necessary to compute the immediate payoff of the option at each node of the tree. We denote it by $I(n) = (K - S(n))^+$. The results are shown in Figure 5.2.

Pricing will be performed in a similar fashion as for European claims, starting from the expiry time and moving backwards. The value of the American put at time n is denoted by $P(n)$ so

$$P(5) = I(5).$$

0	1	2	3	4	5
put payoff					0.0
				0.0	
			0.0		0.0
		0.0		0.0	
	0.0		0.0		0.0
0.0		0.0		0.0	
	10.0		6.9		3.6
		19.0		16.2	
			27.1		24.5
				34.4	
					41.0

Figure 5.2

0	1	2	3	4	5
					0.0
				0.0	
					0.0
				0.0	
					0.0
				1.4	
					3.6
				11.4	
					24.5
				29.6	
					41.0

Figure 5.3

Our first serious goal is to compute the prices at time $n = 4$. At this time the holder of the option has a choice between exercising and waiting till the final moment.

The decision about 'waiting' now depends on the value of the European option with exercise date one step from now. This can easily be computed by means of replication, or, equivalently, by using the martingale probability $Q = (q, 1 - q)$. Suppose the risk-free return is $R = 5\%$, so $q = \frac{R-D}{U-D} = 0.6$. At each state at time $n = 4$ we compute the discounted expected value of the payoff available after one further step, obtaining the numbers as in Figure 5.3.

In the two lowest states at time $n = 4$ it is better to exercise immediately rather than wait and the values of the option are the corresponding payoffs (of course we mean here the positive numbers, zeros are irrelevant from this point of view). In the middle state 'waiting' has positive value while

0	1	2	3	4	5
American put					0.0
				0.0	
					0.0
				0.0	
					0.0
				1.4	
					3.6
				16.2	
					24.5
				34.4	
					41.0

Figure 5.4

the immediate payoff is zero. Figure 5.4 shows the results. The highlighted numbers are those where immediate exercise prevailed.

We can summarise the above in a concise way. The value of the European put at time 4 is the following random variable

$$\frac{1}{1+R}\mathbb{E}_Q(I(5)|\mathcal{F}_4) = \frac{1}{1+R}\mathbb{E}_Q(P(5)|\mathcal{F}_4).$$

Therefore, taking the benefit of an immediate exercise, if profitable,

$$P(4) = \max\{I(4), \frac{1}{1+R}\mathbb{E}_Q(P(5)|\mathcal{F}_4)\}.$$

It is convenient to divide both sides by $(1 + R)^4$, which will lead to the discounted prices satisfying

$$\widetilde{P}(4) = \max\{\widetilde{I}(4), \mathbb{E}_Q(\widetilde{P}(5)|\mathcal{F}_4)\}.$$

The prices $P(4)$ computed above are the true market values of the American put, encapsulating the rights belonging to the holder: immediate exercise or wait and keep the option. As such they represent the possible cash flow at time 4, since the option can be sold. Therefore they form a basis for the next (backward) induction step, moving from 4 to 3. Applying the same argument to this step we obtain

$$\widetilde{P}(3) = \max\{\widetilde{I}(3), \mathbb{E}_Q(\widetilde{P}(4)|\mathcal{F}_3)\}$$

with the numerical results shown in Figure 5.5. (Note that in the *DDU* state the exercise payoff is 6.85 which is lower than the value of 'waiting'.)

0	1	2	3	4	5
					0.0
				0.0	
			0.0		0.0
				0.0	
			0.5		0.0
				1.4	
			6.94		3.6
				16.2	
			27.1		24.5
				34.4	
					41.0

Figure 5.5

0	1	2	3	4	5
American put					0.00
				0.00	
			0.00		0.00
		0.20		0.00	
	1.23		0.52		0.00
4.51		2.94		1.37	
	10.00		6.94		3.59
		19.00		**16.17**	
			27.10		24.55
				34.39	
					40.95

Figure 5.6

In general we have shown how to develop the following **backwards induction** procedure, which for the discounted values has the form

$$\widetilde{P}(5) = \widetilde{I}(5),$$
$$\widetilde{P}(n-1) = \max\{\widetilde{I}(n-1), \mathbb{E}_Q(\widetilde{P}(n)|\mathcal{F}_{n-1})\},$$

resulting in the numbers given in Figure 5.6 completing the example, where in particular we find the current (time 0) price of the American put in question: $P(0) = 4.51$. All numbers here are rounded to two decimal points.

We have constructed an example of a general mathematical object.

Definition 5.1

A sequence $Y(n)$ of random variables is the **Snell envelope** of the sequence $Z(n)$, $n = 1, 2, \ldots, N$, adapted to $\mathcal{F}_n$ if

$$Y(N) = Z(N),$$
$$Y(n-1) = \max\{Z(n-1), \mathbb{E}(Y(n)|\mathcal{F}_{n-1})\}.$$

The notion is defined in a general setting but in applications we will use it for binomial trees with expectation with respect to the risk-neutral probability.

So, as we have seen, $Y(n) = \widetilde{P}(n)$ is the Snell envelope of $Z(n) = \widetilde{I}(n)$, $n = 1, \ldots, 5$ with respect to the martingale probability Q and the filtration generated by the partitions of the probability space of scenarios in a recombining binomial tree.

Directly from the definition we can see that $Y(n-1)$ is $\mathcal{F}_{n-1}$-measurable (i.e. Y is adapted), and

$$Y(n-1) \geq \mathbb{E}(Y(n)|\mathcal{F}_{n-1}),$$

(these two conditions by definition mean that Y is a **supermartingale**), as well as

$$Y(n-1) \geq Z(n-1),$$

so the Snell envelope Y of Z is a supermartingale dominating Z. This turns out to be key to characterising Snell envelopes.

Theorem 5.2

The Snell envelope Y of Z is the smallest supermartingale dominating Z. In other words, if $T(n)$ is a supermartingale satisfying $T(n) \geq Z(n)$, then $Y(n) \leq T(n)$.

Proof We have already observed that Y is a supermartingale and that it dominates Z. Given any supermartingale T with $T(n) \geq Z(n)$ for all n, then in particular

$$T(N) \geq Z(N) = Y(N).$$

We will prove by backward induction that this property holds for all n. Suppose, for the induction hypothesis, that this is true for some k, that is, $T(k) \geq Y(k)$. This immediately implies

$$\mathbb{E}(T(k)|\mathcal{F}_{k-1}) \geq \mathbb{E}(Y(k)|\mathcal{F}_{k-1}).$$

The sequence T is a supermartingale, so

$$T(k-1) \geq \mathbb{E}(T(k)|\mathcal{F}_{k-1}).$$

Putting these two inequalities together we get

$$T(k-1) \geq \mathbb{E}(Y(k)|\mathcal{F}_{k-1}).$$

In addition, as T dominates Z, we have $T(k-1) \geq Z(n-1)$, so

$$T(k-1) \geq \max\{Z(n-1), \mathbb{E}(Y(k)|\mathcal{F}_{k-1})\} = Y(k-1)$$

(the last equality is the definition of the Snell envelope), which completes the induction step and so the proof.   □

Exercise 5.1   Find the price of an American straddle, i.e., the derivative with payoff $I(n) = |S(n) - K|$ for $N = 4$, where $S(n)$ follows a binomial tree with $S(0) = 50$, $U = 12\%$, $D = -6\%$, $R = 5\%$, $K = 50$.

Exercise 5.2   Investigate the dependence on the strike K of the difference between the prices of European and American puts on the same stock.

5.2   Stopping times and optimal exercise

Going back to our numerical example, suppose we bought the American put for $P(0) = 4.51$. The problem we are facing at all times is the decision whether to exercise this option or not. (Refer to Figure 5.6 for the option prices computed at each stage.)

Consider first the strategy of exercising at the earliest possible time when the option price is equal to the available payoff.

Of course, we do not exercise at time 0 since the payoff is 0. Let B_U (resp. B_D) be the set of all paths beginning with a u (resp. d) movement, and similarly define $B_{UU}, B_{UD}, B_{DU}, B_{DD}$ and so on.

• Suppose the stock goes down in the first step, that is, consider $\omega \in B_D$. We exercise the option at time 1, cashing 10, which, as we saw, is higher than the expected profit from waiting.

• Suppose the stock goes up in the first step, so let $\omega \in B_U$. Here we distinguish three cases.

  – If $\omega \in B_{UDDD}$ we exercise at time 4, obtaining 16.17.

  – If $\omega = $ uuddd, $\omega = $ ududd or $\omega = $ uddud, we exercise at time 5 receiving 3.59.

– For other paths we do not exercise the option at all and receive zero. Or, in other words, we exercise at time 5, where the payoff is zero.

We have defined a random variable assigning to each ω the time when we exercise the option:

$$\tau_1(\omega) = \begin{cases} 1 & \omega \in B_D, \\ 4 & \omega \in B_{UDDD}, \\ 5 & \text{otherwise.} \end{cases}$$

This is an example of an important general notion, which we define next.

Definition 5.3
A random variable $\tau: \Omega \to \{1, 2, \ldots, N\}$ is a **stopping time** if $\{\omega : \tau(\omega) \leq n\} \in \mathcal{F}_n$ for all n.

The condition means that the decision to stop at time n will be based on the information available at that moment. This is even clearer in the following equivalent formulation, which you should verify.

Exercise 5.3 Prove that $\tau: \Omega \to \{1, 2, \ldots, N\}$ is a stopping time if and only if $\{\omega : \tau(\omega) = n\} \in \mathcal{F}_n$ for all n.

Going back to the example of the decision strategy for option exercise considered above, we can define a natural modification, related to the early exercise, of the process of the option values. These values fluctuate with time when we observe them along various scenarios. For example, if $\omega = udddu$ we have the sequence

$$P(n, \omega) = (4.51, 1.23, 2.94, 6.94, 16.17, 3.59).$$

In such a scenario our strategy tells us to exercise at time 4. Imagine that we keep the money we have cashed, so the sequence is modified to become

$$P_\tau(n, \omega) = (4.51, 1.23, 2.94, 6.94, 16.17, 16.17).$$

For this particular ω, $\tau(\omega) = 4$, and we left the sequence unchanged for $n \leq 4$, replacing the subsequent values by the value at time 4, so for $n \geq 4$ we have $P(n, \omega) = P(\tau(\omega), \omega)$.

This motivates the next definition.

Definition 5.4
For any sequence of random variables $X(n)$ and any stopping time τ we define the **stopped process** $X_\tau(n)$ by

$$X_\tau(n) = X(\min\{\tau, n\}),$$

or, more explicitly, by

$$X_\tau(n, \omega) = \begin{cases} X(n, \omega) & \text{if } n \leq \tau(\omega), \\ X(\tau(\omega), \omega) & \text{if } n > \tau(\omega). \end{cases}$$

In particular, $X_\tau(N) = X(\tau)$. The stopped process X_τ inherits all the important properties of X.

Proposition 5.5

If X is adapted, then X_τ is also adapted. If X is a martingale (supermartingale) the X_τ is also a martingale (supermartingale).

Proof   First we claim that we can write X_τ in the form

$$X_\tau(n) = X(0) + \sum_{j=1}^{n} \mathbf{1}_{\{j \leq \tau\}}(X(j) - X(j-1)). \tag{5.1}$$

The terms in the sum cancel out (the difference term on the right with $j = 1$ takes care of $X(0)$) so only the last term survives. The index of this survivor depends on the indicator function. If $\tau(\omega) \geq n$, then it is one for all j so we have $X(n)$ left. Otherwise the last j for which the indicator is one is $j = \tau(\omega)$ and the right-hand side reduces to $X(j)$.

The sequence $\mathbf{1}_{\{j \leq \tau\}}$ is predictable since

$$\{j \leq \tau\} = \Omega \setminus \{j > \tau\} = \Omega \setminus \{\tau \leq j - 1\} \in \mathcal{F}_{j-1}.$$

Hence X_τ is adapted since all the terms on the right in (5.1) are $\mathcal{F}_n$-measurable. So if X is a martingale then X_τ is a martingale transform, so by Proposition 4.31, X_τ is also a martingale.

Next, again using the representation of $X_\tau(n)$ given in (5.1), we compute the conditional expectation of the increment:

$$\mathbb{E}(X_\tau(n+1) - X_\tau(n)|\mathcal{F}_n) = \mathbb{E}(\mathbf{1}_{\{n+1 \leq \tau\}}(X(n+1) - X(n))|\mathcal{F}_n)$$
$$= \mathbf{1}_{\{n+1 \leq \tau\}}\mathbb{E}(X(n+1) - X(n)|\mathcal{F}_n),$$

where we used the 'take out what is known' property of the conditional expectation ($\mathbf{1}_{\{n+1 \leq \tau\}}$ is $\mathcal{F}_n$-measurable). Therefore the random variables $\mathbb{E}(X_\tau(n+1) - X_\tau(n)|\mathcal{F}_n)$ and $\mathbb{E}(X(n+1) - X(n)|\mathcal{F}_n)$ have the same sign – they are either both greater than or equal to zero, or both less than or equal to zero. Hence if X is a supermartingale, that is,

$$\mathbb{E}(X(n+1) - X(n)|\mathcal{F}_n) = \mathbb{E}(X(n+1)|\mathcal{F}_n) - X(n) \leq 0$$

then X_τ is a supermartingale. $\square$

Remark 5.6

A **submartingale** is an $\mathcal{F}_n$-adapted sequence satisfying $\mathbb{E}(X(n + 1)|\mathcal{F}_n) \geq X(n)$. The above proof also shows that if X is a submartingale, then the stopped process has the same property.

Going back to the numerical example, we seek a criterion for optimality of the exercising strategy. Since the sum of money generated by such strategies can be random (in our special strategy the decision and the outcome depend on ω), their comparison is difficult. Random variables are functions, and functions are rarely comparable. For this reason we need to associate a single number with each exercising strategy.

A natural candidate as optimality criterion is to maximise the mathematical expectation of the payoff obtained at the exercise time. If the moment at which we exercise is denoted by τ, the money received in a particular scenario ω is the payoff $I(\tau(\omega))$. These sums of money emerge at different time instants, so for economic reasons we should discount them to make them comparable.

We choose the risk-neutral probability $Q = (q, 1 - q)$ for the purpose of computing the expectation. To find the expected value of all discounted payments, note that we receive 10 for $\omega \in B_D$, 16.17 for $\omega \in B_{UDDD}$, and 3.59 for $\omega = uuddd$, $\omega = ududd$, or $\omega = uddud$ so that

$$(1 - q)\frac{10}{1 + R} + q(1 - q)^3\frac{16.17}{(1 + R)^4} + 3q^2(1 - q)^3\frac{3.59}{(1 + R)^5} = 4.51 \quad (5.2)$$

which, remarkably, is the money we paid for the option. (We show the results up to two decimal points, so the equality is approximate, but we will prove that the equality is exact in general.)

As we will see, this is the best we can get. Such a claim could be verified numerically in our example since we have to deal with a finite number of possible strategies, but we will prove it in general.

First we give a formal definition of the optimal exercise strategy.

Definition 5.7

A stopping time τ is **optimal** if

$$\mathbb{E}(Z(\tau)) = \max\{\mathbb{E}(Z(\nu)) : \nu \text{ is a stopping time}\}. \quad (5.3)$$

Analysing exercising strategies in general, consider again the discounted payoff $Z(n) = \widetilde{I}(n)$ of the American put option. The Snell envelope Y of Z gives the value of our option at each trading date. If it satisfies $Y(n) > Z(n)$, then it is not reasonable to exercise at time n, since we would be replacing a security worth $Y(n)$ by a smaller amount $Z(n)$. So, a sensible exercise time

τ should satisfy the condition $Y(\tau) = Z(\tau)$. If such an opportunity emerges, then from the economic point of view we should grab it as soon as possible due to the time value of money. Below we prove that this intuition gives a correct solution.

Proposition 5.8
The random variable $\tau_{\min}$ defined by

$$\tau_{\min} = \inf\{n : Y(n) = Z(n)\}$$

with $\inf(\emptyset) = N$, is an optimal stopping time. In addition

$$Y(0) = \mathbb{E}(Z(\tau_{\min})). \tag{5.4}$$

Proof First note that $\tau_{\min}$ is a stopping time since

$$\{\tau_{\min} = n\} = \bigcap_{k=0}^{n-1}\{Y(k) > Z(k)\} \cap \{Y(n) = Z(n)\}$$

and each of the sets on the right belongs to $\mathcal{F}_n$ since the random variables involved are suitably measurable. For instance, for $k < n$,

$$\{Y(k) > Z(k)\} = (Y(k) - Z(k))^{-1}((0, \infty)) \in \mathcal{F}_k.$$

We will show that the stopped Snell envelope $Y_{\tau_{\min}}$ is a martingale. Again using the representation (5.1) of the stopped process we have

$$Y_{\tau_{\min}}(n + 1) - Y_{\tau_{\min}}(n) = \mathbf{1}_{\{n+1 \leq \tau_{\min}\}}(Y(n + 1) - Y(n)).$$

If $\{\tau_{\min} \geq n + 1\}$ then $Y(n) > Z(n)$. By the definition of the Snell envelope, $Y(n)$ as the greater of the two numbers $Z(n)$ and $\mathbb{E}(Y(n + 1)|\mathcal{F}_n)$ must equal the latter: $Y(n) = \mathbb{E}(Y(n+1)|\mathcal{F}_n)$. We insert this in the right-hand side above and compute the conditional expectation

$$\mathbb{E}(Y_{\tau_{\min}}(n + 1) - Y_{\tau_{\min}}(n)|\mathcal{F}_n)$$
$$= \mathbf{1}_{\{n+1 \leq \tau_{\min}\}}\mathbb{E}(Y(n + 1) - \mathbb{E}(Y(n + 1)|\mathcal{F}_n)|\mathcal{F}_n) = 0$$

which proves that $Y_{\tau_{\min}}$ is a martingale. Martingales have constant expectation so for all n,

$$\mathbb{E}(Y_{\tau_{\min}}(n)) = \mathbb{E}(Y_{\tau_{\min}}(0)) = Y_{\tau_{\min}}(0)$$

the initial value being non-random. In particular, $\mathbb{E}(Y_{\tau_{\min}}(N)) = Y_{\tau_{\min}}(0)$ but by the definition of $\tau_{\min}$, $\mathbb{E}(Y_{\tau_{\min}}(N)) = \mathbb{E}(Z_{\tau_{\min}}(N))$ and also $Y(0) = Y_{\tau_{\min}}(0)$. Putting all these together we get $Y(0) = \mathbb{E}(Z_{\tau_{\min}}(N))$ as claimed in (5.4).

Finally we show that $\tau_{\min}$ is optimal. Take any stopping time ν. We know that Y_ν is a supermartingale so the expectation decreases with time and so

$Y(0) \geq \mathbb{E}(Y_\nu(N))$. By the definition of the stopped process, $\mathbb{E}(Y_\nu(N)) = \mathbb{E}(Y(\nu))$ which is greater than or equal to $\mathbb{E}(Z(\nu))$ by the definition of the Snell envelope. So

$$Y(0) \geq \max\{\mathbb{E}(Z(\nu)) : \nu \text{ is a stopping time}\}.$$

But (5.4) holds so $Y(0)$ is equal to one of the expectations on the right. Therefore, we must have equality, i.e. (5.3) holds, which completes the proof. □

Remark 5.9

Optimality of the early exercise strategy follows from simple economic considerations. If at a certain stage the option holder chooses not to exercise while the payoff is higher than the expectation of the future possibilities, then she effectively replaces the security held by an asset which is worth less, so suffers a loss (being the profit to the other party, the seller of the option). This will be seen clearly in the hedging argument presented below.

Putting together (5.4) and optimality of $\tau_{\min}$ (that is, (5.3) holds) we have the following important conclusion concerning the price of the option:

$$Y(0) = \max\{\mathbb{E}(Z(\nu) : \nu \text{ is a stopping time}\} \tag{5.5}$$

($Y(0)$ is the price $P(0)$ if we consider the Snell envelope of a sequence of put option payoffs).

Exercise 5.4   In a binomial tree with three steps consider all possible stopping times and find numerically the one that maximises the expected discounted payoff (expectation with respect to the risk-neutral probability).

Exercise 5.5   Find the optimal exercise time for the straddle described in Exercise 5.1.

Analysing the optimal exercise strategy in our leading example, path by path, we can see that before we exercise, the prices follow a martingale scheme since in the Snell envelope, the maximum of the two is the discounted martingale expectation. After we exercise (i.e. stop), the sequence becomes constant and so it is obviously a martingale. Thus we have found a simple and elegant criterion for optimality, however with little practical

meaning since verification of the martingale condition of the stopped process is not straightforward.

Theorem 5.10
A stopping time τ is optimal if and only if $Z(\tau) = Y(\tau)$ and $Y_\tau(n)$ is a martingale.

Proof See page 133.   □

5.3 Hedging

We keep working within the framework of our 5-step binomial example. Suppose we have written and sold the American put, where $S(0) = 100$, $U = 15\%$, $D = -10\%$, $K = 100$, $R = 5\%$. Having cashed the price, 4.51, we are exposed to some risk. To make our position secure we construct a replicating strategy which, we recall, is based on taking a position in the underlying and completing the portfolio with a position in the money market account. Our position in stock is determined by the **delta** computed by

$$\Delta(0) = \frac{P^{\mathrm{u}} - P^{\mathrm{d}}}{S^{\mathrm{u}} - S^{\mathrm{d}}} = \frac{1.22 - 10}{115 - 90} = -0.350644$$

where superscripts denote the prices resulting from the up and down movements of the stock in the first step. This number is negative which means short-selling the stock. The money market position is then

$$4.51 + 0.350644 \times 100 = 39.579 \cong 39.58$$

so this amount is invested risk free for one period.

Time $n = 1$

Consider the case where the stock goes down. There are two cases: the holder of the option either exercises or not.

• Suppose the option is exercised.

We owe the payoff 10 and we have to repurchase the fraction of the stock to close the short position the good news being that the stock is cheap since we only have to pay 0.35×90. The risk-free investment exactly covers this cost since $R = 5\%$ and

$$-10 - 0.35 \times 90 = -41.56 = -39.58 \times (1.05).$$

• Suppose the option is not exercised.

We compute the new delta

$$\Delta(1) = \frac{2.94 - 19}{103.50 - 81} = -0.71.$$

This means that we have to increase our short position by short-selling additional $0.71 - 0.35 = 0.36$ shares, which will generate some money to be added to our risk-free investment:

$$0.36 \times 90 + 39.58 \times (1 + 5\%) = 74.23.$$

However, we do not need all this money for further hedging since the 'value of waiting' is (with $q = 0.6$)

$$\frac{1}{1.05}(0.6 \times 2.94 + 0.4 \times 19) = 8.92$$

so for replication such a value of our strategy is needed. Therefore to cover our liabilities: short stock position worth $-0.71 \times 90 = -64.4$, and the option: -8.92, we need 73.15 so we could consume $74.23 - 73.15 = 1.08$. This would mean that our strategy would not be self-financing so we prefer not to withdraw any funds, which leads us to suspect that we are superhedging strictly, as will be confirmed below.

Time $n = 2$

Consider both cases of subsequent stock movements following the first step, which is down, and assume that the option is exercised or repurchased in each scenario to close the position.

• Stock goes up to $S^{du} = 103.50$. We pay 2.94 for the option and we have to buy back 0.71 of a share and to cash our savings:

$$-2.94 - 0.71 \times 103.50 + 74.23 \times (1.05) = 1.135.$$

• Stock goes down to $S^{dd} = 81$. We pay 19 as the exercise pay-off. We buy back 0.71 of a share and we clear our money market account:

$$-19 - 0.71 \times 81 + 74.23 \times (1.05) = 1.135.$$

In each case as a result of the sub-optimal policy of the option holder (the option should have been exercised at time $n = 1$) we have a surplus (which is obviously the extra money 1.08 from the previous step increased by the risk-free return).

This is an example of a general fact which we will discuss below in the general setting.

The Doob decomposition

The sequence of prices $Y(n)$ is a supermartingale, as we know. In particular, their expected values decrease. To make such a sequence a martingale one should somehow compensate this 'leakage of mass' by adding some suitable quantities. We will show that such a compensation is always possible, and moreover, that it is unique within a certain family of processes.

Theorem 5.11 Doob decomposition
If $Y(n)$ is a supermartingale then there exist a martingale, $M(n)$, and a predictable, non-decreasing sequence, $A(n)$, given by a recursive formula

$$A(n) = A(n-1) - (\mathbb{E}(Y(n)|F_{n-1}) - Y(n-1))$$

with $A(0) = 0$, such that

$$Y(n) = Y(0) + M(n) - A(n).$$

This decomposition, called the Doob decomposition, is unique in the above classes of the processes M and A.

Proof   See page 134.   □

Writing the decomposition in the form (with $M(0) = Y(0)$)

$$M(n) = Y(n) + A(n)$$

we can see that the role of A is to **add** to Y what is needed to obtain a martingale ($A(n) \geq 0$ since it starts from 0 and is non-decreasing), which justifies the commonly used term **compensator**: the increasing process A 'makes up for' the lack of the martingale property in the given Y.

Corollary 5.12
If X is a submartingale, then it can be written uniquely as

$$X(n) = M(n) + A(n)$$

with a martingale M and a predictable, non-decreasing process A starting from $A(0) = 0$.

Proof   It is sufficient to note that $Y = -X$ is a supermartingale. The Doob decomposition of Y gives $Y = M - A$ so $-Y = -M + A$ and so $-M$ is the desired martingale for the decomposition of X.   □

Exercise 5.6 Find the exact form of the compensator and check that A is predictable for the American put in our 5-step model with $S(0) = 100$, $U = 15\%$, $D = -10\%$, $K = 100$, $R = 5\%$.

Exercise 5.7 Find the compensator for the straddle with $I(n) = |S(n) - 50|$ for $N = 4$, where $S(n)$ follows a binomial tree with $S(0) = 50$, $U = 12\%$, $D = -6\%$, $R = 5\%$.

Going back to the hedging problem, in the notation for the put option we consider the Doob decomposition of the sequence of discounted option prices $Y(n) = \widetilde{P}(n)$, so

$$\widetilde{P}(n) = M(n) - A(n)$$

for some martingale M and increasing predictable A. In the binomial model (or in general, in any complete model) we can replicate any random variable given at any time. We choose to replicate $M(N)$, that means we find a strategy $(x(n), y(n))$ so that

$$\widetilde{V}_{(x,y)}(N) = M(N).$$

Writing and selling the option we receive the price $P(0) = Y(0) = V_{(x,y)}(0)$ so we can start such a hedging strategy. The process $\widetilde{V}_{(x,y)}(n)$ is a martingale so

$$\widetilde{V}_{(x,y)}(n) = \mathbb{E}_Q(\widetilde{V}_{(x,y)}(N)|\mathcal{F}_n) = \mathbb{E}_Q(M(N)|\mathcal{F}_n) = M(n).$$

This implies

$$\widetilde{P}(n) = \widetilde{V}_{(x,y)}(n) - A(n).$$

The value of our strategy for all n makes our position secure since the value of the strategy dominates the option payoff at all times

$$\widetilde{V}_{(x,y)}(n) \geq \widetilde{P}(n) = Y(n) \geq Z(n) = \widetilde{I}(n).$$

The holder of the option may exercise if $I(n) > 0$ but this is not sufficient since if $P(n) > I(n)$ he is better off by selling the option.

If $P(n) = I(n)$ and $A(n) = 0$ the inequality $\widetilde{V}_{(x,y)}(n) \geq \widetilde{I}(n)$ is then an equality and the financial result for us is zero.

In the $A(n) > 0$ zone, the inequality becomes strict, $\widetilde{V}_{(x,y)}(n) > \widetilde{I}(n)$, which means additional profit, which is equal to the value of the compensator.

Therefore the following exercise strategy is of interest: we do not exercise as long as Y is a martingale. If A becomes non-zero, the process Y ceases to be a martingale, so we should exercise just before that instant. At a given trading date we are able to tell whether A is going to become positive at the next step since A is predictable. Of course, if A never gets positive, being zero up to time N, the exercise time has to be the trading horizon:

$$\tau_{\max} = \begin{cases} N & \text{if } A(N) = 0, \\ \min\{n : A(n+1) \neq 0\} & \text{otherwise.} \end{cases}$$

As it turns out, this exercise strategy is optimal but not very relevant from the practical point of view.

Theorem 5.13
The stopping time $\tau_{\max}$ is optimal.

Proof   See page 136.   □

In practical terms, the irrelevance of $\tau_{\max}$ follows from its comparison with a much simpler strategy based on $\tau_{\min}$. For exercise to be truly profitable the payoff should be strictly greater than the value of waiting. This means that if $\tau_{\min}(\omega) = n$, then

$$Y(n) = Z(n) > \mathbb{E}(Y(n+1)|\mathcal{F}_n)$$

and, moreover, $Y(k) > Z(k)$ for all $k \leq n - 1$, which implies $Y(k) = \mathbb{E}(Y(k+1)|\mathcal{F}_k)$. Consequently,

$$A(k+1) = A(k) - (\mathbb{E}(Y(k+1)|\mathcal{F}_k) - Y(k))$$
$$= A(k) = 0$$

and in particular $A(n) = 0$, but

$$A(n+1) = A(n) - (\mathbb{E}(Y(n+1)|\mathcal{F}_n) - Y(n))$$
$$= Y(n) - \mathbb{E}(Y(n+1)|\mathcal{F}_n) > 0.$$

This gives $\tau_{\max}(\omega) = n$ and so here, with strict inequalities above, both stopping times coincide: $\tau_{\max} = \tau_{\min}$. This also proves that $\tau_{\max} \geq \tau_{\min}$.

Exercise 5.8   Show that for a call option the compensator is zero (use the data from the previous exercise or work with a general case) which suggests that it is never optimal to exercise a call before maturity.

Exercise 5.9 Show that in a 4-step binomial model with $U = 10\%$, $D = -10\%$, $R = 0$, a put with $K = S(0)$ can be optimally exercised at time 4. Find $\tau_{\min}$, and explain why this example does not contradict Remark 5.9, despite the fact that $\tau_{\min}(\omega) < 4$ for some ω.

5.4 General properties of option prices

American call options

It will now become clear why our leading example above was a put. Specifically, we show that the prices of European and American call options written on a stock not paying dividends are the same.

Denote by $C^E(n)$ the price at time n of a European call option with exercise price K and exercise time N. The prices of the American version of the same option will be denoted by $C^A(n)$ so $\widetilde{C}^A(n) = Y(n)$ in the general notation.

Proposition 5.14
For all n we have $C^A(n) = C^E(n)$.

Proof First, note that the inequality $C^E(n) \leq C^A(n)$ holds as a result of the No Arbitrage Principle. If $C^E(n) > C^A(n)$ for some n, at this time we buy the American and sell the European call creating a positive cash flow which we immediately invest in the risk-free asset. We do not exercise the American option until time N, when both options are (or are not) exercised, with zero balance in each case.

We thus need to prove that $C^E(n) \geq C^A(n)$. We know that $C^E(n)$ is the value at n of a replicating strategy and so after discounting we have a martingale. In particular, $\widetilde{C}^E(n)$ is a supermartingale and to show that $C^E(n) \geq C^A(n)$ it is now sufficient to show that $\widetilde{C}^E(n)$ dominates the payoff $\widetilde{I}(n) = Z(n)$. Indeed, the Snell envelope $\widetilde{C}^A(n) = Y(n)$ is the minimal supermartingale dominating the payoff so it cannot exceed any other such supermartingale, in particular $C^A(n) \leq C^E(n)$.

So, it remains to see that $C^E(n) \geq I(n)$ and using call-put parity we have

$$C^E(n) = S(n) - K(1 + R)^{-(N-n)} - P^E(n)$$
$$\geq S(n) - K(1 + R)^{-(N-n)}$$
$$> S(n) - K$$

which implies $C^E(n) \geq S(n) - K$. Of course, $C^E(n) \geq 0$ so $C^E(n) \geq$ max$\{0, S(n) - K\} = I(n)$ and the proof is complete.   □

The inequality $C^E(n) \geq I(n)$ gives a model-independent argument since it shows that it is never optimal to exercise the American call option before expiry as the option value exceeds the available payoff at time n.

It may seem that the holder of the American call option has an advantage over the holder of the European option since the latter cannot exercise before expiry. However the European option can be sold at any time for the same amount as can be obtained from exercising the American call.

Finally, we give a simple example showing that if the stock pays dividends, it may be profitable to exercise the American call prior to the expiry date.

Example 5.15

Suppose $S(0) = 120$, $U = 20\%$, $D = -10\%$, and consider a call with $N = 2$, $K = 120$. Assume that $R = 10\%$ and just before time 1 a dividend of 14 is announced and will be paid to the current shareholders soon after time 1 (there is always a gap between these events). This will move the prices at time 1 down by this amount since if the share is sold, the new owner will not receive the dividend, and the resulting tree is shown below

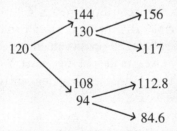

The call gives us some money at time 2 in just one scenario, namely uu. For European call at time 1 in the up state the value is

$$\frac{1}{1.1} \times \frac{2}{3} \times 36 = 21.18,$$

so

$$C^E(0) = \frac{1}{1.1} \times \frac{2}{3} \times 21.18 = 12.84,$$

$$C^A(0) = \frac{1}{1.1} \times \frac{2}{3} \times 24 = 14.54.$$

In this state the payoff of the American call is 24 so it is higher, and the option should be exercised in this state. The initial prices of the options are of course different; nonetheless, the American call, if correctly exercised at time 1, is more profitable.

Exercise 5.10 Investigate the dependence of American call price on a dividend expressed as a percentage of the stock price.

Exercise 5.11 Show that European and American derivative securities not paying dividends have the same prices if the payoff is of the form $h(S(n))$ for convex h: $[0, \infty) \rightarrow [0, \infty)$ with $h(0) = 0$. Find a counterexample if the last condition is violated.

Bounds on option prices

Here we consider some simple bounds on the initial prices of American options, similar to those proved earlier for European options. Arbitrage arguments again provide the principal tool, and a good deal of the detail is left to the reader, as these methods should be very familiar by now. We begin with the relationship between calls and puts.

Recall the call-put parity relation, proved as Theorem 4.41

$$C^E - P^E = S(0) - K(1 + R)^{-N}. \tag{5.6}$$

For American options we cannot obtain an equality, but nonetheless the following inequalities provide useful bounds for the prices of American puts and calls on a stock that does not pay dividends.

Proposition 5.16

Let C^A, P^A denote the initial prices of, respectively, an American call and an American put option, each with strike K, on the stock S (which pays no dividends). Then

$$S(0) - K \leq C^A - P^A \leq S(0) - K(1 + R)^{-N}.$$

Proof Suppose that the first inequality fails, so that $C^A - P^A - S(0) + K < 0$. We construct an arbitrage as follows: sell a put, short a share and

buy a call. Invest the balance $S(0)+P^A-C^A$, which is positive, since the call costs less than $S(0)$, in the money market. Suppose the put is exercised at time n. We can borrow K in the money market to settle the put and use the share we receive to close the short position. Our net position then consists of the call and cash of

$$(S(0) + P^A - C^A)(1 + R)^n - K > (1 + R)^n K - K > 0.$$

On the other hand, if the put is not exercised, we exercise the call at time N and obtain a share for K, enabling us to close the short position in the stock. Closing the money market position we then have

$$(S(0) + P^A - C^A)(1 + R)^N - K > K(1 + R)^N - K > 0.$$

In both cases we have a riskless profit, which implies that $C^A - P^A - S(0) + K \geq 0$, proving our first inequality.

By Proposition 5.14 the American and European call prices are the same, so $C^E = C^A$, while the American put price always dominates that of the European put, $P^A \geq P^E$. Using (5.6) this proves the second inequality. □

Exercise 5.12 Suppose the underlying stock S pays a dividend D at time $n < N$. Show that

$$S(0) - D(1 + R)^{-n} - K \leq C^A - P^A \leq S(0) - K(1 + R)^{-N}.$$

Bounds on the individual option prices can also be found quite simply. For the American call we obtain the same bounds as in the European case. By Propositions 2.45 and 5.14,

$$\max\{0, S(0) - K(1 + R)^{-N}\} \leq C^A \leq S(0).$$

For the put price P^A, note that we must have $K - S(0) \leq P^A$, since otherwise we would buy the put and exercise it immediately, gaining a risk-free profit of $K - S(0) - P^A > 0$. A strict upper bound for P^A is given by K: if $P^A \geq K$ we can sell the put and invest the proceeds in the money market. If the put is exercised at time n we obtain the stock for K and sell it at once for $S(n)$. This leaves a balance of $P^A(1 + R)^n - K + S(n) > 0$, while if the put is not exercised we retain $P^A(1 + R)^N > 0$. We have therefore proved that

$$(K - S(0))^+ \leq P^A < K.$$

Exercise 5.13 Show that the following hold for a stock that pays a dividend D at time $n \leq N$:

$$\max\{0, S(0) - D(1+R)^{-n} - K(1+R)^{-N}, S(0) - K\} \leq C^A,$$
$$\max\{0, K(1+R)^{-N} + D(1+R)^{-n} - S(0), K - S(0)\} \leq P^A.$$

Dependence on the underlying

We make use of the various bounds on option prices obtained above to investigate the dependence of these prices on various parameters. The first results are obvious, although it would be instructive for you to provide a rigorous arbitrage proof. We already know that the call $C^E(S)$ is a non-decreasing function of S, so that, since $C^A(S) = C^E(S)$, the same holds for the American call price. We denote these prices by $C^A(S)$, $P^A(S)$ to emphasise the variable being examined.

Exercise 5.14 Show that the American put option price $P^A(S)$ is a non-increasing function of the underlying S.

We can use our option price bounds to say rather more:

Proposition 5.17
If $S' < S''$ then

$$C^A(S'') - C^A(S') < S'' - S',$$
$$P^A(S') - P^A(S'') < S'' - S'.$$

Proof Using the inequalities in Proposition 5.16 we have

$$P^A(S') - C^A(S') \leq K - S',$$
$$C^A(S'') - P^A(S'') \leq S'' - \frac{1}{(1+R)^N}K.$$

Add, then

$$[C^A(S'') - C^A(S')] + [P^A(S') - P^A(S'')]$$
$$\leq S'' - S' + (1 - \frac{1}{(1+R)^N})K$$
$$\leq S'' - S'.$$

Both terms in square brackets on the left are non-negative (by the above exercise) so neither can be greater than the term on the right.   □

In other words, the (positive) slope of $S \to C^A(S)$ is less than 1, while the (negative) slope of $S \to P^A(S)$ is greater than -1. As the differences on the left-hand side are non-negative, these two functions in fact satisfy Lipschitz conditions with Lipschitz constant 1.

Our final result is left as an exercise.

Exercise 5.15   Show that American call and put prices are both convex functions of the underlying.

Dependence on the strike price

Consider the American call and put prices as functions of the strike K. We denote them by $C^A(K), P^A(K)$ for this purpose. Trivially, the call price is non-increasing (it coincides with $C^E(K)$ so Proposition 2.46 applies) and the put price is non-decreasing since, if $K' < K''$, the right to sell a share for K'' is more valuable than the right to sell it for K'. We again have Lipschitz constant 1 for both functions, as the next exercise implies.

Exercise 5.16   Provide arbitrage arguments to verify the following inequalities when $K' < K''$:

$$C^A(K') - C^A(K'') < K'' - K',$$
$$P^A(K'') - P^A(K') < K'' - K'.$$

Note that Exercise 2.31 provides a stronger result for European options, with Lipschitz constant $(1 + R)^{-1} < 1$ in each case. Finally, we note that $C^A(K) = C^E(K)$ ensures that $K \to C^A(K)$ is a convex function, and prove that $K \to P^A(K)$ is also convex. (For simplicity we again just consider the midpoint.)

Proposition 5.18
If $K' < K''$ then

$$P^A(\frac{K' + K''}{2}) \leq \frac{1}{2}P^A(K') + \frac{1}{2}P^A(K'').$$

Proof   Suppose $2P^A(\frac{K'+K''}{2}) > P^A(K') + P^A(K'')$. Sell two puts with strike $\frac{K'+K''}{2}$, buy two puts with strikes K', K'' and invest the difference risk free. For any $n \leq N$ we have $2(\frac{K'+K''}{2} - S(n))^+ \leq (K' - S(n))^+ + (K'' - S(n))^+$, since the function $f(x) = (x - S(n))^+$ is convex. If the holder of the puts sold wishes to exercise, we do the same and the inequality makes sure that we have sufficient funds. The risk-free investment gives the arbitrage profit. □

5.5   Proofs

Theorem 5.10
A stopping time τ is optimal if and only if $Z(\tau) = Y(\tau)$ and $Y_\tau(n)$ is a martingale.

Proof   Suppose that $Z(\tau) = Y(\tau)$ and $Y_\tau(n)$ is a martingale, which implies (by the constant expectation property)

$$Y(0) = \mathbb{E}(Y_\tau(N)) = \mathbb{E}(Y(\tau)),$$

the last equality holding by the definition of the stopped process. The last number is equal to $\mathbb{E}(Z(\tau))$ by our hypothesis. Proposition 5.8 tells us that $Y(0) = \max \mathbb{E}(Z(v))$, so $\mathbb{E}(Y(\tau)) = \max \mathbb{E}(Z(v))$ and τ is optimal as claimed.

Conversely, if τ is optimal then by (5.3) and (5.5) we have $Y(0) = \mathbb{E}(Z(\tau))$. By the definition of the Snell envelope we have $\mathbb{E}(Z(\tau)) \leq \mathbb{E}(Y(\tau))$. But we know that Y_τ is a supermartingale so $\mathbb{E}(Y(\tau)) = \mathbb{E}(Y_\tau(N)) \leq Y(0)$. Putting these inequalities together we get

$$Y(0) = \mathbb{E}(Z(\tau)) \leq \mathbb{E}(Y(\tau)) = \mathbb{E}(Y_\tau(N)) \leq Y(0)$$

so $\mathbb{E}(Z(\tau)) = \mathbb{E}(Y(\tau))$. In addition, we know that $Z(\tau) \leq Y(\tau)$, so $Z(\tau) = Y(\tau)$.

It remains to prove that Y_τ is a martingale and to this end it is sufficient to show that $Y_\tau(n) = \mathbb{E}(Y(\tau)|\mathcal{F}_n)$. We know that Y_τ is a supermartingale hence $Y_\tau(n) \geq \mathbb{E}(Y_\tau(N)|\mathcal{F}_n) = \mathbb{E}(Y(\tau)|\mathcal{F}_n)$. Then to show that the random variables $Y_\tau(n)$ and $\mathbb{E}(Y(\tau)|\mathcal{F}_n)$ are equal, it is sufficient to show that their expectations are equal:

$$\mathbb{E}(Y_\tau(n)) = \mathbb{E}(\mathbb{E}(Y(\tau)|\mathcal{F}_n)).$$

The right-hand side is $\mathbb{E}(Y(\tau))$ by the tower property The left-hand side is the same as the following chain of inequalities shows

$$Y(0) \geq \mathbb{E}(Y_\tau(n)) \quad (Y_\tau \text{ is a supermartingale})$$
$$\geq \mathbb{E}(\mathbb{E}(Y_\tau(N)|\mathcal{F}_n)) \quad (\text{as above})$$
$$= \mathbb{E}(Y(\tau))$$
$$= \mathbb{E}(Z(\tau)) \quad (\text{as established above})$$
$$= Y(0) \quad (\text{since } \tau \text{ is optimal}).$$

$\square$

Theorem 5.11 Doob decomposition
If $Y(n)$ is a supermartingale then there exist a martingale, $M(n)$, and a predictable, non-decreasing sequence, $A(n)$, given by a recursive formula

$$A(n) = A(n-1) - (\mathbb{E}(Y(n)|\mathcal{F}_{n-1}) - Y(n-1))$$

with $A(0) = 0$, such that

$$Y(n) = Y(0) + M(n) - A(n).$$

This decomposition is unique in the above classes of processes M and A.

Proof To find $A(1)$, which, as an $\mathcal{F}_0$-measurable random variable, must be a constant, we take the expectation of the target relation:

$$A(1) = -Y(1) + Y(0) + M(1)$$

to find

$$A(1) = -\mathbb{E}(Y(1)) + Y(0)$$

since $\mathbb{E}(M(1)) = M(0) = 0$. We must then put

$$M(1) = A(1) + Y(1) - Y(0)$$
$$= Y(1) - \mathbb{E}(Y(1)).$$

Next, to find $A(2)$ satisfying

$$A(2) = -Y(2) + Y(0) + M(2)$$

we take the conditional expectation of this target identity with respect to $\mathcal{F}_1$, recalling that A is to be predictable, to get

$$A(2) = -\mathbb{E}(Y(2)|\mathcal{F}_1) + Y(0) + \mathbb{E}(M(2)|\mathcal{F}_1)$$
$$= -\mathbb{E}(Y(2)|\mathcal{F}_1) + Y(0) + M(1) \quad (\text{if } M \text{ is going to be a martingale})$$
$$= -\mathbb{E}(Y(2)|\mathcal{F}_1) + Y(0) + A(1) + [Y(1) - Y(0)]$$

having inserted the form of $M(1)$ obtained above. Rearranged, this gives a formula for $A(2)$:

$$A(2) = A(1) - \mathbb{E}([Y(2) - Y(1)]|\mathcal{F}_1).$$

This suggests a general recursive formula: for $n \geq 1$ write

$$A(n) = A(n - 1) - \mathbb{E}([Y(n) - Y(n - 1)]|\mathcal{F}_{n-1}) \qquad (5.7)$$

with the form of M implied by our goal

$$M(n) = A(n) + Y(n) - Y(0).$$

This was an educated guess based on desired properties, and it is time for a rigorous argument. First note that A is increasing since the supermartingale property of Y gives $\mathbb{E}(Y(n) - Y(n - 1)|\mathcal{F}_{n-1}) \leq 0$.

Next, we use induction to prove predictability: $A(1)$ is constant, so $\mathcal{F}_0$-measurable, and if $A(n - 1)$ is $\mathcal{F}_{n-2}$-measurable, it automatically is $\mathcal{F}_{n-1}$-measurable and with the second term on the right of (5.7) also being $\mathcal{F}_{n-1}$-measurable we find that $A(n)$ is $\mathcal{F}_{n-1}$-measurable.

It remains to see that M is a martingale:

$$
\begin{aligned}
\mathbb{E}(M(n)|\mathcal{F}_{n-1}) \\
&= \mathbb{E}([A(n) + Y(n) - Y(0)]|\mathcal{F}_{n-1}) \\
&= A(n) + \mathbb{E}(Y(n)|\mathcal{F}_{n-1}) - Y(0) \\
&= A(n - 1) - \mathbb{E}([Y(n) - Y(n - 1)]|\mathcal{F}_{n-1}) + \mathbb{E}(Y(n)|\mathcal{F}_{n-1}) - Y(0) \\
&= A(n - 1) + Y(n - 1) - Y(0) \\
&= M(n - 1).
\end{aligned}
$$

For uniqueness, suppose on the contrary that we have another such decomposition, with $Y(n) = Y(0) + M'(n) - A'(n)$, so that

$$Y(n) - Y(0) = M(n) - A(n) = M'(n) - A'(n).$$

Then

$$M(n) - M'(n) = A(n) - A'(n)$$

and note that for $n = 0$ we have $M(0) = M'(0)$ since A and A' start from 0. Next, take the conditional expectation on both sides with respect to $\mathcal{F}_{n-1}$

$$\mathbb{E}([M(n) - M'(n)]|\mathcal{F}_{n-1}) = \mathbb{E}([A(n) - A'(n)]|\mathcal{F}_{n-1})$$

which gives

$$M(n - 1) - M'(n - 1) = A(n) - A'(n).$$

So, the equality of M and M' at time $n - 1$ implies the equality of A and A' at time n, which yields equality of M and M' at n. By induction on n this proves the uniqueness.   □

Theorem 5.13
The stopping time τ_{max} is optimal.

Proof   First, directly from the definition, τ_{max} is a stopping time since the set $\{\tau_{max} = n\}$ is determined by $A(n + 1)$, which is $\mathcal{F}_n$-measurable.

Next, again by definition, $A(\tau_{max}) = 0$, so $Y_{\tau_{max}}(n) = M_{\tau_{max}}(n)$, and $Y_{\tau_{max}}$ is a martingale.

To complete the proof it is sufficient to show that $Y(\tau_{max}) = Z(\tau_{max})$. Fix arbitrary ω and denote by j the instant $\tau_{max}(\omega)$. Insert the Doob decomposition into the definition of the Snell envelope

$$
\begin{aligned}
Y(j) &= \max(Z(j), \mathbb{E}(Y(j + 1)|\mathcal{F}_j)) \\
&= \max(Z(j), \mathbb{E}(M(j + 1) - A(j + 1)|\mathcal{F}_j)) \\
&= \max(Z(j), M(j) - A(j + 1))
\end{aligned}
$$

since M is a martingale and A is predictable.

Next, by the definition of τ_{max}, $A(j) = 0, A(j+1) > 0$. Since $M(j) = Y(j)$, we have $M(j) - A(j + 1) < Y(j)$. So $Y(j) = \max(Z(j), M(j) - A(j + 1)) = Z(j)$.   □

6

Modelling bonds and interest rates

6.1   Zero-coupon bonds
6.2   Forward rates
6.3   Coupon bonds
6.4   Binary tree term structure models
6.5   Short rates
6.6   The Ho–Lee model of term structure

In the previous chapters we used the money market account to represent the risk-free part of a portfolio. Recall that with a discrete time scale based on evenly spaced instants denoted by $n = 0, 1, \ldots, N$, we had $A(n) = A(0)(1 + R)^n$ determined by the single-step return R. To be more precise, let us denote the length of each step by h and write the return over that time period as R_h. Typically, we take $h = 1/m$ to be a fraction of a year due to the convention that the unit is taken as the whole year. The rate of return for the year is called the **interest rate**, denoted by r, so that

$$(1 + R_{1/m})^m = 1 + r. \tag{6.1}$$

In particular, for $h = 1$ we have $R_1 = r$.

Given interest rate r we can construct the money market account by reversing the above computations. Take the step length to be $h = 1/m$ and define $R_{1/m}$ by solving (6.1).

The return $R_{1/m}$ can be annualised (scaled) by writing $r_m = mR_{1/m}$ so that, for $n \geq 1$,

$$A(n) = A(0)(1 + \frac{1}{m}r_m)^n$$

and we say that the rate r_m corresponds to compound interest.

> **Exercise 6.1** Show that $r_m < r_k$ if $m > k \geq 1$ (taking $r_1 = r$).

For each particular step we have returns of the form $R_{1/m} = \frac{1}{m}r_m$, or $R_h = hr_m$, representing the so-called **simple interest rule**: the annual interest rate is linearly scaled to the period of length h. This reflects the fact that no transactions take place between consecutive steps. The total growth is best described as a product of single-step growth factors $1 + R_{1/m}$ since after each step the interest is added to the account, so that $A(n + 1) = A(n)(1 + R_{1/m})$, the interest being $A(n)R_{1/m}$. The increased sum is the basis for the next step.

When we are only concerned with the value of a risk-free investment (or a loan) at a future instant n, with no cash flows in the meantime, then the simple interest convention is used to annualise the return and the rate which is quoted for such transactions is given by

$$r(0, n) = \frac{1}{nh}\frac{A(n) - A(0)}{A(0)}.$$

For $h = \frac{1}{m}$, $n = m$ we have $r(0, m) = r$. Note that above for each step we in fact employ the simple interest convention as the expression $1 + \frac{1}{m}r_m$ for the single-step growth factor shows ($h = 1/m$, $n = 1$).

> **Exercise 6.2** Find the formula expressing $r(0, n)$ by means of the interest rate r. Show that the sequence $(r(0, n))_{n \leq N}$ is increasing.

If the investment or loan is planned to commence at some future time k, the rate $r(k, n)$ that applies at that time cannot be known now (at time 0) and our goal in this chapter is to build models of such future rates as random quantities.

6.1 Zero-coupon bonds

A **zero-coupon bond** with **maturity date** $n \leq N$ and face value F is a contract that guarantees the holder to be paid an amount F on that date.

A **unit bond** is a zero-coupon bond with face value $F = 1$. In practice the face value of a bond is a round number like 1000 but we may assume that it is 1 without loss of generality. The bond is traded at times k up to its maturity date n when it is exchanged for one unit of cash. We call such a

bond an *n*-**bond.** We assume that for any trading date *n* the market includes tradeable *n*-bonds.

The **(spot) price** of an *n*-bond at time $k \leq n$ is denoted by $B(k, n)$ with $B(n, n) = 1$. For $k < n$ we will have $0 < B(k, n) < 1$, which reflects the principle of the time value of money as $B(k, n)$ is the value at time k of a sure unit at time n.

The dependence of the bond price at time k on its maturity n steps into the future is described by the function

$$n \mapsto B(k, n + k)$$

which is referred to as the **term structure** of bond prices, or the **bond price curve** at time k. We would expect bond prices to increase as the time to maturity decreases, as the following example illustrates.

Example 6.1
Current term structure $h = 1/12$, $N = 12$, $k = 0$

n	$B(0, n)$
1	0.9991
2	0.9974
3	0.9956
4	0.9939
5	0.9921
6	0.9903
7	0.9884
8	0.9866
9	0.9847
10	0.9829
11	0.9810
12	0.9791

We would prefer to capture the information provided by the bond prices by means of interest rates, which are more intuitive and convey a clear message. The determination of these rates is conventionally achieved via the London Interbank Offer Rate (LIBOR), which is the rate at which deposits are exchanged between banks. The simple interest principle is applied (there is no cash flow between now, *k*, and maturity, *n*) and for a bond

$B(k, n)$ we denote the annualised LIBOR rate by $L(k, n)$, so that,

$$B(k, n) = \frac{1}{1 + (n - k)hL(k, n)}.$$

If we buy an n-bond at time k and keep it till maturity, the return on this investment is

$$K(k, n) = \frac{1 - B(k, n)}{B(k, n)},$$

which shows that $L(k, n)$ is the annualised return

$$L(k, n) = \frac{1}{(n - k)h} \left(\frac{1}{B(k, n)} - 1 \right). \tag{6.2}$$

Exercise 6.3   Find the rates $L(0, n)$ implied by the bond prices of Example 6.1. Compute the bond prices $B(1, n)$ assuming that the rates stay constant: $L(1, n) = L(0, n)$, $n > 1$.

Let us now consider briefly what would happen if future bond prices were known with certainty.

Proposition 6.2
Suppose that the future bond price $B(k, n)$ is known at time 0 where $0 < k < n$. Then

$$B(0, n) = B(0, k)B(k, n).$$

Proof   We prove this by an arbitrage argument. Suppose first

$$B(0, n) < B(0, k)B(k, n)$$

and then at time 0
- buy an n-bond,
- sell the fraction $B(k, n)$ of a k-bond,

with a positive balance. This will be our arbitrage profit since at time k our bond will be worth $B(k, n)$ and the short position in k-bonds will require exactly this amount to close.

The case $B(0, n) > B(0, k)B(k, n)$ can be dealt with similarly.   □

Observed market prices for bonds do not display such regularity, so that realistic models should allow the future price $B(k, n)$ to be unknown (random) at each time $0 < k < n$. A simple model of this kind will be proposed later in this chapter. The possibility of interest rate fluctuations introduces risk. These fluctuations are less spectacular than the variations of stock

prices. However, due to the large sums of money involved in bond trading, the resulting possible gains or losses may be substantial.

If the future price were as given by the proposition,

$$B(k,n) = \frac{B(0,n)}{B(0,k)},$$

then the investment: buy an n-bond at time 0, sell it at time k, would have the following return, in view of (6.2):

$$K(0,k) = \frac{B(k,n)}{B(0,n)} - 1 = \frac{1}{B(0,k)} - 1 = khL(0,k).$$

In other words, the return would be the (scaled) implied risk-free rate:

In general the return is, again via (6.2):

$$K(0,k) = \frac{B(k,n)}{B(0,n)} - 1 = \frac{1 + nhL(0,n)}{1 + (n-k)hL(k,n)} - 1$$

which is a decreasing function of the future rate $L(k,n)$.

We do not incur any risk if we keep the bonds until maturity, since then the amount received is certain; this is the particular case $k = n$:

$$K(0,n) = nhL(0,n).$$

Exercise 6.4 Using the results of Exercise 6.3 find the rate $L(1,12)$ required for $B(1,12)$ to fall below $B(0,12)$.

Exercise 6.5 An investor gambles on a decrease in interest rates and wishes to earn a return $K(0,n)$ higher by 1% than the current rate $L(0,n)$. Sketch the graph of the function $k \mapsto L(k,n)$ which would allow one to achieve this at any $0 < k < n$. First try the data from Example 6.1.

6.2 Forward rates

Forward price of a unit bond

We saw in Section 2.7 that a forward contract is a derivative security, namely an agreement to exchange an asset at a certain delivery time for an agreed price, the forward price. The forward price is the price at which

it costs nothing to enter into the forward contract at the time when it is struck. Suppose now that the asset concerned is a bond. Since bonds are related to interest rates, a contract of this kind is called a **forward rate agreement**. It gives protection against movements of interest rates.

Suppose the forward contract on the n-bond is struck at time k with delivery time m, where $k < m \le n \le N$. The corresponding forward price $B(k, m, n)$ is given by the following theorem, which applies Proposition 4.43 (more precisely, Corollary 4.44) in this situation. For clarity we revisit the proof, replacing the price $S(k)$ of the stock by the spot price $B(k, n)$ of the bond. The ratio $\frac{1}{B(k,m)}$ below corresponds to the risk-free growth factor present in the stock version of the theorem. Note that here the **extended market** will now include trading in forward contracts on bonds, and our No Arbitrage Principle is again extended to cover portfolios which contain these derivatives.

Theorem 6.3
The forward price of an n-bond is

$$B(k, m, n) = \frac{B(k, n)}{B(k, m)}.$$

Proof The proof is close in spirit to the proof of Proposition 6.2. Suppose that

$$B(k, m, n) > \frac{B(k, n)}{B(k, m)}.$$

In this case we could construct an arbitrage strategy as follows:
At time k

- take a short forward position – the cost is 0;
- buy one n-bond, paying the amount $B(k, n)$;
- sell short the number $\frac{B(k,n)}{B(k,m)}$ of m-bonds, receiving the amount $B(k, n)$.

At time m

- sell the n-bond for the forward price $B(k, m, n)$;
- close the short position in all m-bonds held, paying their face value, namely, $\frac{B(k,n)}{B(k,m)}$.

The arbitrage profit would be $B(k, m, n) - \frac{B(k,n)}{B(k,m)}$, contradicting the no-arbitrage principle.

If the reverse inequality holds,

$$B(k, m, n) < \frac{B(k, n)}{B(k, m)},$$

we could follow the opposite strategy:

- At time k, take a long forward position, sell one n-bond, receiving $B(k, n)$, and buy $\frac{B(k,n)}{B(k,m)}$ m-bonds with these proceeds – net cost $B(k, m, n)$.
- At time m, receive one n-bond for the forward price $B(k, m, n)$ and use the bond to close the short n-bond position, while cashing the m-bonds for $\frac{B(k,n)}{B(k,m)}$. This yields an arbitrage profit of $\frac{B(k,n)}{B(k,m)} - B(k, m, n) > 0$. As both inequalities lead to arbitrage, the identity is proved.   □

Exercise 6.6 Find the forward prices $B(0, m, 12)$ for the data from Example 6.1.

Note that if, for $m < n$, the future bond price $B(m, n)$ is known in advance at time m, Proposition 6.2 implies that $B(m, n)$ equals the forward price $B(0, m, n)$, since both are given by $\frac{B(0,n)}{B(0,m)}$. In other words, the No Arbitrage Principle provides a forward price which matches the price that would be charged if the bond price were independent of any risk assessment.

Forward rates

We can now examine how this forward price leads to **forward interest rates**, that is, interest rates, determined at time k and assumed to hold over the future time interval $[m, n]$, $k \le m$, which would reproduce the forward bond price. For this, we use the relations found between bond prices and spot rates as a guide.

Definition 6.4
The **simple forward rate** $F(k, m, n)$ from m to n contracted at k is the rate implied by the forward bond price by

$$B(k, m, n) = \frac{1}{1 + (n - m)hF(k, m, n)}.$$

Theorem 6.5
For simple forward rates the following hold, where $k \le m < n$:

$$F(k, m, n) = -\frac{B(k, n) - B(k, m)}{(n - m)hB(k, n)},$$
$$L(m, n) = F(m, m, n).$$

Proof We compute the forward rate from the definition and then insert the formula $B(k, m, n) = \frac{B(k,n)}{B(k,m)}$ for the forward bond price:

$$
\begin{aligned}
F(k, m, n) &= \frac{1}{(n-m)h}\left(\frac{1}{B(k, m, n)} - 1\right) \\
&= \frac{1}{(n-m)h}\left(\frac{B(k, m)}{B(k, n)} - 1\right) \\
&= \frac{1}{(n-m)h}\frac{B(k, m) - B(k, n)}{B(k, n)}.
\end{aligned}
$$

Next we substitute $k = m$ in the last formula to get

$$
F(m, m, n) = -\frac{B(m, n) - B(m, m)}{((n-m)h)B(m, n)} = \frac{1}{(n-m)h}\left(\frac{1}{B(m, n)} - 1\right)
$$
$$
= L(m, n).
$$

$\square$

Exercise 6.7 Illustrate this theorem using the data from Example 6.1. Are the rates $F(k, m, n)$ non-negative?

Exercise 6.8 Is it possible to have $F(k, m, n) < 0$? Give an example. Formulate a property which would guarantee $F(k, m, n) \geq 0$.

Definition 6.6
The (instantaneous) **forward rate** with maturity at step $n < N$ contracted at step k is defined by

$$
F(k, n) = F(k, n, n + 1).
$$

We have, using our notational conventions,

$$
F(k, n) = -\frac{B(k, n + 1) - B(k, n)}{hB(k, n + 1)},
$$

so that

$$
hF(k, n)B(k, n + 1) + B(k, n + 1) = B(k, n),
$$

that is,

$$
[1 + hF(k, n)]B(k, n + 1) = B(k, n).
$$

We obtain the inductive formula:

$$B(k, n+1) = B(k, n)\frac{1}{1 + hF(k, n)}.$$

Our goal here is to determine whether or not the forward rates determine the bond prices. This formula is the first step in this direction and applied to $n = k, k+1, \ldots, N-1$ it gives

$$B(k, k+1) = \frac{1}{1 + hF(k, k)},$$

$$B(k, k+2) = B(k, k+1)\frac{1}{1 + hF(k, k+1)}$$

$$= \frac{1}{1 + hF(k, k)}\frac{1}{1 + hF(k, k+1)}$$

and so on. After a finite number of such steps we arrive at the maturity time n of the bond in question.

We conclude that the forward rates determine the bond prices:

$$B(k, n) = \frac{1}{1 + hF(k, k)}\frac{1}{1 + hF(k, k+1)} \cdots \frac{1}{1 + hF(k, n-1)}. \qquad (6.3)$$

Exercise 6.9 Find the forward rates $F(0, n)$ for the data from Example 6.1.

Exercise 6.10 Assume that for all $k \leq n$, $B(k, n) = (1 + r)^{-(n-k)}$ (with $h = 1$). Compute all simple forward and spot rates at time k.

Definition 6.7
The **short rate** is defined by

$$R(k) = F(k, k).$$

When $h = 1/360$, then $R(k)$ is the overnight rate, under the convention that divides a year into 12 months of 30 days. Recall that

$$F(k, n) = -\frac{B(k, n+1) - B(k, n)}{hB(k, n+1)},$$

so

$$R(k) = -\frac{B(k, k+1) - 1}{hB(k, k+1)}.$$

Definition 6.8

The **money market account** is defined by

$$A(k) = A(0)(1 + R(0)h)(1 + R(1)h) \cdots (1 + R(k-1)h).$$

At each step we know the current short rate, so we know the value of the investment in this account at the end of the period. But we do not know the next short rate, so the subsequent values are random. Thus the money market does not represent a 'riskless asset' when dealing with fixed income securities.

6.3   Coupon bonds

Fixed-coupon bonds

There are normally few zero-coupon bonds traded in the market, and they have a relatively short time to maturity, typically up to a year. The majority of bonds, especially those with longer times to maturity, are coupon bearing. The simplest kind are **fixed-coupon** bonds, providing predetermined payments (called coupons) at fixed dates.

The precise description of a fixed-coupon bond is:
- The holder of the bond receives deterministic coupon payments $C_1, \ldots, C_J$ on the corresponding deterministic dates $0 < k_1 < \cdots < k_J \le N$.
- On the maturity date k_J the holder receives the deterministic face value F. The face value is received in addition to the final coupon due on that date.

Both zero-coupon bonds and fixed-coupon bonds are fixed income securities. We shall assume, for simplicity, that the interval between coupon dates is constant, $k_{j+1} - k_j = c$, $j < J$, with $k_1 \le c$. The first coupon date indicates the day when the bond was issued, which is $c - k_1$ units before today. So for instance with $h = 1/12$, $k_1 = 2$, $k_2 = 8$, $k_3 = 14$ (semi-annual coupon) we are dealing with a bond issued four months ago.

It is easy to compute the price of a fixed-coupon bond. The cash flow of fixed-coupon bond payments can be replicated by investing, at time 0,
- $C_j B(0, k_j)$ in k_j-bonds (to receive C_j at time k_j), $j = 1, \ldots, J$,
- $F B(0, k_J)$ in k_J-bonds (to receive F at time k_J).

We know these dates and the amounts at time 0. We can use zero-coupon bonds with the corresponding maturities. Their prices are known, so we

can manufacture an investment replicating the coupon bond cash flow with certainty.

The total value of the replicating investment is the initial bond price:

$$P(0) = \sum_{j=1}^{J} C_j B(0, k_j) + F B(0, k_J). \qquad (6.4)$$

In practice unit bond prices are only known for short times to maturity (because zero-coupon bonds with longer maturities are rarely traded), whereas coupon bond prices are known for longer maturities. Therefore in practice in (6.4) $P(0)$, C_j, and F will be known and $B(0, k_j)$ will have to be computed. To this end we need a sufficient number of equations, in other words we need information about sufficiently many traded coupon bonds. The procedure of finding the structure of zero-coupon bonds with long maturities, known as **bootstrapping**, is illustrated by an example.

Example 6.9

Suppose that
- a one-year zero-coupon bond with face value £100 is trading at £91.80,
- a two-year bond with £10 annual coupons and face value £100 is trading at £103.95,
- a three-year bond with £10 annual coupons is trading at £105.15.

This leads to:

$$B(0, 1) = 0.9180,$$
$$10B(0, 1) + 110B(0, 2) = 103.95,$$
$$10B(0, 1) + 10B(0, 2) + 110B(0, 3) = 105.15.$$

Solving, we find

$$B(0, 2) \cong 0.8616,$$
$$B(0, 3) \cong 0.7941.$$

In reality, the data may be scarce or irregular and the number of variables may be larger than the number of equations. The solution is to assume additional conditions based on linear interpolation.

Exercise 6.11   Assume that the unit is one month and find the zero-coupon bonds implied by a 4-month zero-coupon bond trading at 98, and two coupon bonds with semi-annual coupons of 10, one maturing after 14 months trading at 101, and one maturing after 12 months trading at 103.

The coupons are typically constant, $C_j = C$, and often determined as a percentage of the face value, called the **coupon rate** (not annualised)

$$\frac{C}{F}.$$

Exercise 6.12   Let $h = 1$ and prove that the coupon rate equals the implied interest rate if and only if $P(0) = F$.

The price of the coupon bond at time $n \in [k_i, k_{i+1})$ according to the cash flow replication as presented above will be

$$P(n) = \sum_{j=i+1}^{J} CB(n, k_j) + FB(n, k_J) \tag{6.5}$$

$$= \left(\frac{C}{F}\sum_{j=i+1}^{J} B(n, k_j) + B(n, k_J)\right)F. \tag{6.6}$$

This price is sometimes called the **dirty price**. Note that this price is not quoted in the markets.

Accrued interest is defined by

$$AI(n) = C\frac{n - k_i}{k_{i+1} - k_i},$$

which reflects the fact that between the coupon dates the holder should be compensated for the time the bond is held. For simplicity this is done in a linear way. The **clean price** is then defined as

$$CP(n) = P(n) - AI(n).$$

Variable-rate bonds

These are bonds for which the value of the coupons is not fixed in advance, but reset for every coupon period.

Definition 6.10

The **coupon of a variable-rate bond** is

$$C_j = \left(k_j - k_{j-1}\right) h L(k_{j-1}, k_j) F.$$

The value of the coupon due at each time k_j is determined one step earlier according to the rate $L(k_{j-1}, k_j)$. The future rates are random so at the beginning we only know the first coupon.

Recall that with our conventions

$$L(k_{j-1}, k_j) = \frac{1 - B(k_{j-1}, k_j)}{(k_j - k_{j-1}) h B(k_{j-1}, k_j)},$$

so

$$C_j = F \frac{1 - B(k_{j-1}, k_j)}{B(k_{j-1}, k_j)}.$$

Theorem 6.11

The initial price $P(0)$ of a variable-rate bond is equal to F.

If the bond price is equal to the face value then we say that the bond **trades at par**. According to this theorem, a variable-coupon bond is trading at par at time 0. Before we prove the theorem, we consider an example.

Example 6.12

Take time steps $k_1 = 1$, $k_2 = 2$ with constant rate $L(0, 1) = L(1, 2) = R$. Then the coupons are given by $C = RF$ and

$$P(0) = \frac{C}{1 + R} + \frac{C + F}{(1 + R)^2} = \frac{RF}{1 + R} + \frac{RF + F}{(1 + R)^2}$$

$$= \frac{RF}{1 + R} + \frac{F}{1 + R} = F.$$

This simple example illustrates the main idea of the theorem. Observe that the coupon rate must be computed according to simple interest, otherwise this argument would not work.

Proof of Theorem 6.11 If $J = 1$, then $C_1 = F\frac{1 - B(0, k_1)}{B(0, k_1)}$, so

$$P(0) = B(0, k_1)(C_1 + F) = B(0, k_1) F \frac{1 - B(0, k_1)}{B(0, k_1)} + B(0, k_1) F = F.$$

If $J = 2$, then $C_2 = F\frac{1 - B(k_1, k_2)}{B(k_1, k_2)}$. The previous step yields

$$P(k_1) = B(k_1, k_2)(C_2 + F) = F.$$

This is the key point. At time k_1 the bond price $P(k_1)$ represents the value of the cash flow at maturity, here time k_2, namely the final coupon and face value. The holder of the bond will receive this amount with certainty in addition to the first coupon, so

$$P(0) = B(0, k_1)(C_1 + P(k_1)) = B(0, k_1)(C_1 + F) = F.$$

Induction gives the general result for any number of time steps.   □

Exercise 6.13 Having sold a variable-coupon bond with face value F design a hedging (replicating) strategy.

Interest rate swaps

Now we briefly consider **interest rate swaps**, which are contracts between two parties to exchange cash flows according to agreed criteria. For interest rate swaps this means the exchange of a floating-rate loan to a fixed-rate one, or conversely – this is usually called a **plain vanilla** swap. One party agrees to pay the other fixed-rate interest computed using the **swap rate** R_{swap} on a notional capital sum, while the second pays the first interest on the same sum and in the same currency, but at a floating rate determined by market conditions. The floating rate is usually based on the London Interbank Offer Rate (LIBOR), which acts a reference rate for Eurodollar bank deposits. Interest rate swaps can also be **floating-for-floating**, in which case two different reference rates are used to calculate the exchange payments. In both instances the **principal** acts simply as a notional sum used to calculate interest payments. The condition which will enable us to find the swap rate is that the contract is initiated at no cost.

Thus a swap is a portfolio of forward contracts, with initial and final value zero. If there is no default, the swap reflects the difference between a fixed-rate and a floating-rate bond, and this fact can be used to price the swap. The fixed-rate buyer, in effect, has a long position in the floating-rate bond, and is short the fixed-rate bond underlying the swap. The value to him is the difference of the values of these two bonds. The position of the floating-rate payer is exactly the reverse. Swaps are used by banks to adjust the cash-flow characteristics of their assets or liabilities.

The party paying the fixed-rate stream (and receiving the floating-rate stream) is called the **payer** and the party receiving the fixed-rate stream (and paying the floating-rate stream) is called the **receiver**.

A swap amounts to exchanging at time 0 a fixed-coupon bond with constant coupon rate r_{swap} (annual) for a floating-coupon bond, at no initial cost. The two bonds have the same face value F and coupon dates $0 < k_1 < \cdots < k_J$. If you swap a fixed rate for a floating rate in that way, at time step k_j you will receive the floating coupon $FL(k_{j-1}, k_j) h_{coupon}$ where $h_{coupon} = (k_j - k_{j-1})h$ is the time (in years) between the coupons, constant as we assumed above, while you will have to pay the fixed coupon $F r_{swap} h_{coupon}$.

The **value** $\Pi(0)$ of a swap to the receiver is the difference between the variable rate bond price

$$P_{variable}(0) = F$$

and the price

$$P_{fixed}(0) = F \left(r_{swap} h_{coupon} \sum_{j=1}^{J} B(0, k_j) + B(0, k_J) \right)$$

of a fixed-coupon bond with constant coupon rate r_{swap}, as given by (6.3) with $n = 0$:

$$\Pi(0) = F - F \left(r_{swap} h_{coupon} \sum_{j=1}^{J} B(0, k_j) + B(0, k_J) \right).$$

Since the initial cost of a swap is to be zero, we must have $\Pi(0) = 0$. This allows us to compute the swap rate:

$$r_{swap} = \frac{1 - B(0, k_J)}{h_{coupon} \sum_{j=1}^{J} B(0, k_j)}.$$

It should be noted that there are other (similar) versions of the swap contract. The one described above is called a **forward swap settled in arrears**. The swap rate depends on k_J so we introduce the self-explanatory notation $r_{swap}(0, k_J)$.

Exercise 6.14 Find the swap rates $r_{swap}(0, n)$ for the data from Example 6.1. Perturb one of the rates obtained by adding or subtracting x and reconstruct the bond prices. Analyse the impact of x on the prices obtained.

We have shown here that a swap can be decomposed into a portfolio of bonds, and so its value is completely determined by the bond price curve.

However, in practice, the swap market is so liquid, at so many maturities, that it is in fact swaps (through various swap rates) that drive bond prices!

6.4   Binary tree term structure models

The observed unpredictability of interest rates leads to mathematical models where interest rates and bond prices are stochastic processes. We begin with binomial branching, which as we know has the significant advantages of simplicity and completeness. However, these features are specific to the model of stock prices and we first discuss the modifications needed for bond markets.

The main type of underlying asset studied is a zero-coupon bond. It has finite life-time and becomes deterministic at maturity. Thus we need models where the randomness of prices ceases at maturity. The fact that some future prices are known in advance means that the Cox–Ross–Rubinstein (CRR) model cannot be applied, since there the range of possible values increases with time. In particular, should we apply the uniform binomial tree (i.e. with the same structure of returns at each step) to model bond prices, after some steps we would have values greater than 1 with positive probability, which is unacceptable. So, if we are going to use a binomial model, it has to be more sophisticated.

Another important feature is dependence of the bond price upon maturity. Bonds with different maturities are separate objects, like many stocks, but clearly their dynamics are closely correlated. In a simple binomial tree this correlation is perfect, which creates problems. In particular, without due care the model may allow arbitrage opportunities, which is to be avoided.

General binary tree framework

Consider the data available at time 0. In contrast to the CRR model, where only the stock and risk-free asset prices are known at time 0, we now have the entire spot term structure of bond prices, that is, the spot prices

$$B(0, 1), B(0, 2), \ldots, B(0, N).$$

In practice, many of these unit bond prices will be computed by bootstrapping from coupon bond prices.

At times $0 < n < N$ there remain all the bonds which have not yet matured. At the final time step N only one bond, maturing at N, remains.

Future bond prices are modelled as random variables, except for the prices of maturing bonds, which are equal to 1.

To specify the bond price $B(k,n)$ as a random variable we have to describe a suitable probability space. Let

$$\Omega = \{u, d\}^N$$

so $\omega \in \Omega$ is a sequence $(\omega(1), \ldots, \omega(N))$ with $\omega(k) = u$ or $\omega(k) = d$. For ease of notation we will omit the brackets and commas, writing, for example, $\omega = ddudu$ rather than $\omega = (d, d, u, d, u)$.

We introduce **nodes** $\omega_k = \omega(1) \ldots \omega(k)$ representing the history of the movements up to time k and in particular providing the exact location on the tree. Given a node ω_k, the next possible node is either $\omega_k u$ or $\omega_k d$. We will use nodes to describe random variables in the sense that if we write X^{ω_k} we mean $X(\omega)$ for any ω where the vector of initial k coordinates coincides with ω_k. In other words, the notation X^{ω_k} implicitly assumes that X is constant on all such ω's.

Thus for a bond maturing at n we write $B^{\omega_k}(k, n)$, where $k < n \leq N$; and of course $B^{\omega_k}(k, k) = 1$. The tree has binary branching, with 'up' and 'down' successor nodes and the bond prices will be written as $B^{\omega_k u}(k + 1, n)$ and $B^{\omega_k d}(k + 1, n)$. We adopt the convention that $\omega_0 = \emptyset$ so that the above notation makes sense for $k = 0, 1, \ldots, N - 1$. A simple example best illustrates the idea: $N = 3$

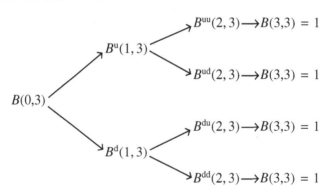

Strictly speaking, we should include two branches in the last step, but these are reduced to one since the final results are the same and consequently we drop the notation for the last node. The example shows another difference between term structure models and the CRR model which is that we allow the tree not to be recombining, which means that bond prices may be path dependent.

The probabilities of the branches will be denoted by p^{ω_k}, where

$$p^{\omega_k u} + p^{\omega_k d} = 1$$

so

$$\omega_{k+1} = \begin{cases} \omega_k u \text{ with probability } p^{\omega_k u}, \\ \omega_k d \text{ with probability } p^{\omega_k d}. \end{cases}$$

The change of bond prices from time k to $k + 1$ is described by the probabilities $p^{\omega_{k+1}}$:

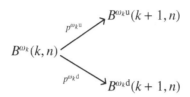

As a result the 'up' and 'down' movements at different times are independent. Note that the probabilities $p^{\omega_k u}$, $p^{\omega_k d}$ are in fact conditional probabilities of landing at the specified node provided we start from the node ω_k.

As we noted above, we should discuss the whole family of bonds with various maturities rather than a particular one. An extension of the tree for $B(k, 3)$ presented before would include the bonds maturing at 1 and 2. The initial point is a vector of current bond prices, the whole term structure.

A binomial tree of bond prices, shown here for $n = 3$, therefore looks like this:

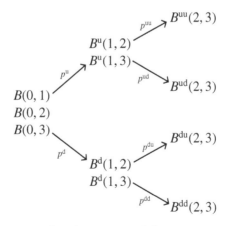

As time progresses, some bonds mature and the vector gets shorter (though some new bonds will be issued and an alternative would be to add $B(1, 4)$ at time 1 and $B(2, 4)$, $B(2, 5)$ at time 2).

Note that unlike in the CRR model we discuss the prices rather than returns. This is a matter of convenience since doing this makes it easier to see that the basic requirement, namely keeping bond prices below 1, is satisfied, so that an apparent violation of the No Arbitrage Principle does not emerge (sell short a bond for $B(k,n) > 1$ and wait till maturity to pay just the unit).

The next step is to give a concrete example consistent with the No Arbitrage Principle. This requires some further discussion.

Risk-neutral probabilities and arbitrage

In the CRR model it is easy to give examples since the specification reduces to finding three returns: a risk-free return R and risky stock returns with $-1 < D < U$. For a single asset all that is needed to eliminate arbitrage is to make sure that $D < R < U$. The starting point is similar here but we have to recognise the fact that we are modelling many assets simultanously, namely bonds with various maturities.

Example 6.13
Let $N = 3$ and take the time step as $h = 1/12$ (one month). We construct the first step of a tree of unit bond prices. The time 0 prices are known, so suppose they are

$$B(0,1) = 0.9966,$$
$$B(0,2) = 0.9932,$$
$$B(0,3) = 0.9897.$$

(Typically the bond prices will by computed from LIBOR rates for the corresponding period.)

We seek the following five numbers: $p = p^u$ (which determines $p^d = 1 - p$), $B^u(1,2), B^u(1,3), B^d(1,2), B^d(1,3)$ – the last four as shown in the diagram:

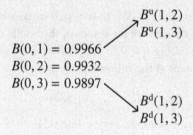

The first step is to find the risk-free return and this is straightforward. This number is provided by the price of the bond maturing in one month:

$$R = \frac{1 - B(0, 1)}{B(0, 1)} = 0.0034116.$$

For each of the two assets: $B(k, 2)$, $B(k, 3)$, treated separately, the no-arbitrage restriction on the returns must be satisfied, i.e. writing

$$U_2 = \frac{B^u(1, 2) - B(0, 2)}{B(0, 2)}, \quad U_3 = \frac{B^u(1, 3) - B(0, 3)}{B(0, 3)},$$

$$D_2 = \frac{B^d(1, 2) - B(0, 2)}{B(0, 2)}, \quad D_3 = \frac{B^d(1, 3) - B(0, 3)}{B(0, 3)},$$

(the subscript here indicates the maturity) we need $D_2 < R < U_2$, and $D_3 < R < U_3$.

With many parameters at hand we could impose some conditions based on the historical data:

$$\mathbb{E}(B(1, 2)) = m_2,$$

$$\sqrt{\text{Var}(B(1, 2))} = \sigma_2,$$

$$\mathbb{E}(B(1, 3)) = m_3,$$

$$\sqrt{\text{Var}(B(1, 3))} = \sigma_3,$$

and employing the formula for the variance of a binomial random variable we arrive at

$$pB^u(1, 2) + (1 - p)B^d(1, 2) = m_2,$$

$$\sqrt{p(1 - p)}(B^u(1, 2) - B^d(1, 2)) = \sigma_2,$$

and similar equations for $B(1, 3)$. We have a pair of two independent systems of simultaneous equations for the prices of the bonds. To find a unique solution we simplify by taking $p = 0.5$. Suppose we have estimated the historical trends and variances at the following levels

$$m_2 = 0.9966, \quad \sigma_2 = 0.00018,$$

$$m_3 = 0.9931, \quad \sigma_3 = 0.00021.$$

This gives the equations

$$0.5(B^u(1,2) + B^d(1,2)) = 0.9966,$$
$$0.5(B^u(1,2) - B^d(1,2)) = 0.00018,$$
$$0.5(B^u(1,3) + B^d(1,3)) = 0.9931,$$
$$0.5(B^u(1,3) - B^d(1,3)) = 0.00021,$$

yielding the prices

$$B^u(1,2) = 0.99678,$$
$$B^d(1,2) = 0.99642,$$
$$B^u(1,3) = 0.99331,$$
$$B^d(1,3) = 0.99289.$$

The solutions can be easily verified against the basic no-arbitrage conditions: $D_2 = 0.00324205 < R < U_2 = 0.00360451$, $D_3 = 0.0032232 < R < U_3 = 0.00364757$.

Obtaining a no-arbitrage condition for each bond separately is actually not sufficient if we recall our discussion in Section 2.4 where we considered two stocks in the binomial model. The situation here is similar since we also have two risky securities in a binomial model and the name (stock or bond) of the underlying does not matter. Theorem 2.13 says that the risk-neutral probabilities determined by these two assets must coincide to avoid arbitrage. Therefore, writing

$$q_2 = \frac{R - D_2}{U_2 - D_2}, \quad q_3 = \frac{R - D_3}{U_3 - D_3}$$

we must have

$$q_2 = q_3.$$

It turns out that the numbers obtained in the last example do not satisfy this condition:

$$q_2 = 0.46777934,$$

$$q_3 = 0.44395229.$$

Exercise 6.15   Find an arbitrage strategy for the above example.

In this example we have assumed that $p = 0.5$ since we had too many variables (five variables with four conditions only). We could try to refine the example by changing the probability, but as the following exercises show, this does not work in general: only if the historical data satisfy some additional conditions will we have no arbitrage, independently of p; otherwise altering p does not help.

Exercise 6.16   Within the scheme of Example 6.13 show that if $B(0, 2)(1 + R) = \mathbb{E}(B(1, 2))$, $B(0, 3)(1 + R) = \mathbb{E}(B(1, 3))$ then $q_3 = q_2$ for any p. Formulate a condition linking the expectations and variances of $B(1, 2)$ and $B(1, 3)$ so that $q_2 = q_3$ for all p. Show that if this condition does not hold, $q_2 \neq q_3$ for any $p \in (0, 1)$.

So a modification of the probability does not lead to elimination of arbitrage and to rectify the model we have to change at least one of the four prices at time 1 to make q_2 equal to q_3, but this will cause some of the four conditions to be violated.

Exercise 6.17   Change the value of $B^u(1, 2)$ in Example 6.13 so that $q_2 = q_3$ and analyse the expectations and variances after the change.

In practice the estimation of expected returns (or the expected future price, which boils down to the same) is not reliable so we take a different tack in the next attempt.

Example 6.14

We assume that $p = 0.5$ and we abandon the conditions concerned with the expected bond prices. On the other hand, we assume that the **risk-neutral** probabilities are not only equal for various maturities but

specifically they are both equal to 0.5, which is much more stringent, but quite convenient.

We take the variances from Example 6.13, so the equations are of the form

$$\frac{B(0,2)(1+R) - B^d(1,2)}{B^u(1,2) - B^d(1,2)} = 0.5,$$

$$0.5(B^u(1,2) - B^d(1,2)) = 0.00018,$$

$$\frac{B(0,3)(1+R) - B^d(1,3)}{B^u(1,3) - B^d(1,3)} = 0.5,$$

$$0.5(B^u(1,3) - B^d(1,3)) = 0.00021,$$

and we immediately get

$$B^u(1,2) = B(0,2)(1+R) + 0.00018 = 0.99676840,$$

$$B^d(1,2) = B(0,2)(1+R) - 0.00018 = 0.99640840,$$

$$B^u(1,3) = B(0,3)(1+R) + 0.00021 = 0.99328646,$$

$$B^d(1,3) = B(0,3)(1+R) - 0.00021 = 0.99286646.$$

The model is of course free of arbitrage due to the assumed equality of risk-neutral probabilities for different maturities.

Another approach to the task of building an example is to use some available market data for derivative securities.

Example 6.15

Let $q_2 = q_3 = 0.5$ which gives two conditions which can be conveniently written in the form

$$B(0,2)(1+R) = \frac{1}{2}(B^u(1,2) + B^d(1,2)),$$

$$B(0,3)(1+R) = \frac{1}{2}(B^u(1,3) + B^d(1,3)),$$

so the construction boils down to finding $B^u(1,2)$ and $B^u(1,3)$, say.

Suppose we know the price of a call option written on 2-bond with strike price $K = 0.9965$ and exercise time $k = 1$. Consider $100\,000$ options and assume that the price of the package is 20. With q at hand this gives the

equation to complete the 2-bond details

$$100\,000 \times \frac{1}{1+R} \frac{(B^{\mathrm{u}}(1,2) - K)^+ + (B^{\mathrm{d}}(1,2) - K)^+}{2} = 20$$

resulting in

$$B^{\mathrm{u}}(1,2) = 0.99690136,$$
$$B^{\mathrm{d}}(1,2) = 0.99627544.$$

Next, to make the story more interresting, suppose that we know the price of the following derivative involving both bonds. Let the payoff $H(1)$ be the annual interest on the sum of $100\,000$ according to the higher rate of the two rates implied by the 2-bond and the 3-bond (payable at time 1). The annual rates on the 2-bond are (simple compounding is used)

$$12 \times \left(\frac{1}{B^{\mathrm{u}}(1,2)} - 1 \right) = 3.7299\%,$$

$$12 \times \left(\frac{1}{B^{\mathrm{d}}(1,2)} - 1 \right) = 4.4862\%.$$

Suppose that the price of this derivative security is 4200 and this, as we shall see, requires taking

$$B^{\mathrm{u}}(1,3) = 0.9939233,$$
$$B^{\mathrm{d}}(1,3) = 0.9922296,$$

since then

$$6 \times \left(\frac{1}{B^{\mathrm{u}}(1,3)} - 1 \right) = 3.6683\%,$$

$$6 \times \left(\frac{1}{B^{\mathrm{d}}(1,3)} - 1 \right) = 4.6987\%,$$

the payoff is

$$H^{\mathrm{u}}(1) = 100\,000 \times 3.7299\%,$$
$$H^{\mathrm{d}}(1) = 100\,000 \times 4.6987\%,$$

and clearly

$$\mathbb{E}_Q \left(\frac{1}{1+R} H(1) \right) = B(0,1) \frac{3729.9 + 4698.7}{2} = 4200,$$

which agrees with the price assumed.

Multi-factor models

Recall that the trinomial model with two risky assets is typically complete with a unique candidate for the risk-neutral probability (common for both assets). Despite its uniqueness we cannot guarantee that this candidate probability will be genuine and nondegenerate (i.e. all branching probabilities lie in the interval $(0, 1)$), as shown by the examples given in Chapter 2. We now consider a model of this kind with two bonds, as shown in the diagram:

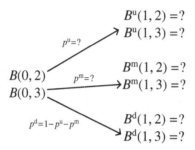

A substantial advantage now is that the bond prices do not have to be perfectly correlated and we can insist on some nontrivial correlation between the prices, perhaps close to, but not necessarily equal to one. There are eight parameters to find and following the scheme based on historical data, six conditions can be formulated based on:

- 2 expectations,
- 2 standard deviations,
- 1 correlation.

From the point of solvability we are here in a good position having many variables and few equations. However, this requires some ad hoc decisions since typically there will be infinitely many solutions.

Example 6.16

As before, the simplest assumption is to take the three probabilities to be equal, $p^u = p^m = p^d = 1/3$. This arbitrary choice is again guided by the fact that for option pricing the original probabilities are irrelevant and only the risk-neutral probabilities are used. Let us try to use the data from Example 6.13. We leave it as an elementary numerical exercise to check

that with some accuracy, the following prices fit the scheme

$$B^u(1,2) = 0.996820,$$
$$B^m(1,2) = 0.996600,$$
$$B^d(1,2) = 0.996379,$$
$$B^u(1,3) = 0.993310,$$
$$B^m(1,3) = 0.993176,$$
$$B^d(1,3) = 0.992814,$$

the correlation coefficient is $\rho = 0.964$ and the risk-neutral probabilities are $q^u = 0.3533$, $q^m = 0.2409$, $q^d = 0.4059$.

We will not pursue other methods of fitting the tree to the data which were outlined above, such as using the current prices of derivative securities, which is arguably the most promising, since it is related to current market data. However, the work involved in formulating the conditions and solving the equations is similar as before.

Suppose we admit an additional bond $B(1,4)$ maturing at time 4. In real markets many bonds with different maturities are traded, so this is an inevitable direction for the development of the model. We are working in the trinomial model, so we have 11 parameters:

- 9 bond prices,
- 2 probabilities,

and 12 conditions:

- 3 expectations,
- 3 standard deviations,
- 3 correlations,
- 3 equalities for risk-neutral probabilities.

Here we have too many conditions, and with our experience we can arrive at the conclusion that we should consider more branches in the tree, for instance a quadrinomial model. However, this becomes very complicated and bearing in mind that we are considering just the first step, this does not seem a viable path for further development. As will be seen in a later volume in this series, continuous-time interest rate models, though in principle more sophisticated, provide a more tractable approach to this problem.

Multi-step models

We have seen that introducing more complex models leads to complications and does not really solve the problem. We have to make simplifying assumptions in order to build some viable examples.

We would like to follow the general approach of the CRR model where the returns determine the prices and the returns in all steps are the same. Here we can apply this only partially and some extra care will be needed.

The general pattern is this: at step 1 we build binomial trees for various bonds (with various maturities). These trees have the following form

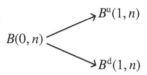

where $n = 2, \dots, N$. At each step the time to maturity decreases by one for each bond. We would like to apply the same scheme in each subsequent step, using appropriately structured changes related to the distance to maturity.

So, for instance, with $N = 4$ we have three trees related to the bonds of maturities 2,3,4 and their times to maturity are reduced to 1,2,3, respectively. We have at our disposal three schemes, which could be denoted by 2to1, 3to2, 4to3. Now at time one, at the up state, we have the prices $B^u(1,4)$, $B^u(1,3)$, $B^u(1,2)$. The last bond requires no action since it will become the unit at the next time. For the design of trees for the first two bonds we now use the 3to2 and 2to1 schemes. In other words, the structure of the tree

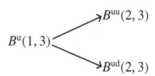

will be the same as the structure of the tree

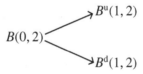

Our task is to identify this structure. Among the many calibrating methods available we choose the one based on taking all risk-neutral probabilities to be $1/2$. This implies the following structure of returns

$$U = R + \varepsilon,$$
$$D = R - \varepsilon,$$

where R is the risk-free return. Let us explore this with a numerical example.

Example 6.17

We will continue Example 6.15 and we recognise the form of the structure related to the 2to1 tree. The risk-free return for step 1 is

$$R(0) = \frac{1}{B(0,1)} - 1 = 0.3412\%.$$

For the 2to1 reduction we use the bond prices computed before

$$B^u(1,2) = 0.99690136,$$
$$B^d(1,2) = 0.99627544,$$

which are related to returns at time 0 for the 2-bond

$$U_{2to1} = \frac{B^u(1,2)}{B(0,2)} - 1 = 0.3727\%,$$

$$D_{2to1} = \frac{B^d(1,2)}{B(0,2)} - 1 = 0.3096\%,$$

and clearly

$$U_{2to1} = R(0) + 0.0315\%,$$
$$D_{2to1} = R(0) - 0.0315\%,$$

hence

$$\varepsilon_{2to1} = 0.0315\%.$$

Similarly, employing $B(0,3)$ and $B^u(1,3)$, $B^d(1,3)$ we can find

$$\varepsilon_{3to2} = 0.0856\%.$$

Now we will design the prices $B(2,3)$ at time 2 (there are four of them). Recall that earlier we found the values

$$B^u(1,3) = 0.99408791,$$
$$B^d(1,3) = 0.99206501.$$

Consider two cases:

(i) 'Up' move at step 1. First note that we have the risk-free return

$$R^u(1) = \frac{1}{B^u(1,2)} - 1 = 0.3108\%.$$

We need two prices $B^{uu}(2,3)$ and $B^{ud}(2,3)$ and we build them by applying the above structure and requiring that

$$\frac{B^{uu}(2,3)}{B^u(1,3)} - 1 = R^u(1) + \varepsilon_{2\text{to}1},$$

$$\frac{B^{ud}(2,3)}{B^u(1,3)} - 1 = R^u(1) - \varepsilon_{2\text{to}1},$$

so that

$$B^{uu}(2,3) = B^u(1,3)(1 + R^u(1) + \varepsilon_{2\text{to}1}) = 0.997326,$$

$$B^{ud}(2,3) = B^u(1,3)(1 + R^u(1) - \varepsilon_{2\text{to}1}) = 0.996699.$$

(ii) 'Down' move at step 1. The risk-free return is

$$R^d(1) = \frac{1}{B^d(1,2)} - 1 = 0.3738\%,$$

and working in the same manner (using the same perturbations $\pm\varepsilon_{2\text{to}1}$) we get

$$B^{du}(2,3) = B^d(1,3)(1 + R^d(1) + \varepsilon_{2\text{to}1}) = 0.996252,$$

$$B^{dd}(2,3) = B^d(1,3)(1 + R^d(1) - \varepsilon_{2\text{to}1}) = 0.995626.$$

To summarise, here is the complete tree:

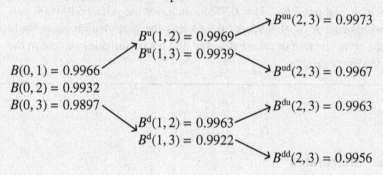

In general, at the first step, assuming $q = 1/2$, we have the perturbations $\varepsilon_{n\text{to}(n-1)}$, $n \leq N$ and then at time k, in the state ω_k we design single-step trees for all bonds using the same risk-free returns, and appropriate perturbations, the same for each step, depending solely on distance to maturity

$$B^{\omega_k u}(k+1,n) = B^{\omega_k}(k,n)(1 + R^{\omega_k}(k) + \varepsilon_{(n-k)\text{to}(n-k-1)}),$$

$$B^{\omega_k d}(k+1,n) = B^{\omega_k}(k,n)(1 + R^{\omega_k}(k) - \varepsilon_{(n-k)\text{to}(n-k-1)}).$$

One important final comment is related to the No Arbitrage Principle. Using $q = 1/2$ seems to guarantee lack of arbitrage but one has to be careful, since in general the bond prices might increase beyond 1. Should this happen in the model, we must find appropropriate adjustments to deal with it.

Remark 6.18
If we adopt the method of using the first step structure at the subsequent stages, the first step is crucial. An alternative to assuming a value for the risk-neutral probability arbitrarily, as we have done, is to take the historical variances (or standard deviations) related to bonds with various maturities. Such a sequence of standard deviations $\sigma(0, k)$, $k \leq N$, is called the **initial term structure** of volatilities. Clearly their sizes are related to the corresponding perturbations $\varepsilon_{k\text{to}(k-1)}$. The binomial distribution gives a simple formula for the standard deviation and if $U = R + \varepsilon$, $D = R - \varepsilon$ then ε is the standard deviation of the returns but computed with respect to the probability $q = 1/2$: $\sigma = \sqrt{q(1 - q)}(U - D) = \varepsilon$. If we have the historical standard deviations we have to remember that they correspond to physical probabilities, not the risk-neutral ones.

Exercise 6.18 Build the initial tree for a bond maturing at time 4 with initial price $B(0, 4) = 0.9859$, such that the price of 100 000 puts with strike $K = 0.9898$ is 80 and find the perturbation $\varepsilon_{4\text{to}3}$. Build the complete tree of prices $B(k, 4)$ using the perturbations found in the previous example.

6.5 Short rates

The bonds maturing at the next time instant determine the short rates. Here we assume simple interest but other methods can also be used. Previously we used the returns, but here the returns are annualised in line with general convention, providing the rates of interest.

The short rate is defined by

$$r(k) = \frac{1}{h}\left(\frac{1}{B(k, k + 1)} - 1\right)$$

and it is a random variable except the case $k = 0$ (we use r since R is reserved for returns, with simple compounding applied these differ by the factor h).

Example 6.19
The tree of bond prices $B(k, k + 1)$ with $h = 1/12$ constructed in Example 6.15 determines the tree of short rates. Note that the short rates for any given month are determined at the begining of the period.

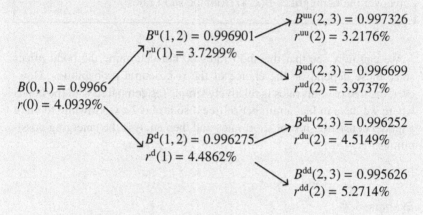

$$B^{uu}(2,3) = 0.997326$$
$$r^{uu}(2) = 3.2176\%$$

$$B^{u}(1,2) = 0.996901$$
$$r^{u}(1) = 3.7299\%$$

$$B^{ud}(2,3) = 0.996699$$
$$r^{ud}(2) = 3.9737\%$$

$$B(0,1) = 0.9966$$
$$r(0) = 4.0939\%$$

$$B^{du}(2,3) = 0.996252$$
$$r^{du}(2) = 4.5149\%$$

$$B^{d}(1,2) = 0.996275$$
$$r^{d}(1) = 4.4862\%$$

$$B^{dd}(2,3) = 0.995626$$
$$r^{dd}(2) = 5.2714\%$$

A natural question emerges: given a tree of short rates, can we compute the bond prices? As a first step in this direction we will recover the bond prices we already know.

Example 6.20
Given short rates as in Example 6.19 we can immediately find the bond prices $B(k, k+1)$ applying the definition. Then, bearing in mind the method of Example 6.15 we can complete the tree using the risk-neutral probabilities as assumed, i.e. $q = 1/2$, and performing no-arbitrage option pricing, i.e. taking the discounted risk-neutral expected payoff. So we get the two missing prices of the 3-bond

$$B^{u}(1,3) = \frac{1}{1 + \frac{1}{12}r^{u}(1)}\left(\frac{1}{2}B^{uu}(2,3) + \frac{1}{2}B^{ud}(2,3)\right),$$

$$B^{d}(1,3) = \frac{1}{1 + \frac{1}{12}r^{d}(1)}\left(\frac{1}{2}B^{du}(2,3) + \frac{1}{2}B^{dd}(2,3)\right),$$

and also

$$B(0,2) = \frac{1}{1 + \frac{1}{12}r(0)}\left(\frac{1}{2}B^u(1,2) + \frac{1}{2}B^d(1,2)\right).$$

Exercise 6.19   Find the short rates $r(3)$ following Exercise 6.18 and recover the bond prices $B(k,4)$ from the short rates.

We can now see that the short rates do not determine the bond prices since these depend on the choice of the risk-neutral probabilities. However, the tree of short rates is relatively simple (as compared with the bonds where we have in fact a number of trees) so it may be worthwhile to build a model consisting just of short rates and then analyse the emerging possibilities.

Example 6.21

Suppose we have, by some method, built a different tree of short rates (with the same $r(0)$ as before), yielding

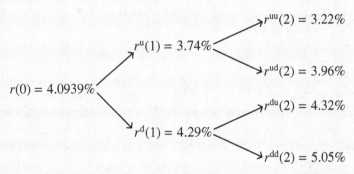

The one-step prices $B(k,k+1)$ can be found using the definition and with these, assuming $q = \frac{1}{2}$, we can complete the bond price calculations. In particular, we obtain

$$B(0,2) = 0.993277,$$
$$B(0,3) = 0.989864.$$

However, these numbers cannot be arbitrary since they are known current market values. If these are as before, namely

$$B(0,2) = 0.993200,$$
$$B(0,3) = 0.989700,$$

the model is not consistent with the data.

We can save the day by allowing a flexible choice of risk-neutral probabilities. Our tree consists of three single-step subtrees so in general we can use three probabilities (these are risk-neutral probabilities of the up movement at each node)

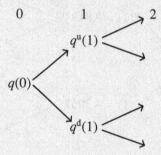

Assume $q^u(1) = q^d(1) = q(1)$ so that they depend on time but are not random. It is now routine to see that the choice

$$q(0) = 0.330928,$$
$$q(1) = 0.607029,$$

gives the initial bond prices as required.

Exercise 6.20 Find the tree of bond prices in the above example taking $q = 0.5$ and then taking the above values of $q(0), q(1)$. Extend this to the case considered in Exercise 6.18.

In summary, given risk-neutral probabilities and short rates, we can find all bond prices by moving backwards from the maturity payment. But the initial prices must, crucially, agree with the market data. The model must be sufficiently flexible to allow adjustment to fit the current market data, represented by the whole sequence of initial bond prices. As we have seen, this can be done by adjusting risk-neutral probabilities. but of course

this is just one possibility. The other one is to adjust the model of short rates.

Example 6.22
Assuming the risk-neutral probabilities are again $q = 1/2$ we find a tree of short rates by adjusting their values to fit the initial prices. A simple application of the Excel program Solver to find the six numbers representing rates at time 1 and 2 gives a possible solution:

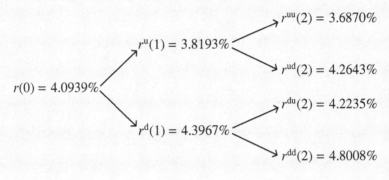

For trees with many steps it would be convenient to have some structure to limit the number of parameters. We give examples based on discrete versions of well-known continuous-time models of short rates.

Example 6.23
Suppose that the short rate follows a binomial tree with

$$r^{\omega_k u}(k + 1) = r^{\omega_k}(k) + ah - \sigma \sqrt{h},$$
$$r^{\omega_k u}(k + 1) = r^{\omega_k}(k) + ah + \sigma \sqrt{h},$$

for some real values of a and σ, and given $r(0)$, which corresponds to the Merton model. With risk-neutral probability $q = 1/2$ at each node, we can adjust the parameters a, σ so that the initial bond prices agree with the data. It turns out that in general we can do this only approximately – the structure of the tree is not sufficiently rich. The same is true for the

more sophisticated Vasicek model, where for some positive a, b, σ we postulate

$$r^{\omega_k u}(k+1) = r^{\omega_k}(k) + (a - br^{\omega_k}(k))h - \sigma\sqrt{h},$$
$$r^{\omega_k u}(k+1) = r^{\omega_k}(k) + (a - br^{\omega_k}(k))h + \sigma\sqrt{h},$$

with some initial rate $r(0)$ given. Here on average the rates will be pushed towards a since if the previous rate is low the drift coefficient $(a - br^{\omega_k}(k))$ will be positive and negative otherwise (with exact relationship subject to the choice of b).

An obvious weakness of these models is that they allow negative rates which gives some bond prices above 1 with immediate arbitrage.

Exercise 6.21 Consider the above models with $h = 1/12, k = 0, 1, 2$ and try to calibrate them to the initial bond prices $B(0, 2) = 0.9932$, $B(0, 3) = 0.9897$ taking the rate implied by $B(0, 1) = 0.9966$ as the initial short rate.

Finally, we observe that if the tree of prices of the bond with the longest maturity is built, then this together with the short rates will determine the remaining bond prices with maturities $m = 2, \ldots, n - 1$ via a replication procedure. Indeed, the bond prices with maturity n together with the short rates determine the risk-neutral probabilities by

$$q^{\omega_k}(k) = \frac{\frac{1}{B^{\omega_k}(k,k+1)} - \frac{B^{\omega_k d}(k+1,n)}{B^{\omega_k}(k,n)}}{\frac{B^{\omega_k u}(k+1,n)}{B^{\omega_k}(k,n)} - \frac{B^{\omega_k d}(k+1,n)}{B^{\omega_k}(k,n)}}. \tag{6.7}$$

Since the bond prices at maturity m are known to be equal to 1, the risk-neutral probabilities can then be used to compute the bond prices prior to maturity m using the martingale property

$$B^{\omega_k}(k, m) = \frac{1}{1 + r^{\omega_k}(k)}[q^{\omega_k}(k)B^{\omega_t u}(k + 1, m)$$
$$+ (1 - q^{\omega_k}(k))B^{\omega_t d}(k + 1, m)]. \tag{6.8}$$

The following exercise illustrates this procedure.

Exercise 6.22 Let $h = 1/12$, let $n = 3$ and let the short rates and the prices for the bond with maturity 3 be as in the following tree:

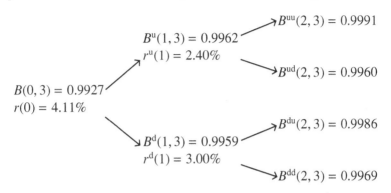

First, compute the risk-neutral probabilities $q(0)$, $q^u(1)$, $q^d(1)$ (of upward movement) using (6.7) and then compute the prices of the remaining bonds.

To summarise, we have seen that for short rates to give the bond prices we need more information. The short rates alone do not suffice for this purpose. However:

- Short rates and n-bond prices give prices of m-bonds for $m \le n$. We illustrated this with an example, but it is clear that the procedure can be applied in a binomial tree with arbitrary size. The most natural method here is the replication by solving systems of simultaneous equations to obtain the replicating strategy by going backwards step by step.
- Short rates and martingale probabilities together give all bond prices:
  - the terminal payments are known (=1)
  - we go backwards through the tree computing discounted expected values
  - discounting uses the short rate
  - the expectation is taken with respect to martingale probabilities (for $B(m-1, m)$ just discounting is needed).
- The n-bond tree gives the risk-neutral probabilities for times $k \le n$ and vice versa.

An important observation: given the long-term bond prices the martingale probabilities can easily be computed in the binomial model and then

they can be used to compute the prices of other bonds. These in turn generate the martingale probabilities which agree with the probabilities generated by the long maturity bond.

We now examine a term structure model where the binomial trees recombine, determined by few parameters.

6.6 The Ho–Lee model of term structure

This is the simplest term structure model, bearing many similarities to the Cox–Ross–Rubinstein model of stock prices. It was developed in 1986 and is largely regarded as the first successful model of term structure (successful, but not without problems).

Model set-up

The **Ho–Lee** (HL) model is based on a recombining binomial tree, which means that bond prices in this model are **path independent**. So the price at a given node depends only on the number of up and down movements between the root of the tree and the given node.

We know that the forward price, contracted at time n, of an m-bond to be traded at time $n + 1$ is

$$B(n, n + 1, m) = \frac{B(n, m)}{B(n, n + 1)}.$$

To model random bond prices Ho and Lee modified the forward price by setting

$$B^{\omega_n u}(n + 1, m) = \frac{B^{\omega_n}(n, m)}{B^{\omega_n}(n, n + 1)} h^u(m - (n + 1)),$$

$$B^{\omega_n d}(n + 1, m) = \frac{B^{\omega_n}(n, m)}{B^{\omega_n}(n, n + 1)} h^d(m - (n + 1)),$$

for some functions h^u and h^d, called **perturbation factors**, which depend on the time to maturity $m - (n + 1)$. The exact form of these functions will be established in what follows. In other words, at time n at node ω_n, the risk-free growth factors are perturbed by factors depending on the time to maturity only. So in this spirit the above formula can be written as

$$B^{\omega_{n+1}}(n + 1, m) = \begin{cases} B^{\omega_n}(n, m) \frac{1}{B^{\omega_n}(n, n+1)} h^u(m - (n + 1)) \\ B^{\omega_n}(n, m) \frac{1}{B^{\omega_n}(n, n+1)} h^d(m - (n + 1)) \end{cases}$$

Remark 6.24

The expressions $\frac{h^{\mathrm{u}}(m-(n+1))}{B^{\omega n}(n,n+1)}$ and $\frac{h^{\mathrm{d}}(m-(n+1))}{B^{\omega n}(n,n+1)}$ in the HL model are analogous to the factors $1+U, 1+D$ in the CRR model. However, in contrast to the CRR model, the factors in the HL model are not the same throughout the tree (not even for all bond prices at the same node). Formally they depend on both n and m, although in fact they depend only on their difference.

Remark 6.25

This model is close in spirit to the principle we applied before where we assumed a uniform scheme of reduction of time to maturity. Before, we would perturb by adding and subtracting some number – which is a matter of style rather than of principle – so that the above formula corresponds to what we called the $(m-n)$to$(m-n-1)$ reduction of time to maturity. However, the present approach is more efficient since it will lead to a simple form of the perturbation factors and we postpone a concrete numerical example till we confirm this result. We will also see that, owing to the assumptions imposed on the growth factors, it is less flexible than the previous scheme.

For the present we simply note some relations for the initial steps

$$B(1,2) = \begin{cases} B^{\mathrm{u}}(1,2) = B(0,2)\frac{1}{B(0,1)}h^{\mathrm{u}}(1) \\ B^{\mathrm{d}}(1,2) = B(0,2)\frac{1}{B(0,1)}h^{\mathrm{d}}(1) \end{cases}$$

$$B(1,3) = \begin{cases} B^{\mathrm{u}}(1,3) = B(0,3)\frac{1}{B(0,1)}h^{\mathrm{u}}(2) \\ B^{\mathrm{d}}(1,3) = B(0,3)\frac{1}{B(0,1)}h^{\mathrm{d}}(2) \end{cases}$$

$$B(2,3) = \begin{cases} B^{\mathrm{uu}}(2,3) = B^{\mathrm{u}}(1,3)\frac{1}{B^{\mathrm{u}}(1,2)}h^{\mathrm{u}}(1) \\ B^{\mathrm{ud}}(2,3) = B^{\mathrm{u}}(1,3)\frac{1}{B^{\mathrm{u}}(1,2)}h^{\mathrm{d}}(1) \\ B^{\mathrm{du}}(2,3) = B^{\mathrm{d}}(1,3)\frac{1}{B^{\mathrm{d}}(1,2)}h^{\mathrm{u}}(1) \\ B^{\mathrm{dd}}(2,3) = B^{\mathrm{d}}(1,3)\frac{1}{B^{\mathrm{d}}(1,2)}h^{\mathrm{d}}(1) \end{cases}$$

and in particular

$$B^{\mathrm{ud}}(2,3) = B^{\mathrm{u}}(1,3)\frac{1}{B^{\mathrm{u}}(1,2)}h^{\mathrm{d}}(1)$$

$$= B(0,3)\frac{1}{B(0,1)}h^{\mathrm{u}}(2)\frac{1}{B(0,2)\frac{1}{B(0,1)}h^{\mathrm{u}}(1)}h^{\mathrm{d}}(1)$$

$$= \frac{B(0,3)}{B(0,2)}\frac{h^{\mathrm{u}}(2)}{h^{\mathrm{u}}(1)}\frac{h^{\mathrm{d}}(1)}{h^{\mathrm{d}}(0)}.$$

This suggests a general formula.

Proposition 6.26

The price at time step $n \geq 0$ of a unit bond expiring at time step m (where $n \leq m \leq N$) at a node ω_n reached by a path $\omega_n = \alpha_1\alpha_2\cdots\alpha_n$, where $\alpha_1,\ldots,\alpha_n \in \{u,d\}$ is given by

$$B^{\omega_n}(n,m) = \frac{B(0,m)}{B(0,n)}\,\frac{h^{\alpha_1}(m-1)}{h^{\alpha_1}(n-1)}\,\frac{h^{\alpha_2}(m-2)}{h^{\alpha_2}(n-2)}\cdots\frac{h^{\alpha_n}(m-n)}{h^{\alpha_n}(0)},$$

where $\omega_k = \alpha_1\cdots\alpha_k$.

Proof This is just a matter of applying the single-step formula a number of times or using mathematical induction

$$B^{\omega_n}(n,m)$$
$$= \frac{B^{\omega_{n-1}}(n-1,m)}{B^{\omega_{n-1}}(n-1,n)}\,\frac{h^{\alpha_n}(m-n)}{h^{\alpha_n}(0)}$$
$$= \frac{B^{\omega_{n-2}}(n-2,m)}{B^{\omega_{n-2}}(n-2,n)}\,\frac{h^{\alpha_{n-1}}(m-(n-1))}{h^{\alpha_{n-1}}(1)}\,\frac{h^{\alpha_n}(m-n)}{h^{\alpha_n}(0)}$$
$$\vdots$$
$$= \frac{B(0,m)}{B(0,n)}\,\frac{h^{\alpha_1}(m-1)}{h^{\alpha_1}(n-1)}\,\frac{h^{\alpha_2}(m-2)}{h^{\alpha_2}(n-2)}\cdots\frac{h^{\alpha_n}(m-n)}{h^{\alpha_n}(0)}. \qquad \square$$

The perturbation factors

We now turn to determining the exact form of the functions h^u and h^d. Observe that $B(m,m) = 1$ implies

$$h^u(0) = h^d(0) = 1.$$

Next, we consider conditions for the absence of arbitrage. We know that the lack of arbitrage is equivalent to the existence of a probability measure that turns the discounted prices of all assets, in particular all discounted unit bond prices, into martingales. Here discounting is by means of the factors $B(n,n+1)$. As a result, at each n and each node ω_n there is a probability $q \in (0,1)$ such that for each $m > n$

$$B^{\omega_n}(n,m) = B^{\omega_n}(n,n+1)\left[qB^{\omega_n u}(n+1,m) + (1-q)B^{\omega_n d}(n+1,m)\right],$$

which gives

$$1 = qh^u(m-(n+1)) + (1-q)h^d(m-(n+1)). \tag{6.9}$$

Furthermore, it is assumed that q is independent of n, ω_n and m, thus is the same at each node throughout the tree.

We can obtain a further condition by assuming that prices follow a re-combining tree. Starting at any node ω_n, the bond prices after going up-down in the next two steps must be the same as after going down-up,

$$B^{\omega_n \mathrm{ud}}(n + 2, m) = B^{\omega_n \mathrm{du}}(n + 2, m).$$

The left- and right-hand sides of this equality can be written as

$$B^{\omega_n \mathrm{ud}}(n + 2, m) = \frac{B^{\omega_n \mathrm{u}}(n + 1, m) h^{\mathrm{d}}(m - (n + 2))}{B^{\omega_n \mathrm{u}}(n + 1, n + 2)}$$

$$= \frac{B^{\omega_n}(n, m) h^{\mathrm{u}}(m - (n + 1)) h^{\mathrm{d}}(m - (n + 2))}{B^{\omega_n}(n, n + 2) h^{\mathrm{u}}(1)},$$

$$B^{\omega_n \mathrm{du}}(n + 2, m) = \frac{B^{\omega_n \mathrm{d}}(n + 1, m) h^{\mathrm{u}}(m - (n + 2))}{B^{\omega_n \mathrm{d}}(n + 1, n + 2)}$$

$$= \frac{B^{\omega_n}(n, m) h^{\mathrm{d}}(m - (n + 1)) h^{\mathrm{u}}(m - (n + 2))}{B^{\omega_n}(n, n + 2) h^{\mathrm{d}}(1)},$$

so that for any $m \geq n + 2$

$$\frac{h^{\mathrm{u}}(m - (n + 1)) h^{\mathrm{d}}(m - (n + 2))}{h^{\mathrm{u}}(1)} = \frac{h^{\mathrm{d}}(m - (n + 1)) h^{\mathrm{u}}(m - (n + 2))}{h^{\mathrm{d}}(1)}. \tag{6.10}$$

The above properties can be summarised as follows:

$$q h^{\mathrm{u}}(k) + (1 - q) h^{\mathrm{d}}(k) = 1, \tag{6.11}$$

$$\frac{h^{\mathrm{d}}(k + 1)}{h^{\mathrm{u}}(k + 1)} = \frac{h^{\mathrm{d}}(k)}{h^{\mathrm{u}}(k)} \frac{h^{\mathrm{d}}(1)}{h^{\mathrm{u}}(1)}, \tag{6.12}$$

for each integer $n = 0, 1, 2, \ldots$ (Use $k = m - (n + 1)$ in (6.9) and $k = m - (n + 2)$ in (6.10).) Putting

$$\delta = \frac{h^{\mathrm{d}}(1)}{h^{\mathrm{u}}(1)}$$

we find from (6.12) that

$$\frac{h^{\mathrm{d}}(n)}{h^{\mathrm{u}}(n)} = \delta^n,$$

and from (6.11) that

$$h^{\mathrm{d}}(n) = \frac{\delta^n}{(1 - q)\delta^n + q}, \qquad h^{\mathrm{u}}(n) = \frac{1}{(1 - q)\delta^n + q},$$

for each $n = 0, 1, 2, \ldots$

As we can see in the next proposition, the HL model is fully determined by the initial term structure of bond prices $B(0, 1), \ldots, B(0, N)$, that
is known at time 0, and the two parameters q and δ, which can be obtained
by calibrating the model. All the remaining quantities can be expressed in
terms of these. Because we are working in a recombining tree, the bond
price does not depend on the actual shape of the path but only on the number j of down jumps along the path.

Proposition 6.27
If the symbol d *appears* j *times in* ω_n *then*

$$B^{\omega_n}(n, m) = \frac{B(0, m)}{B(0, n)} \delta^{j(m-n)} \frac{(1-q)\delta^{n-1} + q}{(1-q)\delta^{m-1} + q} \frac{(1-q)\delta^{n-2} + q}{(1-q)\delta^{m-2} + q} \cdots$$

$$\cdots \frac{(1-q)\delta^0 + q}{(1-q)\delta^{m-n} + q}.$$

Proof Such a path can be denoted by $\omega_n = d^j u^{n-j} = \alpha_1 \alpha_2 \cdots \alpha_n$ and by
Proposition 6.26 we get

$$B^{\omega_n}(n, m) = B^{d^j u^{n-j}}(n, m)$$

$$= \frac{B(0, m)}{B(0, n)} \frac{h^d(m-1)}{h^d(n-1)} \frac{h^d(m-2)}{h^d(n-2)} \cdots$$

$$= \cdots \frac{h^d(m-j)}{h^d(n-j)} \frac{h^u(m-j-1)}{h^u(n-j-1)} \cdots \frac{h^u(m-n)}{h^u(0)}.$$

We have j occurrences of $h^d(k)$, with various k, and after we replace each
by $\delta^n h^u(k)$ we have

$$B^{d^j u^{n-j}}(n, m) = \frac{B(0, m)}{B(0, n)} \delta^{j(m-n)} \frac{h^u(m-1)}{h^u(n-1)} \frac{h^u(m-2)}{h^u(n-2)} \cdots \frac{h^u(m-n)}{h^u(0)}$$

and the claim follows inserting the particular shape of h^u. $\square$

Exercise 6.23 Build a concrete model for $N = 3$ with initial term
structure determined by the familiar bond prices: $B(0, 1) = 0.9966$,
$B(0, 2) = 0.9932$, $B(0, 3) = 0.9897$, taking $q = 1/2$, $\delta = 0.99923$.

Exercise 6.24 Adjust the δ in the previous exercise so that the pack
of 100 000 calls written on 3-bond with exercise time $n = 2$ and unit
exercise price $K = 0.9964$ is worth 24.47 today.

Short rates

Consider short rates for continuous compounding

$$r(n) = -\frac{\ln B(n, n+1)}{h}.$$

In particular, we can use the above results to compute the short rate in the HL model. First, we obtain

$$B^{d^j u^{n-j}}(n, n+1)$$
$$= \frac{B(0, n+1)}{B(0, n)} \delta^j \frac{h^u(n)}{h^u(n-1)} \frac{h^u(n-1)}{h^u(n-2)} \cdots \frac{h^u(2)}{h^u(1)} \frac{h^u(1)}{h^u(0)}$$
$$= \frac{B(0, n+1)}{B(0, n)} \delta^j h^u(n)$$
$$= \frac{B(0, n+1)}{B(0, n)} \frac{\delta^j}{(1-q)\delta^n + q}.$$

It follows that the short rate is given by

$$r^{d^j u^{n-j}}(n) = -\frac{1}{h} \ln B^{d^j u^{n-j}}(n, n+1)$$
$$= f(0, n) - \frac{j}{h} \ln \delta + \frac{1}{h} \ln((1-q)\delta^n + q).$$

Next we derive the recursive equations for $r(n)$:

$$r(2) = r(1) + \mathbb{E}(r(1))h \pm \sigma \sqrt{h},$$

$$r(3) = r(2) + \mathbb{E}(r(2))h \pm \sigma \sqrt{h}$$
$$= r(1) + \mathbb{E}(r(1))h + \mathbb{E}(r(2))h \pm \sigma \sqrt{h} \pm \sigma \sqrt{h},$$

$$r(n+1) = r(n) + \mathbb{E}(r(n))h \pm \sigma \sqrt{h}$$
$$= r(n) + f(0, n)h - (\ln \delta)n\frac{1}{2} + \ln\left[\frac{1}{2}(\delta^n + 1)\right] \pm \sqrt{n}\frac{1}{2}\frac{1}{\sqrt{h}} \ln \delta.$$

The expectation of the short rate is given by

$$\mu_{r(n)} = \mathbb{E}(r(n))$$
$$= f(0, n) - \frac{1}{h} \ln \delta \sum_{j=0}^{n} j\frac{n!}{j!(n-j)!}(1-q)^j q^{n-j} + \frac{1}{h} \ln((1-q)\delta^n + q)$$
$$= f(0, n) - \frac{\ln \delta}{h}n(1-q) + \frac{1}{h} \ln((1-q)\delta^n + q),$$

where we have used the well-known formula $\mathbb{E}(X) = n(1 - q)$ for the expectation of a random variable X with binomial distribution.

Similarly, we can compute the variance of the short rate:

$$
\begin{aligned}
\sigma^2_{r(n)} &= \mathrm{Var}(r(n)) \\
&= \frac{(\ln \delta)^2}{h^2} \left(\sum_{j=0}^{n} j^2 \binom{n}{j} (1 - q)^j p^{n-j} - (n(1 - q))^2 \right) \\
&= \frac{(\ln \delta)^2}{h^2} nq(1 - q),
\end{aligned}
$$

using the formula $\mathrm{Var}(X) = nq(1 - q)$ for the variance of a random variable X with binomial distribution.

Observe that the variance $\sigma^2_{r(n)}$ of the short rate is proportional to n. In other words, the short rate has **constant volatility**. This is an important property of the HL model.

Exercise 6.25 Find the short rates, and compute the expectations and variances following Exercise 6.23.

Problems inherent in the HL model include possible negative values of interest rates appearing after a sufficiently long time n, as well as the perfect correlation of the moves of the term structure curve, which is unrealistic, as perfect correlation is not usually observed in practice. The model proposed earlier is more flexible in some respects but since it is also based on binomial trees, it shares the HL model's principal limitations when it comes to modelling realistic correlations.

Index

180

Printed in the United States
by Baker & Taylor Publisher Services